Reflections on Three Oceans

Hugh Richards

REFLECTIONS ON THREE OCEANS

Canadian Cataloguing in Publication Data
Richards, Hugh, REFLECTIONS ON THREE OCEANS
ISBN: **978-0-9867393-0-9**

1. Richards, Hugh; 2. Voyages and travels — Pacific Ocean, Indian Ocean, Atlantic Ocean; 3. Family adventure — a special experience; 4. People and places visited around the world.

Contact:
Hugh & Christine Richards
reflectionsonthreeoceans@gmail.com

Published by:
GreenPark Productions
GreenPark-Productions.com
greenpark.productions@gmail.com

For Christine

This book is dedicated to my wife Christine with whose help, support, companionship and encouragement this dream came true.

Also to my three sons, Nicholas, Christopher and David.

PREFACE

Welcome to the world of adventure

This book is not a lexicon for would be cruisers. It is a book with which to relax as you read the story of the fulfillment of one couple's dream to sail their own boat across the oceans of the world.

If you love the sea, are afraid of it, or wonder whatever possesses people to set out in a small boat, read on and enjoy.

FOREWORD

This is the story of a childhood dream. A dream born in a landlocked valley in North Wales that was home for the first twelve years of my life. I can vividly recall standing on a long forgotten hillside looking at the encompassing hills on three sides, letting my eyes be drawn to the distant triangle of blue, twelve miles away at the valley's mouth, where the River Clwyd joined the sea.

As we spent our summer holidays at the family cottage in Anglesey, the dream was emancipated to one of seagoing adventure, pirates and all, as I sailed our leaking dinghy around the small islets in our sheltered bay. Occasionally my father would take us to Cymyran – a name spoken softly. For it was through this narrow gap that the tide would rush in and out of our bay with mesmerizing ferocity. The ensuing day at Silver Sands brought the excitement of huge waves crashing on the beach after picking up strength crossing the Irish Sea.

Never in my wildest dreams while growing up, then living the daily routine of a life of learning and working, did I think that my childhood dream would come true. That I would sail my own boat into exotic harbours of which I had only read, San Francisco, Tahiti, Auckland, Zanzibar, Capetown and more. What romance!

Yet, after a lifetime of totally unrelated work, where sailing was restricted to dinghy sailing and later extensive coastal cruising, I found I had the greatest asset of all. Christine, my wife for over forty years, threw herself wholeheartedly into making my dream a reality. I cannot express adequately how proud I am of her courage, and how much I admired her mastery of sailing and her ability to adapt all her skills ashore to a life at sea. To her I shall always be grateful.

So this book is for dreamers. Those who hang over harbour walls looking at the boats below; or those, some of whom we would meet on our journeys, who are landlocked yet, for some mystical reason, dream of the sea. I hope this book will be savoured during the quiet times of many busy lives. For not only is it a book of our discovery of this magical planet and the people who, by chance, make it their home, but it is also a voyage of discovery of ourselves. Through the isolation and challenges of ocean passage making, we learnt about ourselves and each other, which in itself is a priceless reward.

So come with us and share some of our adventures and then, who knows, maybe you will be tempted or encouraged to take up the challenge yourselves.

DEMELZA'S VOYAGE

TABLE OF CONTENTS

VANCOUVER 32 PILOT CUTTER

Length Overall	32'0"
Designed Waterline	27'6"
Beam	10'7"
Draught	4'6"
Displacement	14,000 Lbs
Ballast	6,000 Lbs
Head Room	6'6"
Mainsail	221 sq. ft.
No. 1. Jib	374 sq. ft.
No. 2. Jib	240 sq. ft.
Storm Jib	75 sq. ft.
Staysail	139 sq. ft.
Genoa	435 sq. ft.

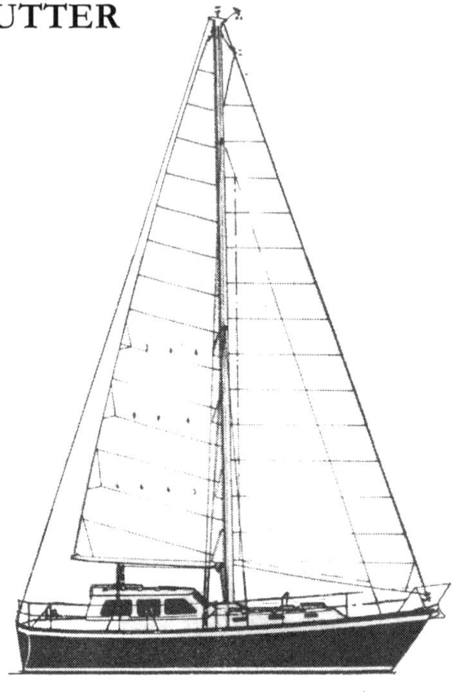

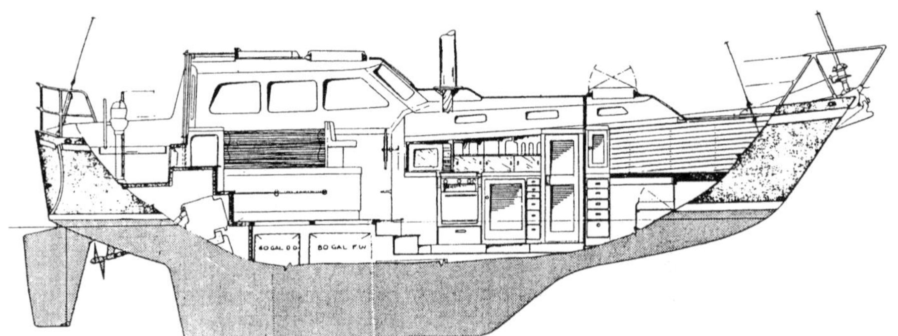

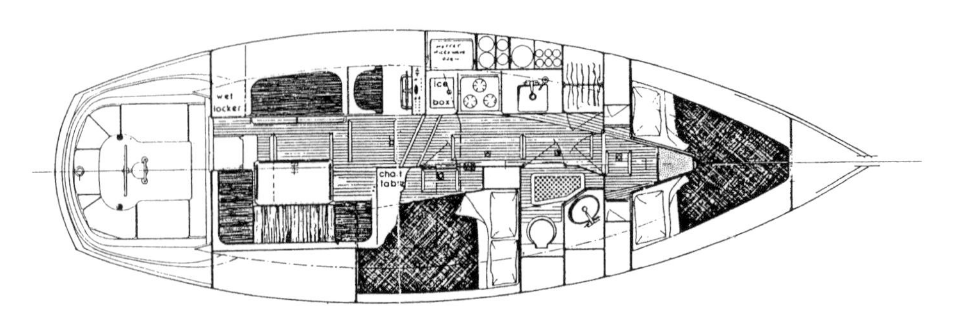

Demelza

CHAPTER 1

The chance of a lifetime

We had seen better days in Melanie Cove on the West Coast of British Columbia. The rain, drumming on the coach roof of our Crown 28 sailboat, *Morwenna*, reminded us that another precious day of our short summer holiday was over. Huddled in the confines of *Morwenna*'s cabin, lulled by the steady hiss of her kerosene heater, we dreamed of sitting at anchor in the heat of some exotic tropical lagoon, wearing the scantiest of clothing, slipping into the warm blue waters whenever we wished, and sipping cool drinks in the cockpit watching the sun set below the horizon on balmy nights in paradise.

Morwenna tugged at her rode as she hunted from side to side in the strong breeze. Overhanging pines shed their needles all over the deck, and seagulls screamed with delight as they negotiated the updrafts above a nearby rocky promontory. Little did we realize that our dreaming was the germ of a six and a half year voyage around the world.

How it developed into a firm commitment is less clear now, but I do recall that it was an intermittent and tortuous process of elimination and planning. There seemed to be so many good, sound and sensible reasons for not going. What about our young family struggling to get established in the work world? What about my job? Could I afford to retire early? What about our lovely German shepherd. Could we leave her behind? What of the expense involved? Would we like offshore sailing? Could we live together in such a cramped space for so long? Was it safe? Did we know enough? Were we physically and mentally strong enough to handle the inevitable stresses and strains of passage making? The list seemed endless.

We didn't talk about all these things endlessly, probably because we were busy doing other things. But over time, reading lots of nautical books and magazines, meeting people who had been "out there," and just anticipating the challenge, we found our enthusiasm building and our resolve hardening. It seemed almost casual, as we went about each day's mundane tasks, that our decisions were more and more directed toward making this adventure a reality.

Renting out our home seemed feasible, and storing our belongings possible. Family and friends were supportive and becoming just as enthused about the whole idea. "Rather you than me" more frequently became "You lucky things" as we talked over our plans.

The advertisements in the *Latitude 38* and *48 North* boating magazines were titillating. No firm commitment yet. Just a great interest. A myriad of knowledgeable, talented and experienced contributors to sailing magazines vied for our attention. Tales of woe, of horrendous storms at sea, of miraculous survival and heroic deeds, were counterbalanced by vivid descriptions of tantalizing destinations, exotic foods, and welcoming people all over the world. Books by the Smeetons, Pyes, Hiscocks and Roth, to name a few, became required reading. It was a classical case of the more we read the less we knew. We became acutely aware of our shortcomings and determined to do something about them over the two years that we had decided it would take to prepare ourselves.

More often than not, our spare weekends were spent meandering up and down marina docks looking at the seemingly endless variety of boat designs, construction and prices. Some were obviously too light, some too heavy. Some just didn't look right. We went through periods of great enthusiasm and some of despair as we failed to find our "ideal boat."

Then came the day that we saw a boat out on the water that we really liked. After some initial inquiries, we decided to visit the boat builders concerned in California, to see for ourselves how well this boat was built. The assembly was as clean as a commercial kitchen. Everything had its place. The newest staff member had worked there for twelve years. The staff was so accommodating. On a conducted tour, for the best part of a day, we saw every part of the operation. The price for the complete boat was well out of our range no matter how we crunched the numbers. Home we went to start all over again.

As I scanned the advertisements a week later, I noticed a repeat one from the previous Fall for a Vancouver 32 Pilothouse cutter at a reduced price. With a name like Vancouver it had to be followed up. I caught the first ferry to Vancouver where the designer, Robert Harris, lived. For half a day he fielded all my questions about the boat's design, compromises made, construction and sail requirements and seaworthiness. Finally he assured me of the boat's sea kindliness and fast passage-making.

"This is a boat that can take you in safety anywhere in the world." he said. Procrastination was no longer an option. We flew to Los Angeles where the boat was berthed, petrified she would sell before we got there.

Bob, the owner, was heavily into bananas for one of California's large grocery chains. After I told him of our arrival he said he would leave the keys for us to look over the boat the next day. He would join us later.

Christine and I looked into every nook and cranny. We inspected every fitting and joint that we could access. We tried out all the equipment. We even tried the bunks for size and comfort. We could find nothing major to complain about. So the deal was eventually done and we flew home, realizing that now there was no turning back. The boat survey was carried out by a very pernickety Frenchman, who produced the most detailed reports I had ever seen. Soon the boat was on her way north, and our excitement was tempered only by the sadness of selling our faithful *Morwenna* to friends Nancy and Ray, who we knew would look after her well.

CHAPTER 2
Preparations

The wait for our new boat's arrival from Marina del Rey in Los Angeles was almost unbearable. It was akin to waiting for the birth or our first child.

"What shall we call her?" Christine asked.

As I had had my pick of a Welsh girl's name for *Morwenna*, it was only fair that Christine, whose family comes from Cornwall, should choose a Cornish girl's name for our new acquisition. Finally she thought of Winston Graham's heroine of the Poldark novels, *Demelza*. She was a feisty young lady from humble beginnings who, with courage, tenacity and a fair bit of luck, managed to achieve a great many of her dreams.

Demelza is a compound name in Cornish derived from *de* meaning "your" and *melza* meaning "sweetness." It is also the name of a small hamlet in Cornwall, a county in southwest England, consisting of a few houses, a church, and a pub. On all counts *Demelza* seemed a perfect name, and augured well for a successful outcome to our adventure.

Demelza village sign post, Cornwall, England

Soon, it was the weekend of *Demelza's* arrival in Anacortes, Washington. I was working, so Christine hitched a ride on her sister's boat to await the arrival the following day. That morning she woke up to see a huge transporter drawing in through the entrance to the boatyard. Excitedly she ran across to meet the vehicle. Anxious that all had gone well, she called up to the young, bronzed Californian driver.

"Did the trip go well, and how's the boat?"
"Just great," he replied "these little ones are never any problem."

Demelza's arrival in Anacortes, Washington.

Crushed by his assessment of the size of our beautiful new boat, Christine observed her offloading, along with the myriad of bits and pieces that had been taken off for her journey north.

As the boat was swung out over the water, Christine offered a silent prayer that this obviously hazardous procedure would go well. When she phoned me that evening, she reported a successful launch and that *Demelza* was lying in flat water waiting for us to put up her mast. One of the things that had worried me was that the launching site was exposed to a long fetch from the north, and that, should a sudden December north wind blow into the bay, stepping the mast would be difficult.

My good friend David and I arrived by ferry the next day and with Christine, her sister and brother in law, we got to work spreading out and reassembling all the rigging and putting the whole puzzling mass together again. In retrospect, I should have supervised the dismantling of the boat's rigging, labeling every piece as it was taken off. Finally all was orderly, and the mast was hoisted over the boat. We juggled it into place and *presto*, before we knew it, she looked like a sailboat again.

We paid our bills, and set sail for Roche Harbor on San Juan Island on the way home to Sidney, British Columbia. That evening as darkness fell, we christened our new boat *Demelza* before retiring for a well earned rest on our first night aboard.

By morning Christine had acquired her first injury, a black eye resulting from walking into one of the fitted mosquito screens over the main hatch. The bilge was filling with water, as the stuffing box was not tightened sufficiently. Once that had been sorted out, the journey to Sidney went smoothly, and Canada Customs were pleased to relieve us of the required Import Duty on landing.

So there we were, safely in home port, everyone anticipating our forthcoming adventure, and me silently wondering what on earth we had let ourselves in for.

Over the next few weekends, we took *Demelza* on several cruises in local waters under variable winter conditions. Nancy and Ray on *Morwenna*, David and Colleen on *Checkmate* and Ray and Barb on *Carina* often accompanied us. All these wonderful people gave help and encouragement as the inevitable glitches surfaced and were resolved. We began to relax and enjoy ourselves.

The brisk January winds gave us an opportunity to put *Demelza* through her paces, and to savour the new found comfort of the pilothouse. In the northwest, the winter wind is heavy and wet, and we were impressed by the boat's comfort and stability. However we soon found that getting in and out of the pilot house let in too much rain. So a dodger of some kind seemed essential. So began the "must do" list in preparation for our journey.

Christine and I took turns at leaving and re-entering the dock, to get used to *Demelza's* ten foot six inch beam without scouring the hull's gel coat. The full length teak and brass rub rail helped in these first few weeks. We were also impressed with how close to the wind *Demelza* sailed with both the jib and the staysail set, but noticed that it took a five to ten knot breeze to move her seven tons along at hull speed. The cutaway keel gave good maneuverability in tight spots, an asset which proved invaluable later as we steered through reefs, and into and out of crowded anchorages and moorings.

Gradually we made headway on all the jobs, making the boat more convenient to sail single handed should the need arise. Going downwind, we needed a whisker pole for the staysail and a bigger pole for the Genoa. We could then sail wing on wing, with the sails set on either side of the boat. Much of the boat's wiring had been set up with connectors. I decided to replace these with soldered joins wherever possible to make them more reliable.

In February '93, we bought an Autohelm 3000 and fitted it to our wheel steering in the cockpit. After many hilarious outings weaving about the bays adjusting it, we finally had success, and were delighted at the prospect of relief from lengthy periods of hand steering the boat on long passages. We included its extra electrical draw in calculating any generating shortfall.

The boat had come equipped with a complicated electronic package for measuring wind strength and direction as well as water speed, temperature and depth. However we decided to heed the advice of our sailing mentor, Peter Coombs.

"Keep it simple Hugh. It will save you a lot of pain and anxiety."

We made up a lead line using a fishing weight at one end, and stored away a few pieces of wool for tying to the shrouds to give us the wind direction should the electronics fail. I often thanked Peter for his sound advice, because the depth sounder later malfunctioned, and a booby, sitting on top of the mast while we were off Madagascar, chewed its way through our plastic wind vane.

As a fall-back for measuring our speed through the water, I bought a handy little gadget consisting of an L shaped graduated clear plastic pipe with a table tennis ball inside. When pointing the mouth of the short arm of this pipe in the direction traveled, and inserting it into the sea, the ball would ascend the long arm of the calibrated pipe, indicating the speed traveled through the water. Peter would be proud of us.

To boost our courage, we installed a sixteen mile radar, mounting the scanner on the mast at the upper cross trees to give us maximum range over the horizon.

In March, it became evident that the Chinese batteries with which the boat was equipped were not holding their charge. A further review of our electrical needs and generating capacity led me to replace the alternator on the engine with a larger one, and to insert an ammeter to measure the amps flowing into the batteries. I also set up a separate bank of deep cycle house batteries, and at a later date, installed a solar panel on the stainless steel arch above the aft rail which constantly trickle charged the starter battery bank.

Originally I had thought of installing a wind generator but, in spite of their popularity on cruising yachts, I felt they were too noisy and worked best in windy anchorages, which we hoped to avoid. We compromised by buying a tow generator, which could be adapted to use as a wind generator if need be, by substituting an enormous two bladed propeller for the normal sized water propeller before hauling it up into the rigging. In full flight, this was an awesome and potentially dangerous beast.

By now, the energy equation of demand versus generating capacity seemed more balanced. I had looked at a friend's boat and envied his ability to fast charge batteries by manually regulating the alternator's output. However budget constraints ruled out this very handy option. Another item that I really would have liked was an electronic battery charge status monitoring device.

I have gone into a fair amount of detail on the choices we made concerning batteries. It is such an important feature of life on a cruising boat equipped with refrigerator, steering gear, alarm systems, navigation lights, navigational aids, water-makers and radios. In all we had a house battery bank of three hundred ampere hours capacity, and an engine cranking bank capacity of one hundred and eighty ampere hours. We did not use our refrigerator at sea as the risk of all its contents spoiling should the refrigeration fail was too great. Instead we would rely on dried and canned goods for our passages.

March continued cold and blustery. *Demelza* had no heating in the cabin. Although we were planning to sail in the tropics, we both felt it better to have some source of heat if only to dry wet clothes. We went back to the boat journals to review all the different types of heating systems available and settled for a forced air diesel heater. Firstly it could deliver hot air to all cabins on demand. Secondly it would run off the diesel oil from the main tank avoiding having to find, carry and store another type of fuel. Thirdly, it was a safe method of heating. Lastly, the compact heating unit could be located in the storage area at the stern of the boat, well out of the way. Space, or rather lack of it in the living areas, was rapidly becoming an issue. We transferred the engine's air intake to one of the cockpit lockers, and put a shut off valve on it to prevent seawater getting into it. These cockpit side lockers also had fabric covers to prevent water getting into them, a type of double insurance.

Ben, my trusty diesel engine mechanic, overhauled the Yanmar engine, supplied a wealth of basic spares, and found me a shop manual for the engine. I agonized over whether or not to keep the propane cooking stove because of its inherent explosive potential should leaking gas accumulate in the bilge. It is such a quick, easy and clean fuel, readily obtainable almost anywhere in the world, and it was already installed. So we decided to keep it. To improve safety, we installed a new gas detecting and alarm system as well as a solenoid shut off valve at the tanks in the cockpit locker, operated from the cabin. Lastly, we had a detailed professional inspection of the installation to ensure it was sound.

At the beginning of April, we organized a work bee with some of our friends. *Demelza* was hauled out of the water for a close inspection. We checked the through hull fittings for signs of electrolysis, and the cutlass and rudder post bearings for any sign of undue wear. We replaced the anodes, two on the propeller shaft, and two plates bolted to the hull aft which were connected to the boat's bonding system. We replaced the two-blade eighteen inch diameter nine inch pitch propeller, for a three-bladed sixteen inch diameter eleven-inch pitch model. The propeller shaft was not tapered, so we replaced it with a standard tapered one on which we could fit a replacement propeller if needed. A small leak at the base of the skeg showed a potential structural weakness. Given the huge stresses to which the skeg would be exposed while under way, we fibreglassed in a stainless steel reinforcement which cured the leak.

After a good bottom clean and two coats of antifouling paint, *Demelza* was ready to be put back into the water. We felt that another "last time job" had been completed.

Friends' work bee

Bob and Mary were committed to join us on the Victoria to San Francisco leg. Both were relatively new to boating, but we had spent a glorious three weeks together in the Desolation Sound area during the previous summer. They were eager for the adventure, and both had a lot to offer on the journey south.

David was committed to the leg from Mexico to the Marquesas. An experienced sailor, he was a great handyman and an accomplished player of the mouth organ for those evenings sitting on deck watching the sun set over a glassy sea.

Ray, also an experienced sailor, was keen to join us for the leg from Tonga to New Zealand, a passage that we anticipated might give us the most trouble from inclement weather. We appreciated the thought of having another pair of experienced hands to deal with whatever Mother Nature delivered on that approximately two week passage.

Throughout April preparations continued, such as putting extra lighting in the main cabin, attaching holders, lee cloths, hooks, shelves and anything else we could think of to make life easier afloat.

To assist with downwind sailing we installed a track mounted spinnaker boom on the mast. I thought that being able to store the boom on the mast would free up working space on the foredeck, making sail handling more manageable at sea.

The boat was equipped with a thirty-five pound CQR anchor, and a friend had donated a forty-five pound Danforth. We had kept a twenty-five pound Danforth from *Morwenna* and I bought a fifty two pound CQR as a storm anchor. With all this weight distributed around the boat, and convinced we needed chain, I was concerned about adding too much additional weight. So the decision was made to install three hundred feet of 5/16th forty grade high tensile chain, which would be lighter and easier to handle, along with an appropriate electric capstan.

The problem then was where to store all this equipment. The thirty-five pound CQR I left on the bow roller, the fifty two pound in the large bin under the berth in the bow, the twenty-five pound Danforth in a cockpit locker and the forty five pound Danforth under one of the main cabin seats. As for the three hundred feet of galvanized chain, only half of it would fit into the chain locker at the bow under the electric capstan. Aft of this was a large locker under the front double berth. So I bored a hole from the anchor locker and inserted a hawse pipe of sufficient diameter and length to carry half the chain aft before securing the bitter end at the foot of the mast. All this weight distribution was checked against the trim of the boat as we went along so that she remained level, and assured no listing to either side. To avoid any anxiety about drinking water shortage in countries where its quality was suspect, we installed a small desalinating water-maker to provide drinking water only. Lastly we put *Demelza's* name and port of registration in gold letters on the transom. Now all systems were "go" and she was ready for sea.

While all this boat preparation had been going on, we were preparing ourselves for the long offshore voyage. Being long standing dinghy and coastal sailors, we felt we would benefit from acquiring some additional skills. Christine spent the final winter and spring taking a course to qualify as a Certified Amateur Radio Operator. Horrified at the prospect of the theoretical and practical examinations involved, she tackled the mathematics and electronics with her usual gusto. During the course, Christine asked the principal of one of our more prestigious local schools if she had any advice for a mature student taking such exams, and was taken aback by her reply -

"Ladies of your age should not even contemplate taking exams."

With the unfailing patience and knowledge of her mentor, Peter Thomas, controller of the DDD (Dreamers, Doers and Doners) Amateur Radio Net, she delighted herself and everyone else by acing the examinations. Following such success it was obligatory to install a Kenwood single side band radio for our newly qualified radio operator. This was located under the navigation station in an enclosed two door locker in the pilot house, and connected to an insulated back stay aerial with an automatic electronic tuner. The grounding was supplied by four lengths of copper strapping laid along the inside of the boat's hull connected to the bronze through hull fittings.

Demelza's radio operator, Christine.

For my part, I enrolled in two of the Canadian Yacht Club's Certification programs as an adjunct to several of the Canadian Power Squadron certificates which I had collected over the years. I enrolled in evening courses on Celestial Navigation and Marine Diesel engine maintenance. These were critical subjects about which I knew very little. While by no means making me an expert, at least I became familiar with the peculiar bumps on the outside of the engine, and of its essential need for clean fuel, clean air and good compression. As for the celestial navigation, the remainder of the class was made up of either very intelligent young men working for their masters tickets, or old salts brushing up their skills when not guiding huge commercial vessels across the oceans. My first practice sextant fix from the Victoria waterfront placed me firmly in the centre of the Indian subcontinent! Immediately I rushed out to buy what I hoped would remedy some of my mathematical limitations, a handheld navigational calculator.

At a minimum my studies would boost my morale and that of the crew, and the knowledge gained might even prove helpful in an emergency. Only sometime later was I forced to acknowledge the value of people who knew what they were doing in solving more serious problems.

My plumbing training was more hands on, known to all cruising sailors as "Fixing the plugged up head." Nothing can destroy morale more quickly than this crisis, solid and immoveable in nature. Preventive advice is freely available from all and sundry without asking. We must have poured gallons of vinegar and cooking oil down the recalcitrant throat of this apparatus over the years. We advised all visitors not to put anything down there that they had not eaten. Inevitably however the days always came when Christine would call from below

"Darling, the head doesn't work." or "Darling, I can hear something dripping." or "Darling, there's water running across the cabin sole."

These cries would galvanize me into taking a most unwelcome tour of the plumbing, hidden in parts of the boat that were never designed to see the light of day. Inevitably I would emerge with blood pouring from a resulting abrasion or two.

Another major concern was the increasing strength and frequency of the *El Nino*, a recurring global weather phenomenon affecting the world's oceans, particularly the Pacific. It causes changing weather patterns, more frequent storms, and a lessening of the Trade Winds. I visited the Institute of Ocean Sciences, where I met with staff having an interest in the subject. Thanks to their expertise and patience I began a lasting and beneficial interest in maritime weather.

With this sustained effort to prepare the boat and ourselves, we both felt tired as the departure time approached. Nevertheless we were pitched into a whole new round of preparations.

The most important of these was stocking up with food and drink. Christine compiled lists of dried and canned foods that would make up the bulk of our diet when travelling and taking over when our stock of fresh food ran out. The variety of dried foods available was gratifying but expensive. Other boats frequently dehydrated and vacuum packed their own food for storage, using a small machine which sucked the air out of and sealed up plastic containers.

In one of Eric Hiscock's books on cruising, he describes in detail how to keep meat in brine. The brine was easily prepared by adding enough salt to water until a potato floated in it, at which time the brine was sufficiently saline. Then Christine chopped up a variety of lean meats into small chunks before immersing them in the brine assuring the meat was totally covered before sealing the jar. We used powdered milk, and we found that fresh eggs turned over daily easily survived our passages.

Each shopping expedition produced another pile of cans, bottles and packages that had to be stored. Christine noted down the location of each item on an inventory of every numbered locker in the boat, so that we could easily find it later. Not only was it just a case of finding room, but we had to be careful to distribute the weight properly to keep the boat on an even keel.

For my part, I commandeered one locker for storing all the tools that we would need. Again this led to agonizing choices of what to take and what to leave behind. Being a small boat, *Demelza* had no dedicated space as a work area, which many of the larger boats possess. Because of this, all bench work had to be done on a plank across the cockpit seats.

On my retirement my colleagues at work, knowing of our plans, had presented us with many useful items. One was a bosun's chair. I did not much like the idea of drilling holes all the way up the mast to attach mast steps, thinking they might weaken its structure. But having tried the exercise of Christine attempting to winch me to the top of our forty plus foot mast in the bosun's chair, we realized that supplementary assistance was required. It was then we saw an advertisement by *Mast Mate* for a flexible nylon webbing mast ladder with an eye at either end to one which the main halyard could be attached, and slides along its length that fed into the mainsail track. This and the bosun's chair provided an easy and accessible way to mount the mast.

Spare parts were another big item, for many of the places we would visit would not have easy access to these. West Marine advertised a round the world delivery service. On the basis of that I reduced a number of the heavier items in the spares bin. Engine parts, filters, rigging wire, cabin lights, piping, wiring, fuses. The list seemed endless, but eventually there just wasn't any more room. I had to decide what the most vulnerable and critical items were to get us back to port, list them in order of priority, and take as many as I could from the top of the list.

Then there was the question of health emergencies, and what we should take. A number of commercially prepared kits were available, but at great expense. So, with the kind help of my good friend Dr. David, and having a nodding acquaintance with the subject myself, we made up our own kit.

The financial side was relatively easy, as our eldest son Nick accepted power of attorney for all our financial matters while we were away. Here I must say a big thank you to Nick for fielding all the emergencies and routines with his usual patient calmness and total commitment to details, including good communication with us all over the globe sometimes in most difficult circumstances.

By this time the storm jib that we had ordered arrived, as did our altered mainsail. In this we had added a deep third reef and had its seams triple stitched. All this was an alternative to a tri sail on a separate track on the mast. This was done to save money. I think a tri sail is preferable, as it provides alternative propulsion should the mainsail be torn in a storm.

Tackling the inventory of needed charts was a nightmare in both choosing which charts, and at what cost. We sought out every possible source of second hand charts and loaners that we could find. The volume of paper increased, so we developed a new flat storage for them under the middle stateroom bunk. This area was for charts not immediately in use for the current passage. Our first inventory comprehensively covered the Juan de Fuca Straits and the west coast of North America down to and including San Diego, California.

I have gone into some detail about planning our voyage and our preparations for it, not in any way putting it forward as a prescription to be followed, but only to illustrate some of the endless considerations that we had to make to keep us safe and happy on our wanderings.

It seemed that, no matter how much we included in our plans, and all our reasons for doing it our way, there were always as many opinions as people on how to do it "the proper way." As with all aspiring cruisers we began by building on what we already knew, derived from as many sources of information and advice as we could muster. I believe that offshore passage making is well within the reach of the many we have met who love the idea of sailing the blue seas but, for whatever reason, are reluctant to take the plunge. With careful planning and preparation, many who fear or feel ill equipped to venture forth would enjoy the life of adventure and the rewards of safe offshore cruising.

Demelza leaving dock

CHAPTER 3
Time to Go

Two years of seemingly endless planning and preparation had suddenly evaporated, and with it the constant niggling apprehension in the back of my mind of critical things we might have missed, and the loss we would feel for those we were leaving behind. But this was tempered for us both by the great excitement of adventures ahead. Our departure from our dock in Sidney was heart wrenching. As we pulled away in the morning light, I particularly remember looking back at the group of family and friends waving goodbye. Especially vivid is the memory our good friend, Catherine, in her eighties, who had got up so early to see us off, and had staggered down to the end of wharf with a deckchair in her hand.

"Catherine, what are you doing here at this time of day?" Christine asked as we settled her in her chair.

"I just couldn't stay at home," she replied. "You'll be away such a long time before I see you again."

It was not to be, for Catherine died before we returned, leaving that last image of her sitting with our friends on the end of the wharf waving as we motored off into the bay, to the accompaniment of blasting fog horns and waving arms.

Our first port of call was Anacortes to visit friends and to install the windvane, which was the very last item we felt we needed. Our friend David, who had accompanied us to Anacortes, spent a significant amount of time hanging over the transom and docksides measuring and boring holes to attach the wind vane to our beautiful *Demelza*, taking care that it was correctly aligned.

Christine fired up her shortwave radio for a first contact with the DDD net in Victoria. We were now one of the "doers." The dulcet tones of Peter Thomas, controller of the net, came through clearly. The radio was working well. An added thrill was to tell Ian, in New Zealand, that we were on our way, and looking forward to meeting him on our arrival in that distant country. With fewer distractions, we put final touches to our preparations. Soon all was complete. We waved David off home, with grateful thanks for all he had done for us. We looked forward to seeing him in Mexico where he would join us for the passage to the Marquesas.

I lay in my bunk that night as waves of apprehension swept over me. What were we letting ourselves in for? Had I remembered everything? Should I have included anything else? Sleep brought relief.

The succession of gales that we had been experiencing at home before we left, continued with lashing rain for the next two days. Local residents Janet and Ed kindly gave us refuge ashore in their beautiful home, as we waited for a better weather forecast.

On May 4th, dawn broke clear and calm. We hustled to store everything ready for sea, waved farewell to our friends, and turned the boat toward the Strait of Juan de Fuca. At Port Angeles we were to meet up with Mary and Bob, who were to accompany us on the passage down the coast to San Francisco. Our new windvane was coping well with the brisk fifteen knot breeze that found its way past all the gear that we had mounted on the aft rail. This was against all advice in the windvane manual. We had two outboard motors on brackets, a life sling, a life ring, and an extension post for the GPS aerial. In addition there were my fishing rod and the solar panel mounted on a stainless steel arch above the push pit.

Christine's first contact with Peter on the radio was so rewarding.

"I'm so proud of you Christine," Peter said "After all that studying and tests, this is what it's all about, and your signal is as clear as a bell."

Across the straits to starboard, we saw Victoria in the sunshine. By evening we were approaching Port Angeles, and the wind had dropped. We motored in passing a Rafiki 37 sailboat that had just arrived from San Francisco.

"How was your trip?" I called.

"It's taken six days," came the reply, "and three hellish storms."

I could feel my heart go "thump." It didn't take much to let loose my imagination on the subject of storms at sea.

After our one fine day, the next was foul as we rode the incoming surge at the Port Angeles dock. We spent that day reorganizing and restoring things around the boat in preparation for a rough passage along the Juan de Fuca, securing the contents of lockers and bookshelves as best we could. We prepared the forward berth for Bob and Mary who were due the following day.

They arrived on the ferry from Victoria, exuding their usual enthusiasm and optimism for the journey ahead. It was catching. Almost a tonic, after all the worrying I had been going through. As we celebrated their arrival with a bottle of champagne to the accompaniment of a howling wind in the rigging above our cozy warm cabin, I pondered whether or not I had chosen too early a date to start out. Maybe we should have left in June. Too late now, we were all assembled. I tried to tell myself to stop worrying.

The following morning was foul, so we delayed our departure for twenty four hours. Twenty knots of westerly wind continued all day, making it impossible to think of beating into it for the seventy nautical miles up the straits to the Pacific Ocean. Two men came into harbour on a boat from Coos Bay, Oregon saying that they had had a very rough passage. They looked it. Oh God! What were we doing?

After leaving at six the following morning, and while testing all systems, we found the radar wasn't working. So back to port we went to find out what was wrong with it.

"Sorry I can't get there until tomorrow." said the technician.

So passed the only decent day we had had for a week. Sure enough he arrived after noon on the following day, to find that there was a join in the coaxial cable over the battery box. This had resulted in corrosion of the wires. So the wires were rerouted, newly spliced, and *Presto* the radar worked.

At three in the afternoon we left Port Angeles for the second time, feeling like race horses being let out of the starting box. As we turned toward the ocean, the headwind began to rise again from the west, and a strong flood tide was against us. Soon the wind had risen to twenty-five knots and we were crashing into big waves. With the engine at maximum revolutions we were getting precisely nowhere, very wet and feeling sick. As darkness fell, and with little headway being made, we turned back yet again. It took us twenty minutes downwind to recover the distance we had gained over the entire afternoon.

Even Bob and Mary looked a bit despondent as we roller coasted back in large seas under staysail only. Green water was pouring over the deck, as Bob worked hard handling the sails. Shafts of lightning and claps of thunder accompanied us as we sped past Ediz Hook with thirty knots of wind behind us. The rigging sang as we reached into the harbour at 2200hrs. We wondered whether we would ever leave the Straits.

In the morning Bob and I chatted to a sheltering fisherman who told us to wait for an easterly wind that was sure to come. I spent time trying to figure out how water was getting into the chain locker. It appeared that the seal on the deck's lid to the anchor locker and capstan in the bow was not adequate to keep water, breaking over the deck in heavy seas, from getting into the locker. Nor was the locker drain large enough to drain this water away. Instead it overflowed through the hawse pipe into the second chain locker below the forward berth and from there into the bilge. The only solution that I could come up with was to tape the lid all around before putting out to sea.

After a most pleasant evening at the movies and a good night's sleep, we felt better the next day, but awoke to an especially foul morning. It was an easy decision to stay exactly where we were. After a hearty breakfast in town, we decided to rent a car to go up to Hurricane Ridge. Later, Mary and Christine went off on a tour of Port Townsend. They followed the seagull shapes painted on the sidewalks, to guide them among the interesting period houses of the town. Lilacs, azaleas, rhododendrons and bluebells flanked their path in an abundance of springtime optimism. By evening the weather looked better, and the wind had subsided. We anticipated a good day to follow.

The 0500 hrs forecast the next day was good, so I roused all the crew to make the best of it. Within an hour we were ready to leave in a gentle breeze from the east, which would push us the way we wanted to go. With renewed optimism, we let go the mooring lines, and waved goodbye to the fishermen on the wharf.

We had a rendezvous planned in mid straits with David, Janet, Ann and other friends on *Island Wanderer.* Underway at last Christine whispered to me

"Let's motor sail to get out of here as fast as we can."

Our meeting with these good friends in mid channel was marvelous. After a brief visit we sadly waved our farewells and set off in a determined frame of mind toward the west, as they sailed back home to Sooke.

By early afternoon a light westerly breeze set in as we passed Pilar Point, and built steadily all afternoon.

"Bob, bring down the jib," I called as the boat surged increasingly into the rising contrary sea. "Let's tack out into the Straits to get a point of sail. We'll put into Neah Bay for the night, then set out into the Pacific in the morning."

Bob leapt into action, taking a reef in the mainsail and raising the working jib. By now the wind was blowing at twenty-five knots from ahead of us, and the sea was coming over the bow in regular sheets of spray. Bob's wet weather gear was running with water, as he struggled to manipulate his safety harness while working his way around the deck.

With all this water coming aboard, Christine took the helm and I went below to see if any water was coming in through the anchor locker. Bone dry. Bob's sealing and securing the deck hatch was working! From now on we would carry lots of rolls of wide tape to seal the anchor locker each time we headed out.

What was not dry was the cabin sole! Indeed it was awash in about an inch of water. Oh God! I thought, we must have sprung a leak. Where to start looking? The bilge pump was not running, and the bilge was dry. So the leak must be above the cabin sole.

With the boat's action so severe, and having no time to get over any feelings of seasickness, I checked all through hulls and hoses that I could find. Just then, a gust caught the boat, and we heeled significantly. This movement was accompanied by the sound of a waterfall coming from the galley. At excessive heel, the fresh water tanks, which were brim full, had refluxed up through the taps, a problem solved by shutting them when at sea. Another lesson learned.

While all this was going on, the rest of the crew were kept entertained by a United States military helicopter doing air sea rescue practice off our starboard side. Firstly a man leapt out of the helicopter into the water, before being retrieved in a lowered net from the hold of the hovering aircraft.

We beat our way into Neah Bay by 1700 hrs, and tied up to the fish packing plant's dock as sheltering fish boats had filled the marina. They kindly gave us permission to stay for the night, as they didn't expect any action in the prevailing gales. For good measure they sold us a gorgeous salmon for our supper. We all retired early to the accompaniment of barking sea lions that had taken possession of a nearby wharf.

What are we doing? I kept asking myself as I lay fitfully dozing through the night. Not even fishermen are going out in this stuff. I was comforted a little by the fact that *Demelza* had performed well in the first serious wind that we had experienced while fully laden.

Good news. The forecast was favourable. We were up at 0500 hrs as a hundred fish boats left for the open ocean. With Bob untying the lines, I pressed the engine starter to get us out of harbour, to no avail! So we tied up again to investigate the problem. What was it my night school instructor had said?

"A diesel engine needs three things to work, clean fuel, air and good compression." A quick check of the fuel filters showed that the fuel and air filters were clean, so it must be a compression problem.

"Bob, if you turn over the engine, I'll let off two of the compression levers to reduce the load on the engine. Once she fires I'll put the compression back on."

This we did with gratifying results and, as the engine leapt into life, we hurriedly disconnected ourselves from the dock and headed out to sea.

On the way at last

Now although this little exhibition must have impressed the crew of my abilities as a diesel mechanic, and helped bolster their morale, my resultant self esteem was tempered somewhat by not having the faintest idea why this malfunction should suddenly have occurred for the first time since we had owned the boat.

Nevertheless we were on our way, heading out between Tatoosh Island and Cape Flattery on a grey rolling sea, a leftover from the storm of the day before. In the absence of wind, we motored out to get away from the coast.

Heading west to the Pacific Ocean

"If you get eighty miles offshore," the local gurus in Victoria had said, "you'll get much steadier winds, and the seas won't be as rough in a blow."

Grey clouds were approaching from the south, and soon we began to feel the first zephyr of a southerly breeze. By mid afternoon we were sailing well in fifteen to twenty knots, forty six nautical miles offshore. Christine and Mary took the afternoon watch, while Bob recovered from his morning's gymnastics on the foredeck, and I tried to stop worrying.

By 1600 hrs the wind was up to thirty knots from the south. Spray was coming over the deck, but the spray sheets were keeping the cockpit dry. By now the sky was a lowering grey, the boat was active, and we were all feeling a bit under the weather.

Demelza was sailing under small jib and triple reefed main when there was a resounding "bang". We looked at one another and my heart almost stopped.

"What was that?" enquired Christine from the main hatch. My eyes quickly surveyed the deck and rigging, to observe the head of the mainsail working its way down the track on the mast. What was left of the main halyard, streamed out over the water and the mainsail began to flog.

"The only spare halyard we have for the main is the topping lift Bob. Can you bring down the main and attach it to the head of the sail?" I asked.

"Sure," said Bob, willingly reattaching his harness. Carefully he negotiated his way along the lurching deck, disappearing into clouds of hissing, stinging spray. As the boat plunged up and down in the frothing sea, he struggled to attach the end of the topping lift to the head of the deeply reefed main. I was truly glad when he finally regained the cockpit.

"Fantastic job." I grinned.

"Just like being on a crazy elevator." he replied, as he peeled off the hood of his wet weather suit. He must have been exhausted by the afternoon's deckwork. He had been at great risk. But here he was, still smiling and able to make a joke or two. What amazing strength and inner fortitude this man had when we needed it. He was the best crew I could have found.

All night we struggled against the wind and mountainous seas. The noise was all enveloping as we plunged ahead, being thrown from side to side with the occasional crash as the boat, after being temporarily airborne, landed against a solid wall of water.

Down below, Mary continued to produce iron ration food at intervals to keep us going. Of us all, she appeared to be the least nauseated. Seasickness pills seemed to have little effect on keeping lethargy at bay, and I felt less and less like doing anything. I had to force myself to concentrate on the jobs at hand between waves of nausea.

I put my head in the main hatch to see that all was well in the cabin, and found Mary lying in her bunk, with the lee cloth firmly secured around her.

"Otherwise it's just like being tossed around in a matchbox," she said. "When I am up, I need both hands to hang on. Everything down here is on the move."

Christine's attempt to connect with Peter Thomas on the DDD net failed as the gale continued to build before midnight.

"I don't know about you," I said, when we were all assembled below leaving the windvane to look after the boat, "I don't think it's any less brutal out here eighty miles off land than closer inshore. We'll see what its like for the rest of the night, but if this storm continues, I think we'll make for a rest stop at Grays Harbor tomorrow."

"Good idea." was the chorus.

By midnight, as Bob and I resumed watch, we could see the lights of fishing boats all around us. Scary tales abound of boats getting tangled up in fishing nets before being towed for miles behind trawlers. At 0100 hrs Mary produced a bowl of rolled oats. It was a fight to keep it down, a fight which I lost. Mary and Christine took over the watch between 0100 and 0400 hrs as we threaded our way through the fishing fleet in very poor visibility and sheets of rain and spray.

Mary woke Bob and me at 0400 hrs with some dry toast, which I managed to keep down. Bob had slept well. He and I struggled up into the cockpit where Christine was stoically still keeping watch.

"This isn't much fun." she declared as my green face appeared above the hatch cover. I could only agree as she disappeared down below.

At 0700 hrs it was a change of watch again. I celebrated by being seasick, and felt unable to even contemplate getting into my bunk, but would rather stay topsides with easy access to the rail. Christine joined me again as we looked at the broiling ocean around us. We braced ourselves against the occasional impact of the hull reconnecting with the ocean's surface after a brief spell of being suspended above it.

At 1000 hrs I went down below to plot a course for Grays Harbor before forcing myself to get some rest in the sea berth below. The contents of our bookshelves covered the bunk and floor. Clearing up was impossible in my condition, so I joined the mess on top of the bunk, and secured myself with the lee cloth.

Christine was exhausted by this time. So Mary and Bob took over at the helm. I lacked the confidence to let the new windvane steer the boat in those conditions, so we hand steered throughout the night. Later on in our voyage we found it steered the boat better than any person in heavy winds and rolling seas.

The miracle was that, although Mary had never had any experience steering a boat in such conditions, she turned out to be a natural. She steered us out of the danger of the bigger waves with an awesome display of expertise. Bob on the other hand tended to wander off the wind, causing the boat to heel uncomfortably close to abeam of the oncoming waves, with the possible resulting chaos of being laid over on our side.

Gradually, as the day progressed, the wind dropped, leaving a huge rolling sea, which instantly made both Bob and Mary sick. Christine, who though very tired, was less nauseated than the rest of us. She steered the boat under power towards Grays Harbor while I tried to tidy up some of the muddle below.

Alternately, we took turns at the helm while the rest of us went below to try to regain some strength. Christine fell asleep on top of all the wet weather gear in the main cabin. Bob went forward to his bunk fully clothed complete with woolly *toque*, while I went to sleep with the latest assortment of books all over my bunk.

As we approached the broad entrance to the Chehalis River, on which Grays Harbor is situated, we followed the long sandbar guarding its entrance looking for the two sea buoys that marked the entrance channel. Christine called up to me in the cockpit

"I've reported our position to Peter on the radio and that all is well."

As we drew up to Westport Boat Haven, we received a great welcome from the harbour master. Later his wife gave us a tour around the harbour in her car. Following this, after hot showers and a fresh prawn supper, we all retired to bed in a still and quiet boat, to sleep undisturbed for twelve hours.

"That has to be one of the worst trips I've ever experienced." I volunteered to the assembled bleary eyed crew next morning over breakfast in bright sunshine. "Perhaps summer has arrived?"

Christine began cleaning up the boat inside and out, while Mary seemed to take almost everything washable to the laundromat ashore. Drying clothes and equipment covered the sun drenched decks, and the warmth revived our spirits, and replenished our energy.

I checked out the engine compartment to see if I could find any reason why it continued to be such a reluctant starter, and was appalled to find salt water in our air filter. The only way to gain adequate access to the engine in *Demelza* was through the main port cockpit locker, which involved emptying all that locker's contents onto the dock, and then proceeding slowly, feet first, into the gloom below. This achieved, I noticed a drip of salt water coming from underneath the bridge deck. Tracing this back to its source, I found that the antisyphon valve on the engine's exhaust loop was leaking.

Bob and I mulled over this latest discovery.

"If the antisyphon valve is not working Bob," I said "then it's quite likely that we have been sucking water into the engine in those huge seas, and that could be the cause of reluctant starting."

"Good." he rejoined with his usual optimism "We'll just replace it with a spare."

Now, as I have previously noted, we had a locker full of spares, which had been the focus of many ribald comments about 'heavy boats.' But not one of the spare antisyphon valves I had would fit the plumbing at that particular location.

Undaunted, Bob set off briskly down the wharf to find a spare in town.

"Won't be long," he called as he scrambled up the ramp to shore, and disappeared on his quest. Mary returned from her third trip to the laundromat, and called to Christine, who was scrubbing the caked salt off the deck fittings.

"What did you have in your pocket?" she asked.

"Why?" asked Christine

"All the laundry came out pink!" she said. Sure enough the culprit was found in a pocket of Christine's shorts, a lipstick! Fortunately the pink dye had been selective in what it chose to permanently colour. For some reason it had concentrated on our underwear. The rest was satisfactorily remedied when Mary relaundered a whole load.

"Well pink underwear is all the rage isn't it?" Christine laughed.

After lunch we felt we had done enough chores, so went exploring. Christine and Mary found a secondhand book shop, and happily disappeared inside. Bob had found a chandlery, but the only antisyphon valve available of the right size was one used on domestic hot water tanks. He was sure it would work just fine until we could find something better. In the meantime he had put in an order for a replacement to be shipped from Seattle the next day.

As fish boats came in to discharge their loads of shrimp, they reported it as being 'very rough' outside. Bob prepared a supper of chili over rice as Mary and Christine rifled through their loot from the book store. After supper, in a perfect sunset, we sat having a coffee beginning to feel human again.

We talked of our experiences to date. Three shots at leaving Port Angeles, engine problems and a snapped halyard. We decided there and then that struggling offshore was not for us. Rather we would plan to hop down the coast. If the hospitality of the local people along the coast was anything like that we were receiving in Grays Harbor, we would have a great time and, with luck, arrive in San Francisco less exhausted.

After a great night's sleep and a fabulous breakfast of poached eggs, Bob and I tackled the job of replacing the snapped main halyard. The one that had broken had not been new, but it had been in good shape when we set off.

"While I'm up there, Bob, I'll have a good look to see if there is any reason why that line should have frayed. Maybe there's something sharp at the top of the mast rubbing on it?" Bob hauled me up in the bosun's chair to feed the replacement halyard down the mast. He then had to fish for its end with a coat hanger through an opening in the mast just above its base. "Gotcha!" he cried at last. The job was done.

The reason for the frayed halyard in strong wind seemed to be that the sides of one of the outlets at the top of the mast was quite sharp. The other three outlets, rigged with spare halyards, seemed smoother. So we settled on one of the spare halyards as the future main halyard, and re rigged a reserve in the old slot, making a note to do a more permanent fix at a later date.

While all this was going on Christine and Mary walked to the Coast Guard Station to get a weather forecast.

"It doesn't look good at all for the next few days," they reported on arriving back at the boat. My heart gave a thud. Maybe summer hadn't arrived after all.

Most of the jobs had been completed and, pending the arrival by express of the replacement antisyphon valve, we spent the next day on an expedition to Aberdeen. Walking along the seawall to catch the bus, a local called out

"I hear you all had showers this morning!"

Oh for a small town! We climbed aboard the bus.

"Where to folks?" asked the driver.

"Aberdeen please." we replied.

"Oh, you must be off the yacht that blew in the other day. Where are you from?"

"Victoria." we responded in unison.

"Ever seen a cranberry bog?" he asked.

"No never."

"Does anybody mind if we take a short detour to show these folks the cranberry bog?" he asked.

"No, go for it." they all smiled.

After the tour and explanation by other passengers about the technicalities of growing, harvesting, marketing and selling cranberries, we received further advice as to the best place for lunch in Aberdeen. With a cheerful wave from the assembled throng, we exited the bus feeling on top of the world.

Later, in the warmth of the sun and local hospitality, and fortified by fresh crab for supper, we decided that this was definitely the way to travel.

Four days later, we were still sitting in Grays Harbor with a series of south-southwesterly gales lashing the coast each day, with a reported thirteen foot sea outside the harbour. Still no antisyphon valve had been delivered by express mail. However on the fifth day, it appeared, only to show that it needed some adaptation to fit our plumbing. Bob and I went hunting ashore again.

"I've never walked so far in my life." puffed Bob as we searched around the streets until we found Junkie, a local treasure of a man, whose many hobbies included fixing up old cars and renovating houses. Sure enough, in the back of his warehouse, he found an adapter which, when installed later in the boat, produced a very satisfactory "fire" on the first turn of the engine.

"Well done Bob." I grinned as we celebrated our success over supper at a restaurant that Mary and Bob had visited a couple of days before.

"Do you realize," said Mary "These folks are up at two thirty every morning cooking breakfast for the fishermen before they take off for the day?" There was a sprinkling of fishermen in the restaurant. They told us that they had been out, but had to come back in again as their gear was breaking in the rough seas.

Day six in Grays Harbor broke with rain and grey scudding clouds. We caught a bus to Westport to restock with groceries and, while Bob and I caught the bus back with all the produce, Christine and Mary decided to walk the three miles back to the boat. By the time they returned, rain was lashing the docks, and the wind screeching in the rigging.

Day seven and we were still gale bound. It was my birthday and, though fair weather was not to be one of the presents, Christine had managed to secrete a nice collection of parcels which I opened, along with a bottle of champagne, later in the afternoon. One of my gifts was a magnet for fishing metal objects out of the bilge. Later we were given a ride to the local theatre to see a performance of *Irene*. This was delightful. Afterwards we were driven back to the harbour by Patty from the dress shop. I noticed the barometer was rising just a little.

By morning the skies had cleared and the forecast was excellent. The low pressure system that had lain over us for the past several days had moved north. At 0715 hrs we left the harbour with the last of the fishing fleet. We motored southwest across the mouth of the Columbia River, where the water was grey from silt brought down from inland. Sloppy seas resulting from the recent storm made for an uncomfortable ride, and the inevitable onset of seasickness which persisted throughout the day. On my watch after supper the wind began to rise again, this time from the north. At least we were being pushed in the right direction. *Demelza* was flying through the breaking seas.

"Things are getting a bit wild, Bob." I said "Can you take down the jib and raise the staysail?" He staggered forward, adjusting his life harness as he went, and again disappeared and reappeared in sheets of flying spray. After securing the jib on deck and hauling up the staysail, we had a shouted discussion about whether or not to take a reef in the main before deciding against it.

"I don't feel happy about steering with the wind vane in this." I said "If we broach in these waves we'll be knocked down." For the rest of the night, *Demelza* slalomed down those waves. Christine was on the helm when I woke up in the morning. She had done most of the steering that night, and her face looked drawn and exhausted when I put my head out to look around.

"We've seen shooting stars and several satellites going over in the night." she reported wearily.

"Good on you. It's time for you to get some shuteye." Thankfully she handed over the wheel as Bob and I resumed watch in the continuing blow. Grey whales were sounding out to sea, and what looked like turtles were lying on their backs in the breaking seas.

By noon we were passing Yaquinna Head and studying the charts, trying to decide how to approach the harbour at Newport, Oregon. Although the wind was still blowing strongly from the northwest, the sun had finally come out. What a difference that made as we motored into South Beach Marina exhausted and wet, but satisfied that *Demelza* had done so well yet again in stormy seas.

Another low pressure system was approaching from the south which presaged more gales. This was the fifth gale since we had left Neah Bay. However in the marina our main concern was having enough 10c pieces for showers.

After spending the day at the wharf on the north side of the harbour closest to town, we had to recross the harbour to its south side before 1700 hrs in the evening as loaded fish boats were arriving to land their catches on the north side. Once settled for the evening, Mary and Christine cobbled together a feast of fresh halibut for supper, before we all retired.

Sure enough the wind and rain returned during the night. After doing the inevitable laundry, we took off to explore the Marine Science Centre and local art galleries.

By next morning the wind had abated and the sun had come out. We left port and headed south in a low swell. As the day wore on, the wind and seas began to rise again. We motored into it, thinking we should make as much headway south as possible. All that night we fought for every mile of progress, with small sails pulled in tight, the motor running and spray flying everywhere.

"Not exactly the sunshine cruise you were promised to San Francisco." I said wryly to the crew.

"You're right," groaned Bob, "I want my money back."

All the next day we clawed our way south, getting thrown about. The cabin was a shambles. Mary provided food from the galley in atrocious conditions. Christine took long spells at the wheel. She kept radio contact with home, a job she really found hard to take, being thrown around below while trying to tune in to weather forecasts.

I was feeling very debilitated, and Bob wasn't too good either. Mary read on her bunk most of the afternoon, trying to fight off nausea. Christine was the only one left feeling semi human.

We were too far from Crescent City by afternoon, so I decided to make for Brookings. Christine called up the Coast Guard on the radio.

"Can you give us the latitude and longitude of the entrance to Brookings Harbor?" she asked.

"Sorry Ma'am," they replied "we're not allowed to do that."

We continued through the afternoon and on into the evening, taking a long detour around hazardous rocks along the way. By now it was getting dark and the seas were rough.

"What are the conditions across the bar entrance?" Christine asked the Coast Guard again.

"Rough, but passable." came the reply.

At last, in the gloom, I caught sight of the entrance between navigation lights that seemed impossibly close together.

"My God! That looks like a small entrance." I said in horror as we surfed down the huge combers coming at us from behind.

"Once we're committed, there's no turning back in these conditions." I said, painfully aware that approaching land in the dark during a storm is not recommended. But the wind was rising and we had the harbour in sight. Facing another night of being beaten up was an option none of us relished.

"OK." I said "Secure everything down below, seal up the boat and everybody hold on for a rough ride."

When the combers were in line with the harbour entrance, we turned the boat toward it, and felt these huge swells increasingly pressing us forward as we closed our destination. More and more the stern of the boat rose up as the huge waves raced shorewards underneath us. The bow rose like a frisky horse, and our stern wallowed in the following trough, anticipating the next huge crest. On either side of us, as we careered landwards in the shallower water on either side of the channel, the successively higher waves were breaking ferociously. All around us spume flew into the air, lit green and red by our navigation lights on the bow.

Faster and faster the waves bore us onward as we approached the narrow entrance at a frightening speed. We passed between the two navigation lights on the breakwater walls, and immediately the water was flat. The only sound, other than the receding roar behind us, was the hiss of *Demelza's* hull cutting through the water. The deepening darkness enclosed us as we poked our way into Brookings Harbor. It was totally quiet. Not a soul to be seen, and only dimly lit wharves most of which seemed fully occupied.

"Where should we tie up?" I shouted too loudly for the quiet conditions.

"Anywhere we can see that's empty." was the crew's rejoinder. They were ready for a break. As we tied up in the first empty space, Christine looked up and said "Look." Pointing at a nearby wharf she had spied a night heron sitting quietly in the soft light, watching for his supper in the calm water below.

Mary had done it again. "Scrambled eggs up." she called as we came in from tying up the boat. We consumed this feast with great relish, before collapsing on our bunks, listening to the QUIET.

By morning we had recovered. We were getting used to being beaten up and recovering. We moved on to Crescent City, twenty miles away, negotiating all the intervening rocks which necessitated going eight miles around Seal Rock. It took us the best part of the day.

The sight of the rough seas breaking over these rocks and their lighthouse had been awe inspiring. For although there was little wind, the swells were still high. Everyone had felt less seasick and was able to read for the first time on a passage. Christine even had time to take photographs.

Night Heron

After booking into the marina, we found the facilities left a lot to be desired. Desperate for showers we prevailed on a nearby motel owner to allow us to use a room and its facilities, for which he charged us $24. Bob had a chance to watch golf on television, and I watched the Watergate affair when it was Bob's turn for his shower.

The owner's wife was interested in our proposed voyage around the world, and asked us to be sure to visit her relatives in Bombay, India and include it in a book of our adventures. Meanwhile her husband was more concerned about a leak in the motel roof, which was understandable given the prevailing weather conditions.

On the way back to the boat, Christine mentioned that *Demelza* seemed to be listing to port. So, after breakfast, we rearranged some of the storage locker contents to redistribute the weight. As usual there was a lot of clearing up to do after a rough passage. We hosed off as much encrusted salt as possible especially around the aluminum toe rail, as it seemed to be etching the metal. Christine impressed us all by washing and waxing the outside of the hull, which soon sparkled again. As our burgees had all been blown to pieces, we replaced them to flutter proudly in the breeze.

Soon a strong southwesterly brought in more rain. Christine and I went up to Glen's Bakery for lunch. Here we saw the most remarkable photographs taken of Crescent City in the aftermath of the tsunami which had been caused by the great Alaskan earthquake in 1964. Whole sections of the town were ruined, submerged by the huge wave. Markings on the telephone poles showed the height to which the water had risen.

Next day, the wind really started blowing, and horizontal rain lashed the streets as we walked around town like a drift of daffodils in our yellow oilskins. Having seen all the sights, we called in at the del Norte Yacht Club, a small shack on the waterfront, consisting of a single meeting room with an attached shower. The members couldn't have been more hospitable as we sat with them watching videos, and munching on popcorn.

The following morning Bob and I went for breakfast at the local Best Western, where we learnt that two inches of rain had fallen during the past twenty four hours. Lynn and John, from the yacht club, arrived to take us on a tour of the Mystic Forest. This was a magical experience on a windy but sunny afternoon. The Cathedral Grove of massive Redwoods and the exhibit of indigenous artifacts were especially impressive. On returning to the boat it was pouring with rain again, and the parking lot was awash. This rain continued for twenty four more hours, and many fish boats continued to come in for shelter.

As dawn broke the next day, the barometer had risen a little, but lowering grey clouds covered the sky from horizon to horizon. We poked out to sea in a light southwesterly breeze, and motored around Trinidad Head, crossing the river bar on the flood tide into Eureka. A coast guard helicopter took a good look at us as we continued up the long sheltered approach to the marina at Woodley Island accompanied by the first pelicans we had seen. Great White egrets, sitting on Eucalyptus trees, occupied the shoreline as the sun set for a clear night.

True to form, by midday it was raining again. Christine and I walked across the long bridge into town to visit the local NOAA weather station. The staff gave us a tour of their weather monitoring devices, and we were depressed to see that the forecast was for continuing strong southeast winds for the next few days.

As the days passed with continued gales, pouring rain and intermittent fog, we kept ourselves entertained by meeting many of the yacht crews that were also sheltering from this unseasonable weather. Tony and Marion brought over hot muffins baked on their Roberts 44. They hoped to run their boat as a bed and breakfast following his retirement as a fire marshal. Margie, on her San Juan 24 came over for drinks before lunch one day, and we met Chuck on his Fantasia 35. He was on his way to Alaska, to meet a friend in Seward who had a Vancouver 32 Pilothouse just like *Demelza.*

With continuing delays everybody met everybody else, and we relieved our frustration by having meals together at local restaurants. Christine and Mary had to replenish our food supplies as we were using them up in harbour. This entailed long walks to the nearest stores and back. Occasionally local cruisers with cars would take pity on us as we carried heavily laden plastic bags in the rain, giving us rides back to the boat.

Finally, after eight days sheltering, we left Eureka at 0800 hrs on an ebb tide, crossing the bar into a calm sea before leisurely motoring around Cape Mendocino. Its notoriety had been impressed upon us by all we had met. Here northerly and southerly weather systems battle for superiority, making this a most unpredictable stretch of water. As soon as we had rounded it, the wind started to build from the north. So we shortened sail as a precaution, and still managed to make a good seven and a half knots over the ground in the right direction. By nightfall it was again blowing at thirty-five knots. Huge waves roared up behind us, their crests collapsing menacingly all around.

"Bob, I think we'd better take in another reef before sunset." I suggested as our speed crept ever upward.

Mary took over the helm to get more experience sailing the boat in heavy seas, and loved every minute of it. However the wind continued to build, so everybody was awake throughout the evening, sitting in the cockpit in wet weather gear, life jackets and harnesses. The wind increased to forty knots at 0100 hrs. I steered the boat whilst Mary kept me awake. Christine and Bob went off watch to rest. Bob was up at 0400 hrs and checked that our course line was sixteen miles out from land. Christine then relieved me at the helm and I went to sleep in my oilskins in the main cabin ready for any problems. By 0800 hrs both Christine and Bob were feeling seasick, so Mary took the wheel, again sharing it with me until 1500 hrs.

"This weather forecasting is all wrong" said Bob.

"You're right," I replied. "Before we do much more sailing, we've got to get our own weather fax so that we can see what's coming at us."

On arrival at Bodega Head the sea was white with spume blowing horizontally across the bay. Rounding the entrance buoy brought us on to a course line broaching the waves. Fortunately these were settling down the closer we got to land, except over the foul ground on either side of us. Gradually our course brought us up more into the wind, which was now funneling out of the bay. Rather than attempt to beat up the narrow channel against it, we turned on the engine, and crept at a painfully slow pace into the bay.

On the radio Christine managed to raise the wharfinger at the Spud Bay Marina. He assigned us a berth as we approached, and soon we were tied up and able to inspect the boat. All seemed well except for the jib's bag which had been lashed onto the foredeck. This had shredded itself on the lifelines to which it had been secured. Mary produced supper, and then we all fell on our bunks at 1900 hrs for a fourteen hour sleep.

"My, we're all looking a better colour this morning." I volunteered on surfacing for breakfast. Appetites had also recovered.

"Harold and Virginia are coming to visit us for lunch today." announced Christine.

She and Mary prepared a lunch of salmon, egg and roast beef sandwiches with salad, to be followed by slices of ginger cake, and washed down with two bottles of wine. Our welcome guests duly arrived, bringing lots of news and a parcel of goodies. Fresh corn, peaches from their orchard, kiwifruit and bananas, a French loaf, summer sausage, cookies and grapefruit. What a bounty!

Virginia and Harold

"There was such a lot of news to catch up on." rasped Christine after our visitors had left for home later in the evening

"What wonderful, generous people they are." added Mary.

The next morning, with the wind still blowing hard, Christine and I hiked over the sand dunes separating the marina from the boisterous sea outside. We were startled to see a large ketch stranded on the sand banks in the approach to the marina's sea wall, and later learned that they had tried to come in after dark to shelter from the gale. They had misread one of the channel markers on the long and narrow approach to the marina entrance.

"It just goes to show that closing land in the dark is not a good option," I mused "But given the promise of a quiet night as opposed to a rough one out at sea, it's a temptation hard to resist."

By afternoon the sun was shining, and it was positively warm for the first time since we had left home. Bob broke out his shorts, to much comment from all around. Christine and I borrowed a car belonging to an air force pilot who was on a nearby Islander 30, to pick up some shopping. He told us of his entry here the previous November in a seventy knot wind from the north plus fog, which made our experiences seem very tame.

That evening the four of us had a long discussion about seasickness and how to better manage the passage making in really rough weather. We needed to keep up nourishment and strength to cope with severe conditions over lengthy periods of time. We had tried a variety of seasick remedies, and none seemed to provide us with the degree of protection we needed.

"Do you know," I said "Before this passage I would never have believed that I would have had a problem with seasickness. But I reckon I'm the most affected of us all."

"But we all felt awful this last leg." rejoined Bob.

"I couldn't bear anything in my mouth" said Christine "though I don't seem to be affected until later than the rest of you."

"Well, fixed hours on watch just don't seem to work," I reflected. "After a couple of hours steering in those seas I'm beat and feel like a zombie."

"So shorter watches, say two hours at a time, would be worth a try?" suggested Bob.

"OK, we'll try that, and try to take even the smallest amount of food regularly during a storm."

Another wild night followed and we were all relieved to be securely tied to a wharf. I made several trips topsides to stop the incessant clatter of the wire halyards against the metal mast, which was driving us all crazy below. The decision to stay was not difficult, although the time that Bob and Mary had available to get to San Francisco was now at a premium.

Christine and I walked to Bodega Head to watch the stormy seas crashing on the sandstone cliffs below. The birds were seeking shelter in the grasses of the surrounding sand dunes, which are a wildlife sanctuary. This is one of the great migratory pathways along the Pacific Coast.

The next morning we awoke to see the red pennants on the seawall flying in the brisk breeze signifying another gale warning. So we decided to take the bus to Santa Rosa, the county seat of Sonoma County. After a twenty seven mile drive through the attractive rural countryside, we alighted in the charming town's square, which was bathed in warm sunshine.

Though an earthquake in 1966 had almost flattened the town, most of it had been rebuilt. We wondered at Dr. Luther Burbank's ability to develop so many unique varieties of plants in his small cottage garden, a genius recognized by many visiting world dignitaries of his day. In all he had hybridized eight hundred species of fruit and vegetables to improve their qualities, and to this day the dictionary immortalizes his name "to Burbank a plant" meaning, "to improve it."

In the past the Russians used to harvest sea otter pelts here. General Vallejo was given some land by the Spanish Government for services rendered to the State when gold was found in California. The Americans later displaced the Spanish and Russians.

By the next morning the wind had gone, so we left at 0500 hrs and motored below the steep rocky cliffs of Point Reyes in two knots of wind. As the sun came up so did a gentle breeze which allowed us to sail easily into San Francisco Bay. We sat spellbound on the foredeck looking at the Golden Gate Bridge spanning the entrance to the Bay shining in the bright sunshine. Pelicans put on a fishing display, diving all around us.

"This is a dream come true," smiled Christine later. "To actually sail our own boat into San Francisco."

"It was everything I thought it would be." I replied. "What a high!"

Golden Gate Bridge

Once in the Bay, we turned to port toward the town of Sausalito, passing many boats sailing in the warm afternoon.

"Welcome to San Francisco." called the crew of one of them as it sailed past us.

"That was friendly." observed Christine.

We found a berth at the Clipper Yacht Club, having weaved our way through a mass of anchored boats in various states of disrepair, some submerged with just the tips of their masts showing above the water.

"This is the home of Scanmar marine, makers of our windvane" I said to Bob. "I plan to pay them a visit to find out exactly what kind of weather that gadget can handle before we experience much more of what we've been through."

Over a bottle of champagne we toasted just about everything, but especially that hardy crew Mary and Bob. Always of good cheer, always willing to help. Christine and I realized we would miss them badly.

Next day we went by bus into San Francisco where Bob and Mary rented a car. They were off to shop for clothes while Christine and I took in the wonderful photography in the Ansel Adams Gallery. Then we went up the fifty two floors to the top of the Bank of America building for its fantastic view of the city and bay below. We spent an hour gazing at it all before descending and making our way through the hustle and bustle of Chinatown. A walk through the financial district took us to the Sausalito ferry and the return trip to *Demelza.*

A visit to West Marine chandlery on the next day netted us a whole new collection of cleaning materials for the boat, while Mary tackled another load of laundry. This done, we drove to Tiburon and walked along the waterfront, calling in to look at the impressive Corinthian Yacht Club on the way.

The following day we drove over to San Raphael to see Frank Lloyd Wright's architectural showpiece, the Marin County Civic Center. It's very modern space aged shape did not impress one of its occupants, who said furnishing rooms with curved walls was a pain, and all inter-office connections seemed to involve walking for miles. We thought it was magnificent.

From here we made our way to the Sonoma Winery, where we sat in the shade of its lovely homestead, enjoying the ambience, and sipping a glass of champagne and nibbling on almonds, all for $14.

We rigged a big tarpaulin over the boat in the eighty degree daytime heat in an attempt to keep the cabin cool. By afternoon it was too hot to do any serious work, so we went to see the Corps of Engineers' working model of the Bay, which is used to study tides and currents.

Finally the day had come for Mary and Bob to go home. They left early for the 0800 hrs flight, and immediately we missed having them around. They had been such good sports and had taken everything the elements had thrown at us in very good spirit.

Our visit to Scanmar Marine was extremely rewarding. We were shown a video of how the vane was supposed to work under various conditions. It was as if a light had suddenly come on. From then on we had confidence in letting it do its job.

A trip to a chandlery turned up a suitable second hand genoa with some spare hanks. I had noticed that the ones on the working jib were already showing signs of wear. Our neighbour on the dock, Mary, seeing that we were now alone, kindly invited us to visit her lovely home in Belvedere. Here we met Debbie, her daughter, who had completed the Ironman Hawaiian race, and was just leaving to compete in the Santa Rosa triathlon in which she later came in second in her group and eighth overall.

Over the next few days we varnished, polished and entered in the GPS waypoints for our next passage to Ventura, three hundred nautical miles to the south. Walt, on the ham radio and much to our amusement, asked Christine for a picture of herself and *Demelza* for his radio shack wall.

"Oh," laughed Christine "It's been years since anybody asked for my photo."

The radar had lost its signals again, so we had somebody come and fix it. The sail bags had been re-stitched and the genoa altered and triple stitched. We calculated that if we left Sausalito one hour before low slack tide, we should be passing out of the Bay under the Golden Gate Bridge before the start of the flood tide.

Early next morning, when many of our new found friends had come down to the dock to wave us off, we started the motor, untied our mooring lines and put the engine into reverse. Nothing happened. We didn't move an inch. Flashing through my mind were all the possibilities. Major transmission failure? Gear linkage broken? Propeller fallen off? Then I looked over the side to see swirling mud in the propeller's wash. We were hard aground!

To say we were embarrassed is an understatement. It gave those ashore a good laugh as we retied the boat to the dock, and regrouped around the coffee pot to wait for the tide to float us off.

In due course that's what happened, and we motored our way into an already significant floodtide under the bridge. As we passed under it, workers were suspended below the span above us, sandblasting the beams in readiness for painting. The strong current inexorably pushed us toward the port side shoreline of rocks and boulders which was covered with spume from waves kicked up by the twenty-five knot breeze. As hard as we hauled in the mainsheet, we still seemed to be setting closer to the beach. One wave reared up on our starboard beam and its crest broke into the cockpit. Fortunately we had remembered to put in all the hatch covers, so no water got into the boat. At last we were able to clear the point to arrive at Halfmoon Bay by nightfall.

The following day we approached Santa Cruz and, as the wind dropped, we motored to a marina in the river. We passed many boats heading out into the bay for the evening's beer can races. On the next wharf was a Cal 39 from Alameda. As I looked out of the cabin window the following morning, her crew was sitting on deck, head between hands, staring towards land. We learnt later that the couple had one year's experience of sailing and were on the start of a cruise, from San Francisco to Hawaii and then on to British Columbia. Outside San Francisco they had broached, swamping the cockpit and making a shambles of their cabin. Their portholes had all been open and a large cooler, stored in the cockpit, had broken free, simulating a missile gone berserk ricocheting uncontrollably, causing damage and personal injury as it went. The crew was not impressed and was dreaming of land, while the skipper was already planning to give the Hawaiian trip another go.

Wishing them luck, we left the next morning, motoring in a very light breeze across the bay to the marina in Monterey. An interesting feature of our stay in this marina was that when we first arrived, I went to check in with the harbour master while Christine began to tidy the boat. She heard a crackling sound and, thinking it might be an electrical short, she quickly turned off the power switch. She inspected wiring around the boat and checked out under the floor boards. It was most mysterious. She couldn't discover what was making the noise. Later we learned that it was caused by crackling shrimp that feed on any small vegetation growing on the outside of the hull.

We took a bus to visit Monterey's excellent Aquarium, and on our way saw the schooner *Californian* swarming with young people getting her ready for a cruise in the bay. During the very hot afternoon we escaped into the coolness of a local movie house to watch Much Ado about Nothing, before visiting the Maritime museum. On the way home the local coast guard station gave us some helpful advice about sailing down the Big Sur. San Simeon appeared to be the only safe haven before Morrow Bay, which is notorious for its sudden fogs.

In the marina, a neighbouring boat was being prepared for trucking up north to Seattle, as it had experienced two blown jibs and a freaked out crew who refused to do any more sailing northward. Another bigger boat had blown out its mainsail two days before, and its crew was busily bagging it up to have it repaired.

For the next two days strong winds continued to blow, so we visited Pebble Beach, driving around its famous golf course and Silverwater Cove. We took a bus to Carmel to enjoy its art galleries and a pub lunch of Cornish Pasties and Whitbread beer. We enjoyed the farmers' market which had for sale lovely fresh vegetables from the Salinas Valley.

With our newfound confidence in the windvane, *Demelza* looked after herself very well in the fifteen knot downwind sail the following day. We were able to cover a respectable one hundred and forty three nautical miles in twenty four hours. At night Christine and I spelled one another off on three hour watches.

First thing in the morning we rounded Point Conception in a light breeze before heading into the Santa Barbara Channel.

As we progressed, fog began to form all around us, and oil rigs loomed menacingly through the gloom as we slipped by. That evening the fog had gone but we had trouble finding the entrance to the Santa Barbara Marina in the moonlight because the city lights competed with the navigational aids on the way in. It was quite noticeable, after rounding Point Conception, that we had moved into summer, as the evening air was warm for the first time.

Oil rig off Santa Barbara

On July 3rd, after three days of total relaxation in the sun and a visit from our friends Jane and Hamish to celebrate Christine's birthday, we moved to Ventura. Here we planned to do a major cleanup on *Demelza* and catch up with routine maintenance. We had time to see much of the surrounding area as Jane kindly lent us her car for a week. We stayed for a month at the friendly Ventura Yacht Club, meeting many of its members, especially Roger and Amy on their lovely old powerboat *Ile Delice*. Also Collette and Chuck, who were later to join us on the leg from French Polynesia to Tonga. The port itself had been beautifully developed as Mariners Village, with open air restaurants and shops set off colourfully by terraces covered with jasmine, lavender and bougainvillea.

Ventura Yacht Club

Here we met Paul and Karen from San Diego, who were later to show us the sights of their home city, and who were experts at the California Shuffle. This entailed utilizing the three days free reciprocal privileges available at California yacht clubs, shuffling from one club moorage to another on the appropriate day.

All too soon our visit was over so, in hot and humid weather, we moved on, to sail across to Santa Cruz Island in the Channel Islands group. Dry scrub oak covered the hills around our anchorage at Fry's Harbor. At night the sea was rolly, but not enough to keep us awake. Exploration here took us to Guervo Valdes where there was a picturesque cave and waterfall, before we sailed down the coast to Little Scorpion anchorage for the night. This was much rollier than the previous night and on getting up in the morning, we found a nearby boat had drifted down on top of us. His anchor rode had crossed our stern anchor line which we had put out to keep our bow facing the swell. Eventually we were able to free ourselves from its grip, while its skipper continued to sleep throughout the whole maneuver.

Anchorage Santa Cruz Island

We motored, and later sailed, the sixty five nautical miles to Catalina Island in a fifteen to twenty knot breeze from the west. We arrived in Emerald Bay on the northeast side of the island, to be greeted by Shirley, the harbour master. She gave us a short lesson on how to pick up the mooring buoys, before allocating us the only spot that had a little protection from the incoming swell. This was behind a large rock out in the bay.

So began two weeks among the mass of vacationers from Los Angeles and other mainland Californian communities. Moored side by side on the mooring buoys, strung along the length of the coves, we were one of hundreds. Everything here had to be well regulated to accommodate the volume of traffic. Every seaside holiday amenity was available either in Avalon, the main settlement, or at the smaller Two Harbors at the northern end of Catalina Island.

We swam, lazed in the sun, went for walks in the barren scrub-covered hills, and visited many of the coves along the island's northeast shore. Most anchorages were rolly, and achieving a reasonable sleep was sometimes difficult. We had the opportunity to meet several people who were helpful and hospitable, especially Nancy and Geoff from the Balboa Yacht Club who entertained us at the Club Outstation in White Cove. Others we met had cruising experience going to Mexico, who kindly invited us to visit their clubs as we moved down the coast.

The day of our leaving broke calm and sunny, so I was glad to have fueled up on our visit to Avalon. We motored twenty six miles across a calm sea to the Bahia Corinthian Yacht Club in Newport Beach which was a wonderful base from which to explore the attractive community of Balboa Island. This resembles a modern Venice in the flat surrounding sand. Opulent homes took advantage of the dredged canals and were surrounded by well manicured lawns and extensive gardens. We loved watching the open electric launches leisurely taking their owners and guests up and down the harbour for evening drinks before supper, their awnings flapping gently in the summer's breeze. A visit to Minnie's, a famous chandlery, was a must for second hand gear.

At this point, we left *Demelza* in the Club's care and took a break from onboard living to visit Virginia and Harold's home in Fullerton. Here we met up with many other longstanding friends.

Once back on the boat we relocated to the Newport Harbor Yacht Club which was founded in 1912. Eric showed us the mooring buoy that had been allocated to us, situated in a quiet part of the bay just below the yacht club's lawn. The routine for going ashore was to hail the yacht club launch by sounding the boat's Freon horn.

Early photographs of Newport harbor show it as a sand bar, with summer cottages along its length. These have now been replaced by multi million dollar homes, with individual docks at the bottom of their beautiful gardens. Prices in 1993 varied from six hundred thousand to three million dollars.

After celebrating our wedding anniversary with Jane from Ventura, who had come down especially for the occasion, we were hailed by John on our way back to the boat

"Hi there," he said "would you care to join my wife and me at the Club for supper tonight, as our guests?" A lovely Datura tree decorated the entrance way to the club house as later we made our way in to enjoy a pleasant evening in their dining room overlooking the bay.

The following morning we joined Ron and Patti for breakfast on the yacht club's deck, watching Etchell dinghies being rigged for the finals of the world championships. Among their crews was a friendly man from the Bay of Plenty in New Zealand who was working in the United States on an extended work permit. He had taken early retirement from his law firm, leaving it in the hands of his son, to enjoy a life of sailing.

Geoff, who we had met in Catalina, arrived in the evening to take us home to Tustin for supper. He had made an ingenious and removable cockpit table for us, in his home workshop, which was to prove very useful. Geoff owned a yacht club mooring which he had bought in 1950 for fifteen hundred dollars. He told me it was now worth four thousand dollars with six hundred dollars per year maintenance levy and four hundred dollars a year for taxes.

One day we heard a loud, continuous blast of a Freon horn from the boat next to us. Thinking there might be something amiss, I went over in our dinghy to see if I could be of help. It transpired that the owner, a venerable dentist of many years standing in the yacht club, was trying to attract the attention of the club's launch to keep an appointment in town. He was so pleased we had responded, that he invited us both to the club for supper that evening.

On another occasion, Geoff called to take us to Minnie's where we bought a "flopper stopper" which we were assured, would reduce *Demelza's* rolling at night in exposed anchorages. On returning to the boat, one of our neighbours was looking steadfastly at *Demelza*. He was employed by the local coast guard auxiliary and was interested in buying a different cruising boat. Later Bruce and his two boys arrived. He had seen our Seven Seas Cruising burgee, and had come over to investigate. He was delighted to hear we were also on our way to Mexico and the Pacific, as that was his family's plan.

At first light, we left Newport Harbor in a shroud of sea fog. Ghostly boat shapes slipped by, seagulls stretched their wings before leaving their roosts on top of the channel buoys before idly disappearing into the gloom for unknown destinations. We moved slowly along in two knots of wind all day. As we approached Mission Bay we were hailed by one of the residents waving a green flag. It was Gloria and her husband asking us to join them for an evening aboard their Petersen 46. They had just returned from a cruise to the Caribbean, Panama, Alaska and British Columbia. However they were now looking forward to life ashore as Gloria had been perpetually seasick and couldn't stand it any more. One of the side benefits of our visit with them was that they sold us their Baja fuel filter, which later proved to be invaluable in keeping a lot of rust, water and dirt out of our fuel tanks.

We left for San Diego, reaching around Point Loma while avoiding the significant kelp beds growing out to sea. We close hauled all the way up the harbour entrance, arriving at Shelter Island by mid afternoon, and tied up at the Silver Gate Yacht Club. A local member of the club had offered us his empty space while he was away cruising. However the wharfinger was not impressed with our private arrangement, and ultimately moved us to an alternative space for $11 a night. We settled in happily to watch a firework display against the backdrop of the city's lights.

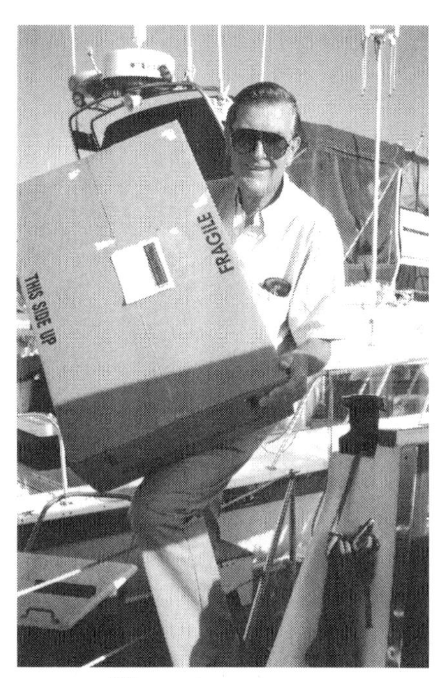

Watermaker arrives

Christine cleans aviation fuel off the rigging

CHAPTER 4
San Diego and onwards

San Diego in the Fall is a unique boating experience. Boats from the north were beginning to congregate in preparation for winter cruising in Mexico and places beyond. Space at the wharves was at a premium, and we observed more of the California Shuffle. Consequently, throughout our two month stay, the whole harbour gave the impression of a large anthill, constantly on the move. Eventually we moved to Shelter Island Marina where our new neighbour was Monty. He spent most evenings sitting on his bridge deck smoking foul smelling cigars upwind of *Demelza*. After one night of this torture Christine exclaimed.

"We've got to move. I can't bear it!"

But in the time it took to arrange an alternative wharf, Christine had made friends with Monty and his wife. As I returned up to the wharfinger to rescind our booking, Monty offered to smoke downwind of *Demelza*.

Local residents Karen and Paul, who lived on their boat *Karen S* and whom we had met in Ventura during the summer, turned up soon after our arrival. From then on they, with the added bonus of their car, helped us tirelessly with all the jobs that needed to be done to prepare *Demelza* for her onward voyage.

For entertainment, the most exceptional experience was going down the harbour in our dinghy to Humphrey's open air concerts, held in the band shell of the hotel's gardens overlooking the harbour. A huge raft of dinghies, kayaks and anything else afloat, would congregate in the bay below, from which there was a most excellent view of the stage. Boaters would enjoy their picnics in the evening sun, anticipating the start of the evening's entertainment. A good natured crowd welcomed Englebert Humperdinck, Tom Jones and Ray Charles on three separate occasions. After the show, under a starlit sky, the rafted flotilla separated, put on their navigation lights and, under the watchful eye of the harbour police, made their way back to their mother ships.

Local maritime businesses put on a series of useful workshops and seminars on a variety of subjects which either Christine or I or both would attend. Weather and weather charts, cruising the Baja and Sea of Cortez, radio and GPS operations, keeping healthy while living on board, deep sea fishing and heavy weather sailing were some of the subjects covered.

These same businesses were doing a brisk trade with the travelers, selling everything from replacement parts to equipment "you just can't manage without." Boxes of food and drink were being delivered each day in bulk for stowage, as though there were no shops to be found south of the border.

Interspersed with all this activity, we took welcome breaks at Humphrey's Happy Hour each day where, for $3, we could pick up a beer or margarita and various selections of finger food in the congenial company of other cruisers.

Christine managed to find time to attend a course of "Conversational Spanish for Boaters," and became quite good at it. The course concentrated on expressions for the boater such as reporting our arrival to Port Captains, and buying food and drinks ashore. This proved very useful in the months ahead.

Karen and Paul took us in their car to experience the Mexican Independence Day festivities at Chula Vista, ten miles south of San Diego. The Mariachi band competed with a gusty wind which blew all the decorative balloons in colourful swirls.

Naturally we had to do some sight seeing. We particularly enjoyed our visit to San Diego's Sea World with friends Jim and Judy from our home yacht club. We visited Balboa Park, built for the 1923 San Diego Exhibition. One evening we sailed with new friends on their Hinckley 43 for a cruise in the twilight down San Diego Harbor to the Coronado Hotel and back. It was a magical experience, passing the shapes of naval vessels moored in the twilight and silhouetted against the twinkling lights of the Coronado Bridge and downtown San Diego.

Virginia and Harold came from Fullerton for a visit which coincided with the arrival of Ann from Victoria, who had flown in to join us for our passage to Mexico. One night we had a memorable supper at San Diego Old Town. At that time a hurricane was threatening Cabo San Lucas, and we were receiving torrential rainfall at its periphery. Our table for outdoor dining was located under one of the many umbrellas on the restaurant's patio. It had an overhead gas heater keeping off the chill. No sooner had we started our meal than the heavens opened and we were surrounded by a wall of water cascading off the umbrella. The poor waitresses dashed from one table to an other clad in plastic sheets, and the mariachi band shuffled under umbrellas between the tables, trying to hold on to both the umbrellas and their instruments. Needless to say their efforts bonded everyone to an appreciative audience, and the sodden little group received rapturous applause.

Our time in San Diego was coming to an end. Boats had already started leaving by ones and twos during the previous weeks. A radio report from *Utopia*, with Sandy and Jack on board, stated that they were having a rough ride down the Baja coast.

Karen and Paul ran us down to Tijuana, across the Mexican border, to meet Jose. He took us to his office, where he issued Mexican Ham Radio Licenses. This was our first view of Mexico, and Christine's first serious need to be able to communicate in Spanish. Poor Jose had been aroused from his sickbed to ferry us around, but he did so with good humour. We were then driven back to the border along streets resplendent with reams of waste paper blowing in clouds and filled with noisy crowds and hawkers.

My visit to the San Diego Customs Office, to obtain a Certificate of Departure from the United States, triggered a surprising response. The Official produced a most impressive document, resplendent with the American crest which declared that 'The good ship *Demelza* had left San Diego on a specified day with the Captain on board (me) and "two good men in ballast" (Christine and Ann). That certainly produced a most gratifying reaction among *Demelza's* crew.

On the morning of 15th November, Dan came down from the San Diego Yacht Club with a weather picture in his hand.

"If you get a move on," he said "you have a couple of clear days coming up, which should get you to Cedros Island. After that, shelter is readily available."

On hearing this we left harbour to the accompaniment of Monty's boat horn, and Dan in his lovely boat to bid us farewell. In a healthy twelve knot northwesterly breeze we made good time through the first night, and talked on the radio to Sandy and Jack on *Utopia.* They were now anchored in Bahia Santa Maria recovering from a rocky ride. Ann began to familiarize herself with going on watch when she joined me at 0300 hrs until Christine took over at 0700 hrs.

Ann takes the helm

The following day, in calm weather, we reached Cedros Island. With Christine keeping regular radio schedules with the boats ahead, and fair seas, we were soon entering Bahia Santa Maria. After five nights at sea we were feeling pleased with our progress. We had seen four freighters during our night watches, and the days were spent leisurely sunbathing on deck watching the flying fish jumping out of *Demelza's* way.

Arriving in Bahia Santa Maria at night was our first attempt at entering a strange harbour using radar. We managed it slowly, as it took us some time to interpret the picture in relationship to the diagrams in Charlie's Charts. After anchoring, we rigged the anchor light, and retired for a good night's sleep.

We stayed a day in this lovely wide bay, which is about five miles across at its entrance. The crews of two other Canadian boats rowed over to say hello on their way to do some fishing. We watched them progress toward the sandy shoreline, and in the evening we joined them for a supper of their catch of the day.

On the following morning's expedition ashore the surf was higher. We managed to jettison Ann overboard from the dinghy while trying to land in the surf. She took it in good part, and even volunteered for a walk into the hills, where we saw some large flowering cacti, hummingbirds and many unfamiliar wild flowers on the sandy, rolling hills.

Bahia Santa Maria to Cabo San Lucas was an easy journey, starting with a lot of wind. This died off at night, necessitating motoring with the autopilot. At dawn we were seventy nautical miles from Cabo, when the wind got up to fifteen knots from the southwest. We were joined by an escort of several dolphins frolicking around the boat. By 2000 hrs, we were off Cabo Falso as the wind again dropped. We had to motor through the night and around the arches at Cabos Arcos, entering the marina in the morning. On arrival, a nice young Englishman tied us up and offered us each a cold beer.

Approaching Cabo San Lucas

Of the three officials we had to deal with, by far the most enterprising was the Customs Officer. He had an ingenious method of deciding which of the hundreds of boats entering Cabo San Lucas he would bother to go down to inspect. On his desk was a cardboard box containing ten coloured marbles, three white and seven green. If after shaking, a white marble first emerged through a small opening, he would inspect the boat. If green, he wouldn't bother. Five times he tried to get a green marble out of the slot, but each time a white one emerged to much hilarious laughter all around. Whereupon he made an executive decision not to bother to inspect *Demelza* anyway and stamped our entry papers to Mexico.

Arriving back at the boat after our American Thanksgiving supper ashore at a local restaurant, *The Giggling Marlin*, we found we had locked ourselves out of the boat. Just as I started banging on neighbouring boats to find a hacksaw, a head popped up from the boat opposite. He said that he was a professional lock smith, and in seconds had *Demelza* picked open.

One of the excursions that we most enjoyed was a visit to the Finnisterre Hotel for drinks on their terrace. From here we watched the total eclipse of the moon over the Pacific, followed by a fantastic sunset. Another was an early morning jaunt in *Demelza* to see the sunrise over the arches at Cabo Arcos, which Christine sketched before taking some photographs.

Fortunately we had arrived during a week of sale prices for wharfage in the Cabo marina. But after five days the sale was over. After a very hot walk along the dusty streets of town to the Port Captain, Immigration and Customs Offices, all located in different parts of town, we booked out of the marina.

The morning sunshine made the famous arches glow as we motored out, and we were surprised to see *Joyride*, the boat we had met in Santa Cruz on his way to Hawaii, anchored out in the bay. Apparently he had finally got the message from his crew and had decided that the calm waters of Mexico would be much more to her liking.

For the whole day we were headed by a two knot breeze from the north as we entered the Sea of Cortez. Mercifully our bimini kept the hot sun off our heads. By nightfall we could see the island of Espiritu Santo in the distance. We turned into Puerto Ballandra to anchor after twenty hours of motoring. This very pretty bay is open to the east, with rocky shores embracing a brilliant white sandy beach.

Accompanied by a good breeze in the morning we left the bay as the wind died again.

"I can't believe how little wind there is." I said as the motor sprang into action.

Soon we were anchored off El Candalero beach on the island of Espiritu Santo. We took the dinghy ashore to explore the grotto and its well, located on the dry hillside above the beach. All that night the boat rolled mercilessly. None of us slept very well. Wide awake by 0700 hrs and looking out to see what all the commotion was about, we could see the wind sweeping down in dust storms over the tops of the surrounding hills, with a resultant swell curving around the point to our north.

Nashira with Bruce, Kris and their two boys, Nathan and Scott, joined us in the bay. We had first met them in Newport Beach, California. After a morning swimming, photography, walking and sketching, we motored over to Bahia San Gabriel where all the fish boats were anchored. We soon realized that they were not getting the swell that we had experienced in the other bay. So we entered the bay and dropped anchor. After a supper of prawns off one of the fish boats we retired for a better night's sleep.

As the northerly breeze had freshened by the next morning we stayed where we were. We went ashore, with Phil and Diane from *Belle Louise*, to explore the remains of an old oyster farm with its lagoon. Nearby were some caves with Indian petroglyphs readily visible. There was a Frigate bird rookery close by in the mangroves, with blue footed Boobies sharing their shelter from the north wind. Heavy grey clouds covered the hills as we took our booty of prawns over to *Belle Louise* for Phil to show us his favourite way of cooking them.

Then, after a one night stop at Caleta Lobos, we made for La Paz where, after motoring up the long channel between El Mototе and the Baja and along the La Paz waterfront, we entered Marina de La Paz. Mary, the owner, checked us in before we went down to the docks to see who else had arrived. *Prologue*, *Sine Tomore, Magic Carpet* and many others that we had met along the way had already settled in. We heard stories of rough rides they had experienced during the past few days while we had been anchored in Espiritu Santo.

Many boats had decided to anchor out in the channel. This anchorage had a fierce reputation. Known as the "La Paz Waltz," anchored boats were at the mercy of the strong tides that washed them one way and then the other. This had the potential danger of dislodging the anchor and flushing them either up the creek or out to sea.

That first evening, we walked over with Phil and Diane to Englebert Humperdinck's resort hotel, *Posada de Englebert.* Here we celebrated our arrival. On return to the marina, Ann and Christine were shown over the sixty five foot powerboat *Jenni* by its owner and crew.

"Now, that's a boat" they both agreed.

After a shopping spree ashore, where Christine bought the Christmas presents for our family which Ann had kindly agreed to take with her, we spent the last five days of her stay cruising some of the bays on the nearby islands. The weather was perfect for her to enjoy the swimming and hiking on the beaches and surrounding hills. However the heat was beginning to affect us all. Christine made Christmas cards for the family and close friends to go home with Ann. By day pelicans kept us entertained sweeping around the boat and, in the evening, diving for their supper in the bay. As different boats came into our anchorages taking time out from "city living" in La Paz, we exchanged visits to enjoy learning of different places and people that we encountered.

We visited the Los Isolottte rocks, home of a colony of vociferous sea lions, and watched their antics just as closely as they watched ours. Ann's time with us was coming to an end. We moved south again to Ensenada Grande before sailing the whole length of Epiritu Santo into a little bay south of San Gabriel for the night. We put into Marina Palmira to meet up with new friends Steve and Veronica, on *Malolo*. This marina was more expensive than Marina de la Paz. A newer facility, it had a substantial sea wall protecting it from the open seaway but was still vulnerable to swells.

Two boats from our home yacht club arrived, *Expediter* with John and Sandy, and *Reiver* with Terry and Christine. They had met up with *Belle Louise* the previous night in Ballandra, sheltering from a gusty wind.

Ann was up early to catch the bus to Cabo San Lucas for the flight home. She looked happy and sun tanned, so we felt she had had a good experience cruising in Mexico. We would miss her company.

On getting back to *Demelza* and relocating to Rocos Lobos, we had a radio call from Marina de la Paz saying that a boat called *Yassu* had been calling us all day. We put out a call and found that Harry, a Canadian of Greek ancestry, whom we had met in San Diego, was incapacitated twelve nautical miles southeast of Punta Coyote. His propeller had broken in thirty-five knots of wind. He was exhausted and could not raise any help on the radio.

Harry, who was from our home port Victoria, planned to sail his twenty foot boat to Greece to claim his inheritance in the Peloponnesus. Passionately interested in the return of the Elgin Marbles from the British Museum to his homeland, he was a man with a mission.

When we had first met Harry and *Yassu* in San Diego, he was in the process of sawing off the end of his boom because it kept catching on his backstay. Small in stature, he possessed an immense personality, personifying for me, a typical Greek. As we had watched him prepare *Yassu* for sea, cobbling together a home made wind vane, I had wondered where we would meet him again. He had installed an armchair in his cabin facing aft, resting against the mast. As he said "I might as well be comfortable." Around him, all available space was stacked with horizontally placed plastic buckets in which he stored everything aboard.

Christine sat at the radio talking to Harry to keep him awake until help arrived. As he had received no response from the rescue service, we hauled up our anchor and told him we were on our way, realizing it would take us some time to reach him under prevailing conditions. Christine was continuing her conversation about almost anything with her sleepy friend, when there was a roar from behind.

A high speed rescue craft sped past us. Its skipper broke into our radio conversation to say that he was on his way to Harry, and would be there in half an hour.

"He heard we were on our way to give Harry a tow," said Christine. "He didn't want to miss out on his $125 fee."

We reentered Rocos Lobos for the night before going the next morning to Marina de la Paz where *Yassu* now lay firmly tied to the dock. After his terrible experiences Harry must have lost thirty pounds. He was very sun burnt and feeling awful. On his arrival the previous night, he had felt so hungry that he had bought a hot dog from one of the street vendors outside the marina. He was having to retire every ten minutes to sort out his insides. Not only that, but he was due to catch a bus up to the American border to meet his wife. She was making for La Paz, but insisted on being met at the Mexican border.

A few days after Harry had departed in his debilitated state on the bus north, we noticed that the wharf beside *Yassu* was piled high with all her contents. Standing beside her, looking dapper in immaculate clothes and a smart haircut, was none other than Harry. His wife, Anita, having first cleaned him up, had busily set about cleaning his boat and was not often to be seen above deck.

Yassu *Harry*

From the terrace of the La Perla Hotel, we, along with Terry and Christine, watched the Christmas Sail Past, put on by visiting American sail boats.. Its proceeds would be donated to the town to improve Christmas for the poor children.

The radio waves were abuzz with a call from an English yacht eight hundred nautical miles off the Galapagos Islands. Its sole occupant, eighty year old Sir Henry, had had violent diarrhea for three days, was unable to keep any food or drink down, and was beginning to lose consciousness. Christine was able to relay some of his calls for help to a boat close to him. From this he was getting advice, but could not always pick up their signal.

Time passed quickly getting the boat ready for our next leg to Puerto Vallarta.

We were visited by friends on cruises to Mexico, or who were camping in the area for the winter. Roger and Amy, from Ventura, came with us on a cruise to Espiritu Santo for a few days over Christmas.

On Christmas Eve, while anchored in San Gabriel Bay, Christine spoke on the radio to a man working at the American Base at the South Pole. He had just won the "Around the World Race" for a bottle of rum, but said he would prefer to have been sitting on a yacht in Mexico. We sent radio Christmas greetings home to our family via Peter Thomas in Victoria. They seemed such a long way away. Christmas day was spent with our friends from *Reiver*, with a Christmas tea of freshly baked mince pies and tinned Christmas cake while listening to their tape of *A Child's Christmas in Wales*. After a walk ashore, we tucked into Christmas dinner of roast ham, *ponsh meip* and white onion sauce, washed down with a superlative red wine, before watching our friends row home to their boat on a perfectly still moonlit night.

Following our one month's stay in and around La Paz, we decided it was time to set off for Puerto Vallarta across the Sea of Cortez, a passage of two hundred and fifty nautical miles. We planned to keep to the Baja side until reaching Los Frailles before the crossing towards Chakala, just north of Puerto Vallarta.

We left on 30th December, putting into Caleta Lobos for the night. On our way to Ensenada de los Muertos, we found ourselves in quite a heavy swell with fifteen knots of northerly wind. This anchorage had a wide crescent shaped sandy beach backed by a low scrub covered plain. In the past it had been the centre for exporting salt and silver. The remains of the old warehouse and wharf were still evident. After a calm moonlit night, we spent a lazy day with the boys from *Nashira*. Just before sunset we were joined by *Nashira's* friends on *Dolphin Amica*, a Tahiti ketch. Walking along the beach in the afternoon sun, we met friends of Beryl and Miles Smeeton and Peter and Anne Pye. Dick and Roz owned a boat called *Because*, which was at home in Victoria while they enjoyed a camping holiday in the sun.

Leaving Los Muertos at 0930 hrs, we immediately faced a twenty-five knot northerly wind which, with jib and main boomed out on either side of *Demelza*, gave us a marvelous day's sailing before blowing us around Punta Los Frailles and into the anchorage. This bay was surrounded by scrub covered sand dunes. Behind the point we found shelter from the significant northerly swell. We postponed leaving for an extra day as it was blowing so hard. The swimming around the reef was clear, and we saw many reef fish and a turtle in the shallows. During the nights we became used to the sound of rays jumping in the bay as they splashed back into the water.

Things had calmed down by the next morning, so we left to cross the Sea of Cortez. The current was setting to the north and, in the calm water; we had to motor at our maximum speed of four to six knots. As Christine monitored the radio, we heard that our friends Coryn and Tony on *Maistral*, who were cruising in the south Atlantic, were sixty nautical miles from Cape Horn in calm weather. In the evening sky we saw the Southern Cross for the first time. This was to be our night time companion for many miles in the southern hemisphere. We watched the Baja sink into a perfect sunset as we motored on toward Chakala, on the mainland of Mexico.

By now we had about five knots of wind from the west. The seawater temperature was 82 F, and the barometer was steady indicating continuing calm weather. We enjoyed having showers on deck under the sun shower as dolphins played all around the boat. We had the jib and main wing on wing, with a preventer rigged so that the boom could not hit either of us in the event of a swell rolling the boat unexpectedly. One of our delights on this calm passage was the arrival of many Spinner dolphins, putting on a display of agility and energy that left us spell bound.

After thirty-five hours of motoring assisted by the sails, we dropped anchor in Chacala Bay at 2000 hrs. As we had sighted land, we had noticed whales blowing on the surface of the calm sea, and small fish boats working along the coast. Chacala is situated just south of Punta Los Custodes, a rocky treed bluff. It had a lovely beach, fringed with Palapa restaurants. Chakala is known for its mosquitoes, so we put up all the boat's screens. This made the temperature in the cabin even higher. As the sun set, the roll of the boat seemed to ease.

By 0830 hrs we had left the bay. Sailing down the coast, edged by densely wooded hills, we turned into the wide anchorage of Punta de Mita in Banderas Bay. The following morning there were twenty cruising boats already in the La Cruz anchorage when we arrived. This small town, nestled under a hill, was attractive with cobbled streets and treed squares. The harbour behind the breakwater was taken up by local fish boats known as *Pa'angas* (aluminum open boats, generally powered by an outboard engine). These were drawn up along the beachfront where Nancy ran the Los Dos Fillipes restaurant. On going ashore, Christine tried out her Spanish to find the location of the bus stop for Puerto Vallarta airport, where our friends from Victoria were due to arrive the next day.

Pat and Bev arrived safely to be whisked off for supper at Los Dos Fillipes. They had brought all our mail from home with them.

Having shown the little town to our visitors, we moved on to Puerto Vallarta Marina. In its enclosed location, it was rather like sailing into an oven. A whole host of boats had just arrived and the crews were going into town for supper. We gave it a miss as we wanted to get settled in.

In the morning, the ladies decided to avail themselves of a free breakfast being offered as a perk for looking at a new block of time share condominiums that overlooked the harbour. However, when they presented themselves to their prospective realtor host, they were summarily turned away because they were all women, and therefore couldn't possibly make a decision to buy in the absence of a man. Arriving back at the boat, they were beside themselves with chagrin.

Feeling we had to put on a better show for our guests, who were both feeling the heat of the enclosed harbour, we decided to go cruising. After suitable preparation we left, motoring south around Cabo Corrientes to Punta Ipala. Cabo Corrientes is a huge rocky headland projecting out to sea and, like Point Conception in California, has a reputation for generating wind and weather of its own. In torpid heat, and in the absence of wind, we had to motor. At 0745 hrs the next morning the overheating alarm went off. Both the oil and cooling water levels were low. After replenishing both, I started the engine, noticing air bubbles rising in the cooling water surge tank. In the absence of any immediate crisis, we motored on to Ipala. Surrounded by steep cliffs, the anchorage lay in a small sheltered cove, in the centre of which were large rocky patches which restricted the places where we could drop anchor. We had been warned in Puerto Vallarta of drug problems ashore, so we did not land but rather enjoyed a refreshing swim in the crystal clear water of the bay.

The six hour sail from there to Bahia Chamela was idyllic, which impressed our guests sitting on the foredeck enjoying the sun. All along the coast, tree covered hills rose toward higher mountains behind. Suddenly Pat called "Look Hugh, right beside us!" We all looked at where she was pointing. Right alongside, maybe twenty feet off our port side, a huge whale eyed us with interest. We were entranced until the whale rolled over and slipped below the surface. Why had no one thought to take a photograph? Pat even had her camera in her hand. What a memorable sight!

Bahia Chamela was bathed in moonlight as we arrived to drop anchor off Isla Colorado. We spent one night in Bahia de Careyitos where there is a Club Med. The bottom of this small bay was covered with rocks and the holding poor. We rolled all night in the swell. The following morning we were up early and motored out of the bay. This was a shame in retrospect for, unknown to us, staying at Club Med, were the two friends of ours who had bought *Morwenna.* They had seen us arrive the previous evening, and had tried to hire a boat from the resort to come out to us. However all the dinghies had been locked up for the night. They had rushed down to the boat house first thing in the morning only to see us drawing out of the bay, and their attempts to contact us on the radio failed as we hadn't turned ours on.

As we motored around Punta Farrallon we heard, on the radio, that Santa Monica had been hit by a six point six earthquake. Passing the Los Frailes rocks, about a mile offshore, we rounded Punta Hermanos into Bahia Tenacatita. Above the shoreline on the way down we saw huge castle like dwellings and Arabic styled homes built on the cliffs. Once settled in the anchorage, along with fourteen other boats, we enjoyed cocktails on the deck in the warm, still evening.

At Tenacatita a brackish stream enters the mangroves which fringe the bay.

It winds its way inland for three to five kilometers. As we dinghied upstream, egrets and herons flitted from tree to tree ahead of us.

Off Punta Chubasco, a protecting reef provided excellent snorkeling to watch reef fish. We spent many hours in the warm clear water enjoying this newfound pleasure. I had the opportunity of discussing our overheating problems with Mark on a neighbouring boat, who came to the conclusion that the head gasket on our engine needed replacing. That evening Christine spoke with Peter Thomas in Victoria on the radio. She asked him to get Ben, our mechanic, to send a spare set of gaskets for the engine with our next visitors who were flying down in a couple of weeks.

On the way to Melaque, in Bahia de Navidad, around Punta Bahia, offshore rocks poked up menacingly out of the water. As we arrived the temperature was in the nineties. A boating institution, Philomena, ran the bar and restaurant *Pelicanos* on the beach at Melaque. This served as the mecca for regular Mexico cruisers from North America. All sorts of boats that we had met previously were congregated here, anchored in the sheltered and capacious bay. Philomena ran a radio net every morning, welcoming newcomers into the bay, telling them what was going on in the village, and where everything could be obtained, from emergency services to vegetables.

In the evenings we would watch the local fishermen casting their nets from the beach and hauling in herring that had congregated there in huge schools. As the herring moved up and down in the shallow water, the fishermen and their children chased along the shore as the fish broke the surface. Huge excitement followed as the nets were cast and hauled brimming with fish on to shore.

From our end of the bay we took our dinghy two and a half miles into a lagoon, which the Mexicans were busily dredging, and beside which they were building a new Hotel. Anchored in the lagoon were Laura and John on *Talitha*, ham radio operators from Victoria, who were leaving for the South Pacific in March. Needless to say we had lots to talk about over a supper of shrimp and octopus in Elray's, the open sided restaurant ashore.

We paid a visit by bus to Las Hadas in Manzanillo, passing coconut plantations, banana palms, papaya and avocado orchards. Manzanillo is a busy port with a naval base and huge commercial docks. The narrow streets of the town were congested with trucks waiting to enter the port area. Las Hadas was a fantasy world resort with white buildings, large terraces, swimming pools and bars overlooking the sea. We had lunch on the terrace watching a boat anchoring at the Hotel's docks below us, snagging a neighbouring boat's anchor in the process and causing chaos. Always a good spectator sport.

Back at Melaque it was time to say farewell to Bev and Pat. They looked well, tanned and relaxed as we saw them off on the bus for Puerto Vallarta airport the following day. They took all our mail for home and memories of a holiday afloat in Mexico. We had enjoyed having them on board.

Christine, Bev and Pat

Christine suffered a "gastrointestinal upset" twenty four hours after our lunch in Las Hadas.

"I should never have had that delicious salad." she moaned. By the next day she was over it and feeling better, which was a great relief.

I filled *Demelza*'s fuel tanks through the Baja filter, with diesel purchased in La Paz. Following this, the filter was full of grit. I prayed that it had kept out anything that would cause a problem. More and more boats arrived in the bay. Among them were Diane and Keith on *Lady Guinevere*. Diane was a French Canadian and Keith British. He announced that he had served in the SAS. They were planning to go on to the Marquesas and eventually on to New Zealand.

The green netting that we had bought in San Diego to cast shade over the cabin came into its own in the intense daytime temperatures.

Neil and Sue on *Shearwater* from Vancouver Island arrived in the bay. We had first met them at a Power Squadron dinner in Santa Barbara the previous July, and then later in San Diego. Along with Steve and Veronica we all enjoyed supper at Pelicanos. John from *Big Toy*, a seventy three foot yawl, came over in his dinghy and offered to set us up with a diesel mechanic, and also to mark our charts of the Tuomotos and Marquesan anchorages with which he was familiar. The next morning we received a frantic message from ashore from a local resident to say that under no circumstances should we use the mechanic recommended as his work was atrocious and his prices too high.

By radio we were able to talk to David, our friend in Victoria who had helped us so much getting ready for the trip, to finalize arrangements for his arrival to crew with us for six weeks on the passage from Puerto Vallarta to Tahiti.

Days passed as we enjoyed our stay at the anchorage, spending the heat of the day in the shade ashore, and the cool evenings on the boat. We exchanged visits and general talk, gathering helpful information from those who had cruised extensively in the South Pacific. On some days we would take a bus ride down the coast to Manzanillo to shop and explore.

Our next visitors were Carolyn and Walt. They arrived with the parcel of engine gaskets, a package of mail and all the news from home which we much appreciated. We introduced them to many of our boating friends at Pelicanos. Then we met Bear, who had been referred to us as a genius with engines. On his arrival in the bay on *Oceania*, he came over to *Demelza*, and agreed that the problem we were having with our overheating engine was a break in the head gasket. What a coincidence that one of the offshore cruisers in the bay should be a diesel mechanic who was prepared to sort out our problem. We left him alone as he struggled with the engine and spent the time ashore walking along the headland before retreating to Pelicanos in the heat of the day.

Anxious to see how Bear had got on, we walked down to the beach on which there was a fair surf running. Our friends, Carolyn and Walt were not boaters, so getting off the beach into the surf was going to be an exercise needing maximum cooperation.

"Now this is the deal," I said as we stowed the bags of groceries into the dinghy. "Carolyn and Christine hold onto both sides of the front. Walt and I will be on either side at the back. We'll wade out as far as we can. Then when I say 'Go', we all jump in, pushing ourselves off. When I shout 'paddle' Walt you paddle like mad with your paddle and I'll do the same. OK everybody?"

We duly pointed the bow into the waves as the dinghy bounced about in the shallows. We all pushed out to sea and at the appropriate time I shouted "Go." Whereupon Walt turned to me and asked

"Now?"

By then the next wave had arrived. The bow of the boat rose to the sky, and everybody and everything was pitched into the water. Oranges from our shopping bobbed merrily in the surf and lay stranded down the beach, rapidly followed by a variety of vegetables. We all emerged from the water full of sand and sea water. Howls of laughter came from ashore. At times like these, watching dinghies in the surf was a main preoccupation of boaters on Phil's patio at Pelicanos.

To be fair, a good many onlookers dashed down to the beach to the rescue. Before long our dinghy, full of bedraggled people and wet shopping, was making its way out to *Demelza*. We felt better seeing that the new gasket had been installed, and set about tidying the boat up before having showers and flushing fresh water through the dinghy's outboard engine after its dunking.

Sitting in the cockpit that evening watching the sun set over the ocean and sipping one of Walter's "Whistlebangers," a fierce concoction of who knows what, our mood was restored before we retired happily for the night.

Our ten days of rest and relaxation in the sun on this delightful coast was over. It had been an adventure, and we had met many of the people and boats that were to cross the Pacific with us. The importance of networking as we progressed along on our voyage had been well and truly learnt, in the interest of safety, repairs, and mutual support in times of crisis. Those we had met were from all walks of life with so many skills. All were committed to generously helping one another if needed.

Walter and Hugh – going fishing

On our leisurely way back to Puerto Vallarta we stopped at Tenacatita to show Walt and Carolyn the trip up the stream through the mangroves, before moving on to Chamela where we anchored and I took Walt fishing along the reefs.

Suddenly Walt jumped up in the dinghy.

"Did you see that?" he asked pointing into the water.

"No Walt I didn't," I said "but for goodness sake sit down or you'll have us over."

"It was as big as a train." he said excitedly, looking anxiously around.

Sure enough behind our idling dinghy engine, and about where our lines entered the water, was the large fin of a shark

"Right, just pull in the lines," I said. "Let's get out of here."

This accomplished, I gently accelerated the engine, and in a little while we lost sight of that fin.

"Never mind," I consoled Walt, "we'll try the other side of the bay." Which we did, until looking behind us we again saw that menacing fin.

"That's it. I've had enough. Let's go home." I said.

Walt and Carolyn wanted a final swim before getting back to Puerto Vallarta the next day. It was interesting to note how close to the ladder they both stayed while in the water and, over drinks, they both admitted to having wondered whether they could both get up the ladder at the same time if it had been necessary.

As we waved our guests off on the start of their journey home to Victoria, it was hard to think of them being home in a day. Now that we were alone again on the boat, we set to preparing *Demelza* for sea. Just as before, the jobs seemed endless and we just had to take them one at a time. Our sail covers had taken a beating in the hot sun and had to be replaced. Among all the boats now congregated were David and Evie on *Enetai*, also from Vancouver Island. They would join the cavalcade to French Polynesia. In fact so many boats were leaving for the Marquesas that someone published a lengthy list, called the Class of '94. *Demelza* was one of the two smaller ones at thirty two feet.

We advertised in local coffee shops and shops' bulletin boards for a crewing position for Anne who was walking the docks looking for a boat willing to take her on. She had been introduced to us by Peter Thomas, over the radio. She lived on Saltspring Island not far from us at home.

We were concerned about the hot sun perishing the Hypalon of our inflatable dinghy, so Christine got out her manual sewing machine and stitched covers for its pontoons. We had noticed that many dinghies were protected in this way. Our son Nick and his wife Aleda confirmed that they would join us in Tahiti in July for three weeks. The water-maker had developed a leak, which had to be fixed before we put to sea. We sent mail to Chuck and Collette in Ventura, and to Ray in Victoria confirming the dates for the various legs they were going to be sailing with us in the Pacific.

On 21st February we hauled out *Demelza* at the Opequimar boatyard in Puerto Vallarta where we had all the preparatory work under the hull done for us. What luxury in the heat. We had the engine overhauled, and the hull polished to restore her colour. After two days, the boat was back in the water and ready to leave. Among the things the boatyard had done was to raise *Demelza's* waterline four inches to accommodate the load she was now carrying. Forty boats and crews attended a meeting of those going to French Polynesia, the average boat length being forty two feet.

Christine then set about sewing covers for all the fuel and water jugs that were secured on deck. This took another two days of hard work in the heat of the marina. Sometimes the Marina offered an evening talk or slide show which we tried to attend. At one of these we met a couple who had been cruising for eleven years. They gave a most informative talk and politely answered our many questions. Another time we saw a video that cruisers had taken on a previous visit to the South Pacific which gave us a good idea of what we were facing.

Sometimes we would catch the local bus into Puerto Vallarta's main street, the Malacon, to have supper and watch the sun setting into the sea. One night, four of us were thrilled to see the green flash that we had previously only heard about. We enjoyed watching the enterprising artists selling their wares along the waterfront. Most was space age type art done with spray cans of glossy paint onto boards laid flat on the paving stones. They achieved the most remarkable effects using saucers and other shapes to create their three dimensional pictures.

Anne had had no response to her advertisements for a crewing position, so came to our boat each morning to mention her availability on the daily VHF Cruisers net. Eventually she was offered a berth on another Canadian boat that was leaving within two days.

On the 1st of March *Demelza* wore her Welsh flag to celebrate St. David's Day, the patron saint of Wales. We were joined by Robert and Roselyn of *Tillicum*, and their two friendly dogs, Otter and Hogan to celebrate the occasion. This coincided with the first boats leaving for the Marquesas to the accompaniment of a lot of cheering and well wishes from those of us who would soon follow.

News spread along the docks of the violent death of the skipper of one of the cruising boats. He had been run over when in his own dinghy near Punta de Mita, by a Pa'anga. His body hadn't yet been found. We all felt devastated. His companion was looked after by various cruisers. It transpired a few days later, that the beautiful boat they had been sailing didn't belong to them, and that the owner was flying in from San Diego to reclaim his boat. The lady had been ordered to leave the boat, and had been left with huge debts that she had no possibility of paying. The man's body was found eventually, and we all chipped in for the cost of his funeral.

On 16th March David, full of energy and enthusiasm, arrived bearing masses of mail and packages of spare parts, including a torque wrench. Having stored his kit in his cabin, he spent the day in the bilge going over the bonding of the through hulls. What an excellent crew. Talk about making a good first impression. By now the boat was groaning with provisions, all of which had to be stowed. We spent the last evening introducing David to the Zapatas Bar where, for the price of a drink, we could sit all evening listening to South American music on pan flutes and other ethnic instruments. The band was made up of music students from the music school in Guadalajara and the leader was their teacher.

Another five weeks had slipped by, and again it was time to move on.

David arrives

Sailing in the Trades

CHAPTER 5
Out into the blue Pacific

On Saturday March 19th we were anchored off Punta de Mita for our first night out. Between securing everything on the boat for our three week crossing to the Marquesas, we had time to reflect on the wonderful experiences we had had and on the great friendships made while cruising Mexico. This was the real beginning of our passage making; our next landfall was twenty seven hundred nautical miles away.

The next morning broke to a gentle northerly breeze. One last check around the boat, then

"OK David, pull up the anchor!"

We were off to a leisurely start across a steady low swell. No storms out there I thought. By mid afternoon, the wind was blowing at twenty knots from the northwest with a rising sea. The seasickness pills that we had all taken were being severely challenged.

"So that we don't get too tired, I suggest we start three hour watches." I said.

In the first twenty four hours we had covered one hundred and twenty four nautical miles which made us feel better about our discomfort. The sea was frisky and the air temperature dropped to 76 F instead of the 84 F to which we had become accustomed in Mexico. The sky was blue, and fluffy clouds drifted across the bow of the boat.

Routines aboard re-established themselves. Christine, *Demelza*'s only certified ham radio operator, checked in with the relevant radio nets which would log our position and progress daily. We also listened to the current weather and sea condition reports from other boats ahead of us. David put all our projected waypoints into the GPS for our charted course to the Marquesas. I adjusted the sails to the position in which we were best balanced for the required course, and then set the wind vane. The ship's clock and the Universal Time clock were both calibrated against the radio time signal from Colorado that Christine provided from the radio.

The northeast trade winds blew a consistent fifteen to twenty knots during the day, falling off to ten to fifteen knots at night. The boisterous seas took their cue from the wind, settling nicely at night to a more comfortable moderate swell. David had been assigned the task of plotting our course six times each day, to ensure that we were on track no matter what the wind was doing. Ocean currents had a knack of taking us off course too, for which we had to make adjustments.

"We've got off to a flying start." I said as David plotted our latest position on the chart. But it was early days. We had yet to cross the Intertropical Convergence

Zone (ITCZ) and the equator with their unpredictable weather conditions. The general consensus of the gurus of passage planning was to steer a course north of 10°N as far as 130°W before dipping south to the Marquesas. This should assure the best winds and fastest passage. However, all things being equal with *Demelza*'s short waterline length, that would add a lot of extra miles, so making our passage longer. I had decided that we would follow the shorter rhumb line and, should we be becalmed, we would motor. We had a Mercator projection chart, so it was easy to plot a straight line.

"*Nashira* broke a stem fitting last night," Christine announced from her position by the radio, "and she's returning to Puerto Vallarta for repairs."

What a disappointment. But they were right. Without a properly anchored forestay they would struggle every step of the way, and maybe not have anywhere to get the work done at the other end.

David was feeling the least sea sick of us all in the early days, so he assumed a lot of the physical work on the foredeck, adjusting and changing sails to meet the different wind conditions. No matter what the challenge, he would willingly clip himself on to the safety lines and go up on deck to do what was needed.

Christine probably had the worst job of all, preparing food for a queasy crew under the most difficult of circumstances, while not feeling great herself. Whales breeched about a mile to port. Huge columns of spray following their rocket-like emergence from the ocean's depths, before they returned to their natural salty environment. Dolphins played around *Demelza*'s bows. Boobies dived on unsuspecting prey below, and flying fish, disturbed by our presence, took off in flocks ahead of us for their short flight in the sun. Small squid landed and died on our decks at night, leaving a blue stain which was hard to remove.

By the third day, our seasickness had gone, and we were beginning to enjoy the calming conditions. A freighter passed two miles to our starboard side. Christine called her up on the radio.

"This is the freighter *Tikini,*" was the reply. "We are bound for Tokyo." With that he altered course to pass astern of us, for which we thanked him.

"It is the rules." he responded.

"Can you see us on your radar?" Christine asked.

"Your echo is very sweet." he replied.

That was a critical item that I had wanted to establish since leaving home. We had installed a Danish radar reflector at the topmost of our two crosstrees, and I had wondered how effective it was.

The wind vane was steering a steady course day and night. It was as though we had an extra crew member aboard. Over long distances, it was able to keep a much more consistent course than we could hand steering.

Our tow generator, hung from the rail astern, was turning out five to eight amps in the steady breeze. This was invaluable in keeping the batteries charged, but its drag did cause a loss of half a knot of boat speed. The extra charge meant that we could keep all instruments and nighttime navigation lights operating without having to use the engine to recharge the batteries.

Amps to spare

During the day, David would try his luck at fishing, though at a speed of five to six knots, I reckoned it would have to be a real speedster to be caught on his hook unless he could snag one as we passed. Petrels and shearwaters glided all around us as they skimmed effortlessly over the ocean's surface. Now they were here, now they were gone. Their company meant so much to us out there in the huge expanse of an otherwise empty ocean.

Christine and I made a tape recording to broadcast over the radio to all my erstwhile working colleagues, sending greetings from the middle of the Pacific. They had been so encouraging before we had set out, and had contributed so many useful items to equip the boat. Later we learned that our message had been received.

By radio we heard that the ITCZ was between 4-7°N . As we were then at 12°N we felt we had plenty of room to keep out of its way. This zone, between the northeast and southeast trade winds across the equator, can move north to south at unpredictable speeds, and is characterized by squally weather mingled with total calms.

We celebrated our first five hundred nautical miles with a bottle of cool Liebfraumilch, lovingly kept in the bilge for just this occasion. One hundred and sixty nautical miles ahead of us was *Mariposa* with Chris and Andy from Berkley, California. Poor Andy suffered from *mal de mer* the whole time he was at sea.

At night, under clear starlit skies, *Demelza* pressed steadily onward. As I lay on my bunk in the twilight zone before sleep's oblivion, I would hear the swish of water passing the hull, and David playing his mouth organ on watch in the cockpit.

In the absence of a salt water tap in the galley, which was later installed, we did our washing up in the cockpit. This was definitely crew work. David would collect two buckets of seawater and an assortment of dirty dishes. After juggling with these in the uncertain world of swells, he managed to produce immaculately clean dishes. Often, as the boat lurched and the buckets took their liberties across the cockpit's floor, we heard our willing crew let off steam in no uncertain terms.

At 9°N we were one thousand and seventy two nautical miles from our destination. Roughish nights were made tolerable by our continued progress along David's course line. We were achieving between one hundred and twenty and one hundred and forty seven nautical miles in each twenty four hours.

By now, we were so used to the boat's motion, and in spite of the bruises that Christine had acquired preparing meals down below, we had our evening's cocktail drink on the foredeck watching glorious sunsets. We celebrated completing the first one thousand nautical miles of our passage with champagne!

At 11N we altered course to the south to skirt a high pressure system to the west of us, fearing that, if we approached its centre, we would lose the wind. Squalls appeared on our radar at 0100 hrs. They ringed us. David took down the pole on the genoa and put one reef into the main. One hour later, the squalls had disappeared. So he went forward to let out the reef and rolled out the genoa again. This procedure was repeated with each approaching squall, an irritating and exhausting process.

Resplendent in our oilskins we responded to nature's squally challenges. Sails up, down, up, down. On and on it went, guarding against the potential danger of knockdown. In the squalls that we did encounter, torrential rain was the norm. Christine called from below

"The ITCZ is well south of us, but it's spinning off convection cells."

Again and again, David upped sails and downed sails as the squalls passed. At last the trade winds re-established themselves, and he retired to his bunk exhausted. Crashing waves against the hull, banging rigging, and lurching boat resulted in him emerging the next morning looking rather the worse for wear.

Hugh and David relax

All at once, the ominous black clouds had gone. Bright blue seas had reappeared, and steady trade winds were pushing us along. We thought this must be the end of the ITCZ as we celebrated fifteen hundred nautical miles under the keel as we passed the half-way point of our journey.

It was not to be. Squalls soon encircled us again. Dark, flat bottomed clouds with rain slanting down to the ocean killed our wind. The approaching hiss of white water, working its way toward us over the surface of the sea heralded the imminent chaos of a squall. Slatting sails, as the wind clocked uncertainly around us, registered the squall's arrival. The boat heeled erratically, first this way then that, as the torrential rain lashed the boat.

Then just as suddenly as it had arrived, it left. Confused seas surrounded us and lobbed us from side to side in the light air, sending everything that was loose on board skating across the cabin, with the crew grabbing for handholds wherever they could find them.

Then gently, oh so gently, a whisper of air would cross the boat. Gradually the whisper would grow. The trade winds would re establish themselves, and we would again be on our way.

Atuona on Hiva Oa island in the Marquesas was now one thousand and fifty two nautical miles ahead on the fifteenth day at sea. The barometric pressure was falling, and the sky clouding over. Large long easterly swells were building as the boat rocked in light air.

We crossed the equator on April 5th, our sixteenth day at sea, two thousand nautical miles from Puerto Vallarta. Given our progress to date, we anticipated arriving in the Marquesas in another eight days.

I had stowed away a bottle of champagne to celebrate our crossing of the equator. It had been given to us by Phil and Diane from *Belle Louise*, for just this occasion. Where else would I store it for safe keeping but at the bottom of the wet weather locker? Do you think I could remember where I had stowed it? I almost turned over the complete contents of *Demelza* before producing it with great ceremony.

Buoyed by the sense of occasion, and no doubt oiled by the champagne, David and I took the plunge over *Demelza*'s side, after stopping her by taking down the sails. Only later did we learn that this was not the greatest idea as sharks, in the open ocean, are known to swim under boats to shelter from the sun.

Cooling dip

Weather forecasts from Hawaii called for thunderstorms over the Marquesas. The ITCZ was supposed to be well north of the equator, but thunderclouds began to build all around us. By evening we were coping with another series of squalls with winds of up to forty knots. Lightning flashed around us in the evening sky, as forked bolts plunged into the sea astern. Rising humidity made life aboard uncomfortable, and the normal train of the ocean swells became confused.

Working on deck in all the spray was too cold to bear, so David and I tried wearing oilskin jackets over our bare skin to stop the water evaporating, draining us of our body warmth. The discomfort of this solution was only marginally better than the problem it solved.

We had lost the trade winds in the confusion of the squalls causing *Demelza* to roll uncontrollably. The sails slatted from side to side, and everything aboard relocated itself several times a minute. But the final straw was when Christine collected yet another bruise when working down below. With that we started the engine.

After half an hour's motoring the wind picked up again. This kept David very busy tending to the sails, setting the wind vane, and redeploying the tow generator. Just when he had finished all those jobs there was a cry from below.

"The head's plugged."

Now I certainly didn't fancy working down there in the bouncing sea, but our heroic crewmember leapt into the breach. After all, the alternative of delay was not all that attractive either. Down he went with a tool box as Christine and I kept the boat going in the right direction. Occasionally we could hear him banging away in the bilges. After two hours, without taking a break, Dave emerged successful but looking slightly bloodied and a general shade of green, to rapturous applause from an appreciative crew.

The storm belt that we had crossed was now affecting the fleet behind us at about 12°N , and the airwaves were alive with the gruesome details of the previous night's experiences.

At one hundred miles distant from landfall we could almost smell land, our anticipation was so great.

Sure enough, as Christine emerged with our coffee the next morning she looked forward and there, rising out of the waves on the horizon, were the tops of the mountains of Hiva Oa Island. At last the Marquesas.

In twenty four days we had successfully completed our first ocean crossing of almost three thousand miles. As we entered Traitors' Bay we could see the port of Atuona below the tall mountains beyond, and the narrow tree clad valleys rising steeply between volcanic cliffs.

We had arrived.

A visiting whale seen on the passage

Landfall Marquesas

CHAPTER 6
Marquesas

Lying at 9S, one thousand miles northeast of Tahiti, this chain of islands is two hundred miles long. Only six of them, Nuku Hiva, Ua Pou, Ua Huka, Hiva Oa, Tahuata and Fatu Hiva, are inhabited. Most of the population of approximately ten thousand people lives in and around the major centers of Atuona (Hiva Oa) Hakahau (Ua Pou) and Taiohae (Nuku Hiva).

There are no outlying reefs protecting these islands as the south equatorial current, in which they lie, is too cold. All the bays are therefore exposed to wind and swell in an onshore breeze but, as the southeast trade winds prevail, the bays on the sheltered sides of the islands provide reasonably calm anchorages most of the time.

The steep craggy volcanic mountains of the interior are frequently shrouded in cloud, and waterfalls tumble down their precipitous black cliffs to disappear in the green foliage of the island's vigorous vegetation below. Fruit trees abound. Lemons, oranges, bananas, mangoes and papaya grow prolifically in the gardens, and thick coconut palm groves grow above the sea shore up into the valleys beyond.

Discovered in 1595 by the Spanish, their existence was kept secret until the arrival of Captain Cook in 1774. After this, white man's diseases decimated the local population until only about two thousand remained in 1923. Polynesian by descent, the Marquesans are large and muscular. Although preferring to speak Marquesan, most can also speak French as France took possession of the islands in 1842. The majority are of the Roman Catholic faith.

The day following our arrival in Atuona, as we were sitting having breakfast in the cockpit admiring the exotic setting of the bay, we were electrified by the arrival, under sail, of a thirty one foot wooden boat from Australia called *Grype Type Thynne*. Diana, with a blood covered face, was at the helm as they approached the anchorage. Barry, on the bow, was ready to release the anchor on the appropriate signal from Diana. Suddenly the bay echoed with Diana's voice "Plant it!" Whereupon Barry let go the anchor and, as it bit into the bay's mud, the boat slewed round into the wind. He dropped the sails, and Diana waved at us before they both disappeared down below. We did not see them again for twenty four hours. We later learnt that, as they had approached the bay, they had put the engine on for the first time since leaving the Galapagos Islands three thousand miles before. The water pump had refused to work, and Diana had banged her nose on the aft rail trying to see if any water was coming out of the exhaust. They had had no choice but to come into the rather cramped harbour under sail, to complete their dramatic arrival.

Within days the first of about thirty boats on the Europa '94 Rally began to appear in the bay. Begrudgingly we felt envious of them, for all their paperwork had been completed, their moorage booked, their reception planned and their sightseeing arranged by the Rally before they arrived. It was only a couple of days later that we heard some of the rumblings among the fleet. The small boats had arrived later than the bigger ones, had missed the planned reception for which they had paid, and were faced with having only one night's rest before starting the next leg. Because of this they had no opportunity to see anything of the island before having to move on.

However bureaucracy was alive and well for us, as we slogged up the hill on foot in the muggy heat and flies to register our arrival with the Gendarmerie (police). We were issued with a green passport book which we had to present for stamping at every arrival and departure point in French Polynesia. The authorities obviously wanted to keep track of these yachties.

Christine had to apply for a French ham operator's license which could only be issued from Papeete, Tahiti by telephone. She duly made application and eventually it caught up with us in the Tuomotos. Lastly we had to buy a bond on entry into French Polynesia, which would be reimbursed when we left. That involved a whole chain of currency exchanges and costs which we never fully recovered.

A lengthy walk up the steep streets of Atuona brought us to the town's cemetery, where Paul Gaugin and Jacques Brel are buried. Both had, in a relatively short space of time, been inspired by the beauty of these islands and had expressed their feelings in their art and song respectively. Their graves are almost hidden among the Mango and Plumeria trees. The walk up the hill was overhung with ripe fruit. David excelled by launching himself off the banks at the sides of the road, snaring the fruit in mid air before returning to earth.

Music was a feature of Marquesan life. In church the congregation sang their hymns in harmony, their voices almost raising the roof. We attended a village dance in the local community center in Atuona, where we had a wonderful view of all the proceedings from bleachers inside the long low community centre. Everybody joined in the dancing, even the small children who were never admonished for getting in the way or making a noise. The dancers were all dressed in their Polynesian finery for the occasion, the men adorned by Marquesan tattoos all over their exposed bodies, and the girls in intricately woven grass skirts with garlands of flowers in their hair.

On the island of Ua Pou we anchored in the northern bay, Hakahau. To us this was the most beautiful of all the islands visited, with its huge volcanic spires thrusting twelve hundred feet into the sky. Ua Pou is thirty miles south of Nuku Hiva with a population of about two thousand. This is the island that Jaques Brel had in mind when he composed his song 'La Cathedrale,' and indeed the whole atmosphere was uplifting as the eyes rose from the island's shores to its lofty peaks.

It was here that Christine met Irene. Born in Tahiti, she was visiting her cousin and was intrigued to look over *Demelza*. She wove a lovely Oti wreath to decorate Christine's straw hat, and in return for the gift of a carved wooden Ukulele made by her cousin's husband, Christine gave her our tape recorder and some batteries. When she left us she was wearing the headset listening to a tape by Bob Marley, seemingly the most popular music among the youngsters of these islands. We later visited the Ukulele workshop, a wooden shed perched on pilings in an open plot of land which I assumed attested to the amount of rain on Ua Pou in the rainy season.

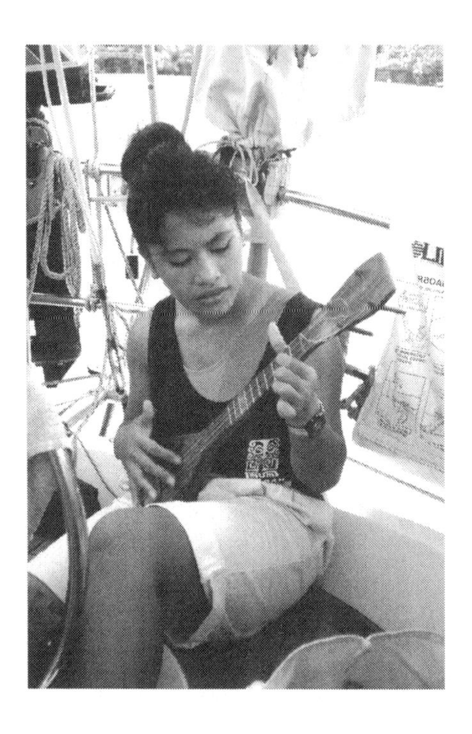

Irene with ukulele

Wherever we explored on the islands, we were followed by an unreasonable cloud of miniscule biting flies, which set about exposed human skin with a ferocity we had never encountered before. It seemed that it was not until the damage had been done, that their presence could be detected. The whole surface of the skin assumed the characteristics of raw meat, and the ensuing pain would last for days. Christine was a particular favourite with these pests and we tried every ointment, deterrent and local remedy to very little effect. On the boat at night they would make their way out into the bay. So we had to secure insect screens across hatches and portholes, which significantly raised the temperature and humidity inside the cabin.

On the smallest populated island of the group, Tahuata, we visited the new Catholic Church, built in 1988 at Vaitahu. The town dance that we had attended in Atuona had been to raise money toward the building of this beautiful church. Made of river rock, it had a tiled floor which kept the building cool, magnificent stained glass windows and a Canadian cedar roof.

Swimming in the bay's clear water, it was hard to think that the tropical fish below us were in water at all. Yellow blossoms adorned the trees up the slopes of the mountain, in stunning contrast to the black volcanic cliffs behind. Huge Hibiscus flowered on bushes along the paths and Plumeria trees grew all around us as we walked among the small village homes.

Wherever we visited, we were overwhelmed by gifts of fruit and vegetables that the islanders insisted we take. Their needs were much more prosaic, a pair of my old reading glasses for an elderly gentleman who hadn't been able to read for years; a Pyrex dish which they had only read about, would be a godsend to them in preparing their meals; fishing hooks, nylon line, and T shirts, which almost had the status of an international currency, were treasured. Christine would find more feminine gifts such as sewing items, soaps, creams and shampoo. A new fruit to us was the pamplemousse, much like a large grapefruit, which grew abundantly on the islands. Its flavour we enjoyed immensely.

Banana anyone?

Inevitably the exchange of gifts would lead to an invitation to the islanders' homes for a meal and to meet the family. On Nuku Hiva, while anchored in Baie d'Anaho, we were introduced to a family that another Canadian boat had visited previously. It was Frederick's sixty third birthday. He was considered elderly, and we were all invited to his feast. He had been out during the day, and had caught some crab and a grouper. A Marquesan oven had been prepared in the garden to cook a goat which had been shot in the mountains that morning. The oven consisted of hole dug in the ground to a depth of two feet. In this, wood had been burnt to hot ash on which rocks were laid in a layer, followed by banana leaves with the goat on top. This was covered with more banana leaves and wet sacking, before being buried with the excavated soil and then left until the feast in the evening.

In all, three boats' crews were in attendance so that, with Frederick's family, fourteen people sat down to a fabulous meal. Breadfruit, taro and banana made up the vegetable component. All this washed down with a local French box wine produced by one of the boats.

We sat under the stars at a long table. Frederick had borrowed the church's generator to provide enough light for his visitors. The family had done everything possible to make it a perfect evening. Following dinner we all relaxed after the children had laid out their mats and gone to sleep. Everything had been cleared away and washed up. Their home had three rooms, two bedrooms and a kitchen, with an open area in the front of the house, and an overhanging roof on one side under which we had had our dinner.

The kitchen was sparsely furnished with one running cold water tap, a gas cooker, and gas fridge which didn't work. They had a long kitchen table and a mesh fronted cupboard for keeping food. There were two windows both without glass.

Frederick had a wonderful time telling story after story about the island, his neighbours, politics, his family and much more. The stories he told amused him more and more as the red wine disappeared. As he said when we left in the moonlight for our walk back through the coconut palms to our dinghies

"That's the best birthday I have ever had."

Our typical day in the Marquesas started at 0630 hrs with a cup of coffee watching dawn light up the mountains around the bay. We'd have breakfast before the heat of the day, followed by a trip in the dinghy to find new rocks to swim over. Then back to the boat to do the day's chores, washing, maintenance, fetching fresh water in jugs from ashore. Then maybe an expedition ashore to see the sights or to hike up into the forest to look for waterfalls for refreshing showers in the heat of the day. On the way out, or on the return home, we would meet some of the locals and share time and information with them, practicing a lot of arm waving and school French in the process. Then a lunch of fruit under the shade trees in the town, or paying a visit to one of the families who had invited us for tea. We'd go back to the boat in the evening, either to put on or to attend a happy hour with other boats before supper. The twilight was short, so back we would go behind the screens for a good night's sleep.

One of the memorable walks, while we were anchored in Taiohaie Bay, was up the hill to the Kekahanui Inn, run by Rose Corser. She and her establishment were well known in the yachting world through books and magazines written about them. Her husband had died a year before our arrival, and she was battling on, keeping the place running by herself. On the deck of the restaurant at suppertime, she had invited a trio of Marquesan musicians, all dressed in their island costumes, to play for her guests. In her library, she had video tapes of interesting bays and places she recommended we visit on the island.

David decided that his holiday time would expire before we were able to get to Tahiti, so volunteered to fly out of Nuku Hiva to Papeete to catch his plane home. The only difficulty was that he hadn't the correct currency to pay for the ticket. Off he went to the local bank, only to learn that the bank in Papeete was closed, and that they were the only people who could authorize the transaction. Thinking fast, he had the brilliant idea of asking Rose Corser if she could change American dollars into French Polynesian Francs. Being Rose, of course she could.

It was sad to see David go. He had been such a stalwart crew, and was fired with enthusiasm about cruising offshore. Uncomplaining, resourceful, energetic and willing, he was an example to all who crew on boats.

Anne, whom we had last seen in Mexico, reappeared saying that all was not well on the boat on which she was travelling as crew. Could she please come with us to Tahiti? Christine and Anne seemed to get on well together, and I thought it would be good company for Christine as I knew she was missing her friends. Anne had already moved ashore from the boat she had been on, and the little house she had rented had a washing machine. So Christine had a field day.

One month in the Marquesas was coming to an end. We could hardly believe the time had gone so quickly. Our weather had been perfect with wonderful hot sunny days, gentle trade winds, and a perfect blue sky with cotton wool clouds.

Tikis

On a few occasions we experienced a tropical downpour and this usually when all the boat's hatches were open. Its onset would be accompanied by a mad dash, in inflatable dinghies, from boat to boat as owners scrambled to get their hatches shut.

We had enjoyed looking at the vestiges of Marquesan culture, evidence of which was everywhere. In Taiohai Bay they had collected a wonderful sample of Marquesan Tikis set in a circle on the shores of the bay. On our walks along the upland valleys we had seen the stone platforms (*paepae*) on which the islanders had built their homes, and the *tohua* made of coral, where ceremonial and important festivals were held.

All the valleys, because of the steep terrain, were isolated from one another. In the early days this had led to intertribal warfare between local hereditary chiefs, and cannibalism had been common. Ironwood clubs, distinctively engraved, were symbolic of this power struggle. Tikis of stone, carved wooden bowls and fan handles are all remnants of the islands long history. The faces of the human carvings are unique to the Marquesas, with large lips parted and large saucer shaped eyes.

As time passed, it seemed that more and more of our companion boats were turning for home rather than persevering out into the Pacific. Job offers, lack of funds, and an inability to find paying jobs along the way were some of the many reasons. It was always sad to see the end of a dream as the boats left for Hawaii and home.

With the end of our stay fast approaching, there was only McKittrick's General Store for reprovisioning. McKittrick had, for many years, catered to travelers and locals alike. His store had everything, or if not everything, then he would either get it or provide a substitute.

We had loved being in the Marquesas. It had whetted our appetite for places we had not yet visited. The people had been welcoming, courteous, helpful and a joy to be with, so we were sad to leave.

To the south of us a lot of wind was being reported on the radio by yachts on their way to the Tuomotos, our next port of call. But by the following day, the weather in the south had settled.

We were off.

CHAPTER 7
Society Islands

Tuomotos

We had an uneventful five day sail to the Tuomotos Archipelago which lies at 23S. It used to be called The Dangerous Archipelago because of its low physical profile, swift currents and poor charts. This isolated paradise had always beckoned. Spread over eight hundred by four hundred miles these seventy eight atolls are home to fifteen thousand people on forty five inhabited islands. Twenty one atolls have a single pass to their enclosed lagoons, ten have two, and forty seven have none at all.

Being in the cyclone zone, shipwrecks litter the atolls. Yet eleven of these coral fringed lagoons sustain commercial black pearl farming.

The Polynesian population has a history of inter island warfare. More recently French colonization, centered in Papeete in the Society Islands, continues to be a significant financial support. The influence of Papeete was readily discernible as the source of outside supplies.

Though appearing to be an easy going and congenial group, we heard of many of the social problems that lie below the surface on these atolls. In spite of the significant export of cultured pearls to Japan, the local population is relatively poor. Jealousy of success is common, and alcohol and drug abuse is a constant problem. Seventy five percent of the island group's population is Roman Catholic and the remainder Mormon.

As dawn broke, we had sighted the coconut palms that covered the atolls, specifically the island of Takaroa. Although this coral island rises only ten feet above water, the height of the trees makes it visible from nine miles offshore.

"I can't believe it," I expostulated on arrival at the village of Takaroa. "Of all the islands we had to land on in the Tuomotos, we would pick a dry Mormon one."

We had arrived at the pass into the lagoon at 0700 hrs. A wicked current can run between lethal coral shoals through this pass which is only one hundred to two hundred feet wide. Judging the time of entry was critical to survival. We were lucky because we had radio contact with *Enetai*, who had entered the lagoon the day before, and who told us what was involved in getting through it. Dave had said

"Once you've sighted the entrance, motor slowly in to test the current. If it's manageable, keep going. Go past the stone wharf at the village for half a mile. Then turn ninety degrees to port. Make sure you get it right because if you go too far you are up on the reef ahead of you."

Carefully we explored its entrance to assess the flow of the current. We estimated it was the end of the tidal flood as it didn't appear to be flowing too strongly. We pressed on into the half mile cut in the coral which looked very narrow from the cockpit. As we continued past the village and its concrete wharf, the current seemed to pick up speed until we were moving along at quite a pace. Imagine my horror, on looking ahead, to see a fisherman paddling up to his knees in water.

"That's got to be the corner Dave talked about." I called to Christine who was on top of the pilothouse at the foot of the mast, keeping a close watch for coral.

Sure enough, after a straight half mile, the current veered sharply to port. I swung the wheel hard over to follow. Heaving a sigh of relief we shot out of the cut into the lagoon beyond, leaving the fisherman on the reef behind us. We could see Dave coming across the lagoon in his dinghy.

"Thanks for all the info on the cut." I called across to him when we were within earshot.

Pulling his dinghy alongside he said

"Welcome to Takaroa. Follow me across the lagoon and I'll get you through all the oyster lines and coral bommies along the way." Most lines were buoyed, but unfortunately although many floated on the surface, others were submerged.

So began our ten day visit to the lovely Takaroa lagoon, anchored off one of the atoll's surrounding *motus* (reef island), called Îles du roi Georges.

On arrival my right foot looked more like a red club, being swollen and painful. I had noticed it just after leaving Anaho Bay, and had started taking antibiotics as it throbbed continuously and seeped an unpleasant blood stained discharge. So my introduction to Takaroa was spent sitting through the heat of the day in *Demelza*'s cockpit under the bimini, trying to keep cool, while the girls went ashore exploring.

Christine met Leonore. She was a pearl seeder at one of the nearby cultured pearl farms. She worked in a single room shack built at the end of a wooden causeway fifty yards out over the lagoon. Here, the oysters were brought for seeding with a synthetic bead and the colourful margin of an oyster's mantle. These were inserted into its pouch before being closed and sent out on the farm's boat, to grow on a line hanging in the warm waters of the lagoon. The shell had a hole drilled in it through which a line was threaded. With twenty oysters to a line, it was lowered about sixty feet into the lagoon and its upper end buoyed. All the buoys were then joined together to make a raft. In this beautiful clear lagoon water the oysters would develop the seeded pearl over two years. During this time each shell would be visited regularly by divers with compressed air hoses, to free the shells of any algal growth.

Approaching Takaroa

Rapid currents at lagoon entrance

Limitless horizon in Fakarava lagoon

Pearl culturing shed

Pearl farm in the lagoon

Cecile and Koro, the owners of the nearby farm, lived in a lovely home on a promontory of land. This kept the mosquitoes, so prevalent on the atolls, at bay in the evenings. Their pearls were grown for the Japanese market and, although the industry was thriving, there was not a lot of money around for the islanders. Christine was thrilled on leaving to receive two lovely black pearls as a gift from Cecile.

We visited Patricia and Jean's home after my foot had improved. Jean was the meteorologist on the island, and proudly took us on a tour of his station. It was their second home, as the first one had been washed out to sea in a cyclone, along with all their belongings. They were in the process of rebuilding. Patricia was a fabulous cook and showed us twelve ways of preparing a coconut to provide all the courses of a meal. She also showed us how to weave a Tahitian hat made from coconut leaves.

On my birthday, the villagers decided to hold a party to celebrate the occasion. Cecile brought two nieces and their friend, visiting from Papeete. After supper Shirley, from the American boat *Slipaway*, produced a birthday cake which we enjoyed to the accompaniment of lovely languid Tahitian dancing and singing by Colette, Paulina and Margo. Gazing over the calm lagoon, we watched a large tortoise in the moonlit water swimming below the wooden walkway as the music continued into the night.

We learnt that there was a problem with a disease called Elephantiasis on the islands, and that a French Army doctor was making his six monthly visit to the island. I thought I would ask him to look at my foot. The Tahitian nurse at his clinic recognized my problem as a Little Scorpion bite, and that the antibiotics I had taken had resolved the problem.

One evening we invited our village friends to supper on the biggest boat in the bay, *Slipaway*. All the boats contributed a dish for the meal, using *Slipaway's* oven to keep the food hot. As my foot still needed to be elevated, I was relegated to the double berth in the main stateroom being fortified with drinks before supper. Suddenly there was a scream from the galley where Evie had opened the oven door without realizing that the oven was gimbaled. The contents of a heavy casserole, which was being heated in the oven, cascaded over her foot. Before I knew it, she was on the bed with me, with her foot also elevated. What the villagers made of this exhibition we will never know. To make matters even more complicated, our hostess Shirley, who had been a barrel racer in her earlier life, wanted to treat both of us with her cold laser apparatus which she maintained worked very well on horses.

Crossing Takaroa lagoon with foot elevated

Our next port of call in the Tuomotos was the atoll of Fakarava, where we planned to meet up with our friends Bruce and Chris on *Nashira*. We anchored off the village of Rotoava after following the well marked channel into the lagoon. After our rendezvous with them, we both moved down the atoll to a lovely isolated beach seven miles away from the village.

Heavy rain showers plagued us during our first evening but they did provide us with water to fill *Demelza*'s tanks. However, because we had left the hatches open during the day, our bedding was soaked. Lightning and thunder was all around us, and we had a disturbed night wondering whether our anchor would drag.

"*Demelza*. This is *Nashira*. I think you have a problem," Bruce's voice announced first thing in the morning on the radio.

"What's that?" I asked.

"On the spot where you left your wet weather gear in our cockpit last night, we found rat droppings. I think you might have a rat aboard."

Panic ensued as *Demelza* was turned inside out. The cabin was chaos as we emptied all lockers, cupboards, and bins looking for signs of a rat. Nothing.

Rats on a boat can cause havoc. They have a predilection for plastic water hoses and electrical wire insulation which can cause incredible damage in a short space of time.

"No luck here." Christine reported to Bruce later that day.

Twelve hours later a further call came on the radio

"*Demelza*, this is *Nashira*."

"Yes, Bruce."

"It isn't your problem after all," he said. "We've just woken up to find the bottom of one of our egg cartons chewed out and broken egg all over the floor."

Poor *Nashira*. Their beautiful boat was full of nooks and crannies in which a rat could hide.

One evening, just when we thought we were experts at cruising these atolls, we dropped one of our wine goblets overboard. Yes, a silver wine goblet. These had been given to us by Mary and Bob before we left home to raise the tone of living on the boat, and we prized them greatly. We immediately buoyed the spot where it had gone over, so that we could locate it in the morning light. *Nashira's* young crew thoroughly enjoyed the expedition the following morning when we used a grappling hook to reclaim the goblet from a depth of forty feet.

Snorkeling around coral heads was fantastic, with beautiful fish clearly visible in the clear water. We spent hours lolling about in the lagoon. The only caution was that the sun was so hot on our backs that we had to wear shirts while swimming.

During this time, Anne was using the radio trying to locate her mail in Papeete. She discovered that Papeete post office would only keep mail for ten days before returning it to sender, which put pressure on us to leave for Papeete as soon as possible.

On our last afternoon in Fakarava lagoon, Christine and I had our first lesson on windsurfing. There was just enough breeze to coax the board along on the rare occasion I was able to stay upright. The greatest incentive of all was that just below the water's surface, nasty pinnacles of coral threatened to cut the incompetent to ribbons if they fell off the board.

Nashira and Demelza in Fakarava lagoon

TAHITI

On June 4th we raised anchor and set sail for Papeete, Tahiti, a projected three days sail. We went through Passe Garue and into calm weather outside the reef. Gradually the wind rose until by the following morning it had picked up to twenty knots with uncomfortable seas. A lot of wind was being reported from boats in many atolls in the Tuomotos. Thirty-five knots in an exposed lagoon anchorage is no fun, so many were putting out to sea.

In two days we arrived in Papeete, dropping anchor in the harbour between two already med-moored boats, before getting a stern line to a bollard ashore. We were one of forty boats strung side by side along the waterfront. The main thoroughfare of the city ran alongside the harbour, creating continuous traffic noise.

Lying to the west of the Tuomotos, Tahiti is one of the windward group of the Society Islands. These are both volcanic and coral in origin, and are populated by people of Polynesian descent, originating from South East Asia in 800 AD as part of a general outward migration across the Pacific.

European interest in these islands began in 1767 when Captain Wallis accidentally found them while looking for Australia. He claimed Tahiti for England, and called it King George III Island. A year later Bougainville landed on the other side of the island. He was unaware of Wallis's earlier claim, and claimed it for France. Captain Cook visited Tahiti four times, the first time to observe the transit of Venus across the surface of the sun, and later on looking for the great southern continent.

Captain Bligh on '*HMS Bounty*' visited in 1788, and in 1791 'HMS Pandora' came looking for the mutineers from the 'Bounty.' Some had fled with Fletcher Christian to Pitcairn Island before they arrived.

There followed the disastrous years of the whalers, sandalwood traders, and pearlers who brought white man's diseases with them and which decimated the islands' population. The French arrived in 1838 and, through subterfuge, took over a number of the islands as a French Protectorate. Bastille Day is still celebrated every July 14th.

Bastille Day celebration

Our first job was to get Anne off our boat's papers and on to those of *Slipaway*, who had agreed to take her for the next leg of the Pacific. We walked along the waterfront and soon had the paperwork successfully completed before taking time to look around this historic city.

Christine and some of her friends from other cruising boats attended the Evangelical Church service on Sunday. Most of this was conducted in Tahitian, and as always Polynesian voices raised in song were awe-inspiring. All the ladies were dressed in their Sunday best which included the customary elaborate hats.

Monday morning brought chaos to the harbour. A rising wind blew across the med-moored boats along the harbour wall, which had the effect of pushing them down on one another. Where an anchor slipped or lines stretched, there was a great deal of excitement as the boats physically jostled one another. Some took the course of least resistance, untying before going out into the harbour to re-anchor. Whereupon they were jumped all over by the harbour police and told to get back in line as nobody was allowed to free anchor in Papeete Harbour. Two boats in the line were blown ashore under the harbour wall as their anchors failed to hold them in the silt at the bottom of the harbour. One reclaimed anchor came up firmly fixed into a piece of ancient carpet, and another found an abandoned shopping cart.

Med mooring along Papeete waterfront

News was rife of a resurgence of the *El Nino*, with its attendant upset of weather systems in the Pacific. A huge storm had occurred in the Western Pacific, affecting many boats sailing in a regatta from New Zealand to Tonga, with the loss of nine boats and the lives of three people. We made contact with the Institute of Ocean Sciences in Sidney, BC to get the latest weather information.

On the way to Tahiti, *Demelza's* depth sounder had ceased to function, and could not be fixed in Papeete. Soundings with a lead line in the coral infested lagoons would take a great deal of effort, and I felt the sooner it was replaced, the better.

By now we were in regular radio contact with *Maistral*, our friends from home. Tony and Coryn were on passage from Cape Horn via the Gambier Islands. They had experienced a lot of stormy weather, and were now only six hundred nautical miles from Papeete. It looked as though a rendezvous of Victoria boats would be possible.

One evening we took a $2 ride on Le Truck and, for the price of a Hinano beer, we watched an evening of Tahitian dancing at the Beachcomber Resort in Maeve Beach.

Our next expedition involved an attempt to return some Hinano beer bottles, bought in the Marquesas, to the brewery just outside Papeete. Having arrived there with our two crates, we had to await the arrival of the manageress. She turned out to be a lady with presence. She sailed in to her office, receiving a good morning kiss on both cheeks from all her staff, before attending to the first business of the day, which was us.

"Je regret," she said apologetically, "that these bottles are a different size to those used in the Marquesas, so we cannot accept them." This was said with such an attractive French flair that I almost forgave her for the ridiculous situation we found ourselves in. She continued.

"However we shall ask Jacques, the warehouse manager, to see what he can do."

Presently Jacques arrived, with the most agreeable solution of all.

"Certainement, c'est possible." he said "but we cannot give you money. Instead please accept a new case of beer."

We were overwhelmed by this display of French logic.

Along with Noel and Natalie from *Elegant Gypsy*, we rented a car for three days in which to tour the island, and on our return journey found a deserted pamplemousse orchard on Tahiti Iti from which we collected enough fruit to fill its trunk.

Load of pamplemousse

Our eldest son Nick, and his wife Aleda, and their two friends Laura and Garry arrived to join us for a three week visit. Nick and Aleda would accompany us as far as Bora Bora. They had just spent a happy week together in Fiji, and were now looking forward to sailing in Paradise.

"Now when you come cruising on *Demelza*," we had said "remember she isn't a cruise ship. Only bring a small amount of luggage."

As they walked down the airport hall, we couldn't believe the size of the bags their friends were carrying, and we spent the next weeks negotiating our way around them in *Demelza*'s small cabin.

Moorea

For our Victoria boat rendezvous we had arranged to meet *Reiver*, *Expediter* and *Maistral* inside Vairere Reef on Moorea to celebrate John and Sandy's wedding anniversary. There we found sixteen feet of water in which to anchor. The passage to a more protected pool looked formidably strewn with coral heads, so I decided to stay outside. That night was a dreadful experience. It blew hard all night, the sea crashing over the reef, and the resultant current behind the reef kept us broadside to the swell.

Expediter, Reiver, Maistral, Demelza at Moorea

In the morning, a small armada of *Reiver*, *Maistral* and *Expediter* appeared over the horizon, led by *Maistral*. They didn't much like the look of where we had anchored, so found a more pleasing place at the other end of the reef. Our second night at this location was no better than the first. But John and Sandy's 39th Anniversary supper on *Reiver* was such a treat, and to be with friends from home meant a lot to us.

Anchored behind the reef, we were subjected to a huge gale in the night. Angry gusts came down from the surrounding hills and continued all the next day, accompanied by torrential rain. The six of us on *Demelza* couldn't conjure up any enthusiasm for going outside, and Christine and I felt so badly that this should be going on when the young ones were with us. After two nights of popping up and down on anchor watch, Nick and I felt exhausted so we decided to relocate into Cook's Bay where all our sensible friends were already anchored.

The storms continued unabated. Everybody was looking for some shelter in the bay. At last the sun came out to raise our spirits a little. But on the radio we heard the wind outside was now blowing sixty knots. One boat in the bay lost its dinghy, so we put our plans to rent a car on hold until the weather settled. So far we had seen little of Moorea, as it had been blanketed in thick cloud and pouring rain. On our second day in the bay we felt confident enough to leave the boat, rent a car, and drive around the island.

Moorea is twelve miles northeast of Papeete. Its white sandy beaches, deep bays and volcanic peaks overlooking enticing bays, make the south side of the island a popular tourist destination. Most islanders live on the windward side. Pineapple, coconut and vanilla plantations are everywhere, and an easily driven road circles the coast. The two main bays, Cook's and Oponohu Bay, deeply indent the northern shores. Of the two, we preferred Cook's Bay, which inspired Christine and Aleda to get out their paints to capture the magic of the hills and peaks. Mount Rotui's three and a half thousand foot jagged peak bisects the two bays, making it an exquisite photographic opportunity along with the four other majestic peaks on this island.

Surrounded by a coral fringing reef, Moorea has three motus providing excellent snorkeling experiences in the crystalline lagoons. Inland, the rich soil supports abundant fruit and vegetable growth, giving Moorea a lush and plentiful reputation.

Discovered by Wallis in 1767, he called it Duke of York Island. It was here that the first Tahitian bible was published in 1817 and thereafter Protestantism spread throughout the South Pacific with disastrous results for Polynesian culture.

News reached us on the radio that *Enetai* had left for Raitaea, and was experiencing forty five knot winds. They had broken three stanchions in huge seas.

"Stay where you are." was David's advice on the radio.

Sure enough the weather deteriorated again, and for the next six days we experienced howling winds coming down off the mountain. Sheets of rain drummed on the cabin roof as we huddled down below, horrified at our children's South Pacific holiday. However they did manage another tour of the island in a rented car one afternoon, before Laura and Garry decided it was time to tough it out in a hotel in Papeete as soon as possible before returning home.

Demelza's young crew —Top – Nick, Laura — Bottom – Aleda, Garry, me

The cruise ship *Wind Song* came into Cook's Bay to shelter from the winds blowing outside the harbour. Christine and I met the Captain in the bar of the Bali Hai Hotel, which was just a stone's throw away from our anchorage. He was not a happy camper. He had a ship full of wealthy Americans on a one week cruise of the Society Islands, three days of which they had spent stormbound, having had to give Bora Bora a total miss

Finally the wind stopped, and the rain lessened. By now we would have done almost anything to get on land. We hiked up to the Belevedere Lookout, and visited the Moorea distillery where papaya, grapefruit and pineapple juices were made from local fruit, and forty percent proof liqueurs were made from coconut, ginger and pineapple.

We saw the *Marae Titiroa*, an ancient Polynesian cultural centre. At one end of the stone structure was a stone sacrificial platform. Stone backrests for the assembled chiefs ringed the *marae* where gifts of food were made to the gods.

About five hundred of these ancient stone structures have been found in this area scattered in the forest nearby, evidence of a strong cultural system at that time. On the hills above the *marae* were archery platforms, where noblemen would kneel to let fly their arrows up the hill, to see who could shoot the furthest.

Cook's Bay, Moorea with Mt. Mouputa

Once the weather had cleared, the tourist industry sprang back to life. We were almost rocked out of our bunks at dawn by hundreds of fish boats roaring through the anchorage at the start of a fishing derby hoping to snag Mahi Mahi, Yellow Fin Tuna and Swordfish. Bruce on *Nashira* gave a vivid commentary of his experiences of their departure past his boat which kept us all amused.

RAIATEA

Finally we had a morning that looked possible for our passage to Raiatea. We raised anchor and, after taking a look around Oponua Bay, put out to sea. What a crossing we had, not so much from the wind, but the sea was a nightmare. Nick and Aleda both felt awful but didn't complain, and we were glad that Laura and Garry hadn't had to experience that night.

We anchored in Hotomuu Bay, at the north end of Raiatea, and in the morning hiked up to see the *Marae Taputapuatea*, one of the best preserved in Polynesia. The coral platform is one hundred and thirty feet long by twenty two feet wide and ten feet high. The courtyard in front of it is paved with volcanic rock which also had stone backrests. From here the Polynesian migration to New Zealand and Hawaii began. All the *maraes* look out to the west, and the view of the island of Maupite across the water was breathtaking.

After leaving the bay we motored to Utaroa, where I checked in at the Gendarmerie while Christine befriended two little girls Tahedani and Tahanne, who sang songs for her sitting on the harbour wall. We relocated to a bay on the northwest side of the island to the accompaniment of drums beating and girls singing. They were practicing for the Bastille Day celebrations as we sat in *Demelza's* cockpit watching the sun set over Bora Bora in the distance.

After a day's stopover at Tahaa, we had a glorious twenty-five nautical mile sail to Bora Bora. As we approached the island the undersides of the clouds over the 'tooth' (the one mountain on the island) were a pale green, reflecting the colour of the lagoon surrounding the island. We discovered that the Autohelm wasn't working again so decided to send it home with Nick and Aleda for repair. As we entered the pass at the west side of the island's fringing reef we dropped Nick and Aleda off at a *motu* with the dinghy for a swim while we continued on to pick up a buoy at the yacht club.

Bora Bora

Mount Ofemanu towers two thousand, one hundred and ninety feet above the blue lagoon, its slopes covered with hibiscus. Both Captain Cook and Charles Darwin visited this island. It was annexed by France in 1895. A twenty-five mile road runs around its perimeter and bicycles, in various degrees of disrepair, can be borrowed for touring.

We pulled in to the Bora Bora Yacht Club, run by Guy, who was probably the man with the fewest social graces we had met on our trip to date. His conversation was monosyllabic, and the operation that he ran was the least businesslike that could be imagined.

The normal moorage fee was $23 a night, but if we sponsored the Yacht Club by buying a $4 beer, this fee would be waived. Ostensibly the Yacht Club anchorage had three houseboats for rent. Two of them had sunk, and the third looked in imminent danger of doing likewise. The location was unique, providing the best sheltered mooring in Bora Bora. Little rental cabins overlooked the gorgeous lagoon. They were very small and primitive, with a single central room with a bed, two chairs and a small bathroom. In the Yacht Club anchorage, there was a very dilapidated raft that had been built by an American living in Bora Bora. On completion he had planned to sail it to the Cook Islands. However the voyage had started as a disaster and he had had to be towed back to Bora Bora. In doing so, the vessel had been damaged, pulled up on the beach and sold for next to nothing to a local boy who still bailed it out every day.

Sadly Nick and Aleda's holiday was drawing to a close. On one of their final days, they rented a moped to tour the island and visited the Club Med. Following this we waved them off on the little boat which took them to the airport on their way to join their friends in Tahiti to catch the flight home.

On our sail down the coast of California we had met Chuck and Colette who had expressed a great yearning to do a passage in the South Pacific. We had agreed. They would join us here for the passage to Tonga. Only two days after Nick and Aleda had departed these two new guests arrived days earlier than expected. Chuck had done some sailing in California but Colette was new to it.

On the 14th July the Bastille Day celebrations started for a week of continuous inter community dancing and song. The winners of the Bora Bora festival would later compete against winners from other islands in the Society Island Championships. The four of us went to Vaitape, the main town on the island, for three days of these competitions. We were so impressed by the quality of Tahitian dancing and music. Each day we walked the mile into town to attend, and happily walked back to the Yacht Club at the end of the evening's performances which was usually around midnight. What was so refreshing was that there was never any public disturbance or drunkenness to be seen, and the families all around us were having a really good time.

When all the celebrations were over, we decided to relocate to a little island off Vaitape called Toopau, anchoring in fifteen feet of water over white coral sand. The snorkeling was unparalleled in quality with crystal clear water over the coral, and plentiful reef fish. After one day's relaxation we received a weather forecast for an approaching weather front. So we moved behind a reef between Toopau and its satellite islet Toopau Iti with the volcanic cone of Bora Bora framed between the two islands. It was a magical location and gave us the protection we needed as the wind changed direction and strength. We were joined by *Nashira* and *Elegant Gypsy*, and we all had a merry time exploring the area, shelling and swimming.

But boat maintenance jobs had to continue. While Chuck and I went up the mast to lubricate the shivs and inspect all the halyards and fittings, Collette and Christine used our hand cranked 1947 Singer sewing machine to patch a chafe in the mainsail. We rigged a downhaul on the boom to prevent further chafing against the shrouds.

The wind was blowing at twenty knots during the day, so we attached the wind propeller to the tow generator and hung it in the rigging. This beast took a lot of taming in a strong breeze as the two-foot blades, spinning at their normal rate, could cause a lot of personal injury if anybody got in its way.

Dave and Evie on *Enetai* had decided to head for home, sailing via Hawaii. We were sad to see them go. Dave asked me to take over the Happy Hour Radio Net that he had begun. It started at 1600 hrs daily and was open to all cruisers in the Society Islands. It proved a most rewarding experience, and it was a way of distracting the many children making passages from some of the more unpleasant features of life on a boat in rough seas. I made many little friends through this program. We would have quizzes, stories, anagram puzzles and jokes. Anything to keep their minds occupied while their parents struggled to keep things going on the boat.

Boats that had left Bora Bora reported stormy weather everywhere. *Enetai*, on their way to Hawaii, had a lot of wind, rough seas, torrential rain and sick crew. Those going to Suvarov and American Samoa were having much the same experience. So we stayed were we were for a few more days.

We borrowed four dilapidated bikes to circumnavigate the road around Bora Bora. My bicycle had obviously never seen oil, and its seat had been designed by a misogynist. The height adjusting nut on the seat was totally frozen by years of rust so that I had to propel this ancient machine while assuming a most unnatural position. Half way around the island, Colette decided that she had had enough. This was not too helpful as there were no other means of transport back to the boat. Frantically Chuck achieved what would normally have been impossible. He pushed Colette's bicycle all the way home in short bursts while she freewheeled!

Raiatea

Our nine days in Bora Bora was over. We had to press on. It was already July and the days were blisteringly hot. The sail back to Raiatea was a fast reach and only took us four hectic hours. The downhaul which Chuck had rigged on the boom, when cinched down tight, improved the shape of the mainsail and prevented it chafing against the shrouds. We anchored off the boatyard in Raiatea in eighty feet of water and managed to get a good set in mud, as the wind howled around us all night.

In the morning we took the boat over to Dominique at the boatyard for him to look at the freshwater leak that had been causing me some concern. He found that it was from a loose clamp on a waterline that both Chuck and I had missed. In the boatyard's dry storage area there was an aluminum yacht that had hit a reef on Huahine. It had been skippered by a qualified charter skipper who had managed to rip the bottom out of the whole length of its hull. Jagged holes had been plugged with bedding, towels and clothes as the crew had frantically tried to staunch the flow. Incredibly they had succeeded in getting the boat back to port.

After moving to the marina at Uturoa, we restocked the food lockers, filled our tanks with fresh water and fuel, and distributed all the fresh fruit that we had been given into hammocks. We hung a huge hand of bananas on the backstay. In retrospect this was not such a good idea, as bananas have this unique characteristic of all ripening at the same time. The only person I have ever known who could consume limitless numbers of this fruit was David, and he had gone home. For a week or two we were left with the gruesome experience of being slapped around the back of the head while in the cockpit in rough weather, by this increasingly ripening fruit. It was most unpleasant. With the passage of time, on a calmish day, we could hear the ripe fruit dropping off one by one into the sea astern, to the accompaniment of a resounding cheer from the crew.

The wind continued to blow at forty five knots in the harbour at Uturoa, so fiercely that I had real concerns that our dock was going to disintegrate. We moved *Demelza* toward the dock's land anchors where it did not seem to be moving so violently. With all the waiting around for a break in the weather, Chuck and Collette's vacation time was running out, which led to the inevitable pressure to leave for Tonga in poor conditions.

To keep ourselves amused, we climbed to the top of Tut Tapioi, nine hundred feet above the town. Here Christine dropped the precious wide angle lens of her camera. We watched helplessly as it rolled down the steep slope at our feet to disappear over the edge of a precipice.

In the afternoons, the islanders were busy practicing for the Bastille Day inter island pirogue races. Teams of muscular brown men toiled away at their paddles, chanting the rhythm as they sped across the lagoon, always attracting an appreciative audience.

And still it blew, with sheets of rain. This was not at all what we had expected in the South Pacific. Christine contacted the Pacific Maritime net, putting a call through to Dan in San Diego to ask him what was going on with the weather. We heard that a boat was hove to fifteen nautical miles off Papeete. That made our decision easy, to stay where we were for yet another day. Dan promised fine weather was on its way within the next twelve hours.

There was great concern among the waiting fleet for boats that had turned home towards North America from the Marquesas and Bora Bora, as a Category 5 Hurricane *Amelia* was heading toward the Hawaiian Islands. The ones with which we were in contact were loping northward south of the hurricane's track. One yacht called us saying

"*Demelza*, *Demelza*. This is the submarine *Njiord*." We felt so sorry for them.

Finally, a perfect morning broke with blue skies and gentle breezes. We checked out of Raiatea, after nine stormbound days, and headed for Tonga. Bora Bora looked wonderful in the sunshine as we sailed past, and for twelve hours we made steady progress.

As the second day at sea came to a close, a dark arch formed in the clouds across the horizon. Huge seas developed during the night and everybody felt seasick. I distinguished myself once again by being prostrated for three days, which was a record. During this time Chuck and Christine took the brunt of the night watches, as I became more and more dehydrated.

"Look behind us." Christine shouted, one afternoon

There in the waves, following in *Demelza*'s wake, was a thirty foot whale showing great interest in our tow generator's propeller. Six or seven times it approached the side of the boat, swimming with ease in the crashing waves before exhaling a cloud of fishy spray and disappearing from sight. We hurriedly looked up our book on whales so that we could describe it to other boats on the radio that evening. The consensus was that it was a Rights Whale.

Wanting to know how we could protect ourselves from a too friendly whale, we solicited advice on the radio from other cruisers. The replies ranged from turning off any music on board, to turning on the engine.

Nevertheless the next day, surrounded by breaking waves, the whale returned. Suddenly there was a huge "bang." The boat shuddered and came to a complete stop in the water. The mast flexed forward in an alarming fashion. We had fallen off the crest of an enormous wave onto the top of the whale. Anxiously I shouted to Chuck from the cockpit

"Chuck, look under the cabin sole to see we are not taking on water."

Following a quick inspection he replied

"All's well down here."

About a hundred yards to port, the whale surfaced, and gave us what I can only describe as a protractedly baleful look before disappearing, never to be seen again.

Apart from a three-day break, our journey to Tonga had been a rough and unpleasant experience. We were all tired, causing havoc to watch schedules and everyone's nerves. I don't think any of us would volunteer for a trip like that again. *Demelza* performed faultlessly, and her sturdiness had been well tested during our encounter with the whale. Christine proved the most stalwart of us all. Chuck was always willing but had tired himself out by the end of the journey. I was either seasick or nauseated, and Colleen retired to her bunk praying that the whole thing might soon end. Not at all the South Pacific cruise we had ordered.

On the tenth day we dropped anchor in Port Refuge in the Va'vau Group of Islands in Tonga.

My log's summary, written on arrival in Tonga, reads:

"French Polynesia. Relief at finding clean restaurants after Mexico. Locals are friendly, the French are not. French officialdom polite, distant and thorough.

Papeete: The least enjoyable place to anchor. Crosswinds in a stern tied anchorage are a potential time bomb.

Marquesas: Lovely, but oh! those biting insects.

The Tuomotos: Delightful and dangerous with difficult anchoring, coral head infested lagoons, clocking winds, lee shores, long fetches and shallow water.

Moorea: Lovely but windy and wet.

Bora Bora: A jewel, lovely reefs, not particularly good snorkeling, good place to practice using a lead line and bamboo pole as depth sounder!

Raiatea: Foul weather limited our exploration.

Our crossing to Tonga: An eleven day nightmare. Foul weather, contrary winds, and blue water over the boat. Huge seas, confused swells from raging storms north and south of us. Eleven days of psychological and physical exhaustion that I could well forget. I failed to manage the watches on our small boat adequately to ensure nobody was too tired. Fortunately the boat was never in danger.

Seasickness: The conventional wisdom is to leave port on the last day of a storm to assure good weather later. The difficulty with this is twofold (1) the crew will certainly be seasick at the start of the passage because of the rough seas, and (2) the last day of a storm seems unpredictable.

CHAPTER 8
Tonga

We tied up alongside a fish boat in the port of Va'vau, after motoring up the five mile channel into its protected anchorage. We completed the formalities for entering Tonga before Collette and Chuck moved up into the Paradise Hotel.

Neiafu is the capital of the northernmost group of Tongan islands, the Va'vau group. There are two other island groups, the Ha'apai with its wonderful beaches and lagoons, and Tongatapu, the largest of the three groups on which the national capital Nukualofa is located. Tonga is a kingdom ruled by King Taufa'ahau Tupou IV, whose ancestors have reigned for over a thousand years.

The Port of Neiafu is overlooked by the town's impressive church and the Paradise Hotel. In the distance, along the fiord-like entrance, we could see the four hundred and ninety foot Mount Talau. Jungle-clad and flat topped, it gives a spectacular view across Lake Tuanaku and many of the nearby islands from its summit.

Of the one hundred and sixty nine islands in the Tongan Kingdom only thirty six are inhabited. They lie at 23°S. About one hundred thousand proud Tongans live here, mostly relatively poor subsistence farmers and fishermen. Under Tongan law, every male over sixteen years is entitled to eight and a quarter acres of land, which is a problem as there isn't enough land to meet all entitlement. However to some extent, that problem is solved by the significant outward migration of Tongans to other countries, especially New Zealand.

Tourism is being encouraged to help the struggling economy. Foreign money is brought in by the sale of copra, bananas and coconut products. Cash aid is a mainstay especially from New Zealand, Australia and Germany.

First discovered by the Dutch in 1616, these islands were visited later by Tasman and Captain Cook, who called them "The Friendly Islands." Intertribal warfare was common before the advent of the missionaries between1820 and 1840, when King George Toupou I was proclaimed king.

The women are skilled at mat weaving, basketry, and making tapa cloth. Like the men, they wear a skirt, *tupanu*, the women's beige ankle length and the men's black and to the knee. The women also wear a decorative waist band, *kiekie*, from which woven or shell ornaments are hung on strings The men wear a woven mat, *ta'avala*, as a sign of respect for the king and elders.

Tongans are Protestant, and on Sunday do no work. Everybody goes to church. The ladies wear black with decorated hats, and the men are smartly dressed wearing their *ta'avala*. The ladies lead church singing with the men joining in almost as an afterthought, with wonderful bass harmony. It was at church that Christine first met Mary. This opened all sorts of opportunities for us to meet local people.

The church in Neiafu was presided over by Father Kevin, an Englishman, who happened to be a ham radio operator. He conducted the whole service in Tongan after greeting us in English. We next met him at his Kava Festival, rather like a Social Club for men, held in the church hall. A number of long tables were arranged around the room, each with an assigned host for the evening. Father Kevin duly introduced us to our table's host, who poured us a generous helping of Kava in a half coconut shell. Made from the ground root of a pepper tree, this liquid has the distinct flavour of what I imagine to be that of wall paper paste. Christine suggested it smelled like nail varnish remover. After drinking a full bowl, my lips began to tingle and I could sense a rather unpleasant detached feeling creeping over me. Apparently Kava is promoted as a tranquillizing alternative to alcohol, the latter making the drinkers uncontrollably aggressive.

Downstairs, in a basement room of the church, a male voice choir practice was in full swing. The harmonies produced were thrilling. Most interesting was the sheet music which was written as a series of numbers from one to nine. Having being given a note by the choirmaster, the singers could follow these numbers to make music. They were practicing for a service to invest the new Bishop of Tonga, which we later attended.

A notable establishment in town was the bakery, which was housed in the most inauspicious looking shack up a side street. As we approached this building we could hear the thumping of the Kava root mills along the way. Once through the bakery door, and on becoming accustomed to its rather gloomy interior, we could see the oven across the dark and stiflingly hot room. All around us were work tables covered in flour, where the dough had been rolled. We waited for the next batch of bread to come out of the oven, while Christine attempted to write post cards. The baker suggested she use one of the work tables as a flat area. As she set herself up, there was an instantaneous wavelike movement on the wooden surface as thousands of weevils scuttled for cover. The Bakery's *piéces de resistance* were huge cinnamon buns, baked on Wednesdays only. These could be smelt cooking all over the neighbourhood, and were a feast for hungry cruisers.

Another establishment important during our stay in Va'vau was the Bounty Bar. This coffee shop/restaurant was run by a New Zealand couple, and was the most significant spot for meeting friends, finding out where things were, and what was going on, as well as for obtaining help if needed. It overlooked the harbour and from here we watched the town's domesticated pigs roaming loose as they snuffled under rocks for crabs on the beach below.

Scattered among the islands of the Va'vau group were a number of anchorages. Some of these had villages nearby, and some were remote. Here we enjoyed the sun, the beaches and unparalleled snorkeling.

Our favourite was the island of Kenutu, on the outer reefs. Here Joanna held sway running the Berlin Bar, a wooden framework building with woven roof, and a deck looking out over the lagoon from its solitary perch on the island. Joanna came from Berlin, and was to become a great friend. In all, during our stay in the Va'vau group, we visited her island nine times. Each time she catered to our needs and we, in turn, helped her with jobs that needed to be done around the property.

Joanna at the Berlin Bar — Kenutu

She ran the restaurant with her friend Leonore. A Tongan man, who caught fish for the restaurant, also brought supplies from Neiafu in his boat. For company she had two delightful black and white puppies called Mosquito and Vollie. During many a sunset over the lagoon, we would play with these delightful little fellows until it was time to make our way back to *Demelza* before dark. They would watch us safely aboard then paddle home for the night. In the morning they were sure to be there on the beach waiting for us to appear. We enjoyed watching them playing, trying to make the time go faster pending our arrival ashore.

Across the island we could hear the ocean waves pounding on the coral and limestone cliffs. Some of our favourite walks were to the blow holes, where surf was compressed before being shot up into the air with a most satisfying explosive noise. To cool off, we would run into the calm waters of the lagoon and swim around the coral looking at the fish or finding vacated shells. A spectacular walk was to the grotto. Bill from *Ramtha* went swimming in its eerie dark water, enclosed by the cave, but my imagination was far too vivid to accompany him.

There was another memorable cave on Vape Island, with a narrow entrance from the sea, called Swallows Cave. We took the dinghy into it and, while swimming around in its dim light, saw our first sea snake alongside. On one side of the cave, a huge buttress of rock stuck out into its chamber. When struck with something solid, it rang like a bell.

In many anchorages on the various islands, the local village would put on a feast for visitors and the crews of anchored yachts. One of these was at Lisa Beach on Maungaui Island, where Aisea hosted the event. The little lane down to the beach was lit by candles, looking so romantic in the warm night air. Unfortunately we heard that, the week before our arrival, Aisea's Feast had been closed down due to an outbreak of food poisoning. Following his reinstatement, we watched from *Demelza* as others enjoyed a moonlit feast ashore. Following Christine's meeting with sixteen year old Mary at Church, we received an invitation from her mother to lunch in the village of Falevai on the following Sunday.

Sure enough Mary was waiting for us after the service. She escorted us through an open glade under the trees where pigs were grazing, and up the hill to her home. There we met her mother Lesieli, her husband, and three more children. They had everything prepared for our visit to their immaculate small wooden home.

A large woven mat was laid on the floor of the main room, and her husband's clothes hung tidily along one wall. On a shelf above them was an assortment of collectables, shells, feathers, jars and the large bottle of shampoo that Christine had given the family as a gift. We had observed families washing their hair in the sea using leaves of a bush. We thought they might like to try our kind of shampoo for a change but have often wondered whether that bottle is still sitting on the shelf.

Lesieli prepared the food in the adjoining room. The meal consisted of a generous helping of piglet, chicken, breadfruit, taro, yam, and a flour dumpling, served by the children. One of the little girls' jobs was to sit to one side making sure no flies alighted on the food. This she did by continuously waving a large palm frond over the meal. Once their initial shyness was over, the family chatted happily, speaking very good English. The paw paw dessert, cooked in coconut milk, was delicious. It surprised us to be invited to take the leftovers back with us to the boat, but we were assured this is their custom.

Mary invited us to visit her primary school's sports day, and to bring any children from the other boats in the bay so that they could join in the fun. We took Ben and Lindsay from *Talitha Koom*, a boat from South Africa. They were on their way to live in New Zealand. Lindsay took a book of South African animals, and we took a pan of brownies and cookies, and a map of the world to show the children where we all came from.

We walked through the school room, which was hung with samples of the children's writing and drawings, out into the field beyond. Here the sports and games were taking place. Some games were familiar, others not. The children soon got the idea and joined in the fray. In the sack race, little Ben tried so hard to progress along the course without much success. A Tongan boy on his team, seeing him struggle, ran onto the course, picked him up, and ran to a creditable third place finish amid lots of laughter and applause. Not only were the children well behaved and polite, but they had a tremendous sense of fun, and were miles ahead of our white children athletically. When all the exertion was over, the children went back to the school room where tea was served including our cakes and cookies.

Teachers at Falevai school

Not content with all this generosity, in the days following, Mary would often walk down to our beach, bringing gifts of vegetables and fruit. In return we gave her mayonnaise for her vegetables, ketchup for the taro and some uncooked popcorn with instructions on how to prepare it when her children next had friends over for a visit. We knew that popcorn would be a huge success as we had already served it to island visitors who came onboard. It was new to them and they enjoyed the popping of the corn.

Some of the best snorkeling of our entire trip was at Ava Island. Here, huge coral walls dropped off into the depths of the adjacent channel. Beautiful fish darted into and out of their special lairs along the walls. Magnificent terraces of many species of coral, of different shapes and colours, radiated out from the cliff into the shallower water. It was a kaleidoscope of colour and variety.

Sheila and Ann arrive at Neiafu airport

Ann and Sheila arrived by plane from Victoria. We had worked hard to make their accommodation on our small boat as comfortable as possible. We took Charlie's taxi to meet them at the airport. He was the local church choir's director so we had a lot to talk about on the journey inland. The return journey with our visitors was more exciting as Charlie's taxi blew a tire on the dreadful road. Taking a look at his tires I found them all completely bald.

"Have you got a spare?" I asked

"Yes, I'll get it on in a minute." he answered from the depths of the car's trunk.

When he pulled it out, it was even balder than the original. At least it had air in it, enough to get us back to the harbour.

Our time with Ann and Sheila was very precious. Good friends, they seemed to enjoy the visits we made to the islands and reefs.

Through the auspices of the Bounty Bar we heard of *Jacaranda*, a beautiful Camper Nicholson yacht. Sandy and Andy were adept at doing canvas work, so we commissioned them to make us a water catcher that didn't leak, to rig over *Demelza's* cockpit. Through them we met Pat Matheson, who very kindly invited us to lunch in her lovely home in Utelei village on Pangaimotu Island. On the appointed day we took *Demelza* around to her home. Pat was an authoress. We had read her book *Utelei my Tongan Home*, which was about her arrival in Tonga as a young teacher, her marriage to the local Scottish doctor, and their life together in Utelei village. It was especially intriguing to meet Tui Fua, a good friend and companion of Pat's. They had known each other for many years.

Tui Fua

Tui Fua had prepared a sumptuous meal. She was so attentive, making sure everything was perfect. During the course of the meal Pat asked me to go to the hospital in Neiafu to meet Ali, the hospital administrator. She wanted a list of items the hospital could use as she was allied to a philanthropic group in San Francisco. She had been trying to get Ali to list his needs for some time.

Unfortunately the end of our visit dissolved into chaos. Pat's dog Rodney, took after a stray pig that had found its way into her garden. During the ensuing chase, first by the dog, then by Pat and the rest of us, we flattened many of her lovely plants in an attempt to catch the intruder. By the time this episode was over, the tide had gone out. In our finery, we carried the dinghy over rough and muddy terrain to get back to the water's edge before returning to *Demelza.*

The next day I walked up to the hospital to visit Ali. He showed me around the wards, where the patients' families were providing supportive care. He took me down to the basement, unlocking a storage room door. Inside were piles of equipment.

"None of it works," he said. "Nobody knows how to fix it, and people steal parts which cannot be replaced. I don't know what to say to Mrs. Matheson."

"Well what would be really useful?" I asked

"Bed pans." he replied. "There are no moving parts."

Too soon it was time for Ann and Sheila to go home and we had to begin preparing for our journey on to New Zealand. The day before they were due to leave we received a tsunami warning. It was due to arrive in Tonga on the day of their departure, so we evacuated them to the Paradise Hotel. From here they would have a great view of *Demelza* lying on the sea bottom should the water drain out of the harbour. Fortunately for us the tsunami failed to show.

We heard that an Agricultural Fair was to be held on the grounds of the High School close to Neiafu's old harbour. Along with the Price family in *Talitha Koom*, we moved our boats to this alternative anchorage, before walking up to the Fairground. All the stalls, loaded with produce and Tongan arts and crafts, were arranged around the perimeter of the grounds. Intricate Tongan woven baskets, skirts, mats, and bags were on display, as well as wonderful wood carvings.

Talitha Koom — Hilary, John and children *Tongan baskets*

A good humoured crowd was gathering as we walked past some of the exhibits, one of which was on heart health. This was of particular interest to the well proportioned King. Because of my own interest in the subject, I spoke to the man who was running the exhibit who happened to be a public health physician. After discussing the problem of obesity and its secondary problems in Polynesian people, he asked

"Would you like to meet the King?"

"I'd love to," I said. "Would you mind if I brought my wife along?"

"No, please do." he replied.

So I dashed off into the crowd to find Christine. She was sitting among the assembled cruisers waiting for the King's arrival to open the Fair. Visitors had been consigned to a particular spot on one side of the field. Waving my arms to attract her attention, she began picking up her belongings.

"Leave all that," I said "Just come."

With the good doctor, we awaited the King's arrival. A respectful hush descended on the festive crowd. He and his son were driven into the Fairgrounds in a Toyota Land Cruiser. They stopped by us, as we waited in line, on their way to the two flower bedecked thrones that had been assembled half-way down the field, one smaller one for the Prince, and a very large one for His Majesty.

The doctor introduced us both.

"I'm very pleased to meet you." the King said, extending his large hand.

That encounter caused a certain amount of joshing among the cruising fraternity in the Bounty Bar when we returned there for supper that night.

Another favourite memory was a visit to Kenutu with Pat and Tui Fua on *Demelza*. On the appointed day, Joanna sent her Tongan helper to collect them by boat from Utelei. They duly arrived at Kenutu where we had anchored, and Joanna treated us all royally at the Berlin Bar. We enjoyed walking around the island together. Tui Fua, who was related to the King, had spent time in her childhood on Kenutu, and told us Tongan fables as we sat on the cliff overlooking the sea.

After lunch on *Demelza*, we all swam in a nearby cove. Three of us were in swimsuits, but Tui Fua fully clothed in a long black dress and underskirts. Tongan girls never learn to swim. She waded in up to her waist before jumping up and down splashing the water with her hands, just as she would have done as a girl. When we returned to the boat Tui did not want to get out of her wet clothes. However Christine and Pat insisted, so I beat a hasty retreat to give them time to sort her out. Later we had a wonderful dinner ashore in the restaurant. Joanna produced a platter of seafood with vegetables from her garden. They slept on the boat, a new experience for both of them, and were a total delight for the two days we had them aboard. Joanna made special meals for us ashore as the puppies entertained us. It was magical.

Another one of our favourite haunts was Diana's Restaurant on Kapa Island. *Telitha Koom* joined us there with a bottle of champagne to celebrate Christine's and my thirty third wedding anniversary. *Chimera* from Australia, with Grant and Robbie aboard, joined us later, and Diana put on a special lunch for us all.

Our experiences in French Polynesia and now Tonga taught us that there were definite understandings in Polynesian culture about giving and receiving gifts. Although nothing was ever said, it is customary to offer guests gifts, and it is understood but not stated, that gifts would be received in return. The giving of leftovers after a meal is also a custom signifying the host's generosity of spirit and therefore not a thing to be refused.

We spent Irish Night at Diana's restaurant in September with many of the cruising boats. Bill played the electric keyboard and Ed, from *Buster*, played the guitar and sang lusty sea shanties. The little Tongan boys from the village loved to dance to the rhythm of the music and kept on dancing well into the night. Afterwards we had to find our way along a dark uneven path through the forest back to the bay where our boats were anchored.

On second visit to Falevai, and before returning to Neiafu, Christine had made a deal with Lesieli, Mary's mother, to buy her a pair of reading glasses at the local store. We were to split the cost with Hilary from *Telitha Koom*, who was going to pick Lesieli up from the village to meet us at the shop in Neiafu where the glasses were sold. Well the meeting with Hilary didn't work out. No one quite knew why Lesieli didn't show up. We heard that she had a daughter working at the Duty Free shop in town. So on the following morning we went to arrange another date for glasses.

At the appointed time a very elegant lady, dressed in a formal black dress, sat outside the store. No sign of Lesieli. After a while Christine walked up to the lady

"Do you know Falevai village?" she asked

"I am from Falevai." she replied

"Do you know Lesieli? Christine persevered

"I am Lesieli." was her reply. That nearly knocked us over. We had the wrong Lesieli.

However, this one also needed reading glasses, so we fitted her out appropriately before she caught the ferry home to Falevai. She agreed to arrange for the right Lesieli to come for her glasses the following day. This was successfully done.

Ray arrived from Victoria to join us for the passage to New Zealand. We caught up quickly with some of the last preparatory boat jobs and squeezed in a final visit to Kenutu island. It was sad to say good bye to Joanna and we saw her waving her German flag on the beach as we lifted the anchor early in the morning on our way to Neiafu for final provisioning.

We called in at Port Morelle, or Port Refuge as it used to be called, the anchorage from which many interesting excursions could be made. One was to Mariner's Cave, an underwater chasm which entailed diving down the face of a vertical cliff for six to ten feet, depending on the state of the tide. Then a horizontal swim along through the rock for about twenty feet, before emerging into the vault of the cave. Five boats' crews, including *Demelza*'s, set out on the elegant fifty two foot *Rascal Fair* for the day's expedition.

When we arrived off the cliff face there was a considerable swell running, mounting up the cliff before subsiding down toward the narrow cave entrance. Only one of our group had been into the cave before. Christine, the only volunteer from *Demelza*, was accompanied by Bill from *Ramtha*, who was a very strong swimmer. While the participants swam from *Rascal Fair* toward the cliff and the underwater entrance, Ray and I took over the running of the boat. There was nowhere to anchor as the water was too deep. One by one, pairs of flippers would emerge out of the waves as the swimmers disappeared into the depths. Suddenly they were gone. The sea was empty of bobbing heads as we idled a few yards from where they had vanished.

Christine went into the cave's opening before Bill and experienced her first free diving along a tunnel through rock. Soon she was in the pool surfacing inside the cave to take a deep breath of air. She later reported that it wasn't totally dark inside. There was a greenish glow coming from the submerged entrance so that they could see each other treading water and examining the inside of the large cave. As the swells rolled in against the cliff face, the level of the water inside the cave would rise. This compressed the air so much that the moisture in the air vaporized, causing a momentary fog that blotted out all visibility. Tongan legends tell of lovers being secreted inside the cave while a hunt was made for them on the island above.

After ten minutes inside the cave, Christine approached the patch of light from below and dived down into the tunnel. This time she had the sensation that it was longer than she had remembered. She began to rise too soon and could feel herself being pressed up against its roof. With a gigantic effort and a few scratches, she forced herself down a bit, then forward and upwards toward the now visible surface of the water outside. It seemed a long way away. Finally she burst through into the sunlight. All agreed it had been a great, if scary experience.

Ray and I plotted our proposed course to New Zealand, entering the waypoints into the GPS. After a final party at Diana's to raise money for a village girl who had lost her fisherman husband at sea, we had one day of rest. We checked the weather charts and filled out our clearance papers before leaving Tonga.

Written in my log before leaving for New Zealand is the following:

"You cannot climb a mountain
Before you walk low ground,
And on the road to wisdom
No shortcut can be found,
Have courage in adversity
You will not strive in vain,
There never was a rainbow
Without a drop of rain."

This was written by Sheryl and Bruce McKarras, on their boat *Isle of Wight* in January, 1994 for Grant and Robbie on *Chimera.* It summed up my feelings about the frequently hazardous journey to New Zealand, in light of the Queen's birthday storm that had occurred in these waters four months previously when nine boats and three lives had been lost. This passage south is notorious for unexpectedly fierce storms, so Ray and I took great care to set the boat up for a rough passage. Christine had food prepared in advance should it become impossible to work down below.

Christine signed on with the various radio nets so they could follow our progress. We relocated from Neiafu to Port Morelle, to complete preparations for the passage in a more relaxed setting. We had a final swim before deflating the dinghy and packing it down below. The following day, at 1430 hrs all was ready. The forecast was good, and reports over the radio from boats underway were favorable. We said goodbye to several friends anchored in the bay. One young man who was single handing his boat *Lady Dashne*, said he would be listening out for us on his radio.

"See you in a couple of weeks." he said.

After a calm and sunny start, the sky gradually clouded over and the wind rose to twenty knots from the southeast by midnight. Ray had put one reef in the main and we were making an easy six knots through the water.

Overnight the wind settled and the clouds cleared. The barometer was rising as we passed Tofua Island five miles to port. This is an active volcanic island at the northernmost end of the Ha'apai Group of Tongan Islands. We continued making between six and seven knots over the ground for most of our second day covering one hundred and thirty nautical miles in twenty four hours.

Leaving Tonga for New Zealand

The clear calm weather continued with eight to ten knots of wind from the east as we crossed the dateline on our third day out. We were now in the Eastern hemisphere for the first time, exactly half-way around the world from Greenwich in England. Almost immediately we lost the wind, so decided to motor. Our plan was to avoid sailing directly to Cape Reinga at the tip of the North Island of New Zealand, as that would later require us to sail down a lee shore to Opua in the Bay of Islands. This shoreline has a reputation for causing trouble. Instead we decided to take a more southerly course, making for Cape Brett at the north end of the Bay of Islands.

However on our eighth day at sea, we began receiving messages that boats ahead of us were experiencing thirty knot winds as they approached New Zealand. John, a ham weather guru living on Norfolk Island, advised us to slow down to let a weather front go past before we continued southwards. Following his advice, we reduced sail and changed to a more westerly course.

By now our system for keeping watch on the boat was well established, Christine doing the 2000 hrs to 0100 hrs shift, me doing the 0100 hrs to 0400 hrs and Ray the 0400 hrs to 0800 hrs. Ray was adept at taking cat naps as the opportunity arose, a skill which I lacked and envied greatly. He spent some of his time studying the new celestial navigation calculator and my sextant, and as the weather continued calm with easterly winds, we both practiced using them. It is one thing to use a sextant in a class room or on the deck at home, but quite another to get it right on a boat rolling and surging in the ocean. I don't think we did very well and were so glad to have a reliable GPS to help us with our navigation.

Ray

To the south of us the bad weather continued. We listened anxiously to the radio reports knowing that we were heading into that same area of the ocean. With five hundred and forty nautical miles to Opua, the storms off New Zealand were beginning to settle. Our wind moved first to the northeast and then to the north as we headed directly for the Bay of Islands. We were moving along at a steady six to seven knots and eating up the miles. At times the sea was so smooth it was possible to sit on the foredeck enjoying reading a book. I replaced one of the slides on the mainsail and Ray made another attempt at taking sun sights with the sextant.

By the eleventh day the sky was full of birds fishing for their breakfast and we were sure we could smell grass.

"No, it's not," called Christine "I think its sheep!"

We rode the gentle north wind and, during the night saw the loom of Cape Brett light ahead of us over the horizon. There was a full moon which shone calmly down as we anticipated seeing land in the morning.

Sure enough, as dawn broke, Cape Brett was silhouetted on the horizon. A family of dolphins played around the boat for an hour as we approached the entrance to the Bay of Islands. A beautiful rainbow stretched like a welcoming archway over the Bay. What a breathtaking arrival.

Nancy had arrived in Opua before us, and had asked Opua Radio if they had heard from us. They were able to tell her our approximate time of arrival. Sure enough when we called them, they told us that Nancy was there to meet us, followed by a cheery "Welcome to New Zealand." The final approach to Opua was past the small town of Pahia on one side, and Russell on the other. We motored along the tree clad estuary, with houses scattered on the gently sloping hillsides and boats moored in the numerous bays.

Nancy was on the customs dock when we arrived and was reunited with Ray after all the formalities were completed. The officials took our last tin of Danish bacon and a can of Mexican insect repellent before saying. "Welcome to New Zealand. We are glad you had a good passage. You may now go wherever you like without any more signing in or out."

We moved *Demelza* to the International wharf for a few days, greeting several friends who had already arrived. We celebrated our safe arrival with a bottle of champagne before Nancy swept us off to her motel for long showers and a delicious supper in a nearby restaurant.

The following day we heard the sad news that the friendly young man to whom we had spoken on our last day in Tonga, had misjudged the entrance to the Bay of Islands, and had been swept onto the Cavelli Islands. He had lost his boat *Lady Dashne*, and had just enough time to grab his passport, wallet and running shoes before clambering onto rocks to watch his boat vanish beneath the waves.

CHAPTER 9
New Zealand

International Wharf — Opua — New Zealand

On our first morning in Opua we walked up the wharf to a chorus of unaccustomed birdsong. This small resort, the entry into the Bay of Islands, was nicely developed. All the essentials for cruising boats were readily available within short walking distance. Here we had our first encounter with a Kiwi staple, the meat pie, which was to satisfy us on many occasions as we traveled about New Zealand by road during the next eighteen months. Our first port of call from Opua was across the bay to the little historic town of Russell.

Called Koroareka by the Maoris, it had been established as a whaling town by the early European settlers. When visited by Charles Darwin, he had been unimpressed by the number of brothels. However today it is a pleasing mix of the old and new. It is a holiday seaside destination whose waterfront is lined by showy Pohutakawa trees that burst into crimson bloom each Christmas. This tree has been adopted as New Zealand's Christmas tree. Russell was the first capital of New Zealand until it was sacked during a Maori uprising in 1845, when the seat of government was moved to Auckland. Above the town is Flagpole Hill, cause of much trouble with the Maoris. At its summit the British flew the Union Jack, to which the Maoris took exception. Under the leadership of Hone Heke, they chopped the flagpole down no fewer than four times. The only buildings to survive the resultant uprising were missionary buildings, including Christ Church. This still stands, scarred by the musket balls fired during the fracas, and is New Zealand's oldest church, built in 1835.

We spent a fair amount of time in Russell as it was a useful base from which to explore the Bay of Islands. We learned a lot more about that area with Nancy and Ray before they left for home. Liz and Allan, Harold and Virginia and Julie and John, all friends from home, visited us at various times and were taken on cruises around these lovely islands during their visits, and all enjoyed the sites and amenities of Russell.

Chris and Andy (Right) — saying goodbye to Nancy

The Bay of Islands lies between Cape Brett to the South and Cape Wiwiki six miles to the northwest. It is studded with lovely islands, many of which have sandy beaches and protected anchorages. It was possible to find a sheltered bay within easy reach no matter what the direction of the wind. Of these islands, one of our favourites was Motuarohia (Roberton Island). Although commemorated as the site on which an early farming settler, Mrs. Roberton, had been murdered by the Maoris, it was best remembered as the first landing place of Captain Cook in 1769. Steep rocky cliffs present themselves to the open sea on the opposite side from its curved sandy beach and sheltered anchorage.

Nearby is the island of Moturoa, which had been used as a hospital camp by the French navigator Marion de Fresne in 1772. It has a number of sheltered beaches and anchorages all around its perimeter, with good holding in mud and sand. Urapukapuka is the largest of the islands in this area. Its northern shore is rocky, but its southern and western shores are deeply indented by four separate bays. Here we had our first swim in New Zealand. It was a very cold experience. Lovely walking trails traverse the pastureland under the watchful eye of thousands of sheep, and the hill tops afford unforgettable views of the surrounding islands whichever way one looks.

Bay of Islands

Coromandel Peninsula

Up the long and shallow Keri Keri Inlet lies the town of Keri Keri, citrus centre of New Zealand. Due to unfamiliar local buoyage, we went astray on our first visit to the town basin at the head of the inlet and ran aground on a sandbar. This necessitated launching the dinghy, with Christine brandishing our lead line to sound out the best way out of our predicament. It all worked out well on the rising tide.

After negotiating the many bends up the inlet, which is fed by a river entering beneath a little stone bridge near the town, we tied up alongside a Dutch boat that was tied between two of the many pilings that are driven into the mud along the river's banks. It was such a delightfully rural setting, with ducklings swimming around the boat. The Stone Store is at the water's edge, and Kemp House is set back a little in its well kept gardens. Looking down from the rising land at the head of the bay is the distinctive small Anglican Church, opposite which is a Kiwi bird sanctuary.

Kerikeri Town Basin — Stone Store and Kemp House

On a bend in the river, just before reaching the town basin, an unusual sailing boat lay firmly secured between two pilings. This was the *Totorore*, owned by Gerry Clark, made famous by her daring adventures in the Southern Ocean. We had read his book *The Totorore Voyage* before leaving home, and so were delighted to see this small vessel. With clipper bow and bowsprit, the raised foredeck allowed for two port holes through the hull to lighten the forecabin. Light blue in colour, this thirty two foot single masted vessel sported a very tall radar arch over the lazarette, and a transom mounted wind vane. She was cutter rigged with roller jib, staysail and mainsail.

Built of Kauri wood, the incredibly strong and durable native wood of New Zealand now restricted in use as a conservation measure, she had double diagonal planking over close stringers to give her extra strength. Because she had no side decks, the only way forward was to clamber over the coachroof. She was twin keeled with a large skeg carrying a transom hung rudder connected to the tiller. Gerry was an interesting man in his seventies when we met. An ornithologist by profession, he spent his time making expeditions down to the Antarctic Islands on *Totorore* to count birds. As we rounded the river's bend, he was putting the finishing touches to preparations for his next trip south, and was awaiting the arrival of his crew of two.

Sure enough, two days after our arrival, at the height of a storm, we heard Gerry telling John on Keri Keri Radio that if he had waited for every storm to pass, he would never leave harbour. We waved him goodbye as he puttered out of the basin and took his place between the pilings. He only managed to get out into the Bay of Islands before wisely deciding to let the weather settle before continuing.

Since then, we were sad to hear that Gerry and *Totorore* had been lost in an Antarctic storm, and that apart from a few pieces of his boat washed up on a desolate shore, no other trace was ever found.

Totorore

Kemp House was named after one of the first three New Zealand European settlers in 1819. He was a blacksmith. The house was built for the first ordained minister in New Zealand, the Reverend John Butler. The third of the trio was a schoolteacher. They bought a piece of flat land from the local Maoris for forty eight axes, and called the settlement Gloucester. The lovely gardens that surround the house were planted by the Reverend Butler to provide cereals, vegetables, fruit and grapes. They also raised sheep.

The Stone Store was built between 1832 and 1835 and James Kemp became the Store keeper. It was under serious renovation when we arrived in the basin.

The town basin is connected by a steep road to Keri Keri town site, which we were to climb many times to collect bags of provisions for our cruises out to the islands. To one side of this road is the little Anglican Church where, on the first Sunday of our visit, a new stained glass window was being dedicated by the bishop. It had been designed by a local artist and depicted many indigenous plants and animals of New Zealand. Through this congregation we were introduced to many local residents who were to prove so hospitable to us throughout our stay.

South of the Keri Keri inlet is the Waitangi Reserve where an unsuccessful attempt had been made in 1816 to start a mission. James Busby was appointed British Resident in 1833 and built a house there. In 1840 a treaty was signed between the British Crown and forty five leading Maori chiefs. What is now called Treaty House, and its surrounding land, was presented to New Zealand in 1933. We spent a hot afternoon looking over its extensive grounds.

Within weeks of our arrival, New Zealand and its surrounding waters were hit by ferocious gales causing all sorts of problems to both local and visiting boats. Forty knot winds, with gusts up to fifty knots, lashed the coast for several days while we were securely hidden away in the Keri Keri inlet. A local chartered yacht out of Whangerei was capsized and the upturned hull eventually located by a New Zealand Air Force Orion. The two occupants were later found washed up, dead, on an isolated beach nearby. We heard of several other boats caught out in the South Pacific. One lost its mast. Another took a wave inside the boat, losing the use of its generator. A third had engine failure due to sludge from the bottom of its diesel fuel tanks clogging up all the fuel filters, and yet another was approaching Opua under jury rig having lost its mast.

Out of the group of boats that had been travelling with us across the Pacific, we heard on the radio that *Lady Guinevere*, with Diane and Keith on board, was calling for a fuel drop three hundred and ninety miles out to sea. Later Keith requested a tow when he was two hundred nautical miles out. For a while there were no volunteers as the weather was so terrible. Eventually the Maori owner of a fifty foot fishing vessel, aptly named *Extreme Limits*, set out in appalling weather because conditions on *Lady Guinevere* were deteriorating. All power had been lost, as had their wind generator (blown away) and emergency gas generator (flooded). She was taking on water through a broken hatch on deck, and had blown out all her sails. She was now lying ahull in storm conditions after two weeks of unrelenting wind, and the three crew members were exhausted.

We found out later that they had been towed into Manganui Harbour close to the North Cape, where they had been taken ashore by their rescuer, and put up in his own home to recover. It transpired that the third crew member was Diane's sister, who had never been on a boat before, and had been anticipating a pleasant summer's cruise in the Pacific.

We drove up to Manganui, with Betty from the church congregation, to see if there was anything we could do to help. *Lady Guinevere* was anchored in the harbour with her sails, in tatters, streaming out in the wind. Over several pints in the historic Manganui Hotel, Keith related the tale of their disaster. His rescue boat had attempted to get a tow line aboard on two occasions. The first time, the line had parted, and the second time the Maori skipper had made two attempts to get a heavier line aboard. Unable to throw it, he had dived into the raging sea with his life jacket on. Finding he could make no headway, he returned to his boat, shed his life jacket, and dived in again with the line to successfully connect the two boats. By the time we met Keith he had recovered a little, and was starting to get things organized. He was to spend the next year putting *Lady Guinevere* back in order at an Auckland boatyard.

After a month's stay in the Bay of Islands, our visitors had all come and gone. We were anxious to get to Gulf Harbour, just north of Auckland, before Christmas. We headed south around Cape Brett, then along the east coast of the North Island in ten knots of northerly wind. With the breeze from behind we had time to watch the seabirds and dolphins. We spent nights in Whangamumu Harbour, Tutukaka, Urquhart Bay (around Whangerei Heads at the entrance to Whangerei Harbour), Bream Head, Cape Rodney (with its diving display of gannets from the colony ashore), and Mansion House Bay on Kawau Island, before sailing into Gulf Harbour. This is situated on the Whangaparaoa Peninsula, fifteen miles north of Auckland.

Although not the most conveniently situated marina, involving a one and a half mile hike up the hill to the little town of Manly for all shopping, it had all the facilities we needed for a lengthy stay. The Gulf Harbour community was in the initial stages of development. Although the boat yard and marina were completed, the master plan of the whole development called for a bustling seaside community of seven thousand people, with its own town centre built opposite the marina, and homes occupying eight hundred acres of gently rolling countryside. Sporting its own golf club, which was completed during our stay, and with spectacular views over the Hauraki Gulf, its success seemed assured.

It was our intention to buy a campervan, transfer some of the useable gear from *Demelza* into it, and leave for an extended tour of both the North and South Islands of New Zealand.

On the afternoon of our arrival in Gulf Harbour, we hitched a ride with a carpet fitter to Manly to buy a bottle of champagne with which to celebrate the safe arrival of the Price family on *Talitha Koom* to their new homeland. This accomplished we asked, in the shop, if anyone was driving back towards the marina, and a very nice lady said she lived along the way so would be happy to take us as far as her house. That is how we first met our Kiwi guardian angels, David and Val. Not only did they take us all the way to the boat, but once there, they stayed for a glass of wine with us, and invited us to their house for supper the following day. It was the beginning of a wonderful friendship that Christine and I continue to enjoy.

Val and David

Demelza was hauled out of the water and put into the dry storage area where we could still live on board. Then began a period of concentrated maintenance on the boat, and the purchase and upgrading of a rather old Toyota HiAce Campervan.

The Automobile Association's prepurchase inspection of the van stated that the engine was well used, the steering was worn, and there was some rust. David had driven us all over Auckland looking at vans advertised in the newspapers, and after a long day's search, this little canary yellow van was the last one on our list. It took us an evening at Val and David's lovely home overlooking the Hauraki Gulf, to decide that the price was right and that we should go for it.

Campervan

That done, not only did we have a huge list of items to deal with on *Demelza*, but now a more urgent list of items on the van to complete before setting off on our tour.

Again Val and David stepped into the breach, offering a room in their basement to store our electronics, sails and several other items from the boat. This done, we had room to do some of the upgrading, which included sanding and re-varnishing the cabin sole, replacing the foam cushions, rewiring the fore-cabin lights and replacing some of the bonding wire and connections. Christine and Val re-stitched *Demelza*'s name on the spray sheets, which was a huge job, while David and I made new transom bracket mounts for the outboard engines in the luxury of his home workshop.

The gel coat was inspected by the local fiberglass guru, Allan. He was of the opinion that the fiberglass hull below the waterline was dry, but that the gel coat could do with a coat of waterproof sealant following the removal of nine layers of old antifouling paint.

Andy and John, travelling on *Sara of Hamble*, a Ferro cement boat which was sitting in the corner of the yard, had a reputation for being delightful but a bit shambolic. They had been allotted the most isolated spot of the boat yard, whereupon they had distributed all their boat's belongings around the base of the keel in a nightmarish assortment of keepsakes. I first met John as he was standing atop a most unstable ladder, poking at his boat's underparts with a very large screwdriver. I hadn't the faintest idea what he was doing. On our second meeting the following morning, he dashed over as I was cleaning off *Demelza's* rudder.

"I say," he panted "I think I've got a bit of a problem. Would you come and have a look?"

We walked over to his boat and I noticed a gaping hole in his boat's hull where none should have been.

"I was scraping off the paint," he explained, "when suddenly my paint scraper went through the hull into one of the boat's lockers, and salt water poured out."

Aghast, I peered at this hole from the top of his ladder, and gingerly probed its depths with my finger.

"Have you a flashlight?" I asked.

He passed one up and I shone it into the inner gloom, fearing the worst. Sure enough, the metal mesh over which the cement had been laid was riddled with rust, which might well have compromised the integrity of the hull.

"John, rust has eaten into the mesh here. I strongly advise you to have some professional advice before doing anything. It should be treated."

He was quiet for a while.

"Well, thanks for coming to take a look." he said as I left him to attend to my own chores.

In the event, John bought a tin of proprietary fiberglass filler, plugged up the hole as best he could, and painted over the top of it making the boat look as new. The last we have heard of them, eleven years later, is that he and Andy are still enjoying the cruising life in the Mediterranean.

Throughout all the preparation for our land cruise, Val and David fed us, cleaned us up, stored vital equipment, ran errands, took us out to their favourite eating places and viewing spots, and indeed did everything and more to settle us into life in New Zealand. We cannot ever adequately repay them for their kindness.

Gradually we came to understand the blemishes of our newly acquired van. The first problem was that it did not record the mileage covered, as the cable to the odometer was broken. For how long, we wondered? A short unrecorded ride to the dealership in Warkworth produced a replacement cable which was duly installed to make us legal again.

We soon realized that our van was seriously underpowered when fully loaded with our gear, and that Kiwi drivers did not measure distances in miles or kilometers, but rather in the time taken to motor from point A to point B. Listening to a radio talk show one day, my impression that Kiwi drivers undergo a personality change behind the wheel of a car was confirmed by the generally expressed opinion that driving seventy five miles per hour along New Zealand roads was quite acceptable.

Our driving experience was totally changed after a conversation we had with a couple waiting for the Cook Strait ferry. They advised us to display a Canadian flag in the back window. The instant we did this, tailgating ceased, we received friendly waves from passing drivers, and road manners improved beyond all expectation.

Otherwise the little van never let us down. She may have leaked a bit when it rained, but with a plentiful supply of sealant, anything could be fixed. By the time Christine had cleaned it up, the van looked ready for anything. With a spare end of new carpet replacing a tired one, she looked almost new and certainly smelled better. She took us on a tour of New Zealand over the next thirteen months without any major catastrophes and gave us a wonderful experience from a comfortable home. Apart from visits to *Demelza* in February '95 and March '96, we lived in the campervan and did a comprehensive tour of the North and South Islands.

Throughout our journeys in New Zealand, it was impossible to get away from the presence of Captain Cook, given the plethora of place names he had left to significant points on his voyage of discovery. His instructions from the British Admiralty in July 1768 were to travel south, further than a previous voyage by Wallis. The latter had thought he had seen mountain peaks to his south stretching from horizon to horizon, which he concluded was the long sought Terra Australis Incognita or The Great Southern Continent.

At first sight, Cook thought the East coast of the North Island resembled the chalky Sussex coast with the South Downs beyond. His reception by the Maoris was little short of a disaster, as several of them were killed by the musket fire of his crew in the numerous exchanges that occurred when Cook landed exploring New Zealand's bays. Their primary purpose in landing at Poverty Bay was to replenish their water supply and food stocks. This was not achieved. From here Cook sailed south along the shore to Portland Point at one end of Hawke's Bay, with its white cliffs and sandy beaches. The rolling hills beyond are now the site of much of the country's wine industry.

After an attempted hijacking of one of the ships crew at Cape Kidnappers, he turned his ship back to Poverty Bay where he succeeded in loading water and wood. Continuing northward they passed East Cape, the most easterly point in New Zealand, to Cape Runaway named because of an incident where grapeshot from *HMS Endeavour's* guns had scared away some advancing war canoes.

As the expedition moved along the coast, Captain Cook continued to record and name salient features. The weather was foul in October when they landed to watch the transit of the planet Mercury, naming the bay, Mercury Bay. They then rounded Cape Colville at the tip of the Coromandel Peninsula before struggling, in foul weather up to the North Cape. This they rounded at the end of December before proceeding down the West Coast, naming the easily observed Mount Egmont as they sailed past.

He sailed into Queen Charlotte Sound at the north end of the South Island, and from the top of a hill, verified the presence of Cook's Strait which confirmed the existence of the North Island of New Zealand.

He continued his journey south along the east coast of the South Island as he had been instructed by the Admiralty, giving name to what he thought was an island, but which in fact was the Banks Peninsula. He made his second mistake in thinking that Stewart Island was attached to the South Island. By March they were at the South Cape, some crew still believing they had reached the Great Southern Continent. The arguments onboard raged, as did the weather, until they rounded the Cape which incontrovertibly confirmed the existence of the North and South Islands of New Zealand.

We had decided to make our way to the South Island first, to make the best of the Southern hemisphere's summer. Of particular interest to the sailor were Wellington Harbour, at the centre of an eroded volcano, with its beautiful vistas and strong winds; Christchurch, the jumping off point of Scott's and subsequent expeditions to the Antarctic; Dunedin, a university town with its sheltered harbour behind the Otago Peninsula and Bluff, at the southernmost point of the South Island with its views across the Foveaux Straits to Stewart Island.

South Island

We remember so many unforgettable places, including the magic of Milford Sound, accessible by car through the Hobart Tunnel and held under the spell of Mitre Peak; the beauty of Golden Bay, with its charming town of Nelson, home territory of our good friends Muriel and John. Then on the North Island, Hokianga Harbour, with its rich history based on the Kauri tree and the beautiful display of its Amber in the local museum; Cape Reinga and North Cape with its desolate miles of golden sand, a trap for the unwary sailor, and the graveyard of many; Whangerei Harbour, deep-set inland from the Whangerei Heads and developed into a thriving town servicing the yachting industry; and lastly the Hauraki Gulf, home of the America's Cup Challenge, playground of Auckland boaters. It is sheltered by the Coromandel Peninsula, and endowed with many beautiful islands, some being carefully nurtured back to their pre European natural state.

Mitre Peak

In a nutshell, and for those with an interest in history and the cutting edge of boating, New Zealand has few contenders. Learning to sail from an early age in dinghy races off the Auckland beaches at weekends, Kiwis nurture some of the world's best competitive sailors. Their Maritime Museums are incomparable, and their sense of maritime history an example to all other maritime nations.

In July 1995 we took *Demelza* with our friends Val and David to watch the return of *Black Magic* to Auckland Harbour following her win at the America's Cup in San Diego. Sitting proudly on the deck of the freighter, which ghosted into Auckland harbour down the Hauraki Gulf accompanied by a horde of private yachts, the winner was led in by a water-spurting fire boat. Air force planes performed a low fly past overhead in salute. It seemed the whole population of Auckland was at the harbour to greet the victorious Kiwi team home. Many were resplendent in red socks, made popular by the Kiwi skipper, Peter Blake, during the course of the racing series. The streets were bedecked with New Zealand flags, bands played, and the good natured crowds sang their country's favourite songs.

Black Magic

Later in the year, we sailed in the Hauraki Gulf between the North Island to the west and the Coromandel Peninsula and Great Barrier Island to the east. Waiheke Island, just off Auckland, is a suburban extension of the city, connected by a good commuter ferry service. Geologically, Rangitoto is the youngest island in the area. Appearing as a volcano only eight hundred years ago, it dominates the Hauraki Gulf. Near its summit, lava caves and tunnels are a popular destination for hikers.

Sailing in the Hauraki Gulf

The Great Barrier Island, once mined for gold and copper, and stripped of its plentiful Kauri trees, is roughly twenty-five miles long by two miles wide, the largest of the Gulf's islands. Its laid-back rural community is mostly preoccupied with farming, fishing and some forestry, and provides a base for tourist activities.

But our favourite of all was little Tiri Tiri Matangi Island, near the Whangaparaoa Peninsula. One of the smallest islands, it is now established as an open nature reserve. Introduced predators such as rats and possums have been systematically eliminated, allowing the natural flora and fauna to reestablish without competition. Bell birds serenaded *Demelza* from the trees and shrubs ashore. North Island Saddlebacks, the red crowned parakeet and even the once thought to be extinct flightless Takahe now flourish in their protected environment. It is truly a treasure and a testament to what can be done by a dedicated partnership of government and the public given the effort and will to achieve.

Suddenly it seemed our eighteen month stay in New Zealand was over. We panicked at the thought of having to sell our campervan in time to leave on the next part of our journey. In the event a very nice farmer and his wife from Warkworth decided that it was just the vehicle in which they could enjoy their retirement.

We sailed for Bon Accord Harbour on Kawau Island on 20th March 1996, under grey skies and light winds. Gradually the weather deteriorated. It poured and blew for the next three days, which gave us ample opportunity to test the reinstalled electronic gear, and to study weather patterns on our newly acquired software.

From here we moved to Whangerei. This involved eleven hours of motoring in the absence of any wind, finally arriving at the Town Basin. As our battery banks had not survived the neglect of the past eighteen months, we replaced them with new batteries.

Demelza was hauled out just before the arrival of a tropical depression that came down from New Caledonia. Winds outside the harbour were gusting at sixty knots, and the rain was relentless. Fortunately we were rescued by Diane and Steve, whom we had visited on several occasions whilst camping on the North Island. They took us home to their Tropicana Motel, to dry us out and feed us, extending yet again the unbounded Kiwi hospitality.

With all the preparatory work completed, *Demelza* was put back in the water. We left the next day for Tutukaka, where again a storm moved in for a couple of days. After a further stop at Whangamumu Harbour on Cape Brett, we made for Keri Keri town basin for a reunion with our friends Betty and her daughter Liz and son in law Tony. The last stop in New Zealand was at Russell for a week. Here we rented a private mooring for ease of mind in the unsettled conditions, so that we could visit friends in the area and take David and Val cruising in the Bay of Islands.

On 22nd April, after completing all the official paperwork, we left for a predicted seven day passage to New Caledonia. A previous month of poor weather pictures, with an established low anchored over New Caledonia, had righted itself. We were free to leave.

We left Russell on a beautifully clear day with a brisk twenty-five knot following wind. The barometer continued to rise, foreshadowing fair weather. As the wind settled into the south and fell to ten knots, the sea remained restless. We covered one hundred and thirty seven nautical miles in the first twenty four hours and by the fourth day, when we had found our sea legs, the wind had dropped to five knots or less, and the sea had become oily under a leaden sky. However it was only a short break as the sky cleared, the southeast trades reappeared, and we resumed our boisterous sail. In the evenings, squalls moved across the horizon from east to west, but none ever reached *Demelza* as she scurried to the northwest. An albatross flew around us, looking quizzically down as it glided past.

On the seventh day of an uneventful passage, we spotted the high ridge of mountains that runs down the spine of La Grande Terre, New Caledonia. A short while later the light on Amadee lighthouse, marking the entrance of Passe Boulari through the fringing reef of the south lagoon, was visible on the horizon. This lighthouse, which stands one hundred and thirty feet tall, was shipped out of France in 1865.

Amadee Light — New Caledonia

After running alongside the barrier reef, we entered the pass with fifteen feet of water below us. To port were the remains of a shipwreck on the reef, and the white sandy beaches of Amadee Islet on which the lighthouse stands, were to starboard. The Islet was occupied by day trippers from the capital city Noumea, sunning themselves in the hot sun. Twelve more miles across the flat waters of the lagoon brought us to Noumea, where we tied up in a modern marina, and received a warm reception from its staff. The officials came down to *Demelza* and filled out the necessary forms in a typically thorough and courteous French manner. They informed us that the courtesy flag that Christine had made was the Kuni Independence flag and should be replaced with the French tricolor.

"We are France." they said.

CHAPTER 10
New Caledonia

New Caledonia lies just north of the Tropic of Capricorn between 18°S and 22.5S. The main island, Grande Terre, lying on a northwest/southeast axis, has its capital city Noumea at its south western extremity. Its affluence is mainly due to the continuous exploitation of one of the world's richest nickel deposits, refined just outside Noumea. Grande Terre is two hundred and fifty miles long and thirty miles wide. The highest point is Mount Panie at four thousand eight hundred and eighty four feet and lies one thousand nautical miles northwest of New Zealand. Besides Grande Terre, New Caledonia consists of many island groups including the Loyalty Group, Ile des Pins (The Isle of Pines), and the Belep Islands to the north. It also includes scattered reefs, such as Chesterfield, Walpole, Surprise, Huron and Mathew. Unlike the Marquesas, New Caledonia is surrounded by a six hundred mile long barrier reef which is the second largest in the world.

Lapita pottery traces the earliest known settlement of these islands, by Melanesians, back to 2000 BC. In September 1774 Captain Cook landed on the North Coast of Grand Terre, calling it New Caledonia because it reminded him of Scotland. Within a couple of weeks he had also found Iles des Pins. In the years following, explorers and merchants arrived looking for a source of sandalwood. Missionaries continued to arrive between 1840 and 1843. France took possession in 1853. The capital city Noumea was founded in 1854 and was originally named Port de France. From 1864 to 1897 the French used the islands as a convict colony. Rich nickel deposits were discovered in 1863 and these have been exploited since 1870 to the present day.

During the Second World War the harbour was critical to the American Campaign in the Pacific, and four large American air bases were established in the area. Of the indigenous animals on the island perhaps the most interesting is the flightless blue coloured bird, called the Cagou. It barks like a dog, and has a long plume of feathers hanging down its neck which stand up erect when alarmed.

A month before our arrival, Cyclone Betty had ravaged many of the farms on the main island, with the loss of a lot of the fruit crop. The new marina survived the storm because of its robust construction, helped by sailors taking the pressure off the docks by running additional lines ashore.

We found the city friendly and cosmopolitan, European in style, with excellent shops and French restaurants. The busy port imports goods, and in exchange exports nickel, cadmium and chromium. Noumea has a population of sixty thousand, and is the only city on the islands. New Caledonia's total population is one hundred and sixty five thousand, a third of which is of European descent.

The diurnal tides of about three feet give a dramatic visual effect as the extensive coral reefs in the area dry out. Exposed beaches have lovely coral sand, whereas many of the sheltered anchorages provide excellent holding in deep red mud. Every bit of this had to be removed from ground tackle coming aboard, as it stained everything it touched.

The best weather in New Caledonia is expected from May to November, with the southeast trade winds blowing strongest in July and August. However gales infrequently occur into September and October. Cyclone season is any time between November and May, with most occurring in January and February. This predicted cycle set the clock for our visit. We planned to move on to Vanuatu after our stopover in New Caledonia, before escaping the cyclone season towards Queensland on Australia's east coast.

Throughout the islands, thirty different dialects of the Melanesian language are spoken. However French is the working language. During our two month stay we began by finding our way around Noumea. Its excellent public market was a stone's throw away from the marina, which made our shopping very convenient. It was here we met one of the many very wealthy businessmen, an Australian importer of wines, who took us out on a day's cruise to a nearby reef, Ilot Croisant, on his sixty foot powerboat. Powered by two, four hundred horse power Caterpillar diesel engines, it held a thousand gallons of fuel in each of its two tanks. The contrast with *Demelza*'s twenty seven horse power and sixty gallons of diesel fuel was startling.

The reinforced trade winds kept us in Noumea at the start of our holiday as I did not fancy sailing around unaccustomed reefs in boisterous conditions. Report of damage to boats on their way from New Zealand indicated severe weather offshore following our arrival here. By the end of our second week, the trades had settled, so we set out for the Isle of Pines (Ile des Pins). This involved sailing around the southern end of Grande Terre, and stopping off at Ile Ouen after transiting the attractive Canal Woodin between the main island and Ile Ouen. Penetrating the canal's north shore into the main island is the Baie du Prony which resembles a narrow inlet. Its east and west shores have well sheltered anchorages, and at its head is the local hurricane hole, the Baie du Carenage.

Here a small river runs into the bay over sun warmed rocks, forming a very popular warm water swimming pool before its clear water joins the red waters of the bay. Refreshing waterfalls and pools are found along the course of this river as it makes its way down into the bay, and we spent many happy hours cooling off there during the heat of the day.

Once out of Canal Woodin we dodged behind Ile Ouen, anchoring between it and a reef in a small pool of deep water, to shelter from an approaching tropical low. For three days we sat in torrential rain, watching the red mud cascading down the sides of the main island's hills into the sea. For three days there was no sight of an animal or human, as we safely circled our anchor in the howling wind, thankful for the sticky red mud at the bottom of our pool. The sea around us had turned red by the fourth morning when the dark clouds, that had shrouded the hills, gave way to that familiar blue sky again.

As the anchor reluctantly emerged from the pool's depths, great gobs of gluey red mud splashed back into the sea. Although I had done my very best to clean every link of the anchor chain before it came aboard, the red stain of the sea water marked its presence on our white foredeck.

As we sailed across the reef-strewn course thirty nautical miles south towards the Ile des Pins, we enjoyed a gentle breeze, anxiously watching out for the telltale change in the water's colour indicating coral heads below the surface.

The island is known as Kunie to its Melanesian inhabitants and the New Caledonian Araucaria pines gave a unique profile to the island against the blue sky. Following its colonization by the French in 1853, the island's western half became a political convict settlement while the eastern half was left to the islanders. These convicts were made up of doctors, writers, cabinet makers, sculptors. All had one thing in common. They had rebelled against the Paris Commune in 1871. The first of three thousand convicts arrived by sailing ships in 1872, and for the next eight years, before their pardon, they spent their days building roads, prison buildings and a water tower. Following their departure, petty criminals arrived who remained until the prison was abandoned in 1920. We found the decaying buildings being reclaimed by trees and vines and decorated with purple wild bougainvillea.

Araucaria Pine

The village of Ouro was established to service the nearby prison and is located beside the Baie de Kuto. This is where we anchored, at the southwest corner of the Ile des Pins. The island is a huge block of coral, and its sharp eroded cliffs are dotted with grottos containing spectacular stalactites. The island is a Kunie reserve, and the local population is very sensitive about its ownership. The bays around its perimeter are a navigator's nightmare, as the passes through the coral reef are shallow and tortuous. One wrong move might earn a very long stay indeed.

The Baie de Kuto is a beautiful bay, with an impressively long white sandy beach. While we were at anchor there, a pocket cruise ship arrived. In eager anticipation the islanders had set up stalls along the beach, laden with crafts they wished to sell to the passengers. The ship had anchored far out in the bay in a howling wind, and only two of its passengers braved going ashore. So the dancers, decked out in their finest costumes for the ships arrival, had to content themselves dancing for these two passengers and those of us who were anchored in the bay.

We hiked the trek to Pic Na, the highest point in the Isle of Pines. From here there is a fantastic view of the whole island with its surrounding reefs and bays. The breathtaking colour contrasts of pale turquoise lagoons, shades of creamy brown coral in the shallow water, azure blue of the deep water, and the dark green columns of the New Caledonia pines were truly awesome.

In Kenemera Bay just south of Baie de Kuto we joined up again with the Canadian Ladies Pirogue Paddling team whom we had first met at the World Championships at Ansa Vata beach in Noumea. They were spending four days rest and relaxation after their strenuous efforts, in a local Gite (guest house) on the beach. Having heard it was my birthday, they invited Christine and me to a birthday supper they had prepared outside their bungalow. It was a memorable occasion, and it was sad to say goodbye to them at the airport a couple of days later for their journey home. As they entered the small plane we played the audio tape they had given us of *O Canada*, which had been played on the occasion of the team's gold medal win at the championship regatta. It was our farewell to a wonderful group of people.

At the local hotel we rented bicycles, and cycled the twenty-five mile circuit around the island, stopping at some of the settlements where stalls selling sandalwood carvings had been set out for visitors. In these beautiful surroundings, life for the local islanders could still be hard, and we saw several old ladies carrying firewood faggots on their backs to cook their evening meal.

We sailed gently around to Baie d'Ugo with the wind behind us all the way. Creeping carefully into the bay with only four inches of water under our keel was hard on my nerves. However once in, the iridescent water of the lagoon was heaven and the snorkeling perfect. As the wind had picked up again outside the bay, we stayed a few extra days. We walked along the limestone cliffs with two French couples from two boats which were also anchored in the bay. Fish eagles were nesting on a nearby mushroom shaped islet, and Spoonbills flew around us and along the shore.

Going to School — Baie d'Ugo

Christian and Jean Jacques and their wives Anne Marie and Danny were school teachers in Noumea. They had been impressed that we had taken *Demelza* through such shallows into the lagoon, as this was usually only attempted by those with local knowledge. But then they hadn't met Christine. They were going to continue on northwards along the island's shoreline to their favourite anchorage in Baie de Gadji, and asked us if we would like to join them. So with the sails set on a broad reach, we followed Christian through the reefs. I didn't find this trip as harrowing as going into Baie d'Ugo but, on arrival, had the greatest difficulty getting the anchor to set. With snubber and kellet on the anchor chain, I let out a scope of 8:1 in twelve feet of water in the centre of this vivid azure lagoon. We spent several days exploring its islets, snorkeling around the coral heads, speaking our school French, and luxuriating in the French food and wine which our new friends insisted we should share with them. It was a marvellous time for us. But they had to get back to school and so left us on our own to enjoy our isolation in this paradise.

Bag O'Winds sailing through the reefs to Gadji

After six wonderful days, tempered by the continuing accelerated trade winds, we eased our way out of Baie de Gadji through the pass. Dark clouds hung over the mountains of Grande Terre and, having picked our way back to the Baie de Prony, we collected rainwater to replenish our tanks. Anchoring in the *Carina*ge was so peaceful after our exciting experiences among the reefs of the Ile des Pins. It reminded Christine of anchoring in Roscoe Bay in British Columbia.

Our sail back to Noumea on the flood tide through Canal Woodin was windy, with gusts coming down off the surrounding hills. Many of the cruising boats had spent time up the west coast of Grande Terre so, on arrival we shared our experiences of different anchorages with the help of some French wine and local beer. News arrived of a British boat being lost on a reef in Fiji. Thankfully the people on board had been rescued. Also a German boat off New Zealand had hit a rock, but its crew had been lifted to safety by a freighter that had been diverted to pick them up before the boat went down.

Our invitation to Christian and Anne Marie's home at Dumbea, in the hills above Noumea, was so precious. Their living room windows looked out over the valley and Mount Kougi, an unspoilt vista of tropical beauty.

On the Ile des Pins we had met a Kiwi kayaker attempting to circumnavigate the island. However as the trade winds had been so strong, she was having difficulty getting past some of the headlands. She arrived at *Demelza* one evening at the marina and offered to show us around the freighter in the harbour on which she was working. She had the job of cooking for a crew of twenty-five in rather basic accommodation. Her kayak was safely stowed on deck for her next adventure. On the freighter we met the Indian engineer who showed us proudly over his antique engine room. He was adamant that we should visit his mother when we arrived in Mombasa, Kenya. His diesel engines were polished until the brass components gleamed, and the bearings were beautifully greased.

Other information that we picked up concerned the Chesterfield and Huron reefs, on the way to Australia, where we could take refuge if caught in a storm. The harbour was full of boats with useful information about our trip ahead. We were given charts of these reefs and of Vanuatu that other people had used, on condition we passed them to other boats when we had finished with them. Again it was time to leave, to say goodbye to new friends, to promise to write, to visit, to phone. In this way we could keep alive the many wonderful friendships we had made along our journey. On June 25th we left the marina as staff and other friends on the docks waved farewell. Our destination was the islands of Vanuatu, or as they used to be known, the New Hebrides.

The weather south of New Caledonia was appalling as we left harbour from Prony. We spent the night at Port Boise, which was sheltered with good holding. The next morning, on a gentle breeze, we set out along the infamous Havannah Passage on an ebb tide. The first thing we saw was the wreck of a Japanese yacht, sitting on a coral reef well out of the water to one side of the channel. This yacht had gone aground while we were in Noumea as a result of a misunderstanding between her Japanese crew and captain. They had been sailing up the passage when a crew member on the bow noticed ruffled water ahead. He had called out a warning to the captain at the tiller, who thought it was the effect of wind off the nearby mountains. Again the lookout shouted a warning, and again it was dismissed just before the boat hit the reef. As is Japanese custom, nobody had queried the captain. He decided to abandon his boat, leaving everything behind. Now she lay stripped of any useful contents, a testament to carelessness.

At dusk we put in at Baie de Kouakoue. Dense tropical vegetation lined the shore. It was well sheltered from the trade winds. The next morning we sailed through the solitary South Pass of the fringing reef, and made for Lifou in the Loyalty Islands, seventy nautical miles to the north. Unlike Grande Terre, these islands rarely rise above three hundred feet. Land on them may only be owned by islanders. Chepenehe is the main anchorage, and the original settlement on the island. Besides Lifou there are five other islands in this group, Mare, Ouvea and Loyaute, Beautemps Beaupre and Tiga. Ouvea is renowned as one of the most beautiful atolls in the Pacific. Our anchorage in Chepenehe Bay was overlooked by a rounded headland with a white church on the top that glowed in the moonlight as we turned in for the night.

At 0020 hrs, the wind suddenly changed to the southeast so that we found ourselves on a lee shore. Waking Christine, we took up the anchor and set out on the one hundred and ninety nautical mile journey to Port Vila in Vanuatu. For thirty six hours we had a rollicking reach in most uncomfortable cross seas.

Anchorage at Chepenehe Bay, Lifou

Lapita pottery

CHAPTER 11
Vanuatu

Port Vila is on Efate Island. This island has two of the best deep water anchorages in the country, Vila Bay and Havannah Harbour. We tied up to the quarantine buoy, flying our Practique flag, to clear customs and immigration. This took place after we had waited until the next morning for the launch to bring the officials out to *Demelza*. A boy in a dinghy then guided us to a mooring buoy in the harbour, which lay in three hundred feet of water, costing $35 US a week. It was worth every cent to avoid having to do an anchor watch every night. Many of the familiar cruising boats had arrived before us, so it was a great reunion. We went ashore to apply for a local ham radio license, and to buy fruit from the excellent local market. All the local women were dressed in brightly coloured Mother Hubbard frocks with decorative ribbons, bows and puffed sleeves.

Over supper at the Waterfront Restaurant, and after talking to the other sailors, we decided to fly to Tanna Island. We had heard many fascinating tales about it, and especially wished to see the active volcano Mount Yasur. This island is situated upwind from Efate, so rather than beat against the reinforced trades prevalent at the time, we would go by air.

Vanuatu was pushed up from the sea bottom twenty two million years ago, creating the northern islands of Santo, Malakula and the Torres Group. Next, Maewo and Pentecost Islands appeared about seven million years ago, and the rest more recently. This upheaval and active volcanoes continue to reshape the land.

The Ni Vanuatu people originated in Melanesia about 3000 BC, and belong to the Lapita culture as do the Kuni of New Caledonia. Lapita pottery is a distinctive relic of those early days having characteristic pinhole incisions in its decoration. These people brought yams, taro, pigs, poultry and dogs with them as they spread out by canoe from South East Asia into the Pacific. A later wave of Polynesian people from the East arrived around 10AD. These intermarried with the established population, injecting some of their cultural attributes into current folklore and custom practice.

Our first few days were marked by almost incessant rain, so we spent the time exploring Port Vila. The shops were arranged around the town's main street, Kumul Street, commemorating the New Guinea troops who were brought in during the 1970s to sort out squabbles between opposing political groups over independence for the country. Independence was finally achieved on 30th July 1980.

Prior to Independence the country had been governed by a joint British/ French Condominium. We went to the 16th Independence Day celebrations, after watching islanders from all over the country offloading their wares on the docks nearby. Market stalls were set up all along the waterfront, with food concessions cooking up a storm on open fires at the back of their stalls.

The ceremonies were held in the large British paddock, a field surrounded by shade trees, into the branches of which local children climbed to watch the fun. The President and Prime Minister arrived with great fanfare. Everybody was treated to the sight of the two platoons of the Vanuatan Armed Forces, along with many groups of children, marching past the President's reviewing platform accompanied by an enthusiastic military band. There was also a platoon of French Gendarmes from New Caledonia and a French Naval band from a ship in port. After the parade, a group of French parachute troops from Noumea dropped from planes flying overhead. Only one lost the plot, landing somewhere else in town. The rest of the day was for dancing and partying.

One day the first of thirty six boats involved in the Around the World Rally arrived from Fiji. Anchorage was at a premium and some of it, being on coral, was very insecure. Their crews soon discovered the Waterfront Bar and Grille, which is where Christine and I had celebrated her birthday with a happy crowd of fellow boaters. There was a lack of indigenous music, as the islanders only have rhythmical drumming to accompany their custom dancing.

We took the dinghy across to Iririki Island which lies to one side of the anchorage. The house atop the island used to house the British Resident, but sadly it was not open for viewing. In its surrounding grounds we found evidence of steps down from the hilltop residence to the white beaches below, and many trails through the trees. Following one of these we found the abandoned isolation hospital.

On a day tour of Efate Island with a local bus company, we stopped for lunch at the Beachcomber Resort and swam off Samoa Point in Havannah Harbour. Other than this, the tour along the rough roads did not offer a lot except views of the ocean, of which we had seen plenty.

Our next adventure, which we shared with Betty and Neville, was the flight to Tanna Island. We had promised to deliver a slab of cheese to the island's physician, a doctor from Victoria, who was doing a locum for six months. Both he and his wife were physicians. They had just arrived with their three small children. His first patient had an arrow through his throat, not a common condition at home. They very kindly entertained us to supper in the 'doctors' house where we were able to hear of their recent experiences.

Our flight to the island had been on a small six-seater plane. Huge cumulus clouds made it a very lumpy one hour's trip against the reinforced trade winds. We landed on a grass airfield that was none too long, running uphill, as an ingenious way of stopping the plane.

We were met by the driver of the 4 wheel drive truck that we had arranged for in Port Vila. This had two plank seats in the open box for Neville and me, while the ladies sat in the cab. Never had I traveled so far on my cushioning hands over such appalling roads.

Our first stop was in the small village of Lanakel, at our agent Eileen's house. Coral roads were lined with dozens of people walking hither and thither in bare feet. There were no other vehicles except the occasional oxcart. We picked up John, our driver for the day, who took us to the Paradise Bay Guest House. This was an old coconut warehouse, at one end of which two rooms had been constructed using shoulder high boards. At least this made talking to Betty and Neville very easy indeed. There was an ancient but workable toilet and shower next to it.

I had bought a large, treated, WHO mosquito net in Vila before our departure, which we hung from the single light bulb in the centre of the ceiling. The remainder of the warehouse was divided into the Co-op Store, library, bank, and restaurant. The latter was full of villagers intent on scrutinizing all new arrivals at the Guest House. The finer points were discussed loudly in the local version of Bislama, an abused mixture of phonetic English and French.

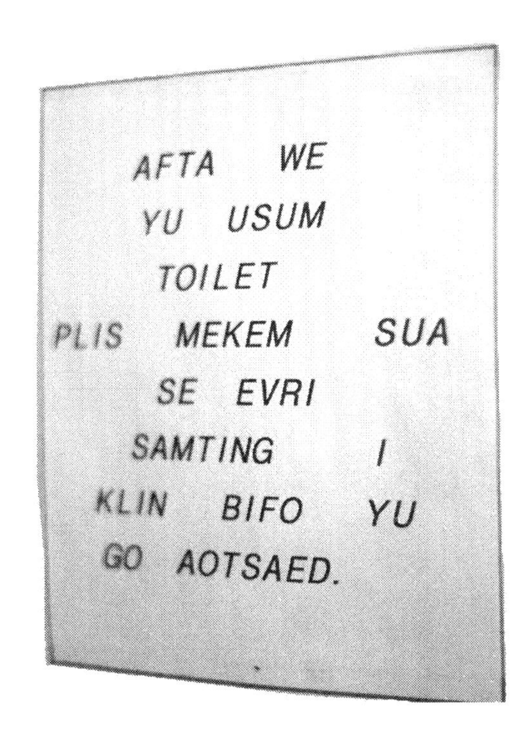

Paradise Bay Guest House

In a flurry of dust, after settling in, we left in our truck up the coral track leading out of town into the Middlebush area and close to a Custom village. Here men walked around naked, apart from a penis wrap, and the women wore green coloured fibre skirts made from the banana tree. In other parts of the island skirts were made from wild hibiscus bark, which had been soaked in seawater, then dried and dyed. Their houses had woven fiber walls with thatched roofs which covered a flattened black earthen floor. We found the people shy, but the women and children smiled willingly enough if spoken to. The children all seemed to have runny noses.

We walked through a patch of Kava (pepper) bushes up to a higher area of level ground where huge banyan trees formed a canopy overhead. Here people were sitting in family groups on the ground, each with displays of crafts for sale. There were woven articles, carved wooden objects, and necklaces made out of grey beadlike seeds with a circular boar's tusk suspended from them. The tusks either had a single or double curvature, the double one being twice the price and a third even more. It takes a boar seven years to grow a single curved tusk. The tusk is a sign of great wealth, and proudly worn by the men.

The men of the village appeared from the shadows, formed a rotating circle and began dancing while chanting and clapping to the rhythm of their chant. It was a singularly unmusical event. The women formed a block on one side of the clearing, and they jumped up and down on one spot, with skirts swishing and their arms clasped firmly across their ample bosoms.

Dancing is for all ages

As time progressed, the dancers seemed to get into the swing of it, becoming more expressive by the minute, until finally the whole thing came to a sudden end with a thundering stamping of the men's feet on the ground. When it was all over, the villagers lined up and filed past us four visitors, shaking our hands.

The next village we visited was celebrating a circumcision ceremony which had been going on all day. This was part of the initiation of twelve year old boys into manhood. First, the boys were sent to live alone to survive in the forest for two weeks. They were then circumcised prior to a feast, when pigs were killed and roasted to celebrate the occasion.

We had arrived after two boys from the village had emerged from their circumcision, and the village feast was being prepared. Gifts were displayed all around the open area. The villagers were dressed in their finest. Huge bundles of roots, baskets of fruit, mats, sugar cane, fish and trussed up pigs were there to be appreciated. The mothers of the boys were parading around with painted faces wearing high headdresses, dresses with long trains and huge grass side panniers.

The party would go on all night and, as we made our way home in the dark, we saw groups of people walking along the track from their villages to the party carrying flaming reefer torches to light their way. The following day, as we toured more of the island, we saw them straggling back home after the night's celebrations, still wearing their finest clothes and carrying their sleeping mats, with painted faces and feathers still in their hair.

We drove along impossible tracks toward Mount Yasur, which Captain Cook had used in his detailed survey of these islands in 1774. He had wanted to climb it, but the islanders forbade him to do, as it was *tabu* (not allowed).

One thousand feet high, Mount Yasur is approached by road over an extensive ash plain, which shakes with increasing strength as the volcano is approached. We drove to within five hundred feet of the volcano's base to the accompaniment of regular blasts from its active summit. The hike up the slope from the parked van was littered with lumps of solidified lava, and took about an hour. As we plodded warily up the eastern slopes, the blasts from its vents occurred every few minutes, spewing hot ash and lumps of red hot lava a thousand feet into the air above us.

Neville at volcano's rim

The strong southeasterly trade winds blew the toxic gases, ash and steam to the far side of the crater as we emerged over its rim to peer down into the red hot fumaroles below. It was like looking into the portals of hell, and was mesmerizing, until the next huge blast and explosion brought us back to reality. With the ground jumping under our feet, we didn't stay up there very long. It was an experience never to be forgotten.

Looking into the crater — one of four fumaroles

Once back in the truck, we reentered the jungle, crossed a valley, and climbed up into Imayo village. This was sited on a plateau overlooking the jungle-clad valley towards Mount Yasur, which was booming and belching flame and ash five miles in the distance. We parked the truck at the bottom of a steep incline covered with trees. As we commenced the climb to the village a small boy ran to one of the larger tree's buttressed roots, and belabored it with a stout stick. The tree boomed satisfactorily, warning the villagers that strangers approached. In a while, a man in a grass skirt took over from the lad and, in time, villagers began to congregate around the village clearing as we approached.

Sounding the alarm

This was a Jon Frum village, a cult which had its beginnings in the 1930s, when villagers began to resent the arrogance of European planters and the Presbyterian Church. They talked of a mysterious man, Jon Frum, brother of a god, who had promised them abundant wealth and freedom from European epidemics. At the end of the Second World War, this cult was one of the three main religions on the islands. Cultists do not pay taxes or use government schools. The identity of Jon Frum is a mystery, but some believe he was an American serviceman, wearing a red cross on his arm, who handed out gifts of free medicine to the islanders. Even today the Red Cross is a cult symbol. Many other theories abound, but like much else in these islands, it remains a mystery.

As we approached, more and more villagers appeared until about thirty were gathered on the village clearing wearing long golden grass skirts. The dance began with the men stamping their feet to the accompaniment of Mount Yasur's regular, distant explosions. The ladies bounced on the spot in time with the men's stamping feet, and the children joined in enthusiastically on the outside perimeter. Their dance told of an island clan looking for a place to settle, finding the volcano, and making it their own. The stamping of their feet in unison was so violent that the ground shook. We were told that this often caused bones in the dancers' feet to break.

Dancing to Mount Yasur's Tune

At night the generator in Lanekal was turned off and the lights go out. So we crept back to the Paradise Bay Guest House in the dark. Our hostess had left a hurricane lamp on in our rooms and had put a hibiscus bloom on each pillow. Thankfully we climbed into bed beneath our mosquito nets after the most timeless experience any one of us could ever have imagined.

In Vanuatu, there are one hundred and five different indigenous languages due to the historical isolation of the islands and of the groups living on them. Bislama is their only means of communicating with one another, and we had the greatest fun trying to make sense of it. In all the language only has about two thousand five hundred words, too few to cover anything other than basic needs. The remaining deficit is filled by the ingenious combination of available words.

Back in Port Vila we were interested in the arrival of James Wharram, the English boat designer/builder of the Wharram Catamarans. He was sailing his latest creation, *Spirit of Gaia*, and his arrival caused a great stir in the harbour. We had met a thirty two foot Wharram catamaran in Tonga, and later in New Zealand, with an English family aboard who were emigrating. The two adults, four children and all their belongings had arrived safely without a mutiny aboard, in spite of the restricted quarters. They had alternated between being above and below decks during their watches, hand steering the boat all the way from England to New Zealand.

'The *Spirit of Gaia*' was a totally different scene, carrying four adults and a twelve year old boy. She was solidly constructed with two fiberglass armas (hulls), each with six separate watertight cabins. None of these had port holes. They were accessed through a submarine type hatch lid on the deck. The bilge was also watertight. Between the armas was a slatted platform on which a small enclosed wheelhouse, head and a BBQ pit were located. She was a fast boat, though rather wet when underway as water came aboard from above and below. This is why James had added an enclosed steering station as an afterthought.

Spirit of Gaia

By the end of July the harbour was full of cruising boats from all over the world, most of which were precariously anchored on the reef all the way out to the quarantine buoy in Vila Bay. Ross and Laura on *Elliott* from South Africa were particularly helpful to us, as they spent an evening explaining some of the tricks and hazards of sailing down the East African coast. They also lent us a copy of *The South African Pilot* and some of the detailed charts for bed-time reading.

After a month on the buoy in Port Vila, we thought it was time to see some more of Vanuatu. We motored across to the other side of Melee Bay on the South

West coast of Efate Island to anchor off Melee village's black sand beach. On Melee Island the Hideaway Resort was located. It was known for its exceptional reef diving and snorkeling.

On our second night we relocated a little further off the beach, as volcanic black sand had a bad reputation as far as holding was concerned. On bringing up our anchor we pulled up an attached reef anchor, which I didn't think was heavy enough to hold *Demelza* safely. A passing villager and his two sons in their outrigger canoe happily accepted this as a gift. The boys promised to meet us the following morning on the beach to show us the way to their church.

In the event they didn't show up, and we were given a car ride to a church further up the narrow road at Mele Matt village. Here we met one of the church wardens called Charlie Budget, so named because he used to be the local Budget Rent a Car agent. He kindly asked us home after the church service for lunch. At the service the pastor introduced us, in Bislama, to the packed congregation. This was accompanied by great smiles all around, and led to friendly hand shakes as we left the church.

On arriving at Charlie Budget's home, he introduced us to his wife Sara. She had prepared a traditional lunch of squares of tapioca with a piece of octopus on each one, cooked in a ground oven. Over this, along with a helping of sweet potatoes, we poured a coconut sauce made from un-ripened coconut. We washed it all down with diluted fresh lemon juice. As is traditional in Vanuatu, Sara sat with her children on mats around the side of the room while Charlie sat with us at the table. The conversation was totally fascinating, as Charlie was an expert on all things Vanuatan, ranging from politics, to religion, to *Kastom*. He had an opinion on everything, and was not afraid to discuss it. We particularly liked his fondness for their political system, where each political party was supported by a different family member. This resulted in every family having a say, no matter which local representative was elected to parliament.

Charlie Budget and family

The following day, Charlie brought Sara and their children, Phillip and Christine, for tea on *Demelza*. They brought us a gift of a small fan which we reciprocated from our accumulated gift stocks.

The following day we sailed around Devil's Point, the southwestern tip of Efate Island, before continuing up the west coast between Efate and Lelepa Islands and up the long reach into Havannah Harbour. To port was Samoa Point, which was a US seaplane base in the Second World War, and numerous protected sandy beaches. Sheltered to the west by Lelapa and Moso Islands, which separate it from the Coral Sea, it was easy to see what a perfect twelve mile long harbour this made for the US fleet during the battle for the Pacific. It now provides a beautifully protected piece of water for dinghy and outrigger sailing. As soon as our anchor hit the water in Soma Bay, two lads appeared in their outrigger canoes offering to bring us fruit and vegetables from their gardens. Frank and Ben lived in a village on Moso Island, but their gardens were on Efate Island, where they grew long green beans, papaya, tomatoes, coconuts, green peppers and cucumbers. Vanuatu, or at least Efate Island, obviously did not lack for food. It was their job to paddle over to their garden plot, gather the crops which were ready for picking and transport them to the twice weekly market in Port Vila twenty-five miles away, all by outrigger canoe, and sell them before paddling home.

Port Vila market

At the head of the harbour, a clean river ran into the bay. In this we did our laundry and collected fresh water for both our sun shower and fresh water tanks. Each evening, flying foxes flew from Efate to Moso Island in a black cloud against the darkening sky. The trees around the harbour were festooned with Virginia creeper, introduced as an American camouflage during the war. This smothered indigenous plants, and threatened their survival in a mass of purple flowers. Our search for dugong in the harbour was to no avail, although the villagers told us that three of them had been sighted. We enjoyed finding WW II Coke bottles, or bits of them, on the beaches each one dated on its bottom. They had been carelessly jettisoned by soldiers during the war. An old gentleman from the nearby village was making a living selling them for $5 US or even more for the older ones.

Sailing out of Havannah Harbour through Little Pass in twenty knot trade winds, we rounded Moso Island to anchor on the east side of Undine Bay at the north end of Efate. Here we swam before retiring for a quiet night. In the morning, we sailed over to Nguna Island where the winds were gusting so hard in Utalangi Bay that we decided to keep going over to Emae Island. In the evening we found Sulua anchorage, which was studded with so much coral that it was difficult to see where to anchor. At dawn I looked around, to find *Demelza* so close to a coral head that we had to take in chain to pull us clear.

Emae Island has three mountain peaks. It is six miles long and three miles wide, and home to about a thousand people. At the north end of the island a language similar to that spoken on an island north of Fiji is common. The remainder speak a Melanesian dialect.

As the night had been so uncomfortably rolly, we left for Epi Island in the morning. This island is twenty-five miles long and twelve miles wide, covered with coconut plantations along its coast, with a thickly forested rugged interior. Four thousand people live there, and there are two submarine volcanoes off its south eastern shores.

We put into Lembito Bay, in a lovely nook behind the reef where calm prevailed after our rolly passage. Daniel and Wilson, two children living in a house overlooking the bay, came out to see us in their canoe. They wanted to show us their home ashore. So we got into our dinghy and followed them to the steeply sloping beach. They introduced us to their mother and to an uncle who insisted we take a look at a little piglet they had in a pen behind the house. It had been orphaned when its mother had been shot. It had given them some good meals. Elizabeth and two more of her children later came out to have a look at *Demelza*, taking home a pair of old reading glasses and a couple of magazines that we had on board.

During the night the wind changed direction blowing across the reef, thus putting *Demelza* on a lee shore. I spent all night on anchor watch, and was glad to take the boat out of the pass in the morning light. It was blowing thirty knots as we rounded Cape Foreland on the west coast of Epi Island. The sea was very rough indeed, throwing water all over the place. We tucked in behind Lamenu Island and set a stern anchor as well as our main anchor, to keep the boat facing the incoming swell. As night fell, the sky was lit up by the volcano across the water on Ambryn Island, a magical sight in an otherwise clear sky.

In the morning we walked north along the beach, and eventually found a small clearing in the trees where six women were sitting on the ground, cross legged, plaiting coconut palm fronds into roofing flats. Olly was working close by, cutting up a huge fish. On seeing us, he sauntered over to extend a cheerful greeting. He gave Christine a drinking coconut which he had prepared, and in return Christine handed around some candies that we had brought on our walk.

We were trying to find a short cut back to *Demelza* through the forest. Olly volunteered to show us the way. Off we went along an overgrown path through the forest. At places, clearings had been cut and gardens planted. Here Olly would pause to tell us some of his gardening techniques. His plants all looked very healthy and all the gardens flourishing. Finally we came to a junction in the path, where Olly pointed down the one we should take back to our anchorage. Thanking him, we set off downhill and soon came upon a clearing where a group of men were drying copra on racks in a shed over a wood fire. The men told us that walking on the nearby reef was *tabu* (forbidden).

"How do we know when a place is *tabu?*" I asked

"It is posted by a stick, with a pandanus frond, stuck upright into the reef." they said.

I had seen such a marker at the start of our walk, but had mistaken it for a guide to fishermen walking across the reef when it was covered by the tide.

In the evening, the *Spirit of Gaia* appeared in the bay. James rowed over to ask if I would have a look at his wife's leg which had been swollen for a week. After doing so, I decided that she needed injectable penicillin to control the infection. We didn't have any on board, so I volunteered to walk up the hill to the small hospital at Vaemali to see if they could help us. They did so willingly, and after a few days, there was great improvement in her condition.

Christine and I were given a tour of *Spirit of Gaia*, and were both amazed to find it had no plumbing and no electrical appliances. The cooking was done in centre cabin of the starboard arma, which had no ventilation. Freya, the young Canadian crew, had an aft cabin on the port side to herself, which she had made into a very attractive, comfortable den where she loved to play her flute.

The following morning David met Christine on the beach and took her home to meet his wife Sylvana, where a selection of her fruit and vegetables had been laid out on clean coral sand. Sylvana was French speaking, having been brought up on Malakula Island where she had attended a French school. Having made her purchases, Christine invited both of them for a cup of Tanna coffee on *Demelza*, where we learned that David had worked in the British Police Force in Port Vila during the days of the Condominium. This accounted for his excellent English. He had met Sylvana when she was finishing High School in Port Vila. After they were married they settled down on Lamenu Island, later moving across to Epi Island, where she had taken a job as housekeeper at the Paradise Sunset Bungalows.

One evening we attended a feast for sixteen people from the visiting boats at the Bungalows. On arrival we were each given a flower to put behind an ear, on the right side if married and behind the left if available. We then walked in line past our hosts to shake their hands, a significant feature of life in Vanuatu. The feast was laid out buffet style, with plenty of chicken, piglet, yams, cabbage rolls and the inevitable slab of Laplap all served on banana leaves. Laplap is made from ground manioc, taro root or yam to form a dough or paste. This is spread on taro leaves and soaked in coconut milk, before a variety of meats are added. Taro leaves are then wrapped around this mixture before being tied with vine and placed in a ground oven with hot stones above and below the food.

Returning home on the evening breeze

The next morning David took us up into the hills above the village to show us his garden. We went along a tortuous steep path through the jungle, passing several clearings where other families were working the ground, before eventually reaching David's orderly plot. Here he had recently planted rows of manioc. He told us of the healing properties of the juice from skin of the papaya fruit against infected wounds, and of the plant's ability to change its sex. If a cut was made by machete through a male sapling's trunk, the plant would heal and in time it would flower and be able to bear fruit.

We followed this visit with a day at Lamenu Island, taking David, Sylvana and Margaret motoring through the pass in our dinghy. This lovely small island is almost totally surrounded by beautiful beaches. At the village, David introduced us to his father and to the village Chief, who was his brother. The island's four hundred residents were assembled for a village bazaar at the Nakamal (meeting house) grounds which were overhung by huge shade trees. Narrow roads, with low coral walls along each side, radiated out to different parts of the island. Everything was scrupulously clean and tidy, and the villagers looked well nourished, and were most welcoming. At the edge of the Nakamal grounds, the old village well, which had been carefully cribbed with stone, had been rendered useless by a recent cyclone as its source of water had been interrupted by landslides. At the north end of the island there were hot springs, from which the volcano on Lopevi Island was clearly visible.

We visited the local school where we were introduced to Mr. Fred, the headmaster. We also went to the village's clinic and church where a notice declared proudly "Dr. Smalley (1902) converted the heathen back to God's ways."

On our return to the village centre, the men had chopped up a bullock, which had been roasted over a big fire. Many pots full of mysterious contents were bubbling away, and the women had been busy making *Laplap*, in huge tureens.

The local craft sale, then in progress, raised money for the youth of the village. By late afternoon the whole place was awash in torrential rain, but the villagers' humour and enthusiasm was undiminished, so that at the conclusion of the feast everybody agreed it had been *'Numba One'* – the Vanuatu way of saying 'the best.'

James Wharram, David and myself

David and Sylvana insisted on loading our boat with vegetables and fruit before we left for the Maskelyne Islands the next morning. We were sad to say goodbye to this friendly couple. It was a short bumpy ride to the Maskelynes, accompanied by the *Spirit of Gaia*. Most of the islets seemed very rugged. But a few had beautiful beaches. The overall visual effect was exceptionally lovely.

The regulator on our alternator was beginning to show signs of chronic malfunction, as sudden bursts of charge to the batteries would occasionally appear on the ammeter. I checked all the leads and tightened the alternator belt, which improved the situation somewhat.

We anchored off Uliveo islet, home to about a thousand people, and for the first time felt some annoyance at the persistent presence of canoes continuously circling both our boats at anchor in the bay. Uninvited, they would draw up alongside, banging into *Demelza's* hull, and standing up to peer in through the port holes. This whole experience put us off exploring the islet and we left *Spirit of Gaia* to the tender mercies of the villagers. The last memory we have of this location was tall James striding up the beach, surrounded by a much shorter but excited crowd of villagers, on his way to visit their Polynesian master canoe builder.

On reaching Awei Island we found the most beautiful anchorage, with excellent coral for snorkeling not far away. The local residents supplied us with fresh caught lobster in exchange for T shirts.

Our next destination was Gaspard Bay on Malekula Island. This was ringed by deep forest down to the shore. Local canoes came out immediately on our arrival. They brought more lobsters which we traded for more T shirts from our dwindling stores. As there was no village close by, we were left in peace to enjoy our day before sailing northward along Malekula Island's eastern shore to round the point into Port Sandwich Inlet. This inlet is about one and a half miles long and has the fearsome reputation for being the most likely place in Vanuatu to be attacked by sharks while swimming. The temperature by day was now in the high 80s°F, and while we were sitting on deck that evening we had the pleasant experience of seeing the tall ship *Soren Larsen*, registered in Colchester, UK, sailing in for an overnight visit to the bay.

We walked from the old wharf along a path to Lamap village. On the way we met Mary and her two children, who gave us some sea shells. We reciprocated by giving them some soap and fishing hooks. This must have been a success because, on our way back past their home, they were waiting for us with arms full of lettuce, green onions, tomatoes and sweet potatoes. Mary took our garbage bag, out of which she salvaged the boxed wine liner as a balloon for the children, and the plastic bags. She burnt the rest. Later we took more plastic bags ashore for her, some real balloons for the children, tea bags and granola bars. All the men were away in the hills working the family gardens and would not reappear until sunset.

That night a cold front passed over us with rain and plenty of wind. On the radio, we heard of boats making their way south in stormy seas. For two days it blew and rained, which confined us to the boat. But then, just as suddenly, it cleared. After being confined to the boat for so long we were ready for some exercise, so walked along the road to Lamap village. On arrival, we were given two drinking coconuts to quench our thirst in the heat of the day. Our kind benefactor was preparing a wedding feast for the following day. He had had to contact the butcher, who lived on Lopevi Island, for him to paddle over to kill and dress the fatted calf. He invited us to join in the festivities. We declined, saying we had to move on.

In the local mission church pictures of sand drawings hung on the walls. Sand drawings are created mainly on the northern islands of Vanuatu. They illustrate local legends or are used to leave messages. The most elaborate forms are done on the island of Ambrym and as far north as the Banks Islands. The technique is fascinating. First the artist draws a sequence of squares or rectangles in the sand using a finger, and then a series of continuous loops or circles is made over this basic framework without raising the finger from the sand. Many of the drawings in the church represented common animals such as the turtle and reef fish.

On our way home Heather popped out of her door, as we passed, with a bag of vegetables and two eggs. Her husband was the local agricultural officer, and they had heard from Mary that we were around. We were so impressed with the generosity of the islanders.

From Port Sandwich we sailed over to the island of Ambrym, a distance of about twelve miles in a stiff twenty-five knot breeze, to anchor in Hot Springs Cove's black sand. At night the sky was lit an eerie red by the island's two volcanoes, Mounts Marum and Benbow, which spewed steam and ash thousands of feet into the air. This ash had, over the years, created a central plain devoid of all vegetation, but elsewhere growth appears in the rich volcanic soil. Seven thousand people live along Ambrym's coastal rim in spite of its history of catastrophic cyclones and several severe volcanic eruptions that had destroyed whole villages. One village had been moved to Efate Island, founding the village of Mele Matt.

We met Etienne and Natalie on the French boat *Jane*, a heavy twenty-five year old steel boat weighing seventeen tons. They used a sixty five pound working anchor! He was a ski instructor in the Swiss Alps, and she a teacher. Together we explored the hot springs ashore on the black sand beach, where the water bubbled up all around us. The impressive canyon of rock, polished smooth by a long vanished stream, leads up toward the volcano above.

From here we moved the boat along Ambrym's shore, arriving off Ranvetlan village where williwaws swept down off the land. As we rowed ashore, two small boys were walking home from school along the beach. They helped us pull our dinghy onto the grassy area above the tide line, and offered to show us the path to their village. This was about a twenty minute walk up a steep slope through the forest. They ran ahead to warn the villagers of our approach, so that by the time we had emerged at the village clearing, quite a crowd had gathered to greet us with smiles and the usual handshakes.

A young man squatted at one side of the sandy clearing. He had overheard us telling one of the elders that we had visited Lamap Village Church, and had admired the sand drawings. In front of our eyes he drew out a series of continuous squares, and then began to draw the characteristic unending circular lines which, when finished, depicted a perfect crab.

Christine bought five beautifully etched and painted bamboo flutes from one of the women in the square. One of these later proved to be home to an enormous spider. Fortunately it only found its way as far as *Demelza*'s cockpit before striking out for shore.

On the way back to the boat we met Joe, who was on his way to the drying shed, to tend his copra oven by adding coconut husks to the fire. He told us that his wife and children were fishing on the rocks below. On our way back to the boat we watched, fascinated, as the boys threw spears at the fish swimming around their feet in the shallow water. Later we heard a whistle from on shore. It was Joe beckoning, and when I went over to him in the dinghy, he presented me with a beautiful fish for our supper.

Another boat came into the bay called *Idunn* with Mette and Julius aboard. They invited us over for supper that evening, and whilst down below, after the sun had set, we heard knocking on the stern of the boat. A face appeared in the darkness over *Idunn's* gunwales, with an attached set of very white teeth.

"Other boat gone walking." the young man said breathlessly.

We looked out to sea and there, very dimly in the distance, was *Demelza*'s anchor light. From the village John had seen her drifting out to sea, before grabbing his small outrigger canoe to paddle out to us. He had noticed our dinghy tied alongside *Idunn.* Julius, John and I jumped into Julius's huge inflatable, which had a big engine, and roared off into the night in hot pursuit of our precious boat. She had gone much further than we thought, but eventually I got on board, started up her engine, and returned to the anchorage to rejoin the others. *Demelza* was none the worse for her adventure. Unfortunately, on backing *Demelza* up to set the anchor, I ran over Julius's dinghy's non floating painter cutting it though. Whereupon he dived off his boat to retrieve his dinghy. The following day I gave John a pair of old Army boots that I had inherited from David in New Zealand, which I had at the time thought might be useful for anchor work on the foredeck. John grinned, hung them around his neck, and dashed off to the village looking very pleased with himself. He must have been the only person on the island with a pair of boots! We later learned that being a guide to the volcanoes is one of the most sought after jobs on the island, so now, equipped with boots, John was all set for a successful career.

From Ranvetlan we moved north along the coast to anchor off Ranon village. Here we took some medical supplies as a gift to the village nurse. We had heard about a local wood carver whom we found and listened to as he played one of our flutes for us. We bought two carvings from him, one a Rom dance mask, and an eight inch replica tam tam. The genuine tam tam is a split pole drum about six feet tall, decorated with a long face and disc like eyes.

Tam — Tams

The Rom dance is Ambrym's most striking ceremony. In August, each village on these northern islands, after practicing for many weeks, demonstrates its dances in neighbouring villages. The Rom dress consists of a tall conical painted banana fibre mask and a costume of banana leaves. The dancer represents a spirit. After each dance, the costume is burnt to destroy the spirit. It is *tabu* to watch a Rom costume being made.

Rom dance

From here we crossed over to Pentecost Island, anchoring in Loltong Bay. It had been another rough crossing for the five and a half nautical miles over the Selwyn Strait. Though blowing hard outside, none of it penetrated into this secluded anchorage. On going ashore the following day we were soon swept up by the villagers. Beatrice gave Christine a soursop and pamplemousse. Willie, who had paddled his canoe over from Wali, offered us more fruit. Walter and Rachel, who led us to their home to meet Philip's mother, Lolowea, offered Christine a beautifully made handbag and a finely woven basket all made from pandanus leaves. Willi claimed to be the champion tower diver on Pentecost Island. He told us he made ten dives a year, and was paid one hundred Vatu ($1 US) per jump.

Before the arrival of Europeans, circumcised islanders on Pentecost Island used to dive off tall banyan trees once every five years, attached by a vine rope around their ankles. Nowadays, each year, twenty villagers jump off towers built of local tree trunks and saplings bound together with vines and anchored to a tree stump. Taking six weeks to build, and about fifty feet high, these towers are located close to an open flat dancing area. The soil below is dug over to loosen it to a depth of about one foot. The towers are believed to be inhabited by the spirit of an ancient tribesman while the diving takes place. Each diver makes his own double vine thong of the exact length to prevent his head hitting the ground. He ties one end to his ankles and the other end to the top of the tower. The first successful jump after circumcision marks the time of achieving adulthood. Only the hair of the diver touches the ground if the thongs are precisely the correct length.

Loltong village was built on a series of terraces up the side of a cleared space on the hill overlooking the bay, with the Catholic community high up, and the Anglican further down. I went to the little church on Sunday. It was quite small, with a coral floor and split sapling bench seats. On being introduced to the local congregation by the pastor I was cheered twice, once for being an Anglican, and secondly for being a Rector's son. The enthusiastic response took me aback. One day we were invited to lunch at Patrick's house. Fish and taro was on the menu. Here we met a beautiful lady from New Guinea, named Elizabeth, who was visiting a B'hai teacher in the village. On our way back to the boat, villagers pressed fruit and vegetables on us.

While Christine paid a visit to Lolowea's home, where she met her daughter Ansen with her twin one and a half year old babies John and James, Etienne and I met Luke, the village chief. He was very insistent that we share kava with him at the Nakamal. I had had enough kava for a lifetime in Tonga. But Etienne went on behalf of us both mostly, I think, to be polite. As the day progressed, we all returned to our boats except Etienne, who had been unable to detach himself from the all male throng. He didn't return until after dark having consumed seven coconut halves of kava. He was feeling very much the worse for wear. Later Chief Luke proudly showed us the 'does and don'ts' book that he had written in

Bislama for his villagers. This set out penalties imposed for specific transgressions which he intended to send to the Minister of Culture in Vila.

We had spent a week at Loltong and it was time to move on. Our next call was at Asanvari Bay at the south end of Maewo Island. This island lies just south of the Banks Islands, and is thirty miles long and three miles wide. It has the dubious distinction of being Vanuatu's wettest island. At the time Captain Cook saw the island, it had twenty thousand inhabitants. However, following the import of European diseases, it now has only about three thousand.

Asanvari Bay

The bay is beautiful, with a waterfall tumbling down off the hillside on to the beach. Here Chief Nelson had built his "Yacht Club," a shack in which to greet the crews of visiting cruising yachts. On our arrival the Chief was in a state of agitation. The following day his village was to host an inter island get-together for the Anglican Mother's Union. The ancient television set in the Yacht Club, powered by a noisy generator throbbing in the background, had chosen that particular day to show nothing but snow on its screen. He enquired whether I or Ron from *Tigger*, could fix it. Well Ron hadn't a clue, and neither had I, but it was obvious that the Chief's expectations of the white man ran high.

After much pensive poking around the back of the set in front of a crowd of villagers who had now gathered to watch the white man's magic at work, we suddenly realized that the Chief had plugged the video tape recorder leads in the wrong way around. The assembled throng had been having a wonderful time chattering and laughing as all this was going on. But, having remedied the problem, the picture of a rock group appeared, and the crowd subsided into a zombied silence.

"That's the worst thing we could have done for this village." I said to Ron as we quaffed one of the appreciative Chief's beers.

It rained all night and all the following day. We collected gallons of water for our water tanks. And still it rained. We read books and talked on the radio to our cruising friends all over the Pacific. And still it rained. Meanwhile, preparations for the Anglican mothers of Ambae, Pentetost and Maewo Islands reunion continued as if nothing untoward was going on. It was a monsoon!

The festivities commenced the next morning at 0745 hrs with a Mass on the football pitch. All the mothers were wearing sopping wet white T shirts and royal blue skirts. The rain poured down on them, but nothing seemed to dampen their enthusiasm. We retired at lunch time to *Demelza* to wring ourselves out. This was "Singing in the Rain" with a difference. In the afternoon most of the dances were unfamiliar to us. In one, a man dressed up as a hunter, mimed his way through stalking his prey, finally dispatching it to resounding applause. It was a very congenial crowd. The children joining in the festivities whatever their ages, and not one of them seemed to notice it was pouring with rain. We beat another hasty retreat back to *Demelza*.

Hunter

The following morning what might kindly be called an ancient coaster came into the bay to pick everybody up. Still it rained as crowds of ladies stood on the beach patiently waiting to be ferried over to the ship moored out in the bay. This would take them home to their various islands. More and more women were packed onto the ship. The cabins below were full, the decks were standing room only, and still they kept ferrying them out from shore. I fully expected the end point to be reached when the ship capsized. But no, the congenial passengers were all accommodated, and the rusty chain and anchor were hauled up. We stood under our cockpit awning as the ship slowly motored around all the anchored boats in the bay as they sang

"Goodbye, God Bless you till we meet again," and they waved smilingly from their cramped standing positions in the pouring rain.

It was another of life's altering experiences as we choked back our emotions.

Our next visit was to Lolowai Bay at the northern tip of Ambae Island. The highest point is Mount Lombenben, a dormant volcano at the centre of the island rising to four thousand five hundred feet. This island is thickly wooded everywhere except for a flat coastal area at its southern end. To our surprise, a short time after we had anchored in the bay, the familiar coaster appeared around the point to drop off the Ambae Islanders who we had last seen leaving Asanvari Bay. Vigorous waving at *Demelza* ensued as they recognized us and we them.

Following a morning visit to Mary and Francis, who ran the Vocational Training centre on the island, we walked along a single track over the hills to the next bay. Here St. Patrick's Secondary School was located in beautiful park like surroundings. Their working day started at 0530 hrs every morning and, after a break in the heat of the day, carried on until 2100 hrs. Fred showed us around the school, which had been founded by missionaries on the Banks Islands in 1902. They were particularly proud to show us a whole caseload of reference books which they had just received from an English benefactor.

On return to the boat we lifted anchor and sailed along the coast of Ambae until it started to get dark. With the very short twilight of the tropics, almost absent in fact, we had no choice but to put into a bay close to Devil's Island. Its bottom was nothing but coral heads. The chain creaked and groaned until midnight when I could stand it no longer. I took in the anchor and we made our way across to Luganville on Espíritu Santo, the largest island in Vanuatu.

The colloquial name for Luganville is Santo, which confuses visitors enormously. Even more confusing is that Luganville is alternatively called "Canal," named after the body of water washing its waterfront, the 'Segond Channel.' The wreck of the SS *President Coolidge* lies in two hundred feet of water here, creating a diving mecca just off Million Dollar Point. She was a 1930 luxury passenger ship, converted to a troopship containing all sorts of war equipment, which was sunk by an American mine guarding the entrance to the harbour during the war.

During the Solomon Island Campaign of World War II, the American forces developed a massive secure forward base at Luganville, from which to resist the Japanese push southwards. At the end of the fighting, Luganville was transformed into a huge military junkyard. Even with the common practice of almost giving it away, vast quantities of this military equipment remained. Much of this was trucked to the waterfront and dumped into the sea. Hence the name Million Dollar Point.

Military Equipment Graveyard

After restocking the boat in Luganville we moved to Palekula Bay which was much more protected but about three miles from town. Glen took us on a tour of old American military sites on the island. Crashed planes that never quite made it back to their airfield, lie abandoned in the overgrown forests just as they had come to rest all those years ago. We visited the site of Bloody Mary's restaurant close by the ruins of the Officer's Mess, which looked across the water to Ambae Island. This view had inspired the movie *South Pacific.* Ambae's profile did not look at all like that in the film, and the local people are of Melanesian descent not Polynesian as portrayed in the film. Bloody Mary had died two years before our visit at the age of one hundred and three. We drove up to Nellie Forebush's hospital site, where only the flat rectangular concrete foundations survive. These are now used for drying coffee beans in the sun.

So ended our memorable visit to Vanuatu. We paid our visiting fee of $51 US for the fifty seven days we had spent in the country, and completed all the remaining required paperwork.

On 25th September we left for Australia after unplugging the head yet again. This always seemed to happen when we were ready to leave. As we set off, the sea was flat and there was so little wind we had to motor for two hours. Gradually a five to ten knot breeze filled in from the south as we set a course to the south west for Gladstone, in Queensland, Australia located at the south end of the Great Barrier Reef.

Although the quiet weather continued, on the third day we heard of a storm to the south of us. We slowed the boat down and circumnavigated Suarez Reef during the night waiting for the storm to pass below us. In the morning we resumed our passage as the wind picked up to fifteen knots from the southeast. *Demelza* was moving along steadily at between five and seven knots, so we were pleased with our progress. By the fifth day the wind had swung around to the north, and the swell was building again. We altered course to the west to keep north of 20°S, along which all the storm cells were travelling. The forecast was for thirty knots from the northwest, so we made for Chesterfield Reef to shelter in Brampton Island Lagoon should it prove necessary.

That night as Christine talked to Peter on the DDD Net, he mysteriously asked whether we had met a particular Canadian boat on our journeys, to which we replied that we had talked on the radio but not met face to face.

"Are you still in contact with him?" Peter asked.

"Yes," replied Christine, "We have a daily "sked" and plan to meet up in Gladstone when we get there."

"Oh good," said Peter, relief in his voice "would you relay to him a message please? Tell him the baby, a little girl, has arrived and mother and baby are doing well."

"Will do Peter. If he comes up on the net we will be sure to tell him."

The airwaves were buzzing with curiosity after that exchange, for the boat in question was being single handed by a most single minded man.

By now we were about four hundred miles away from Gladstone. To our relief the wind began to lighten before disappearing completely. We lay becalmed on an oily sea and, rather than sit about being rolled from side to side, we turned on our engine.

Southward across 20S we plunged into fog and cloud until, after twenty four hours of motoring, the wind suddenly picked up again in the middle of the night. Up on deck the sea was still relatively calm as I took in two reefs in the main and put up the working jib. The wind continued to rise to twenty and then thirty knots as the seas stirred before dawn, to a rough unpleasant froth. The one encouraging thing was that, once the fog had cleared, we were under clear skies, and the barometer was steadily rising. Within twenty four hours, all had settled down, the sail was let out, and the genoa put up to catch a steady ten knot breeze from the southeast. We approached North Reef and the North Channel for Gladstone. The charts of this passage looked quite daunting but, as the alternative was a long detour around Facing Island to enter the easier south shipping channel, we waited for good morning light and incoming tide. We reduced sail to staysail only before poking our noses into the north entrance. Extensive mud banks crowded us on both sides as we carefully followed the twisting buoyage system and day beacons, relying on them to keep us out of trouble. Seabirds sat on top of the day beacons looking unconcernedly at us as we drifted by. Through the narrow "Gut" we passed between the shallows off Quion and Curtis Islands. Then south west through less confined waters to round Middle Bank before entering Gladstone's newly constructed Boat Harbour beside Auckland Creek. Built and landscaped with first rate yachting facilities for two hundred and fifty boats, the site, half-way between Brisbane to the south and Whitsunday Islands to the north, is ideally located as a base for cruising the East coast of Australia.

Auckland Creek,
Gladstone, Queensland, Australia

Tracy

CHAPTER 12
Australian Interlude

As we drew alongside the wharf at Gladstone, the cheery Customs Officer, Tracy, gave us a warm Aussie welcome. After the paperwork had been completed, she sat in the pilot house and, over a cup of tea, regaled us with all the events and goings on in town.

Gladstone is one of the busiest ports in Australia but, from the municipal park and marina across the bay from the port, there was no sign of all that activity. Huge quantities of minerals, agricultural products and coal are shipped out bringing great prosperity to Queensland and to the town. Alumina is processed here from bauxite mined on the Cape York Peninsula in North Australia.

The marina was brand new with superb facilities, serving as a ferry terminal for access to the southern islands of the Great Barrier Reef. This extends northward a few miles offshore. Walking around the town, we saw a campervan for sale which we decided to buy. In Australia the vendor of a used vehicle must have the mechanical, electrical and gas installations inspected and certified before sale. So, putting great faith in the inspection system, we went for it.

Demelza was hauled out of the water, and put in the commodious dry storage area of the boatyard for the cyclone season. Cyclones sometimes hit this area, so we secured her to six substantial ground anchors with our anchor chain tightly looped over the boat several times. We began the process of stripping down all the gear above deck and storing it below to decrease wind resistance. We had to transfer a lot of the boat's contents into the campervan for use during our proposed land exploration of the interior, after Christine had first thoroughly cleaned and re-carpeted it.

Our first visitors from home were Shaun and Penny. On the way to pick them up, the van wouldn't start. So we made our first call to a garage where the problem was diagnosed as a sticky solenoid switch on the starter motor. This was easily solved by giving it a sharp whack with something solid. The next crisis was that the cover of the propane tank locker blew off as we were travelling, necessitating a trip to another garage to get a new one fitted.

John and Muriel, whom we had met in New Zealand, were in the area with their motor home touring Australia. We went with them for our first trial weekend camping trip to the nearby Awoonga Dam. This was a magical experience, with Kookaburras eyeing us from the trees, letting out their catchy cacophony of noise in the evenings as we enjoyed a BBQ.

The van with Shaun, myself, Penny *John, myself and Muriel*

Bill and Robyn Forbes off the boat *Ramtha*, whom we had met in Tonga recovering from their dreadful experience in the Queen's birthday storm, joined us for a camping trip to Byfield State Park, north of Rockhampton. Here we hiked up to the top of Mt Archer for fabulous views over the Great Barrier Reef.

Robyn, myself and Bill *Happy Hour in the boatyard with Betty and Neville*

Another cruising couple we had met in Noumea, Sue and Craig from Mt. Omaney just outside Brisbane invited us to join them for Christmas at their home.

More boats followed us to spend the cyclone season in Queensland. In theory, while being on the southern end of the Great Barrier Reef, Gladstone was far enough south to avoid most cyclone threats. Brisbane, Bundaberg, and Manly seemed to be popular alternative sheltering ports along this coast.

We left Betty and Neville working on their English boat *Wrangler* in the boatyard. They promised to keep an eye on *Demelza* for us before they started their own tour of Australia. We looked forward to meeting up again in the boatyard later in the year.

Following our arrival in Brisbane, we left the van with Craig and his family and took a flying ten day trip to Tasmania. The tourist traffic had come to a complete stop on the island because of a recent murder in Port Arthur, so we had no difficulty finding accommodation wherever we stopped.

The view from the top of Mt Wellington was breathtaking, with a spectacular view of the historic city of Hobart. Its position at the mouth of the Derwent River guaranteed a most interesting maritime history, a lot of which has been carefully preserved and displayed in the city's fabulous Maritime Museum. We visited the Royal Yacht Club of Tasmania and were given a full explanation of the running of the Sidney Hobart Yacht Race, due to start in two weeks time, by the Club's weather guru, Geoff Boyd.

Hobart, from Mt. Wellington

It was here we had the opportunity to visit Peter and his wife Helen. Peter had been such a reliable ham radio contact on our crossing of the South Pacific. We wanted to pay our respects and to thank him for being on the radio for us every day.

On our tour of the island we visited the port of Stanley, on the north coast. This charming little fishing port is situated under a hill, in the shape of a huge boulder called 'The Nut.' Nestled behind the harbour wall we spied the small vessel that had recently been paddled across the Bass Strait from Melbourne. The poor man had suffered from debilitating seasickness on the rough journey, and had decided he wouldn't do it or anything like it again.

At a small yacht club on the Tamar River we saw three men working on a hauled out yacht. We had heard their laughter ringing out in the morning air. The Yacht Club's marine railway had a unique design allowing them to move boats around in the yard, to strategically place them for necessary work. It transpired that the three men had been friends for life. Two of them were in their eighties and the owner, who had been running up and down the ladder for appropriate tools as the others worked below, was the skipper and well over ninety.

Three happy souls

"We don't go out to sea anymore" said the skipper, a small, jovial man. "We just take her out on the river now and then to do a little fishing." They were a charming trio. Long may they continue to enjoy that fine little boat.

A particular favourite was a memorable picnic overlooking Wineglass Bay on the Freycinet Peninsula. The colours there were so clear, and the sea so blue. Another was a day spent at the former penal colony of Port Arthur. In all we had ten enjoyable days touring Tasmania and appreciated its easy going and friendly people.

Returning to Queensland, we motored south into New South Wales to the lovely hill country of Glen Innes before continuing on to the Country and Western heartland of Tamworth. We visited the Warrumbungle Mountains where we heard kangaroos bouncing around our campervan at night. In the hot evenings we were deafened by the noise of crickets, and amused by the antics of the countless Wallabies. Goannas, crested Cockatoos, Emus and Koalas were plentiful.

In the state of Victoria, we drove along the Murrumbidgee River to the Murray River, where we had been invited to spend a few days with Graham and Marianne on their farm near Myall. We had first met them on the flight to Tanna in Vanuatu. They took us on a sunset dinner cruise on the paddle steamer *Wetlander* up Gunbower Creek which is flanked by magnificent red gum trees. We later took a trip on the *Pride of the Murray*, a vintage paddle steamer cruising out of Echucca on the Murray River. This river had played such an important historical role in opening up the interior of Australia for farming.

Murray River boat

We drove on to Mildura, Renmark and Swan Hills along the picturesque Murray River before descending through the lush vineyards of the Barossa Valley to Adelaide. Here Natalie's sister lived in a beautiful home in the hills above the city. We had met Canadians Natalie and Noel crossing the Pacific, and enjoyed a great reunion with them over the next few days. Returning to the coolness of the eucalyptus scented hills after daytime visits to the sights of Adelaide was so enjoyable.

We continued west towards the York Peninsula in South Australia, through the Copper Triangle, worked by miners from Cornwall in the 19th Century. We visited the old Cornish Engine House at Wallaroo as well as the miners' little stone cottages, before driving to Port Victoria on the Spencer's Gulf.

At the head of Spencer's Gulf is Port Augusta, nestling under the shadow of the Flinders Range, established in 1854 as the major grain terminal to load the tall sailing ships heading for Europe. This is also the breeding ground of the Southern Right Whale and the Great White Shark.

At Port Elliott wool from inland farms was brought down to the ocean on Murray River boats, and offloaded at Goolwa. Here it was loaded onto horse drawn rail carts before being taken to Port Elliott. The mouth of the Murray River had silted up, preventing the larger ships sailing into Lake Alexandrina on which Goolwa is situated. From Port Elliott their precious cargo was taken along the Trade Wind sailing routes to Europe.

On the coast road to Melbourne we passed the odiferous salt marshes of the Coorong. Melbourne is situated on the river Yarra, beside which we set up camp in forty degree temperatures for four days, visiting friends and seeing the city, including a visit to the *QE* II which was in port at the time.

We resumed our travels to Mount Beauty through stands of eucalyptus, whose scent was strong after the extreme heat of the previous week. The contorted, elegant shapes of the Snow Gum trees high up on the plateau, opened up to display the beauty of the mountains behind. After going down to Jindabyne, we visited Jack Riley's gravesite, made famous by Banjo Patterson's poem *'The Man from Snowy River.'* Then on to Tom Groggin, where Jack's cabin was built at the headwaters of the Murray River.

Snow Gums

We drove past Mt. Kosciusko in the clouds and descended into Canberra, capital city of Australia, with its broad geometrically laid out streets and wooded avenues. We saw its memorable War Museum and lakeside Canadian Carillon. In spite of its rather lackluster reputation, we found plenty of interest, before moving on towards Sydney.

At Heathcote, we visited Raewyn and her husband Alan. She is the daughter of our friends Val and David in New Zealand. They kindly showed us around the area, including the huge steel mill where Alan worked. By now we were worried about Cyclone Harold, which was revolving menacingly off the Queensland coast.

Trying to be stoic about *Demelza*, we headed for the Blue Mountains, with their spectacular crevices and chasms. After a short pause to photograph the scenery, trying to avoid including the plethora of Japanese tourist buses in our photographs, we continued on to Bathurst through the Wollemi National Park. This is the only place where the distinctive Wollemi Pine trees grow. We visited June Welsh of the Koala Preservation Society and were introduced to 'Precious', a blind Koala baby, that had been found on the Newcastle Airport runway. This little animal, although unable to see anything, had an uncanny knack of knowing its way about June's garden, and could find its way back to its perch in a tree again after going on one of its adventures.

In Forster we looked up another radio ham operator to whom Christine had talked on our passage, to pay our respects. Inadvertently we had left his address on the boat, so we drove around the general area where he lived, looking for the appropriate aerial. However, unbeknownst to us, the television reception in Forster was so bad in places, that many houses had tall, complicated aerials. At the first of these Christine leapt out of the van and banged on the door

"I'm looking for George, VK2OH." announced Christine to a rather bemused old lady. Eventually, when all had been explained, the house owner found a telephone number for us and contact was made. Before we knew it, we were swept up into a local Ham enthusiast's BBQ, and had a wonderful time entertaining them with our stories, and hearing theirs.

Moving on to Coffs Harbour, it was apparent that several of the cruising boats from the Pacific had made this their destination for the Cyclone Season. Along the Pacific Highway through Grafton, which had been half under water a year ago when the Clarence River had flooded, we drove to Byron Bay. Here we had arranged to meet John and Muriel who we had first met in New Zealand, and spent three happy days with them.

At Mount Warning National Park, so named by Captain Cook as a landmark to avoid hitting Danger Point off Tweed Heads, we marveled at what was left of the huge central magma chamber of an ancient volcano, most of which is now covered by the ocean. It is remarkable for being the first place in Australia to see the sun rising every morning.

At Southport Yacht Club we met Jim and Nancy, who drove us to their lovely home in Runaway Bay. We had met this couple in their boat, *Nordlys*, when they visited Victoria a few years previously. In their Yacht Club's yard, on the hard, was *Bolero*, which had just completed a round trip of the five major Capes of the World. Made of wood, she was a fifty five foot Alden ketch, with a beam of twelve feet, and was in fabulous condition. A cabinet maker had spent six years refurbishing and rebuilding the interior. She had sprung two planks of her hull, which was only just discernable to the unpracticed eye.

Among the sites Jim and Nancy showed us during our two day visit, was the Captain Cook Memorial at Tweed Heads, overlooking the horrendous Tweed River bar.

Having heard that *Demelza* had safely escaped Cyclone Harold, we were now starting to worry about Cyclone Justin which was revolving off the Queensland coast, four hundred miles off Cairns. It was the largest cyclone diameter seen in Australia during the past fifty years. We heard, on the radio, of a Canadian couple, now out sailing, having to be rescued from their boat as it began to break up in this storm.

We drove past Tambourine Mountain to arrive, as prearranged, at our friends

Sue and Craig's home in Mount Omany just outside Brisbane. Together we visited Buderim to visit Eileen, Sue's delightful mother, to have lunch in her garden listening to the Butcher bird's romantic calls.

At Maleny we visited Robbie and Grant, whose home on the hill looked out over the Glasshouse Mountains in the wide valley below. We had met them on their boat *Chimera* in Tonga the year before. The Glasshouse Mountains, marking the start of the Sunshine Coast, are a series of volcanic spires rising a thousand feet from the surrounding plain. It was said that Captain Cook named them as he sailed by on his voyage of discovery, because they reminded him of the glass furnaces in his native Yorkshire, in England. This area is home to the Whip bird, with its distinctive call. Many other birds were in full song around the Hammer's beautiful home. We were taken to visit the Kenilworth Forest and the Yaroomba Creek Park to listen to the Bell Birds and to see the Lewin's Honey Eaters. It was here that Christine first heard the Celtic harp being played by Robbie, to the accompaniment of the bird song in the forest. This led her to have an unwavering desire to play the harp one day.

myself, Robbie and Grant
with the Glasshouse Mts.

After a wonderful visit we moved on to Gympie to visit its Gold Mining museum. Then on through Bample where, in 1876, the macadamia nut was first cultivated commercially. We called on Bob, VK4WRB, who lived in Maryborough, another of Christine's favourite voices on the air. On to Hervey Bay where more of our cruising friends were moored, including Bill and Robyn on *Ramtha.*

Cyclone Justin moved inland just north of Cairns causing total havoc in its wake, and yielding twenty four hours of heavy rain at its fringes.

In Bundeberg, it continued raining. For four days it poured without sign of a let up. Finally the weather cleared and we drove through fields of sugar cane to visit Pat and Arthur, friends of neighbours of ours at home, who invited us to stay. We played tennis, and lolled in their most welcome swimming pool which was surrounded by tropical flowers and bushes.

Some friends in Melbourne had insisted we visit and stay at their holiday cottage in the quaintly named village of 1770. This lovely hideaway is a piece of paradise, looking out over the bay below, and surrounded by exotic shade trees of all types. Regular visitors were a flock of Rainbow Lorikeets and Blue Faced Honeyeaters. They just loved the bread that we soaked in honey and left on the bird feeder. It was so hot we slept out on the verandah under mosquito netting, enjoying the cool breeze off the bay at night. Many types of fern and orchid graced their garden as I looked up the origin of the village's name. Captain Cook of course. He anchored his ship the *Endeavour* here on May 24th, 1770. It was his first landing in Queensland as he made his way up the coast.

Rainbow Lorikeets

All things come to an end. Four months after setting out, we were a lot more familiar with Australia and its people. We had met with unfailing hospitality and consideration everywhere in this magnificent country. *Demelza* was safe and untouched on our return.

The Gladstone boatyard was just as dirty as boatyards can be anywhere. Dozens of cruising boats were stored in rows on dry land in the heat. Their owners were either away or busily completing repair or maintenance work. Although the boatyard offered all the skills needed to complete specialty work, pinning staff down to a specific date proved to be totally impossible.

Our reunion with Betty and Neville in *Wranglers'* welcome shade from the afternoon's heat, with a cooling gin and tonic in our hands, was a merry affair. We exchanged stories of the past four months. *Demelza*'s bilge was full of rainwater, due to a leak around the foot of the mast. Otherwise she seemed fine and fortunately the water had not been enough to affect her wiring.

Having obtained the required six month Certificates of Worthiness for the campervan, during which time Christine had done a wonderful job of cleaning up and I had repaired the odd breakage, we put a "For Sale" sign on the notice board in the marina. Boat work commenced. I ordered a new genoa from Ullman's in Brisbane, and a new Australian furling system from a firm in Airlie Beach. I asked the boatyard to install the appropriate new forestay and fitting for the furler. It was becoming more and more difficult to rejuvenate *Demelza*'s green gel coated hull which had bleached out in the tropical sun. However, as usual, there was plenty of advice available from all comers. The cheapest suggested remedy was to wipe down the cleaned hull with dilute oxalic acid, then wash it before rubbing on Penetrol which is a very light penetrating oil. This works well for a while, but treatment had to be repeated.

Gradually we put back everything that had been stored below to above deck, and transferred all our gear from the van back to the boat. By now there were five boats working hard by day and socializing in the evenings, namely Betty and Neville on *Wrangler*, John and Leila on *Serenity*, Mathew and Linda on *Bohemia*, David on *Alice Colleen* and *Demelza*. We became a regular and cheerful group each evening, as we assembled below one boat or another. One feature of the sunset in Gladstone was the nightly migration of thousands of fruit bats flying to roost on nearby islands. The sky was darkened by the sheer number of them as they passed over us.

The bottom of the boat was cleaned and painted, the head taken out and encouraged with some new parts, and all its pipes cleaned out. Christine polished the outside of the hull which, after treatment, had regained a lot of its lovely forest green colouring.

The first snag arose with the arrival of the furler. The boatyard had cut the forestay wire to length, but it would not feed down the foil. Repeated phone calls to the foil's manufacturer ensued. Eventually they agreed to send replacement sections for the parts of the foil giving trouble. The second problem was that a stainless steel rod for attaching the forestay to the boat's stem had been wrongly machined by the boatyard. We couldn't tighten the forestay sufficiently. Back it went to the shop for a second try.

The next concern arose after the obligatory testing of *Wranglers*' life raft led to it being condemned. It had rotted in its deck container due to salt water wicking up the line securing it to the deck. Knowing we also had to have ours inspected, we took it in with some trepidation. Ours had been routinely kept in a valise inside the boat. The Aussie inspector later called it the oldest life raft he had ever passed. This outcome could have been helped by Christine's reaction when we had presented it at the store for inspection

"With a raft that old," he'd said "the best thing to do is put a knife through it before buying a new one."

"That is such a stupid attitude," said Christine huffily, "just test it like any other."

In the event, in spite of having been blown it up to twice the required pressure, it had remained intact, much to our relief and his surprise.

Next I replaced *Demelza*'s electric bilge pump. The original seemed to take forever to clear out the bilge in spite of my having cleaned its screens and otherwise encouraged it to perform.

Two more essential jobs were to acquire a set of charts for the east coast north to Cape York and across to Darwin, and secondly to launder curtains, seat covers and all washable fittings.

The Chaplain of the Australian Armed Services, conducting the Anzac Day service, defined the word *mateship* as "love with its sleeves rolled up" to which we could both relate very well.

The new genoa hadn't arrived, and a on the third attempt, the forestay still didn't fit. The continuing frustration over this in the prevailing heat made life difficult. As usual at times like this, the cruising fraternity rallied around in support, providing the right diversion in the evenings.

Our friends John and Muriel appeared with their motor home on their way north to Port Douglas and were an immense help with jobs around the boat. Muriel helped Christine paint courtesy flags for South Africa, Trinidad, Tobago and Madagascar, as John and I replaced frayed running rigging. We arranged to meet up in Port Douglas in a few weeks as we sailed northwards.

Finally we received an offer on the campervan from Bill on *Sincerity* which we were pleased to accept. To make life even better, the new genoa arrived. We celebrated with a supper put on by John and Leila on *Tranquility*. All the cruisers in the yard came and, as she was a Tayana 55, there was plenty of room.

At last the forestay with its altered attachment arrived. Everybody in the boatyard was there to see it assembled as we successfully raised it into position. However, the jobs were never ending. We had sent our laptop for repair before leaving on our tour of Australia in the van, but it had not yet been returned. We finally received a message that it was on its way. The trace we had put on finally disclosed that it had arrived in Sydney from Vancouver, but was completing the journey by bus, which would take another four days. Some courier service!

Our RAC Queensland insurance rebate would not arrive for a month, by which time we would be long gone, so we arranged to receive it in Darwin. Mail had to be sent, along with our sailing plans, to family and friends at home.

Tracy, our cheerful Customs Officer, came for tea on *Demelza*. We heard that a Canadian boat had arrived from New Zealand without the necessary visa documents, and had been fined two thousand Australian dollars.

Time was passing. Many of our friends had already left for Cape York, while we were waiting for our computer. Five days after arriving in Sydney, and already nine days late, it finally arrived in Gladstone. Eagerly I fired it up to get a weather picture. NOTHING HAPPENED! I was speechless.

It was time to leave. Tracy brought all the necessary papers to the boat, saying she would tell her departmental folks up the coast that *Demelza* was on her way. Again, sad farewells to all the friends and staff who had made us so welcome in Australia and who had kept an eye on the boat while we were away. We were leaving all that was familiar, and heading out into the unknown once more.

Hamilton Island

CHAPTER 13
The Great Barrier Reef — In Captain Cook's wake

The time had come for us to start sailing up the length of the Great Barrier Reef towards Cape York. On 7th May at 0900 hrs, we slipped our moorings in Gladstone to motor out of the boat harbour. Two hours before high tide, the passage through the North Channel was well marked by day markers. On top of these, ospreys were nesting, and they eyed us as we carefully negotiated the narrow channel through Pelican Banks

Soon we were abreast of Cape Capricorn, on the Tropic of Capricorn, heading for the Whitsunday Islands. In the evening sky, the Halle comet was clearly visible over the western horizon as we worked our way north in ten knots of breeze and smooth seas. Passing to the west of Great Keppel Island, with its large resort and tourist traffic, we passed Cape Townshend to port, where we met some tidal action. The weather turned squally, with rain and unpredictable winds from the south pushing us along. We had to keep an eye out for the considerable coastal shipping passing us in the narrow passages.

Captain James Cook in the *Endeavour*, having passed the Keppel Islands and after rounding Cape Townshend on his way north in May 1770, dropped anchor in Thirsty Sound to fill up with water. He found none. On 3rd June he had reached Repulse Bay, just south of the Whitsunday Islands, where they needed maintenance and repair.

The whole area of the Capricorn coast is littered with small islands, and is a favourite cruising ground for local boaters. We passed MacKay, with its large sugar exporting harbour which is notorious for its incessant surge.

After two days of continuous sailing we arrived at Shaw Island off the southern end of the Whitsunday Island Group, two hundred and eighty nautical miles from Gladstone. As we sat sipping a glass of wine in the sunset, we were happy to be joined by Neville and Betty on *Wrangler*, who were also heading northward towards Cape York. They had a date with the "Over the Top Rally" which was starting from Gove in three weeks time. That night the wind in the anchorage increased and by the following morning had risen to thirty knots. I kept letting out more anchor chain in response to this onslaught. The anchor held well for the two days we were there.

We sailed off to Hamilton Island, arriving in calm weather. We passed the commercial jet airport runway which had been constructed from the dredging of the harbour by the island's owner/developer Keith Williams, to whom we were later introduced. The resort on the island was opened in 1984 and was the catalyst for upgrading all the many other resorts in the Whitsunday Islands. Its resort is a small village, with all the businesses run by concessionaires.

We were greeted by Graham who was a longstanding Mediterranean cruising friend of mutual friends, Peter and Monica, from home. Peter was my offshore cruising mentor of "keep it simple Hugh," fame. Graham was most hospitable to us and to the crew of Wrangler. He opened his condominium home to us. This had panoramic views of Mosquito Pass below its balcony. He lent us his electric golf cart, the only type of vehicle allowed on this lovely tropical island, so that we could see the sights. He also donated an invaluable set of charts of North Australian waters for our use on *Demelza.*

Graham advises on cruising the Great Barrier Reef

After an enjoyable two day visit, we continued our travels stopping at Hook Island, the northernmost large island in the group, to anchor in Nara Inlet. Here we met up with a lot of boats who had left Gladstone before us, and who had dawdled their way up the coast exploring some of the hundreds of islands on their way. The weather deteriorated with heavy rain and strong wind. Eagles were soaring over the long inlet, making use of the updraft from its steep sides, as we bounced about in the considerable swell that found its way into the bay.

On Whit Sunday, in June 1770, Captain Cook found his way through this group of islands using what is now called Whitsunday Passage. Ten days after leaving Thirsty Sound, he was still desperate for water, and decided to stop just north of Cape Grafton near Cairns to visit the site on which Cairns now stands.

We felt the need to press on. Almost simultaneously the rain stopped, and the wind dropped giving us a pleasurable downwind sail. One of our two GPSs decided to quit at this stage, so we hauled out the spare. We needed to know where we were among all the reefs. In twenty four hours we had reached Townsville. Betty and Neville had arrived before us. They had just slept for twenty four hours to recover from a rough passage during which, owing to their accidentally having left a hatch open, seas breaking over their boat had soaked everything inside. What made Neville so mad was that his smart new shoes were now acquiring a coat of green mold.

Townsville, the fourth largest city in Queensland, was founded in 1864. Magnetic Island, which lies just offshore, was named by Captain Cook because he was quite concerned that the problems with his compass were caused by the island. We engaged a local sail maker to come down to the boat to find out why our Australian made furling genoa was not working properly. He soon diagnosed the problem. The sail was ten inches too tall! After removing it from our forestay he took it to his sail loft, during which time we explored the town. We enjoyed their weekly market, held in the main street, and had a delicious lunch at a local restaurant, the balcony of which overlooked the busy street below. After lunch we puffed our way to the top of the tall hill behind the town, from which we had a magnificent view of the ocean and reefs. Later we stocked up with food, drink and water ready for the next leg of our journey.

The wind was so light as we sailed up to Orpheus Island in the Palm Group, that a butterfly overtook us quite easily. Past Rattlesnake Island Bombing Range and into Pioneer Bay where we anchored for the night watching a full moon set behind Hinchinbrook Island. On this island, granite mountains rise dramatically from the sea, and the surrounding terrain is unspoilt wilderness and very popular with hikers. The following day we anchored off Cape Richards on Hinchinbrook Island's north coast, where a Coast Watch plane made a sweep over us, asking for our boat's name and destination on the VHF radio.

We sailed onwards to Dunk Island with a helpful westerly breeze off the land. Here we went ashore to explore the resort and to get some aerobic exercise walking around its many trails. It was here that EJ Banfield lived from 1897 to 1923, during which time he wrote the book *The Confessions of a Beachcomber.*

Next we visited Fitzroy Island which took twelve hours of sailing to cover sixty two miles in perfect weather. Another coast watch plane flew over at masthead height, and we went through the same procedure as before. After a night's sleep we crossed to Cairns, where we tied up to pilings in the river, and rowed ashore to introduce ourselves at the Yacht Club. During the morning I had noticed that our alternator was not putting a consistent charge into our batteries. So, on arrival, we arranged to meet Theo the local electrician, who appeared after lunch to take our alternator off to his shop to replace its windings.

Cairns river moorage

Captain Cook had left Cape Grafton at night and had sailed into Trinity Bay, the extreme northerly point of which he called Cape Tribulation. It was off that point that all his troubles began. On a bright moonlit night he set a north easterly course to get into deeper water, and was dismayed to observe that the depth fell from twenty one fathoms to eight. By 2200 hrs he again had twenty one fathoms. But, a few minutes past 2300 hrs, *Endeavour* struck a reef and stuck fast. This reef is now called Endeavour Reef. They had anything from three feet to four fathoms of water around them, with about twelve fathoms a ship's length to starboard. He put an anchor and chain over *Endeavour's* stern to pull her off, but to no avail. Unfortunately they had gone aground at high tide, so the only thing to do was to lighten the ship by throwing cargo overboard. Their guns, iron and stone ballast, hoops, staves and oil jars were jettisoned. At 1100 hrs the next morning, at high water, they were still a foot short of water to float her off in spite of lightening the ship by forty tons. As the tide fell, the ship began to leak, and there was as much water coming in as two pumps could handle. For twenty four hours the seas were flat calm as she lay beached. By 1700 hrs the next day, three pumps were hard pressed to keep up. They had deployed two large anchors off the stern. A fourth pump failed to work. By 2030 hrs water was pouring aboard, and the pumps could not keep up. After much heaving on the anchor they managed to refloat *Endeavour* at 2100 hrs that night, with much water still in her holds. Continuing to pump, they found an error had been made in measuring the amount of water in the holds, making it look as though things were much worse than they actually were. By 0800 hrs the next day, the pumps were gaining the upper hand. They pulled up what anchors they could, abandoning the ones they could not, and headed for land. They sailed past Hope Islands, which they had been hoping against hope to reach before the ship foundered. To help keep the ship afloat, the crew lathered a sail with chopped wool and oakum before spreading horse dung over it. The sail was hauled down over the side and under the hull, to help seal the leaks. The oakum and dung came off the sail underwater, sealing the holes in the hull.

After anchoring Endeavour two miles offshore for the night among shoals, one of the ships boats reported finding a harbour with enough water depth for them to enter. However before they could get in, a gale blew up. Captain Cook decided to stay anchored out. For two days they waited out the gale, fearful that if they raised the anchor they might get stuck on the surrounding shoals. Eventually they took up anchor and sailed into the harbour hitting bottom twice on the way into what is now Cooktown. Here *Endeavour* remained for seven weeks. While repairing the ship, they had their first contact with the indigenous people of the area. During this time survey crews had established that the waters off Cooktown were riddled with reefs, concluding that there was no safe passage north.

For our part, our visit to Cairns was much more enjoyable. We rented a car and drove to the Kuranda Railway station for a train ride up into the Atherton Tablelands for the day. On our return trip we came down by Sky Train in a gondola riding above the canopy of the rain forest. Another memorable visit was to the Royal Flying Doctor Service museum learning about the history of medical care in the early days of European settlement.

Early days with the Flying Doctor Service

It took us seven hours of easy sailing to reach Port Douglas, arriving in the middle of Carnival Week celebrations. As if by some strange coincidence, while transiting Captain Cook's reefs, our depth sounder malfunctioned. In spite of great encouragement it would not come back to life. The following day John and I bought a Fish finder depth sounder to replace our non functional one. We spent many hours installing it. We sprayed our mainsail track with Teflon and taped the ends of the spreaders whose boots had rotted in the sun. With these jobs successfully completed, we took a day off to visit friends Hilary and Laurie. They took us up to Mossman Gorge on the Daintree River for a picnic, and then on to the five star Silky Oaks Resort, where we could just about afford tea.

Again we prepared the boat to leave after a busy week with wonderful friends, and left port in rain and under grey skies the following day. The new depth sounder worked well, and showed us fish under the boat on its display. As there was little wind, we had to motor to Cape Tribulation where we anchored for the night not wishing to motor all the way to Cape York.

Sailing the Queensland Coast

In the morning we sailed around Cape Tribulation and in a lovely fifteen knot wind. Then suddenly our steering jammed. Going around in circles caused chaos with the sails until I hauled them down. All the mechanics of our wheel steering was located in the "hell hole," the only access to which is through a cockpit locker. So, as the boat slewed from side to side in the running swell, we emptied the contents of the big cockpit locker into the pilothouse. I disappeared headfirst into the bowels of *Demelza* to investigate the problem. Feeling rather queasy, I could see nothing that would account for the problem. While all this was going on, a very large coastal steamer was bearing down on us.

"Darling," I said "Can you get on the radio and see if you can raise that fellow. Tell him we have lost our steerage and to please stay clear."

Sure enough Christine was able to raise him.

"He's asked if there is anything he can do to help?" called Christine

"Not at the moment, thank you." she told the ship's radio operator.

"We'll stand by to see if you need assistance." he replied.

"That's mighty decent of him." I said.

He'd stopped the ship, coming to rest about half a mile distant from us.

Meanwhile my search went on, mostly in the upside down position in the cockpit locker. I really didn't feel too good, but as I came up for air, I had a brainwave.

A visit to the Hell Hole

"It's got to be something in the pedestal." I said, and immediately set to, taking out the main compass to gain access. Bits were everywhere, sashaying about in the swell. Lo and behold there in the pedestal was a loose brake pad blocking any movement of the wheel. Easily removed, the steering was restored, as we hoisted the jib.

"Thank you for standing by." said Christine over the radio "We are now under control and the steering is fine."

"Good on you" came the reply, "G'day."

"What amazing courtesy." I said as we resumed our course northward. After all that excitement, we finished our fifty nautical mile journey to Lizard Island in ten hours.

At Cape Direction, Captain Cook was travelling north outside the Great Barrier Reef thinking he was clear of all danger, with open sea ahead of him as he approached Cape Flattery. That was until he went up the mast and saw breaking seas all around. He anchored about a mile offshore then rowed to an island, climbing to high ground from which to view the reefs. This spot he called Point Lookout. Moving slowly northward he again could not see his way clear to proceed, so he decided to row a boat to Lizard Island, the highest island in the area, to climb to what is now called "Cooks Look." The haze was too thick for a good view, so they had to spend the night on the island. The following day he was able to see a clear passage between the reefs off Cape Flattery toward some low islands five miles distant. However, on his way back to the ship, he found an alternative channel on the west side of Lizard Island. This he followed in Endeavour to the open ocean where he was finally out of the reefs' grip.

Being entangled with life threatening reefs for two and a half months, his crew felt relief at being out in the ocean once more. Cook felt badly that he was unable to explore close to the shore which he was convinced was not joined to New Guinea, as was then generally believed. Because of this he decided to go in again towards land as soon as it was safe to do so. In the meantime, being out in the swells had increased *Endeavour,s* leaks considerably.

They proceeded on a northwesterly course to close up to land again fearing that they might miss the gap Cook thought separated Australia from New Guinea. After a full day's sailing, they spied land from the top of the mast and soon afterwards saw breakers between themselves and the land, extending far to the south and to the north, with a small gap between.

As they approached this gap from the ocean the wind died. The breakers on the reef were only a mile away, and they were being swept towards them. With the help of a tow from their small boats, they were able to swing *Endeavour's* bow away from the reef. By 1800 hrs they were only one hundred yards from the breakers and were becalmed in one hundred and twenty fathoms of water, too deep for them to drop an anchor to keep them off the reef. Just then a wisp of breeze passed over them. They again spotted the gap in the reef, one ship's length wide, a quarter of a mile ahead. This was their only hope of escape. With the tide ebbing out through the gap in the reef, the ship was washed past the opening without getting through it. Another gap, a mile wide, appeared ahead of them and, as the tide had turned, they were washed out to sea through it. This gap is now called Providential Channel located off Cape Weymouth.

At the Marine Research Station on Lizard Island we saw a video on the devastation being caused to the Great Barrier Reef by an infestation of the Crown of Thorns Starfish. On our walk back to the beach we saw a Monitor lizard, from which the island takes its name.

Leaving Lizard Island at 0700 hrs we had a magnificent sail to Cape Melville, blowing twenty-five knots for our sixty five nautical mile trip. This cape is a mountain of giant boulders, left over from the last ice age. During the night we had gusts of forty five knots funneling down its steep sides. Our anchor held fast. The area around was totally deserted, an awesomely isolated place. By 0630 hrs we'd had enough, so with gusts blowing across Bathurst Bay, we sailed to the Fly Channel in the Flinders Island Group. Here we anchored in Owen Channel, where the anchorage was totally calm. Aching for a cup of coffee, the solenoid on the stove decided not to switch on the propane. Later we found that this had been caused by a poor electrical contact. From here onwards our laptop computer had decided it would print weather fax pictures again, which was a great comfort on this lonely coast.

The sailing from Owen Channel to Morris Island was exceptionally good. We sailed past Cape Direction, which had a strobe light on it where none was shown on our charts but finally seeing the light on Cape Weymouth. Sailing conditions were good so we kept going past Portland Roads and around Cape Grenville to anchor in sheltered Shelburne Bay. Silica sand dunes shone brightly ashore. Sand bars out in the bay calmed the rollers coming in, giving us a quiet anchorage. Crossing Benman Shoal into the bay we had given ourselves a fright, as there was only one foot of water under the keel, where our cruising guide had said "plenty of water for the average yacht at low tide."

We anchored in twelve feet of water as close to shore as we dared, to get out of the residual swell. *Southern Voyager* passed close by after we had anchored, handing us some mackerel that they had just caught. As we sipped drinks in the evening light, we overheard the following radio conversation between two sailing vessels and a large container ship at sea

Ship: "This is the container ship (name), southbound past (name) reef. May we pass you green to green?"

Yacht: "Just a minute, I'll tighten up a bit."

Pause.

Ship: "This is the container ship (name). I am not familiar with your nautical terminology. Can you explain 'tighten up a bit'?"

Another pause.

Yacht: "Sure, I'm happy to do red to red." said a newly awakened male voice.

Ship: "Well now, I have one yacht green to green and one yacht red to red. What you like we do?"

Ultimately, the container ship veered off fifteen degrees to avoid any chance of a collision with either yacht.

Gradually more yachts joined us in the bay until there were nine anchored along the shore. A huge high pressure system was building in the Australian Bight, which was always a prelude to strong reinforced trade winds covering all Australian waters. Sure enough on the next day, the wind began to rise. We all stayed where we were, and enjoyed a chance to relax and catch up on some reading. Some of the crews went ashore to play *Petanque* (bowls) on the hard sandy beach. Christine joined them and a hilarious time was had by all. The beach was of firmly packed sand with ridges, so the game was most unpredictable. On top of this we had been warned that crocodiles could appear at any time which would send all and sundry flying for their dinghies.

For my part, I spent the hot afternoon trying to expose the engine's water pump, to find out why it was dripping. On her return aboard *Demelza*, Christine kneaded the dough that she had had rising, and soon the gorgeous smell of baking bread filled the boat. By the third day the wind had dropped, though the forecast was for thirty knots. Several of the boats left to get around Cape York. Meanwhile I replaced the packing on the backing plate of the disassembled water pump.

Christine signed on to the Australian Travelers Net on the radio. The reporting of positions on this net was from people travelling on land throughout Australia, giving their locations each night. We were the only boat and later found, on arrival in Darwin, that our journey had become an item of interest each day, especially for those crossing the dry, dusty Outback. A typical report from an inland traveler would be "This is (name) and (name) from water hole 153. We will be staying here for 1 plus 1," meaning they would be there for two days. Christine announcing our Latitude and Longitude and sailing conditions must have sounded very strange to these landlubbers.

The weather settled. On the evening of the fourth day we, along with Paula and Vigo on *Marijke* from Alaska, decided to continue heading north. After sailing through the night we turned into the narrow Albany Channel and were flushed through it on the flooding tide. We sailed in calm water around Cape York, before anchoring off a wide but sheltered beach. After going ashore, we walked over sticky silt to reach the isolated Bamaga Resort, situated in a most attractive rain forest. We were offered cool drinks on their verandah and were regaled with horrific tales of enormous crocodiles lurking nearby. The resort was being run by the local aboriginal tribe. They kindly offered the use of their radio telephone to phone ahead to Darwin to book a berth for us in the marina. We enjoyed walking around this area, clambering onto the rocky, "most northern place in Australia," Cape York. We saw the most enormous ant hills, possibly twelve or more feet high, and lovely tropical trees and vegetation. On Possession Island, close to Cape York, Captain Cook had claimed the east coast of Australia for England in 1770.

Approaching Cape York

Into the Torres Straits we sailed, entering a new set of waypoints into the GPS for crossing the Gulf of Carpenteria to Darwin. We stored away all the charts for the East Coast of Australia and brought out the ones for the North Coast that Graham had given us in Hamilton Island. Our weather forecasts were now coming from Darwin, and they reissued the thirty knot warning for the Gulf of Carpentaria. A boat, already crossing the Gulf, reported they were in thirty-five knots with "ugly conditions." So we, and our friends on *Marijke*, decided to take a day or two to visit nearby Thursday Island.

Paula and Vigo

Thursday Island is one of the Torres Strait Island Group. Seventy in number, they stretch from Cape York in the south almost to New Guinea in the north. The islanders originally came from Melanesia and Polynesia about two thousand years ago. Headhunters, pirates, blackbirders and bands of Japanese pearlers contributed to the island's violent past.

Crossing the rapidly flowing channel on the way to Thursday Island, we had a brisk and wet sail. A huge tide bore us over towards Horn Island. We had to keep checking our position every few minutes. The buoy on Scott Reef had been carried away, so we were glad to have left that area safely behind before reaching a sheltered anchorage off Horn Island. The following morning, we dinghied over to the ferry dock. For $4 Australian were whisked away on the fifteen minute ride to Thursday Island. This community is small and friendly with the luxury of paved roads. The Customs Officers, housed in a lovely old colonial building, told us that Tracy in Gladstone had told them we would be in the area. Good quality hand painted woodcraft, sea shells and paintings were on display in the Community Art Gallery. We walked through rolling fields to visit a World War Two fort, built to defend the island from an expected Japanese invasion that never materialized. Plumeria trees decorate the Japanese cemetery, which contains the remains of two thousand Japanese pearl divers, evidence of the dangerous nature of this occupation in those early days.

On the return ferry trip to Horn Island, we joined up with a group of Queensland Cabinet Ministers who were on an official visit to the area. I had a chance to talk health and politics with the Minister of Health and Local Affairs.

A knock on *Demelza*'s hull that evening revealed Jim, whom we had met in Southport, Queensland during our campervan tour. He was anchored in the bay on a huge power boat called *Idle Wize*, which was on its way to Darwin. Her owner, Erroll, was to be the Communications Officer for the upcoming Darwin to Ambon (Indonesia) yacht race. Erroll's regular job ashore was lockmaster in Darwin, through which we would have to pass to get into the Darwin marina.

After a most interesting week in the Torres Islands we, and three other yachts, left to cross the Gulf of Carpentaria, in spite of a high pressure system that was well established in the Great Australian Bight. Why? Because the other boats, all much bigger than *Demelza*, had decided to go and had persuaded us, against my better judgment, to go with them. It was a seventeen hour crossing to the Wessel Islands with winds of thirty-five to forty knots, incredibly steep seas, several of which we took on board. One lifted us bodily from one spot, to deposit us in another, with a resounding crash. Throughout this turmoil, our wind vane kept us on a steady course, while we observed for most of the night from inside the pilothouse.

We arrived at the deserted Wessel Islands in a maelstrom and, although it was dark, decided we could find our way by radar into a sheltered bay. With an excellent chart, and a copy of John Knight's book on Northern Australia, we convinced ourselves that going into that remote anchorage in a storm was preferable to staying out in the chaos waiting for daylight. In the lee of the island we found the entrance to Marchinbar Island anchorage, and picked our way very slowly into it's apparently hazard free water. To the accompaniment of screaming wind but a completely flat sea, we dropped anchor, turned in, and slept.

In the morning we were surprised to find that the island was only twenty feet above water, with no trees and completely flat land. We could almost see over it. The forecast was for more gales. For three days we sheltered. On the second night we were having supper when Christine looked out

"There's a light out there," she said.

We opened the hatch cover and peered out into the tempest. There, very faintly, we could see a dim light.

"It must be a boat coming in for shelter."

"I'll put on all our nav. lights." I said.

Gradually the dim lights came closer until the boat stopped and we heard a splash as their anchor dropped into the water.

The following morning there was a tap on the hull.

"I've just come over to thank you for putting on your lights for us last night," the young man said. We learned they too had had a rough time in the Gulf.

On July 1st we left our bay with a good forecast. It was two hundred and twenty six nautical miles to Cape Cockburn and we were moving along at just over seven knots under main and jib. The sky was blue, the water rippled. We could hardly believe the contrast with the previous days.

"Let's hope we never have a trip like that again." Christine commented.

"I agree," I said "We should never leave until we are comfortable with the weather." We lazed about in the sun, listening to the radio and recouping our energy.

At that point the plug for the trolling generator shorted out. The fitting was outside the cockpit coaming and, like everything else, had been soaked regularly with sea water. Rather than have to repeat its repair several times, I decided to relocate the plug to a spot inside one of the cockpit lockers.

The wind was getting up again after a day of respite, and by seven the next morning we were taking a reef in the mainsail. The waves were again steep and choppy, throwing a lot of spray about. Everything we touched was encrusted with salt. At midnight we put into Malay Bay on Croker Island, where peace reigned for the rest of the night.

In the early morning, the wind had disappeared so we motored out toward the wide Bowen Strait, hoping that the ebb tide would remain in our favour. The Strait was about fifteen nautical miles long. On entry, we found ourselves being whisked along at six and a half knots toward Point Danger at the end of the Cobourg Peninsula. We put into Alcaro Bay with Cape Don and its distinctive tall pink lighthouse in the distance. At midnight we again caught the tide and, in the absence of any wind, motored all the way to the Vernon Islands. As the night went on we saw many lights moving along fairly briskly in the same direction that we were traveling. Two small naval vessels were escorting a battered, rusty, small coastal steamer which bore no lights. We later learned that the boat was probably full of Indonesian refugees seeking asylum in Australia. These boats were usually equipped with the very best engines. The owners charged refugees a lot of money for the chance of freedom in Australia.

In the morning we noticed the water had changed colour to a soft green. Low, pale looking islands surrounded us. Off Cape Hotham we had the suggestion of a breeze before it died again. However we were covering the ground at eight knots in the tide. It was forty nautical miles to Darwin, and we had to motor all the way across Van Diemen's Gulf on totally flat water. We dropped anchor way out from Darwin's foreshore in Fannie Bay because of an extensive mud flat projecting out to sea.

The British thought the Dutch or French might get a foothold here in the 1820s, so they built two forts, Fort Dundas on Melville Island and Fort Wellington on the Cobourg Peninsula. By the 1850s these forts had been abandoned. Darwin was founded, after many false starts, in 1869. The harbour had been discovered by the *Beagle* in 1839 and named after Charles Darwin. The city is affected by the occasional cyclone and during World War II was attacked by the Japanese sixty four times.

On radioing the Cullen Bay Lockmaster, he confirmed that our berth in the marina was available. We made arrangements to arrive at his lock gates the following afternoon. At the appointed time we entered the locks and were raised twenty feet into the marina pool. The facilities in the marina were top quality, so the first place of call was the laundry. Here we met the lady running it, whose husband was one of Australia's top competitive sailors. He was on his way to Cowes week and the Fastnet Race in England.

Entering Cullen Bay Locks

While berthed in the marina we had several visitors to *Demelza* who had heard of our journey on the Australian Travellers Net and had come to say "G'day!" Many cruising friends had already arrived. The Darwin Yacht Club was a meeting place for all of us, and many evenings were spent sharing stories of our experiences while overlooking the boats anchored in Fannie Bay, and watching the sun setting over the Indian Ocean. The marina was far from town, but a convenient bus service was available. Once in town, there were excellent shops and restaurants to satisfy all tastes and needs. Boat work resumed on *Demelza*, the first one being to replace the water pump, and to have the old one rebuilt as a spare.

By now we had decided to round South Africa rather than up the Red Sea to the Mediterranean. So we set about finding more charts for the Indian Ocean and

East African waters to supplement the ones we already had. I sold all the charts we were carrying of the North Indian Ocean, Red Sea and Mediterranean. We gave away the wonderful charts that Graham had given to us in Hamilton Island to a young Australian family who were heading back down to Queensland.

We paid a visit to the Traveller's Clinic in town to receive the shots we needed for Africa and a good supply of preventive pills against Malaria. On putting waypoints into the GPS, we realized that the distance from Darwin to the Seychelles was four thousand, four hundred and eighty nautical miles. As there would be no supplies on the way, we had to plan everything for the two months it would take us to get there including a short stop either at Cocos Keeling or Christmas Island.

The repaired automatic pilot was returned and appeared to work well. Of all the electrical gadgets aboard the cruising boats this was the one that gave the most trouble. The majority of bigger boats were using them continuously while making passages, whereas we were only using ours when there was insufficient wind to operate the wind vane.

After three busy, happy weeks in the heat of Darwin, all the boat jobs had been completed. The boat was restocked with food and drink. Water, fuel tanks and jugs were topped up. The boat was looking resplendent with its newly varnished woodwork. All systems were "go" as we reversed our transit through the lock into Fannie Bay for the last night before setting off into the Indian Ocean.

CHAPTER 14
Crossing the Indian Ocean

After clearing customs and spending a night at anchor with hundreds of other boats in Fannie Bay, we left on the following morning's tide under bright blue skies.

Later, in a strong breeze we managed to break three of the mainsail's slides on the mast doing a semi controlled gybe. Fortunately by the afternoon, the wind had settled down, and I was able to go on deck to install replacements. A Customs plane did his routine overflight.

"Green yacht heading out of Darwin," he called over our VHF Radio "Identify yourself, the number of people on board, and your destination."

"This is the Canadian yacht *Demelza*," replied Christine. "We have left Darwin, have two people on board, and are heading for Christmas Island."

"Thank you, *Demelza*," he replied as he swept over us at masthead height. "Have a good trip."

During the calm, hot days that followed we relaxed and tried to find our sea legs again. In talking to other cruising yachts in the area on the radio we found that we had met most of them at one time or another during our time in Australia. Hibernia and Ashmore Reefs were eighty nine miles ahead of us, and the Darwin to Ambon race had started. Indonesian fishing boats were working close by us on either side, which surprised us as international waters were many miles to the north.

Gradually the southeast trade winds resumed their welcome assistance at about fifteen knots. Each night the moon was rising later and getting smaller. After a week, we were averaging between six and seven knots over the ground, reaching an occasional nine knots when the wind piped up. With two reefs in the mainsail, we were still doing more than seven knots over the ground with the help of a sea current. Looking at our charts, we realized we were exactly half-way around the world from home.

On 30th July the wind rose and the seas became rough during the night. We lowered the mainsail and proceeded with the poled out jib alone, doing over six knots and rolling violently in huge swells. To the north of us we were passing Bali, and the tidal currents were agitating the sea quite considerably. Dolphins played around us in the darkness, and we could see their luminescent trails as they flashed through the water before surfacing with a "puff."

The next day the wind was still excellent and the sea had become less boisterous. We put up the staysail on the opposite side of the boat to the jib, and poled it out with our whisker pole.

That night, just after Christine had gone off watch, I was standing in the cockpit doing my three-sixty degree scan, when I realized I could see every detail on the boat. Looking up, there were no stars visible in the sky. It was as though there was an eerie daylight bathing us. I looked over the side of the boat, as she slipped quietly through the benign ocean, and realized that the water resembled a huge bowl of milk. The sea was glowing white all around us from horizon to horizon. Mustering up courage, I hustled down below, to gingerly poke Christine, who had only just gone to sleep after her six hour watch.

"Darling, come and look at this."

"Oh no," she said, "What is it?"

"I've no idea," I said "but you've just got to come and look." Poor Christine staggered out of her bunk and followed me topsides to look around, and was spellbound by the sight.

"Can you believe it?" I asked.

"What do you think it is?" she replied.

"I haven't any idea. Maybe we're passing over an undersea volcano."

In our wake, phosphorescence marked our track. But the white, glowing ocean was all around us, having nothing to do with the water being agitated. The phenomenon lasted for about an hour and then, just as suddenly as it had appeared, it disappeared as though a switch had been turned off. We later learned that such a phenomenon had been written up after being observed in the Persian Gulf. Called "bioluminescence," it is caused by microscopic organisms generating light. In the published Persian Gulf sighting, the luminosity had traveled in pulsating waves, whereas ours had been an even and an hour long steady illumination.

The wind moved to the Northeast as we approached a point two hundred and thirty six nautical miles from Christmas Island. The following day, as dawn broke, we saw the island on the horizon, and were surrounded by Frigate birds soaring above us on the morning breeze. Later, Gannets joined the fray above us, making their way out to sea to look for their breakfast. For the first time we saw red tailed Tropic birds, and that evening we observed a black skimmer swooping low over the surface of the settling sea. At noon we sailed into Flying Fish Cove on Christmas Island, where two other boats were already anchored. The bay is dominated by a huge gantry, used for loading cargo ships with the phosphate being mined on the island. All around us high cliffs surrounded the bay, and hundreds of birds circled overhead. Apartment blocks ring the shoreline housing the miners and their families. The bay is over one thousand feet deep, but fortunately there was one buoy still available in a small shallow area close to the beach. We tied to this to the accompanying call of the local muezzin. Our VHF radio sprang into life with a call from the Christmas Island Police. After we had settled, they came with the local Customs Officer and the Health Officer to clear us in.

Flying Fish Cove, Christmas Island

Confusion ensued, for although Christmas Island is Australian territory, we had passed through International waters so we had to check into Australia again. The problem with that was our Australian visa was for single entry, and as this was our second entry, it had expired. A bureaucratic nightmare indeed!

We went ashore the next morning at the invitation of the Chief of Police, to sort out the mess and to find a Laundromat. On our walk from the beach into town we passed an apartment block for Malay workers. Here we met a friendly woman who, after greeting us, informed us that there was no Laundromat on the island.

"Don't worry" she said. "I'll do your laundry, go into town, and call in for it on your way back to the boat."

The Chief of Police couldn't have been more cooperative, and solved the visa problem without any difficulty. The town consisted of a post office, a bank, and a Duty free shop where gin cost $13 Australian for a large bottle. We had lunch at the local café before walking back along the shore. On approaching the apartment block, we were fascinated to see all our washing hanging above the main road outside our new friend's second floor flat. After accepting a bottle of wine for her trouble, she offered to drive us on a tour of the limestone quarry where her husband worked, making bricks, cement and gravel. The phosphate plant is huge, and its phosphate is exported as fertilizer. One theory for its origin is that it was deposited over millions of years by marine animals prior to the island rising from the sea. Another is that it is the accumulation of millions of years of bird guano.

Our Laundry adorns the main street

In the local Naturalist Park, we learnt about the indigenous Abbot Booby bird, and the lovely Golden Bosun Tropic bird. On the following day we were taken to The Dales to view Hugh's waterfall, where thousands of crabs of all colours, scrabbled around among the moist roots of the forest eating all the forest litter, which kept the forest floor scrupulously clean.

After a cooling dip in the waterfall, we went to Martin's Point, where Red Footed Boobies eyed us as we made our way to the Blowholes. Here the incoming surf met immoveable limestone cliffs, into which it had carved huge caverns. These trapped the incoming water and, under great pressure from below, this water shot through holes high into the air with an explosive noise. Above all this tumult, and enveloped by the mist resulting from the blowholes, Malay fishermen deftly negotiated the sharp cliff's surface, casting their lines out into the crashing ocean.

The following day we were walking along the road to the resort and casino across the island, where we had been told we could have a swim and a really good lunch. A police car drew up beside us.

"G'day!" said the Chief of Police "Where are you off to? Can I give you a ride?"

Thankfully, we piled into the back of his very smart car, and were whisked off to the resort. Here we had coffee on the terrace watching a remarkable display of Frigate birds swooping down to the surface of the resort's swimming pool, to pick up a sip of fresh water before soaring up into the sky again, wheeling around, and doing it all over again. This went on all day and every day, no matter whether or not there was anybody in the pool. By some miracle they missed any swimmers. Christine later announced it was pretty scary having those large birds almost landing on her head as she swam about.

On the way back to *Demelza*, our reliable little two horse power outboard, that had served us so well, failed to start for the first time. Panic! As we wrestled with it on the beach, members of the island's Hash Harriers invited us to join them on their next run. We declined the run, but agreed to join the complementary walk the following day. We learnt that the Hash Harriers organization had its origins during the time British Forces were stationed in Arabia. The troops, to get their exercise, ran for miles over the desert in the heat of the day. On Christmas Island, a group of about fifty residents were involved. They made us very welcome, and we enjoyed an interesting walk following the runners. They left us far behind, but the party after all had returned was a lot of fun.

We topped up *Demelza*'s propane and diesel tanks, and posted all our mail before taking the local bus to the Chinese market. There we met friends who invited us to join them at the open air cinema, built as an amphitheatre looking out to sea. We sat on blankets on concrete seats and watched 'The English Patient' as the sun set over the Indian Ocean. Later, when the stars came out, their reflection on the sea created a magical tropical night.

Flying Fish Cove was open to the ocean swells, so we rigged the Flopper Stopper for the first time since buying it in California. After two days the halyard holding it up frayed under the tremendous strain to which it was exposed. After repairs, and using a heavier line, it dampened significantly the violent motion that the waves were creating.

After "checking out" with our friendly police chief and exchanging fond farewells with many of those ashore, we sailed out of the bay on 10th August. We had enjoyed ten days on this interesting small island. Two golden bosun birds sat on the water watching as we headed out to sea for the eighteen hundred and eighty three nautical mile trip to the Chagos Archipelago.

The weather picture south of us did not look very attractive, so we decided to stay north. The southeast trades were blowing consistently at between fifteen and twenty knots and, although the sea was lumpy, our progress was impressive. We were averaging one hundred and twenty nautical miles each day. At times the wind would drop at night, causing the boat to lurch from side to side on the large cross swells. This didn't give the crew a lot of sleep. Many of the boats that we had set out with from Darwin had called in at the Cocos Islands instead of Christmas Island and, although lovely, they had found everything very inconvenient. The anchorage was a long dinghy ride across open water for fuel and food.

During the next few nights we were plagued with many squalls. Our water tanks were full, and we had buckets of fresh water lining the cockpit getting in the way. At times the wind would rise suddenly, switching direction and strength, which made sailing tiring and slow. A huge bulk carrier two miles to starboard, on its way to Cape Town, volunteered that the weather pictures were good for the next two or three days and yes, we were clearly visible on his radar. At the current rate of progress as we crossed 90°E, south of Bangladesh, we estimated that we would arrive in Chagos in about ten days. It was at this point that our brand new, high tech, glued genoa developed a split.

"Do you know," Christine had said dreamily, looking up from her book, "I'm sure I can see daylight through the genny."

Sure enough, one of the glued seams had given way.

"We never should have listened to that fellow," I said "It's OK having a highly aerodynamic jib where the stitches don't get in the way of the free flow of air over the jib, but what's the use, if there's a thundering hole in the thing."

After railing against Aussie workmanship for a while, we rolled it up so not to worsen the situation. There were dark clouds and squalls north of us so we headed slightly south along latitude 8S. We had nine hundred and fifty nautical miles left to reach Chagos.

Squalls at sea

Our attempt at unfurling the genny to allow us to haul it down for repair was not a success in the agitated sea conditions. We were progressing quite satisfactorily under full mainsail and staysail poled out in perfect sailing conditions. Once over the ninety degree ridge on the sea bottom, the surface of the sea seemed to settle, making our progress much more comfortable. In the calmer water, we were able to hang the sun shower bag in the sun and enjoy fresh water showers using the water we had collected in the squalls. What luxury. It made all the difference to our frame of mind. On August 21st we were speeding downwind in twenty knots of wind under clear skies. This was perfect trade wind sailing. Our position each day was being noted by Roy, a ham operator in Perth, Australia, and being relayed home to Peter Thomas in Victoria. Our local weather fax pictures were of poor quality, so we tried to receive pictures from New Delhi. The battery charger plug for rechargeable batteries came apart at this point. We used these batteries for our cabin radios. So I attempted to fire up the propane soldering torch at sea for the first time. This was quite an exercise, serving up a few scorched fingers before the job was done.

Christine kept us well fed and cared for as we sped along below Sri Lanka in glorious Indian Ocean sailing weather. Just as we were relaxing and really enjoying our trip, there was a bang. The forestay had fallen down and was lying alongside the boat streaming in the water. Fortunately it was still attached at the bow. We were three hundred and seventy eight nautical miles shy of Chagos. Five days after we had furled the genny because of a split seam, the whole thing had collapsed into the sea. It happened in mid afternoon so we were able to lasso the trailing end to bring it all aboard. The forestay had broken at the top of the mast.

"Let's take two reefs in the main." I said "This will bring the headboard of the main down to the level of the upper spreader, which is opposite where the inner forestay and staysail are secured. Then we'll take a spare Kevlar halyard forward, and tie it down tightly to the top of the chain plate to support the mast."

Squalls teased us as evening approached, but finally we had secured everything as best we could and although not looking the prettiest boat afloat, we were still making good headway. We refilled our buckets with rainwater off the boom, filled our kettle and water jugs, and even did our laundry. The whole place was awash with rainwater. Huge seas threw us all around the boat, and working on deck was aggravating as I kept tripping over my anchored safety line. Strangely, after a lot of this rough sailing, we both slept well when off watch.

Other boats in the vicinity were quite anxious about how we could manage without the forestay. In fact, once the mast had been stabilized, we were fine. They offered to change course to rendezvous with us to offer assistance should it be required. We were touched by their concern but felt it wasn't necessary.

Stormy conditions generated fantastic cloud effects in the evening sky. Huge cumulus clouds towered all around us, a glowing mix of bright apricot, purple and navy. With three hundred and eighty one nautical miles to Chagos, we wished it would calm down a bit so that we could rest before arriving. Almost as though we had ordered it, the wind calmed and the seas went down sufficiently for us to bring down the main sail. Christine could repair some stitching that had chafed against the shrouds. No sooner had we finished and raised the sail than a huge squall was on top of us, sending us careering off toward Chagos.

One hundred and sixty one nautical miles from Chagos, with squalls all around us, we were roaring along one minute, and battling changing wind direction the next, soaked to the skin, and very cold. On the radio Tony in Kilifi, Kenya was as clear as a bell. He told us that they too had been experiencing rough weather. He offered to order a new forestay from West Marine, which we would be able to pick up in the Seychelles. We thought this was a great idea, and gave him all the details of the size and length of wire needed, and details of the fittings to accommodate our Isomat mast.

A passing ship going from Durban to Singapore, kindly passed on the latest weather forecast. It looked so stable in the maelstrom around us, and was soon gone over the horizon. After it had disappeared, the wind suddenly stopped and we sat with the sails slatting to and fro driving us insane. Unable to bear it any longer, I fired up the engine and we motored for several hours to get within fifty three nautical miles of the Chagos Archipelago.

The southeast trades filled in for the last stretch. We were making such good time, that we hoped to reach the outer anchorage before nightfall. Tony was coming in loud and clear on the shortwave radio, saying he had ordered the replacement forestay, and that it should be waiting for us in the Seychelles.

Approaching Chagos Archipelago

After a seventeen day passage we motored through the Ile de la Passe into the lagoon of the Saloman Atoll in Chagos. This is surrounded by atolls up to seventy feet high. We motored across to the anchorage off Ile Fouguet, where we slept for twelve hours. Peter, a South African, off a boat called *Folly* also in the anchorage, rowed over offering to help fix our forestay. He had arrived five days before us, and had heard of our dilemma on his radio.

As he and I began playing with the forestay the next morning, we were joined by two other men, Graham, one of Peter's crew, and Bart from *Sous le Vent*. Graham was up the mast in no time, and stayed up there for such a long time jury rigging the forestay back into place, sufficient to support the mast as far as the Seychelles. It was a tricky job and depended on wire clamps holding sufficiently well to take the tension.

"The problem is," he said on returning to the deck, "that there is no toggle at the top of the forestay, so all the bending of the wire was going on just below the swage fitting, until it broke."

"But the manuals all say a toggle is essential." I said, fretting because the Australian sail maker of aerodynamic fame was obviously just as bad a rigger as he was a sail maker.

Meanwhile Christine had been talking to a Dutch girl who was crewing on one of the boats in the bay. She had confided that she was so unhappy with the way she was being treated that she had decided to jump ship and hide on one of the atolls until her boat sailed away. Christine suggested we offer the girl a ride to the Seychelles on *Demelza*. This was agreed between our two boats so Tanya was thrilled.

A number of the boat crews in the anchorage met one evening on Diane and Bart's boat, *Sous le Vent*, to celebrate our thirty sixth wedding anniversary. What a happy occasion that was, and in such beautiful surroundings, a deserted atoll in the Indian Ocean.

One of the boats in the anchorage was a small Finnish boat, *Aku Anka* with Aria aboard. She happened to be a sail maker with an industrial sewing machine on board. She offered to triple stitch every seam of our glued, or rather unglued, new Australian genoa.

After much thought and several trips up our mast, we decided not to use the genoa until the forestay had been properly replaced, and only use the staysail and double reefed main. In the strong winds we had experienced for most of the time with this rig, we expected to make good progress, at lesser risk.

Tanya moved aboard *Demelza*, and before long we realized that we had acquired a willing and competent cook.

"I haven't any money," she said, 'But may I do all the cooking?" Christine beamed with pleasure.

Sure enough the morning after she had moved aboard, we woke to the smell of porridge cooking on the stove. Ah heaven!

A few other boats in the anchorage were from South Africa, and when we met for evening BBQs on the beach, we had a chance to pick their brains about sailing down the East African coast to Cape Town. Most of the boats leaving Australia were going up the Red Sea into the Mediterranean and had taken the northern route through Indonesia and Sri Lanka.

Christine made a tracing of Kilifi Creek in Kenya from one the other boat's charts because that was where we planned to leave our boat, before flying home for a visit to the family during the upcoming hurricane season.

One worry, as Tanya transferred to our boat, was that her bedding and clothes might contain cockroaches or their eggs. Her previous boat had been infested with them. She took all her possessions ashore and spent a whole day washing them thoroughly before hanging them out to dry in the hot sun. It must have worked because we continued to be free of this pest on *Demelza* for the rest of the passage.

The beaches on the atolls are pristine white, with overhanging palms. They are a typical picture of tropical islands in the sun. As there were plenty of empty sea shells on the beach, Christine was in her element picking up samples of those she did not already possess. Fairy terns were everywhere, being most upset if we approached their nests. The other common bird was the White Capped Noddy.

Demelza anchored off pristine beach

One morning, as Tanya was busily baking bread listening to the radio, we heard of the death of Princess Diana. What a shock. It reminded us of the world beyond, with all its joys and sadness, making us feel very isolated.

After a few days we raised the anchor, motored carefully across the coral infested lagoon, to Boddam Island, where there was said to be a plentiful supply of fresh water in a well. This had been used to supply the village before it had been evacuated. The Chagos Archipelago, part of the Ocean Territory of the British Isles, had been evacuated of its three hundred Indonesian residents when the British leased one of the atolls, Diego Garcia, to the Americans as a naval base in the Indian Ocean. Many attempts have been made by these displaced people, who had been taken to Mauritius, to get permission to return home, but to no avail. Visiting yacht crews had cleared pathways through the overgrown forest to reveal the eerie remains of the village, including its little derelict church. The Diego Garcia Naval base is the only permanent habitation on the Archipelago, and includes a small British Army contingent. Some of these soldiers came over by inflatable boat, to inspect our passports and check us into British Indian Ocean Territory waters. They also added Tanya to our boat's crew list.

British Army visit

The weather turned windy and overcast, frothing up the shallow lagoon in no time at all, blowing the boats at anchor toward shore. With swinging room at a premium because of coral heads, it was not a comfortable position to be in. Huge squalls passed over us, with heavy winds and copious rainfall. Tanya took a mass of laundry ashore, taking shelter in an old copra shed deep among the coconut palms. In weather like this it would be difficult to get out of the lagoon because of the huge seas pushing water over the surrounding reefs, causing very fast currents through the passes.

Because of the continued unsettled weather and the insecure nature of the Boddam anchorage, we moved back to Ile Fouquet, where the land was higher, giving us better shelter.

In all we had spent eleven days exploring this lovely lagoon, before motoring out of the pass in calm weather and good visibility, which made the deeper water easily visible. With some trepidation we raised the staysail and, as the mast didn't fall down, also raised the single reefed main. We sailed past a neighbouring atoll, Perros Banhos. Yachts that had anchored there, reported that it proved to be a very unsatisfactory anchorage in rough weather. It had few islands to give shelter, and was littered with coral heads in the shallow lagoon.

After twenty eight nautical miles of fast sailing in smooth water behind the atoll, we emerged into huge seas. In spite of all the agitation, our jury rig was holding. Tanya, even in the worst weather, insisted on making us food and tidying up the cabin as things flew around in the bumpy conditions. We were enjoying having her aboard. Christine and she shared pleasant evenings in the cockpit discussing life as they shared a watch until Tanya headed for bed.

Tanya at work

On the radio we heard that the boats that had chosen the north Indian Ocean route through Indonesia and Sri Lanka, had arrived in Galle. The harbour was being depth charged by the Sri Lankan Navy, which had succeeded in removing some of the bottom paint off a few nearby yachts. One of the vessels affected complained to the authorities about the incident, and was refused permission to leave the country. Whereupon all the other yachts refused to leave without him. Ultimately, the standoff was resolved and they were all cleared to leave, but without being allowed to replenish their water supplies. This proved no problem because of heavy rain.

After four days of brisk sailing, we were six hundred and fifty two nautical miles from Victoria, capital of the Seychelles islands. The wind stopped, the Autohelm stopped working, and we had a shocking night rolling around in the large residual swell. Two hours of motoring brought back the wind, and we roared off into the night. Squally winds continued making it a very busy boat, shortening and letting out sails, adjusting the wind vane, and setting the sails for the varying wind directions. Christine worked the radio at scheduled times so that we kept reliable contact with our shore stations. She gave our position and weather conditions, and obtained weather forecasts. Weather fax pictures were hard to come by on this leg of the trip. Either the stations did not come up at the appointed hours, Pretoria was particularly bad for this, or the pictures were very poor when they did arrive.

No matter what Mother Nature threw at us, Tanya kept the meals coming regularly, which maintained our energy levels. She had no hint of seasickness, and whatever we didn't finish she willingly obliged. For a whole week squalls continued, and the morning skies were almost purple in colour. In the calm periods between the squalls, a silvery smooth sea prevailed, with confusing swells coming at us from all directions. At one point in the night the windvane was so confused that, when I went out for my usual three sixty degree look around the horizon, I happened to glance at the compass to find that we were pointing back in the direction we had come.

On one calm morning Black Petrels came to take a look at us. We could see their reflections in the water as they flew a few inches above its surface, their wingtips almost touching the sea. Round and around they would silently glide, to disappear over the crest of a swell as quickly as they had appeared. Finally, after two days of this mediocre and spasmodic progress, the Trades suddenly returned. The slatting sails billowed out and we were off. A huge school of fleeing tuna broke the surface of the sea ahead of us, thousands of them leaping in fearful panic, seeking safety from a group of dolphins in hot pursuit. We watched fascinated by their unbelievable maneuverability in the water as they turned and streaked past *Demelza.*

Two nights before sighting the Seychelles on the horizon, we were hit with the worst thunder storm yet. Vivid flashes of lightning played around the top of the mast, and frequent bolts came out of the black starless sky, hitting the water all around. "We had better disconnect all our electronics," I said, leaving Christine to supervise our progress. The radio, radar, GPS and other navigational instruments were disconnected in a hurry. Smaller items were wrapped in tin foil, which we had been told might offer some protection. I think Christine hid her precious radio in her bunk.

As dawn broke the storm clouds moved away as if by magic, and blue sky and a steady twenty knot trade wind returned. Down into the cabin I went to reverse the previous night's work, connecting everything back together again, and hoping it would all work. Sure enough Christine picked up Kilifi loud and clear. "You'll be interested to hear," Tony said, "that one of the yachts, calling into Eritrea on its way from the Red Sea into the Indian Ocean, was stolen while the owners were ashore. She later cleared into the Seychelles but booked out again before anyone realized she had been stolen. A sharp eyed policeman on one of the outer islands spotted her and escorted them to Victoria. You may see her when you get there. She's flying Norwegian colours. Apparently as soon as they got into harbour the robbers jumped ship and haven't been seen since. The owners have flown back from Norway to reclaim their boat, but the Seychelles authorities are not too keen to let them have it until they have found the thieves and taken them to court."

Again the wind failed us so we had to motor through the night. Now that there were only one hundred and ten nautical miles to our destination, I was no longer anxious about using up our diesel fuel. This part of our journey seemed to have been endless, with all the interruptions to progress along the way, as well as broken sleep schedules to accommodate the squalls. As we brought the mainsail down, Christine noticed that a seam was coming unstitched, resulting from it flogging during the squally winds. I retrieved some magical patching material from my "spares" locker and Christine hand stitched and reinforced the affected area. We noticed that the cotter pin holding the boom's gooseneck in place, had sheared off in the night. I replaced it with a stainless bolt. On our last night out, just when we thought we were arriving in paradise over the Seychelles bank, a huge squall hit us. Squalls were marching one after another across our radar screen. They were everywhere, so there was no chance of avoiding them.

Surprisingly a fine day dawned and we could see the island of Mahe in the distance. Later that morning we motored into the harbour, attaching ourselves to the quarantine buoy as instructed on the radio by the harbour authority. Victoria harbour looked wonderful. The sunlight shone on the surrounding high granite hills, a backdrop to the houses scattered among lush green trees. We waited for the Immigration and Customs Officials to come out to the boat. Three smartly dressed men paid us a quick ten minute visit to fill out the entry forms. As they left, they told us where to anchor in the harbour and that our Seychelles courtesy flag, that Christine had made in Australia and was now fluttering on the spreader, was no longer the correct flag. It had been changed the previous year. After a couple of tries we managed to find a good anchoring spot. It was a tricky place, as there was only one area where there was enough shallow water in which to anchor a small yacht, and naturally that was already full of boats.

Spanish Tuna Fleet at entrance to Victoria's Harbour

In the evening we walked up to the Seychelles Yacht Club to have a celebratory supper with the crews of a lot of yachts that had arrived before us.

Victoria is a very pretty little city, at the centre of which is a miniature replica of Big Ben. The period buildings are clean and well maintained, and the main streets busy and prosperous looking. We had our films developed and printed as we were so anxious to see the photographs we'd taken in Chagos. They were fabulous. We saw a poem written about the Seychelles. It reads as follows:

Seychelles looks like the world as God meant it to be,
Happy Seychelles – happy homes beneath the coconut palms,
Not much money in it, perhaps, but peace, contentment and companionship,
With quickening earth and blue, blue sky,
And new mornings, and quiet enclosings at evening time.
When you will have strayed far
Think of all the little Seychelles, the peaceful land,
Remember the rustic peace which enshrines itself behind the tropical hills.
James R Maucham

The Seychelles Island group consists of three bigger islands, Mahe, on which the Capital city of Victoria sits, Praslin, and La Digue, as well as countless other little islands scattered over the Seychelles Plateau.

We made contact with Jenny's mother. Christine had met Jenny at her store in New Zealand when she was buying material to make courtesy flags. The following day we walked to the Car Hire firm where we met her charming Seychellois mother, and Jenny's husband Trevor. The family lived in a beautiful home high on the hill overlooking the sea. We also met Mike, one of Jenny's brothers, and rented a mini moke from him for a two day tour around Mahe.

"Jenny is here, on the island. She and Trevor have come here to live." her mother told us happily. We made plans to meet up later before setting off into town to do some shopping. I took the Autohelm to a workshop to see if they could fix it, and the Furuno expert in town came to look at our radar, which had been playing up. The solution to the radar was simple. During all the agitation at sea, one of the pins in the aerial cable plug had worked loose.

In the market, where seafood was fresh and abundant, Egrets were climbing all over the produce, pecking at the clouds of flies that alighted on the dead fish. Christine ordered a wrap around skirt in local material from Mrs. Coupidou, who said that she would have it ready in a couple of days. Our replacement forestay had not arrived as we had expected, and later we received a relayed radio message from West Marine saying that they were out of stock and that we should reorder in a couple of weeks. That wasn't much use to us. We were so disappointed. Other boats had ordered replacement parts from the UK and were having better luck.

Having accepted Tanya on *Demelza* as crew, we were now legally responsible for getting her off the islands. Fortunately she was a girl with plenty of initiative. She returned to the boat one day to tell us that she had been able to secure a job on a Dutch schooner, operating out of the Seychelles. We completed all the formalities with Immigration and Customs, successfully taking her off our crew list and transferring her to the schooner's papers.

After completing a two day tour of Mahe in our minimoke with Diane and Bart, we all caught the ferry over to Praslin. It was easier than taking *Demelza*, as we had been told there was limited sheltered anchorage there. It was a fifteen minute ferry ride to Praslin, and a further half hour to La Digue. Here we found beautiful beaches of peach coloured granite sand, dotted with huge pink, granite, rounded boulders. We all swam in the crystal clear water and thought we'd gone to heaven. We visited a copra factory before walking up to Valle de Mai, where a particular type of indigenous coconut, shaped like a woman's torso, called Coco de Mer, was to be found.

News came through that night on the radio that a boat called *Yao*, from Australia, had sunk en route to Mauritius. Fortunately, the family had been rescued by a Liberian registered freighter that had picked up their S.O.S.

The following day several new arrivals appeared in the harbour from South Africa. They had experienced seven hard days beating into the wind from Zanzibar, and all looked a bit the worse for wear. It convinced us that sailing against the Trades was not our idea of fun cruising.

Christine happily sits on a granite boulder

Jobs on the boat continued. All the varnish had to be redone as the old coat had been blasted off by salt spray. We booked a haul out at the local Navy boatyard, and later were very pleased with the care they took of *Demelza.* A diver was in the water throughout the operation to see that everything was correct. By the following morning all the underwater jobs had been completed and the boat went back into the water.

One of the girls working in the Yacht Club, Marie Elaine, asked if we would like to accompany her to the *Reef Resort* to hear her boyfriend, Alain, playing drums in his band, "The Tropics." He duly arrived in his van that evening, and we all piled in among his drums. The evening's entertainment was Creole music and dancing. Marie Elaine made a valiant attempt to teach me the *Sega*, a Creole dance. This involved a lot of hip swaying, with which she had no problem at all, but which I found a little difficult.

The Sega

On 4th October, we left Mahe in perfect sailing weather for our eight hundred nautical mile journey to Kilifi in Kenya. This was Tony's home. As controller of the East Africa Ham Radio net he had talked to us on the radio almost daily, ever since we had left Australia. We were stocked with fresh bread, eggs as well as lots of lovely vegetables and fruit. We had enjoyed eighteen wonderful days in these beautiful islands.

With the East African current running northwards up the coast of East Africa, we headed south of Kilifi toward Mombasa so as not be taken too far north. The sailing was excellent, and we were covering one hundred and twenty nautical miles a day. We saw oil tankers from the Persian Gulf making their way to the Cape of Good Hope at the southern tip of South Africa.

When we were ninety nautical miles off the Kenyan coast, the wind dropped. That was not a problem, as we wanted to approach the fringing reef in daylight the next day. That night a red footed Booby decided to roost at the top of our swaying mast. The aerobatics he performed to alight on the swinging masthead was marvelous to watch as he patiently tried again and again to get his landing right. As anticipated he left us his calling card in the morning.

CHAPTER 15
Kenya

During the night, the three quarter moon had shone brightly, and the loom of Mombasa's lights had been visible in the distance. In the short tropical dawn, the low lying coast was clearly visible ahead of us. As we approached the land, rondavel thatched houses could be seen among the trees. Our excitement at arriving in Africa mounted, as did our anxiety about finding the entrance through the reef into Kilifi Creek which leads to its landlocked lagoon.

Kilifi is a small town thirty miles north of Mombasa, and is a perfect port of entry to Kenya. Once through the reef, following the rather hard to spot range markers on shore, we turned ninety degrees to starboard along the narrow northward entrance parallel to the shore. Dilapidated leading lights, partly obscured by vegetation, helped us approach the creek. Recent buildings had obscured a critical beacon at the creek's entrance. We navigated carefully over the shallower parts, being raced in by a small fishing dhow which was making good speed in the morning's breeze. Ahead was the span of the road bridge, and close by it, transmission lines were strung across the creek. To pass under these we had first to find deep enough water close to the southern shore as well as enough room to pass under the low wires.

As the mast slipped beneath the wires Christine shouted "OK, we're clear." Next a ninety degree turn toward the centre of the creek brought us to the highest point of the road bridge's span. Ahead of us, as we motored on, the beautiful lagoon came into view. On the surrounding hills, red roofed houses were scattered among the tropical growth right down to the shoreline. To port we passed the local boatyard, and to starboard the old ferry landing complete with ancient ferry, abandoned when superceded by the new road bridge.

We made our way across the lagoon toward Tony and Daphne's house before dropping anchor in twenty feet of water. Several boats were anchored at the boatyard, but only two other cruising sailboats were located in our anchorage. The lagoon was twenty miles long and five miles wide, with high banks topped by trees. Its western end was wide and shallow, with mangroves along its shoreline.

After settling in, we inflated the dinghy and rowed ashore, leaving the dinghy tied to the branch of a mangrove bush. We climbed the steps up the steep bank to reach the graceful lawns surrounding Daphne and Tony's lovely home. "Welcome to Kenya." Tony called over his outstretched hand.

Demelza in Kilifi lagoon

It was just like meeting an old friend. His voice was so familiar after talking to him during our passage across the Indian Ocean. As we talked on the lawn Daphne appeared, and was so generous in her greeting. Their home was to become our base for the next seven months. We could use their living room at any time, and often joined them for evening gatherings.

"This is your home," said Daphne. "We have a cruiser's fridge in the garage where you can keep cold drinks, meat and so on."

"Sometime, we need to clear you through customs." said Tony "I'll drive you into Kilifi in the morning if you'd like."

Our first ride into town in Tony's small red truck was an experience. The sandy road was deeply rutted, and wound its way up and around small hills, passing groups of palm fronded houses with attendant chickens, brightly coloured bushes and coconut palm trees. We sat in the back of the truck waving to people walking along the sides of the road. I particularly enjoyed seeing villagers carrying their wares on their heads, whether it was a water bucket, a water melon or, on one occasion, a lady's handbag. Wherever we went, we were greeted with a friendly call of *Karibu* meaning "welcome" in Swahili.

Tony, who had been a pilot with East African Airlines, was a fount of local and East African knowledge. He knew the places to shop and stay in every town, city and village from Nairobi to Mombasa. He and his wife opened their doors to all cruising sailors that were in the vicinity, hosting many evening soirees either in their capacious living room, or around the swimming pool before the mosquitoes took flight at sunset. We sat in their living room some evenings with mosquito coils smoldering under our chairs, while newly arrived cruisers brought yarns from all parts of the world, recounting their seagoing dramas to a very receptive audience.

Tony Britchford

Tony's extensive library had a number of fascinating books on the history of East Africa, which he readily lent out. In spite of the rule of the Omani Sultans in the fifteen century, the colonizing battles of the European nations, and the brutal exploitation of the slave trade, the heart and spirit of the African people prevailed. Yet they seemed to show us no malice.

We had arrived in the lagoon before the beginning of the short rains. A week after our arrival it began to pour. Not a gentle pitter patter, but rather a steady stream of water which began quite suddenly after a glorious week of sunshine, and continued without taking breath for three whole days. In the first twenty four hours, we received twenty four inches of rain, and a total of thirty six inches in three days.

The lagoon turned from a beautiful turquoise into a chocolate brown soup. Torrents of water poured down the steep cliffs, with trees tumbling down them in a flow of mud. The pathway up the bank to Tony's house began to slide down towards the beach, and his neighbours' swimming pool and deck disappeared before our eyes into the lagoon. The noise of this rain on our coach roof was deafening as the torrent continued. We watched the destruction going on around us framed by the aperture of our main hatch.

The road to Mombasa was washed out, as was the road north to Malindi. So Kilifi was cut off. The little rutted path from Tony's house into Kilifi turned into a torrent of water that ended up washing through the courtyard of the local Resort Hotel before running out into the lagoon.

The neighbour's yard came tumbling down

With ninety eight percent humidity and twenty six celsius temperature, the inside of *Demelza* rapidly began to resemble a sauna. Meanwhile Daphne's leather furniture in her living room was assuming a healthy growth of mold. The explanation for all this tumult was that the Inter-tropical Convergence Zone was moving north a trifle early, bringing the so called "Short Rains" of the north monsoon with them.

As we were planning to leave the boat for our Safari to the Masai Mara and then on to Canada for Christmas, we decided to remove all electronic gear that we could from the boat, storing it in Tony's "dry room." This was located in a well aerated enclosure under the metal roof of his house. The rain continued. Eleven bridges were washed out, as was the main highway from Mombasa to Nairobi. The only way to get out of Kilifi was by air. Food supplies in a nearby town were running out, and our road to Kilifi was submerged under three feet of water and closed to traffic.

In the rare breaks in the downpour, we cruised around the lagoon in our dinghy, looking at the dramas unfolding around us, and anticipating more houses coming down the cliff into the lagoon, followed by their swimming pools, decks and gazebos. A forty foot retaining wall had tumbled down before the rain stopped.

Then the sun came out. The torrents all stopped, and at an African pace, a few locals appeared with shovels, to begin the task of repairing the roads as they emerged into the sunshine.

Tony and Daphne were philosophical about all the chaos, taking it is their stride as though nothing unusual had taken place for the past week. However it was the main topic of conversation between neighbours for a few days.

We paid a visit to Mombasa to clear Immigration.

"I'll have tea ready for you when you get home." offered Daphne before we left.

The trip to Mombasa involved being driven by Tony into Kilifi to catch either a bus, considered to be a lethal experience, or a *matatu* which was generally referred to by everyone as a "flying coffin." A matatu is a twelve seat mini bus that doesn't start its journey until there are at least twenty-five people on board. Before leaving Kilifi, a youth hung on to the door of the vehicle, leaning out and calling stridently to the jostling throng, enticing them to join the already overloaded vehicle for the trip to town. Finally, having packed us in until there was no room to breathe, he slammed the palm of his hand on the roof. The engine roared and we were off at a breakneck speed down the main street, dodging the inevitable livestock which had the uncanny knack of getting out of the way at the last moment.

Mombasa lies at 4S, and was second only in importance as a trading centre to the coastal town of Kilwa, in Tanzania, in the sixteenth century. Here the silks and spices of Persia, India and China were traded. It was invaded four times by the Portuguese, who finally took it over in 1589. They built the huge Fort Jesus as an island fortress which helped them retain control until 1698 when, after a three year siege by the Omani Arabs, it finally succumbed. The Mazuri family ruled until 1837 when the Oman threatened to take over. A deal was made for British protection on condition that all slave trade would be abolished. In appreciation of this the Omanis were given a two hundred mile strip of coastal land running from Mombasa north. The British did not live up to their agreement, so the Omani took over in 1849 and the coastal strip became part of the Sultanate of Zanzibar. The British established the colony of Kenya in 1888, moving its capital to Nairobi in 1906. They built the Mombasa to Lake Victoria railway, via Nairobi, to improve access to the headwaters of the Nile, considered to be militarily vulnerable to German attack.

Walking the streets of Mombasa we were the only white faces, which made us feel extremely exposed as a minority group. It was not a comfortable feeling. We picked our way through the potholed main thoroughfares, jostling with crowds of people going in every direction, and often found ourselves pressed off the uneven sidewalks into the streets. Along these cars, buses, bicycles and the inevitable matatus, honked their way to destinations unknown. The sidewalk congestion was not helped by the many vendors who sold everything imaginable, from pirated music tapes to shoes made from recycled tires. "If you feel threatened at any time," Tony had told us "go into any shop that is run by Indians. You will be safe there."

The once elegant colonial style buildings surrounding one of the city's squares, looked completely run down, seedy, and in need of repair. The square outside the Mombasa Cathedral had long since lost its grassy lawns under the African shade trees, to be replaced by plastic bags blowing in the wind, and mountains of pop cans filling the gutters.

The officials, who processed our papers after our lengthy walk through city streets, were polite and efficient. With suitably stamped papers, we beat an exhausted retreat to an Indian restaurant which had been recommended by Tony. "You are most welcome." said the beaming old Indian gentleman as we entered into the peace of his establishment. Courteously he showed us to our table. Tony had primed us with information on which dishes to order. This we did, receiving the greatest attention from the old gentleman's son.

In due course our meal was served, which we enjoyed immensely. So much so indeed that Christine asked the owner if she could meet his wife who, we had been told, had prepared our meal. He was rapturous at the thought, and escorted Christine toward the kitchen. They entered with suitable aplomb. Whereupon all the flies that had settled on the food preparation surfaces rose up in an angry cloud obscuring the view of Madame at the rear of the kitchen. Christine emerged a while later, looking a little pale. "I'm so glad you didn't see that," she said "You'd never have eaten here." Needless to say, our exceptional meal had no untoward after effects.

At a later date we joined up with Ken and Margaret from the yacht *Tomorrow* and Rosemary and Mike who were sailing on *Reality*. We traveled up to Nairobi by the overnight train. We had been advised, by Tony, to find our own tour guide and to make sure we had the vehicle to ourselves. The following morning we asked around the streets of Nairobi, and found a friendly Kamba driver and his mini van at our disposal for a five day trip into the Masai Mara and Samburu Game Reserve. Our Safari was everything we had hoped it would be. We saw the Big Five animals and enjoyed the contrasting lifestyle from that of life aboard.

As this was the cyclone season, we took the opportunity to fly home from Nairobi, to meet all our friends and family and to attend the christening of our youngest granddaughter. Leaving the boat on a mooring under Tony's eagle eye, with an *askari* (guard) sleeping on her each night, we enjoyed a wonderful holiday.

The return journey to Kenya was remarkable for our brush with bureaucracy. We had bought a replacement forestay with fittings, along with other odds and ends, for *Demelza*. On arrival in Nairobi we found that one of the bags had popped its end and some kind airline worker had bound it up with tape to stop all our possessions spewing out over some unknown airport apron or aircraft hold. Knowing the amount of stainless steel that we were carrying, I was in a mild state of anxiety as we collected our baggage and approached the customs lineup. A very large, fierce looking female African Customs officer, after establishing that this entire battered luggage was indeed ours, asked me to open the largest one. This I did, aware of the possible one hundred percent import duty. What I had not realized, was that Christine had packed several packages of dried peas in the same bag. One of these had ruptured en route as a result of rough baggage handling, so that immediately I unzipped the bag, a green avalanche of dehydrated peas cascaded out of its container all over the lady's counter and cubicle floor.

"Close it!" she cried as she eyed this continuing flood with some apprehension. I gladly obliged, and the flow of peas stopped. Without further inspection she proclaimed icily

"You may go."

The Fairview Hotel in Nairobi was an experience which just has to be recorded. An oasis of sanity, it had been recommended by Tony. We were greeted by the owner/manager Charles, and immediately knew we were in the right place. Both he and Edward, the Director, welcomed us on our arrival and ushered us to our room. The hotel was set in two acres of well manicured lawns, flowering tropical shade trees, and well tended flower beds. The Fairview retained that faded elegance of an era long departed. Our well appointed room, complete with faded chintz covered armchairs, overlooked the rose garden, where an African family entertained its happy, chattering guests at their daughter's wedding.

We had planned a detour to Cape Town, to visit Christine's brother Nicky, before returning to Kilifi and the boat. The day before our flight, we visited the Nairobi airport to negotiate the release of our new mainsail. Importing the sail, which had been made in Hong Kong, proved more difficult than we had anticipated. We contacted the courier service, and later met their representative at the airport, who carried a mass of application forms. The baggage agent at the airport was most reluctant to find our package, or even to look for it. Fortunately he had left the door to the storage locker behind the counter slightly ajar. This was sufficient for me to spot our package among the pile of goods awaiting collection. There followed a protracted discussion about the suitability of our forms. He contended that, if we used the ones we had, we would have to pay one hundred percent import duty, even though it was for a "yacht in transit." This is a world wide convention for avoiding import duty on goods for transient vessels.. For a small financial consideration, however, he would supply a different form for cargo transfer on which no duty was required. My refusal to cross his palm led to a whole day's standoff. He relented petulantly the following day, handing over the sail at no charge. The courier agent, who had been most helpful throughout these negotiations, agreed to take our package and deliver it to Margaret, in Kilifi, for us.

All this had taken so long that Christine and I had to run to catch our plane, which was waiting for us. We dashed up the steps onto the South African Airlines Airbus 320 just before its doors shut. It took off almost before we had the chance to sit down. It was an unforgettable flight, flying over the snowfields of Mt Kilimanjaro poking up above the surrounding clouds. We flew over the Zambezi River and Lake Malawi. The pilot happened to be a keen sailor so, on hearing of our cruising exploits, he sent a steward back to ask if we would like to join him in the cockpit. Here we had a most interesting time. We were given headphones to wear, so that we could hear the exchanges between the plane and the air traffic controller in Johannesburg. The weather closed in as the flight progressed, and shortly before the descent into the darkness above Johannesburg, we dipped into the clouds, with flashes of Lightning streaking all around us. The nose of the plane was lit up with the eerie light of St. Elmo's fire. We were thrown around as we descended, and then, suddenly emerged from under the cloud to see the lights of Johannesburg below.

"See if you can find the runway," said the pilot. Try as we may, we couldn't. "It's over there." he said, pointing to a dark strip just ahead of us. As he said it, the runway lights came on and we were gliding smoothly in to land in pouring rain.

The next morning, after a night in a very comfortable hotel in Sandton, we boarded another plane, which took us to Cape Town. We had our first look at the lovely mountains surrounding that city, and on arrival we were greeted by Nicky and his wife Penny. During our visit we borrowed Nicky's car to tour the old Cape Road, Chapman's Peak Drive, and Cape Town's developing waterfront. On another occasion we all visited Franshoek and Stellenbosch, where we bought delicious wine from one of their vineyards for $3 a bottle, before visiting the memorable Huguenot's Museum.

A visit to Simon's Town acquainted us with False Bay Yacht Club, where we planned to bring *Demelza* later in the year. We met all the staff and arranged for moorage.

A particularly enjoyable day was spent with friends of Monica and Peter from Victoria, who lived in a classic Dutch style house in Somerset West. Bill and Irene were authorities on roses and had an extensive rose garden, which surrounded their home. The scent was almost overpowering as we sat in the still evening air enjoying a glass of South African wine together. On another occasion we visited the Kirstenbosch flower show, where Bill was judging the roses. He demonstrated what he looked for, and described the good and bad points that he used in making his decisions.

We have so many wonderful memories of this beautiful city. The visit to the huge Rhodes memorial on the lower slopes of Table Mountain, now occupied by the University of Cape Town; climbing Lion's Peak with a bottle of champagne to celebrate our ascent to its summit; the walk along the contour path with the tablecloth of cloud streaming above us, and the magnificent panorama stretching out two thousand feet below. We enjoyed the unfamiliar plants and birds, and the drive over Bains Kloof to Tulbach, with its charming Dutch gabled homes. One day we drove to Langenbaan and Soldanha Naval Reserve, where Penny had rented a cottage on the beach for a couple of days. We were so happy to know we were to revisit this area in a few months time.

On our return to Kilifi, we heard that Margaret had received our sail from Nairobi, but noticed that Tony had a slightly wary look about him.

"Now before you hear it from anyone else, I'll tell you what happened," he said "*Demelza* grounded on the beach in a recent blow. She had been sitting out a storm comfortably when *Just in Thyme,* on the next mooring, broke free with Jenny on board. As she was blown ashore Jenny panicked, tied her boat to *Demelza* and tried to winch her boat away from the beach. This resulted in *Demelza*'s mooring breaking. So I phoned the boatyard to request a powerboat to pull both boats off the beach. This was successfully accomplished with no damage to either boat." *Demelza* was none the worse for her experience. We don't think she had been in very shallow water when she grounded, as a thermos flask, sitting in the open hanging locker, had not fallen over. We had left all the lockers open when we went away to keep the air circulating throughout the boat, as mold is a big problem in the warm and humid air.

Working in Tony's garden was a man from the local village, named Rafael. He had been our askari, looking after *Demelza* during our absence. At our first meeting, he had stretched out his hand saying

"My name is Rafael, and I am a Christian. Are you Christians?" He had asked us to bring him back a T shirt with a Christian emblem on it, which we eventually had found, with 'Jesus loves me' emblazoned on it.

The weather was hot as we prepared *Demelza* for her journey south to Cape Town. In the heat of the afternoon we often took Bundy, a bright little Bichon Frise dog belonging to a neighbouring boat, for a walk on the beach. We scavenged for fossilized sharks teeth that had been deposited there. We experienced huge rain squalls with lots of wind, which continued off and on for the best part of a week. Margaret took Christine shopping to stock up the boat while I worked on boat maintenance.

On one of our trips into Mombasa, across from the island on which the city stands, rests the Freedom Bell. In the days of slavery this rang every time a slave escaped to freedom by swimming off the island. If they survived the swim, they were given sanctuary in Mombasa's local churches.

On Sundays we attended the Kilifi Anglican Church with Tony's neighbour, Doreen, whose husband had been chief engineer on P and O liners. It was here we had first met Margaret, who lived in a lovely, modern home overlooking the Indian Ocean. She had extensive lawns on which two enormous baobab trees stood, named Beelzebub and Methuselah. We had many a happy visit, listening to local gossip and the song of the exotic birds.

Margaret shows off Beelzebub

At night, we found it increasingly difficult to sleep, as the temperature never dropped below eighty five farenheit. In an attempt to make the boat more comfortable, I rigged up two small twelve volt fans. Following the rain, the lagoon water remained murky. This made it difficult to dive under the boat to free it of all the growth that had accumulated on its bottom since our arrival in Kilifi five months previously. The propeller had totally disappeared into a solid block of barnacles, which I had to tackle with a large screw driver in an attempt to prize it apart. All the through hulls had become blocked with growth and, on examination, the whole of the outlet pipe from the head had clogged with a tenacious salt deposit. This necessitated the removal of all the piping, taking it ashore in lengths in the dinghy and beating it against the stone wall to unblock it. The resulting pile of salt was most impressive.

One of our rides back to Kilifi from Mombassa took place in a torrential downpour. Packed into the interior of the *matatu*, and surrounded by sweating, cheerful locals in torpid heat, we hurtled along the unkempt roads at a frenetic speed. At one point Christine, sitting by a window, was dismayed when, after a particularly violent jolt, found herself holding the window pane in her lap with rainwater pouring in on top of her. The other passengers found this very amusing, but one kind man did his best to replace the glass in the hole as we continued on our way. About half-way home the *matatu* took another violent lurch to one side and we ended up, at a perilous angle, in the ditch beside a field of flax. Roars of laughter greeted this event as all the passengers scrambled out.

"Come on," I said to Christine "We'll give them a hand." But on trying to do so, a couple of the men made it clear that in no way were we to assist. So we waited while the other passengers floundered around in the mud, eventually managing to heave the vehicle back onto the road to continue our journey.

The new bridge at Kilifi is one of the sites shown to visitors. It is the substantial structure that we had sailed under into the lagoon. The story goes that the Japanese donated it to the Kenyan government, and that some local entrepreneur had the brilliant idea of setting up a toll booth at either end for his own benefit. Apparently this went unnoticed for a few years, after which the government put a stop to it.

Kilifi bridge

The boatyard in Kilifi Lagoon was owned by Judy and run by her son Phillip, who was an irregular attendee. Labour was provided by an assorted mixture of expatriates and local African residents. I must have come away from our first visit with enough confidence to ask them to replace our broken forestay. Eventually we took *Demelza* across the lagoon, and secured her to a sea wall. Here, when the tide fell, the bottom of the keel settled in the mud. We could clean and then paint the remaining exposed hull. In the event, having tried in vain myself to wield a brush in mud up to my knees while bent double under *Demelza*, I hired Kahindian, Gambo and Mambo, three local boys, who happily accepted the challenge. They spent the better part of three days, during low water, cheerfully lying on their backs on the mud cleaning and painting *Demelza*'s bottom.

Demelza on the sea wall

Along the wall from us was a German boat, which had arrived in the boatyard some time before us. Her owner regaled us with the story of his arrival. On the first night his boat had been boarded by a swarm of rats. So the next day the boatyard had laid down copious amounts of rat poison, which had fixed the problem nicely for our arrival. Thankfully, we didn't see one rat during our time there. We knew from *Nashira's* experience with a rat on board, what damage they could do. So we put rat guards on all our lines to shore as a precaution. The boatyard also sported a very nice thatched bar, at which local residents spent convivial evenings with their neighbours and visiting yachties, in the eighty five degree heat before mosquitoes drove everyone home.

The more time we spent in Kilifi, the more problems we had with our electronic gear. A particular disappointment to us was the failure of the hard drive in our laptop computer, on which we depended for weather charts via the radio.

On getting the boat back to Tony's mooring, we took some time off from all the hard work in the boatyard, and accepted Margaret's invitation to visit Hemingway's Hotel, and the ancient Arabic Gedi ruins built of coral blocks in the thirteen century. A palace with small houses and a mosque attached, surrounded the well and bathhouses. Along with a granary and council chambers, it made an impressive settlement. In the excavations a lot of old Arab and Chinese pottery and glass had been found.

Work on the boat continued, threading new halyards to replace worn ones. We had to truck the diesel jugs to Kilifi in Tony's truck to fill up our tanks, which involved several round trips of five miles each way for twelve gallons at a time. We made a thorough check of all standing rigging and fittings.

While in Kilifi, I officially retired from work at the age of sixty five, and spent the morning up the mast replacing the topping lift. We then found that the slides on our new mainsail were a fraction too big for the track on the mast. So I spent the rest of my day cutting them to size with a hacksaw. In the evening we went up to Tony and Daphne's house, where I found Christine and Daphne had organized a wonderful birthday supper for me. Eleven people attended. Doreen had made a birthday cake, and presented it with an appropriate limerick. A second cake that she had made for us to eat on the boat had been devoured by one of her dachshunds. We washed it all down with South African champagne. The party was a huge success and went on well into the night. Our host and hostess, their neighbours, cruisers and their visiting families, joined by Bundy, wished me a happy birthday, so making it a very special day.

One afternoon a small boat, that looked as though she had put many sea miles under her keel, sailed into the bay. At the tiller was eighty two year old Harry from Norfolk, Virginia, who put the boat into the wind to stop her before going forward to let down the sails and pay out her anchor chain. All this was accomplished with the minimum fuss and dogged determination. We could see that Harry had a routine for everything and that it was executed with considerable skill, slowly and well. Later in the day we met him. He had preceded us up to Tony's house, having inflated his eight foot battered dinghy, put on his back pack, and slowly rowed for shore. He had circumnavigated the globe with his wife some years before, after which she became ill and died. His children, now in their sixties, were suggesting he might like to live in a care home. He rebelled and announced his intention to circle the world again, this time on his own. Telling this story over the supper table, Harry said "If I fell off the back of the boat, at least I'd be smiling as I leave this earth."

On many trips up the path to Tony and Daphne's house we would meet Raphael working in the garden. He was always cheerful, and more than willing to help with any job. On our return from Canada, Christine had brought a swatch of brightly coloured curtain material for Raphael's wife who, Tony had told us, owned a sewing machine. This was a rare item in rural Kenya. Raphael was building a new home for his family, and later invited us both to visit his village, to meet his family, and to see his nearly finished home. On the appointed day, we went with him along the well beaten path, through tilled fields, to the village.

On approaching, we first heard and then saw a crowd of people gathered to greet us. Great excitement and laughter accompanied all the introductions. We were introduced to his wife and three small daughters, all wearing dresses made of the colourful curtain material that Christine had given to them. Rachel was an excellent seamstress. At one end of the village square, the villagers had placed a table, decorated with Christmas tinsel, and two chairs for us to sit on during our visit. As we took an escorted tour of the village, the table and two chairs followed at a respectable distance.

"You know," I muttered under my breath to Christine "this is what cruising is all about." It transpired that the new house did not yet have any windows, so Rachel's use of the curtain material to make dresses suddenly made sense.

Rachel's family with Christine and the curtain dresses

With all this activity, interspersed with Christine's many rides into Mombasa to buy provisions for the boat, the time to leave was suddenly upon us. We retrieved all our electronic gear from storage in Tony's dry room, and reconnected it to the boat. Our evening get-together with the other cruisers anchored in the lagoon, along with the group of local expatriates that had befriended us whilst here, assumed a sadder tone as the inevitable parting of friends approached.

Finally it was the last day ashore. We telephoned our family in Canada to tell them we were leaving, shared a last walk on the beach with Bundy, bade farewell to our friends ashore and returned down the cliff path for the final time to our boat.

As we pulled out of the lagoon in the morning, our radio was alive with calls of "farewell" and "safe sailing."

We motored under the bridge and power lines, along the paths of the leading lights, through the gap in the reef and out to sea. Dorothy was on shore, waving to us as we passed her house. Suddenly it was over. It was just the two of us again, wandering on a huge ocean. The wind was blowing from the south, the current was against us, and the sky clouded over. It was a somber reintroduction to our travels on the sea.

CHAPTER 16
Kenyan and Tanzanian coasts

In spite of storing our electronics in Tony's dry room, the laptop would not work. I could not receive a weather fax picture. Instead Christine tuned into the short wave radio three times a day to glean what she could about the current weather situation. Tony was very helpful as he could pull up all sorts of information on his computer, before relaying a composite picture to us by word of mouth. We also started talking to Alistair, a friend of Tony's in Durban, who ran the Indian Ocean Ham radio net. He would take over if we lost contact with Tony.

We were working south against a three knot current, so decided to travel as close to the outside of the reef as we safely could to minimize its effect. We were happy to see that the reef showed very clearly on our radar, so that we were able to maintain our desired distance from it in the dark.

The weather worsened as we motored south, blowing twenty-five knots from the southeast, which made it too difficult to enter Mutwapa Creek for shelter. We battled on against the large seas, finally entering Mombasa's Kilindini Harbour, about twenty-five nautical miles south of Kilifi, to anchor in eighty feet of water off the Mombasa Yacht Club. Here it was totally calm. We were surrounded by huge ships disgorging their cargoes all night under bright lights. We had been advised not to linger, as the last visiting cruising boat had been attacked by a knife wielding man. We left before dawn the following morning, sailing two miles offshore outside the fringing reef. As we passed we could see the lights of the Diani Beach resorts. As dawn broke, the Shemba hills rose behind them in the morning mist.

The major break from the contrary wind and current came as we passed Chale Point. We rounded Ras Wasini into the calm of the Wasini Channel between Wasini Island to the south and the mainland to the north. Here we anchored close to the south shore of Wasini Island, below a low eroded coral cliff. This was fringed with row after row of baobab trees silhouetted against the blue sky for as far as the eye could see. Opposite was the little town of Shimoni, which had been the gateway to the East African slave trade. Radio contact with Alistair was good, but we had lost contact with Tony for the first time. Alistair said he would relay our position to Tony. Our radio also gave us news of other cruising friends. *Shemali Blue* was leaving Chagos, and *Tomorrow* was at Asmara in the Red Sea. We were the only offshore cruising boat on this part of the coast.

In the calm of the channel, Christine thought it would be a good place to strip down, clean and grease the winches. One of our boat maintenance books suggested putting all the little bits into the compartments of an egg carton. This way they could all be tipped overboard at the same time!

Wasini Channel

An Australian ham radio operator reported that, in Zanzibar, eight men had boarded a French boat that was based in Kilifi. The boat had been anchored off the harbour seawall at Stone Town, capital of Zanzibar. It had been boarded at night, and the skipper attacked with machetes. The men had stolen everything moveable from the boat and had left the owner bleeding but without harming his wife. He later needed thirty stitches to his face and neck. Christine said "Tony warned us not to go near Stone Town because of all the drug problems. So what were they thinking of?" Unfortunately it was true. Stone Town was well known as a problem area. This episode made us feel quite apprehensive about our dreamed of visit to Zanzibar.

We spent a happy time swimming and walking on one of Wasini Island's lovely beaches. We made friends with two German Shepherd dogs belonging to one of the cliff top resorts. One day as we made our way back to *Demelza* we noticed a Kenyan navy patrol boat anchored out in mid channel, which made us feel quite secure.

One afternoon we took our dinghy across to Shimoni. There we were met by a pleasant man who took our garbage, and promised to guard our dinghy while we looked around. The Simoni Reef Lodge was closed as it was out of season. On the beach, small dhows were pulled up on the sand and, above the tide line, rows of fishermen were busy mending their nets in the shade of overhanging trees. Fish eagles soared as we clambered up the steep bank between poor houses built along the waterfront. The most popular occupation seemed to be sitting around and talking. Most villagers looked at us with curiosity, calling out *Jambo* (hello) as we passed.

While we were in Kilifi, Christine and I had made an effort to pick up a few words of Swahili so that we could converse with the local merchants in the market place. *Habari* (how are you) could lead to a whole lot of trouble, as it invited a torrent of a rejoinder from the villagers. *Mzuri* (fine) was our usual reply. *Kwaheri* (goodbye) was useful and often spoken in great haste to break off an encounter, and *Pole* (sorry) was occasionally useful, as were *Ndiyo* (yes) and *Hapana* (no).

We looked over the Arab ruins and the slave market around which the village was built, and of which Roger Whittaker sang so evocatively in his song 'Shimoni.' Small food stalls were interspersed among the muddy pools of dirty rainwater, an invitation to mosquito breeding and malaria. With our few remaining Kenya shillings we bought cassava root and a loaf of bread.

Arab ruins of Shimoni

Having walked a mile along a track above the beach, passing the National Park Headquarters, we arrived at the Pemba Channel Fishing Club, headquarters of one of the most spectacular marlin and swordfish sport fisheries on the east coast of Africa. Again it was out of season so Peter, the owner, had time over a cup of coffee to tell us all about his life. We had first met him in the owner/managers office at the Fairview Hotel in Nairobi, where he had extended an invitation to us to visit his resort on our way down the coast. The charming cabins and rondavels were empty of tourists, and for the modest sum of two million US dollars the resort could be ours.

It was sad saying goodbye to our German Shepherd friends who had come down to the beach each day to play. We pulled up the anchor and called "Go home!" which they eventually did, trotting homeward up the cliff path but stopping occasionally to look back over their shoulders.

Motoring along the Wasin channel in little wind, we passed the town of Wasini to port.

"This whole place is dotted with reefs," Christine murmured as she pored over the chart "We'd better keep a good lookout."

She went up to the mast and, with the rising sun behind us, could readily pick out the brownish colour of the coral and the dark blue of the deeper channels.

We were now across the border into Tanzania. Five hundred miles of this coastline abound with beautiful anchorages, all within a day's sail of one another, and in relatively protected water. Many river estuaries and coral islands beckoned to be explored, and a lifetime of cruising could be spent here. Some of the world's best diving is to be had on the reefs of this area.

Tanzanian reef island

We learned from the radio that the yacht that had been boarded off Zanzibar had left without navigational instruments and had been wrecked on a reef off the coast of Tanzania. Tony asked us to keep an eye out for her as we cruised down the coast. The owners had made their way home to Kilifi by bus after their disastrous trip.

Motoring among the reefs we stopped for sheltered nights, and spent the days exploring some of the little islands, enjoying cooling swims off deserted pristine beaches. We arrived in Tanga, dropping anchor just at the entrance to Tanga Bay off Ras Kasone. A shallow reef stretched out into the bay for half a mile, giving the impression that we were anchored in the middle of the channel between Tanga Island and the point.

Christine was up early and, on looking out of the cockpit hatch, shouted "You'd better come and look at this." I leapt out to see a huge dhow bearing down on us as she entered the harbour on the morning's breeze. Ungainly yet graceful in appearance under its huge sail, we watched her with some trepidation as she got closer and closer. Finally she passed us about fifty feet away. We had a close-up view of the crew wearing the boat around on to the opposite tack before making its way back toward Tanga Island again.

"Oh, look!" called Christine, pointing toward the entrance buoy. There, two more huge dhows were close hauling into the bay, heading off the boat that had just passed us, and seemingly doing a better point of sail against the very light breeze.

"I can't believe how fast these heavy looking boats are going in such a light wind." I said as we watched them enthralled for an hour or more. They tacked back and forth across the bay making for the port of Tanga further in the bay. Finally one gave up as it was making so little progress, gathered its sail around the mast, and dropped anchor a few yards behind us. Meanwhile the first boat caught a lifting breeze along Tanga Island's shore and inched its way past the reefs to reach its destination.

Dhows from Zanzibar

We later learned that these were commercial dhows sailing between Tanga and Zanzibar, carrying cement. Their owners were fiercely competitive sailors, as the first to reach port received a better price for his cargo.

"I think we'll move out of their way and look for the Yacht Club anchorage." I said. This done we had a wonderful reception at the clubhouse, where we stayed for a week. Here we learnt that *dhow* comes from the Swahili, *dau* (boat). The most common variety of bigger dhows has a square transom, a Portuguese adaptation of the original design. They are called "Sambuck" dhows.

John was the immigration officer. He produced our visa in half a day, during which time he gave me a complete tour of the town on foot. He later invited us to join him for tea at the Meridian restaurant. Sure enough, as we walked up the steep street from the harbour into town, John's smiling face greeted us from a balcony above. He came running down to escort us up to the table that he had reserved on the terrace. He and his friends from the immigration office were most attentive, as the waiter brought a bowl of water with soap to the table for us to wash our hands before tea.

In return we invited John to visit *Demelza* for tea the following day and collected him from the wharf in our dinghy. He was carrying a leather briefcase and was smartly dressed in a suit and new, very dressy leather shoes. We had a very pleasant visit with him, but were saddened when, as he looked around the boat he said,

"You know, I work hard and I save as much as I can, but I shall never be able to afford a place like this."

Taking him back to the wharf, I carefully brought the dinghy to the foot of the ladder up the harbour wall. After saying goodbye, he stepped onto the first rung of the ladder and found himself suspended half-way between the wall and the dinghy. Slowly the dinghy moved away from the wall. With a terrible splash, our beautifully dressed civil servant fell into the void, and the last I saw, as he disappeared beneath the oily surface of the water, were his immaculate black leather shoes. He would not accept my plea that he return to *Demelza* to dry out before catching his bus home.

"I thought he'd gone for good." I told Christine breathlessly on return to *Demelza*. "He had his new official leather bag in one hand, which could have taken him to the bottom. I was so thankful when his spluttering, cheerful face broke the surface, as he struck out for shore. What a way to treat the local immigration officer."

Too soon it was time to leave. After completing all the usual paperwork in triplicate by hand, accompanied by much conversation and laughter, we headed out into the bay. It was a testing night as we threaded our way in moonlight through the reefs off Yambe Island. The dhow skipper I had talked to in Tanga had said "You'd better leave before the wind blows."

Sure enough, we were battling through heavy seas in winds from the south. By the following afternoon, we were anchored in the shelter of Mkokotoni Harbour at the north end of the island of Zanzibar, totally exhausted and ready for bed. The morning dawned fine and we spent the day sailing down the west side of this lovely island. We arrived at Changuu Island anchorage, one mile northwest of Stone Town. Changuu had been built as a prison in 1893, but had never been used as such. We anchored in fifty feet of water in the shelter of the island. Here the wind seemed to veer wildly as a series of squalls passed over us, just as the dhow captain in Tanga had predicted.

After a night's rest we left, beating against continuing southerly winds through English Pass. We were content to see Stone Town's waterfront at a distance of about three miles as we sailed past. Along it a new large hotel was being built. We continued along the west coast of Zanzibar, then across the straits to Dar es Salaam. The wind had picked up to fifteen knots from the south west, heading us again, so we spent a rough night beating upwind to arrive, rather tired, in the anchorage off the Dar es Salaam Yacht Club by midmorning the next day.

Stone Town waterfront Zanzibar

The Dar Yacht Club anchorage is at the entrance to Msasani Bay. The elegant one story building faces out to sea overlooking an idyllic sandy beach. Its great disadvantage is that the ocean swells find their way into the bay, making it difficult to take the dinghy ashore. Instead yachts are invited to call for the yacht club's tender. This flat bottomed boat would leave a concrete groin that extends out into deep water. It is always on call for those whose boats are anchored out in the bay. Hot showers, good food and a well stocked bar, made this a pleasant stop as temporary members, a privilege extended to all visiting cruising boats.

On arrival the usual formalities of signing in had to be observed. After telling Gertrude, at the reception desk, that we would like to go to town, she suggested we catch a bus outside the yacht club gate, and to be sure to pick up C13 Clearance Form from the Harbour Master's Office in the port.

We bounced along the potholed road into town. Much of its condition stemmed from the local people digging up buried water pipes supplying the houses nearby with drinking water. Arriving in the dockyard there was no sign of the harbour master or his office. We waved and shouted to be heard above the general commotion of the bustling crowd on the dock until Juba Saire, the harbour master, finally arrived. He was on his way to lunch at the local railway station restaurant, and invited us to join him "We'll do the paperwork later." he said. "The railway station now serves very good food. It had to stop being a railway station because several bridges further up the line have fallen down." That kind of logic merited a first prize, even by African standards.

The Yacht Club's broad verandahs were a popular meeting place. It was here we met Paul, a South African dentist from Richards Bay, and John, who ran a white water rafting operation on the White Nile in Uganda. John regaled us with many stories of his life, and also insisted we should visit his parents when we arrived in South Africa.

"You're just like my parents," he said. "You'll get on like a house on fire."

Weekly entertainment was provided at the local American Marine Base every Friday evening. This included a film and BBQ supper. We were invited to attend and had a marvelous time meeting a lot of aid workers and NGO staff as well as military personnel.

Just along the coast from the Dar Yacht Club was a commercial shorefront development called "The Slipway." Here, there were shops and an outside restaurant. We browsed in the new and well stocked bookstore, and bought copies of recommended books. *The Ice Cream War*, about early days in Tanga, and *A Good Man in Africa*, both by William Boyd, helped us understand the history and events of the country. We sampled the delicious produce of the bakery and later, while enjoying an ice-cream in the sun on the terrace, were joined by an English couple. They appeared to be in a state of culture shock. They were visiting for their son's wedding to a local Tanzanian girl. It was the day before the wedding, and their job was to look after the 'bride to be' for the day. On the previous day they had experienced unbelievable prenuptial formalities in the nearby town. Endless ceremonial had been the order of the day. Jean and Bob were expected to present the bride's mother with a good quality blanket and a goat. In the event, they were so nonplussed by the challenge of producing a goat, that they were excused that requirement in lieu of an appropriate amount of cash to enable the family to buy one themselves. They had spent the night in a farming community outside the town, in accommodation they described as "rustic but clean." This had not prevented them being mercilessly bitten by mosquitoes all night, which had reduced Jean to a state of acute anxiety about the likelihood of contracting fatal cerebral malaria. After a while she was able to calm down enough for us to enjoy a lunch of fresh cheeses, buns and coffee. When the wedding was over, they planned to take a ten day safari, the last three days of which were to be spent in Zanzibar.

The availability of getting cash on a credit card was limited to only two outlets in the city. One of these we located and immediately we booked two nights at the recommended Mazson's Hotel in Zanzibar for the following week. At lunch, we met a Canadian geologist and his wife who had lived in Dar for six months, helping install water systems for outlying communities. They recommended that when in Zanzibar, we should dine at the Emerson's Hotel for an exceptional experience.

CHAPTER 17
Zanzibar and Lindi

Our safari to Zanzibar began at six the next morning when we were collected by the yacht club tender to catch the bus into town before walking to the ferry. For eight dollars US each we bought tickets for the ninety minute fast catamaran ride to Zanzibar's port of Stone Town. The formality of having to go through customs again was a surprise as Zanzibar is part of Tanzania. However, with a persisting sense of history of the old Sultanate days, the Zanzibaris consider themselves different. Once through, we caught a taxi to our hotel and were glad we did so as we would never have found it on our own through the maze of complicated alleyways and narrow streets.

Zanzibar's narrow streets

The Mazsons Hotel had an interior courtyard around which the two storied accommodation was built. The large rooms had high ceilings and tiled floors for coolness. The hotel looked out on a plaza which had a central fountain. Off this led narrow, inviting alleyways each with beautifully carved doorways to buildings along its length which themselves opened into intriguing dark interiors where all sorts of exotic foods, materials and art work were on sale.

300 year old doors

We walked to the Emerson's Hotel for supper. As we had been told that the restaurant was on the roof, we began to climb the steep stone stairway found inside its main entrance, to emerge on the rooftop. Here peach silk drapes, strung above the whole open area, wafted gently in the evening light. Soft, brightly coloured cushions, on which the patrons sat, were scattered around the sides of the carpeted floor. As the sun set in the western sky, a host of surrounding minaret towers that pierced the canopy of rooftops below, broke into the familiar cacophony of the muezzins calling the faithful to evening prayer. As the light faded, electric lights were turned on above the billowing silken drapes, giving the place a most exotic atmosphere. The waiters, in Arabic costume, brought the food and drinks, which they set on the low tables beside us to the accompaniment of quiet Arabic music.

Sitting next to us was a couple from Montreal who entertained us during our meal with an account of their recent ascent to the top of Mount Kilimanjaro, which had turned out to be a six day hard climb. We tried to ignore the American child nearby who was demanding a hamburger in a very loud voice..

Emerson view over Stone Town

Christine enjoying her Emerson experience

On our second day our friend Tembo, the taxi driver from the previous day, took us for a five hour tour. This included a visit to the cathedral that had been built over the old slave market. In front of the altar was a disc of red marble which marked the spot where a tree had grown. To this tree the slaves had been tied while being whipped to keep them in line. Below, in the dungeons, we looked at the appallingly small, dark chambers into which they had been crammed to await their sale, before being shipped to all parts of the world. To one side was a crucifix made from the wood of the tree under which the explorer Livingstone's heart had been buried in Zambia. This had been removed later for burial in England at Westminster Abbey.

Food Market

Cathedral

The food market was a jumble of stalls jammed with shoppers and traders. A strong smell of spices, mixed with the noise of humanity en mass, filled the air.

Dhows under construction

Further north we visited a village where dhows were being built, using ancient techniques passed down over the ages from father to son and using traditional tools. Then we drove to the farming area where spices were grown. We learnt about growing cloves. These thin, tall trees have flowers which give off a strong characteristic smell. At the bottom of each blossom was the clove, greenish white and later red which, when dried, turns the familiar black. We learnt how to remove the cloves by pulling an almost closed hand over each cluster of fruit. The iodine bush bleeds iodine when its trunk is scratched. Cinnamon bark is shed from its tree trunk before being crushed into small pieces, or being powdered. The root of Cumin, which resembles that of ginger, is crushed and used for colouring. Black pepper was picked off a vine, not a bush or tree as we had expected. Star fruit, lemon grass and many other plants grew in abundance. When it started to rain Idi our guide, cut down banana leaves to create an umbrella and later, as we waited for the rain to stop, he made us an intricate basket out of palm fronds.

The ancient Arab fort was being used as an open air concert space surrounded by a tier of artisan stalls. Emerging from it, we were pestered, for the first time, by a young man who wanted to act as our guide, for a fee. He just wouldn't take 'no' for an answer. In the end, we bought him off for $1 US, and felt guilty that we had succumbed to his insistence, but much preferred the freedom and peace of exploring by ourselves.

Following all these visits we wanted to relax a bit, so retreated to the newest hotel in town, which we had noticed as we sailed past in *Demelza*. Situated on the waterfront, the Hotel Serena had a stone flagged, colonnaded terrace. Here we ordered drinks while watching dark clouds scudding over an equally dark grey sea below. Two Canadian women, holidaying at the hotel, joined us. One was a nurse taking a break from a tour of duty in Saudi Arabia, and the other her sister Tracy, owner/driver of a transport truck based in Toronto. A third girl, an effervescent Australian, made up this most entertaining trio.

On the way home through Stone Town we explored the alleyways and shops, picking up mementoes of our visit. These included an exquisitely carved trivet, a hand sewn cushion cover and a pot of deliciously fragrant Ylang Ylang hand cream.

Suleyman our trivet maker

The next morning we set off for the Jozani Forest with Tembo in his taxi. Here, Red Colobus monkeys hold sway. Beautiful big mango trees, planted by an early princess, line one stretch of the road south. Long tails hanging vertically down from the branches of the trees gave away the presence of slumbering monkeys overhead. Along a two mile boardwalk through the mangrove forest, small baskets of charcoal lined the pathway. Charcoal is made by the local population by burning mangrove wood slowly for two days. This information was gleaned from the Director of Tourism, whom we visited on our return to Stone Town. He was a personal friend of Tembo's, and was fascinated by our journey on *Demelza*. Of particular interest to him were our impressions of visiting Zanzibar.

Charcoal arrives at the market

"What yachts really need in Zanzibar," Christine told him "is good security. Yachts just won't come if they hear of attacks like that on the French couple from Kilifi. Word soon gets around the cruising fleet, and they'll stay away." He was most receptive and courteous, saying he would follow up with the local police, though we were told later that much of the problem is drug related in Stone Town, and that the police were often related to the perpetrators of the violence.

Our return to Dar on the ferry was exciting. Boarding was held up pending the arrival of a television camera crew who wanted to take pictures of the passengers boarding and walking around on the ferry. They were making a publicity film. A charming man sat next to me on the journey. He was from Mtwara, south of Dar, on the border with Mozambique. Watching the on board movie, he became quite excited, and was crushed when we arrived in Dar before its conclusion. Vowing to buy a video of the film so that he could see its end, he bade us farewell. Giving us one of his business cards, he extended an invitation to visit him in Dar if we had time before we left. It was only later, when we were on *Demelza* again and had paid off Mr. Lucan, our askari, that I looked at the card, to discover that he was a High Court Judge in Tanzania.

Hank, who we met at the yacht club, worked at the Dutch Embassy in Dar. He and his wife Beppie invited us to a farewell gathering at the US Marine's Club. They offered to take us to town to collect our exit permits from Tanzania. On the way, we drove past Dr. Koch's internationally renowned Tuberculosis Clinic and hospital, where so much of his pioneering work was done on the diagnosis and treatment of this debilitating and frequently fatal disease.

Dr. Koch's T.B. Clinic

Our visit was coming to an end, with visits from Uwe and Gabby who were on the boat *Aragos*, Irmgard and Oscar on *Telstar*, and Richard on *Mambo*. There followed a shopping expedition to stock up the boat, and several trips ashore to fill our diesel jugs. At a small ceremony at the Dar Yacht Club, we exchanged yacht club burgees with the Vice Commodore, in appreciation of their kindness to us during our stay.

On leaving the bay, we passed a lone fisherman paddling his hollowed out log canoe.

Asante sana Mama (thank you very much Mama) he said as we slowed *Demelza* down dropping a length of nylon fishing line and some fishing hooks in his boat as a gift. We sailed off towards our next waypoint at the mouth of the bay. Our hearts sank when we saw the size of the swell outside. Either this was a hangover from the storms we had had in the past week, or they were an indication of bigger storms out at sea. Huge ships were at anchor outside Dar es Salaam's main harbour. They were waiting for their turn to unload. We tacked our way through these sleeping giants, whose only sign of life was a continuous stream of water from one or more outlets in their hulls.

Heading south, we passed a series of lovely deserted coral islands with untouched beaches as we entered the Mafia Channel. After sailing past Bowejun, we crossed the mouth of the Rufiji River. This river, arising in Africa's largest game reserve, the Selous, winds its way seaward for four hundred miles to emerge in a vast swampy delta. It was here, at the beginning of the First World War, that the German cruiser *The Koenigsberg* sought refuge after sinking *HMS Pegasus* off Zanzibar. After entering the river and scraping over the sandbars, Commander Max Looff removed the ship's boiler, taking it a hundred miles through the bush to Dar for repair. He dismantled the smaller guns, and placed them in appropriate positions guarding the river mouth. After ten months of cat and mouse warfare between torpedo boats and the German shore battery, the cruiser was finally spotted from reconnaissance aircraft. Gun barges were sent upriver to disable her. Finally when there was no hope of escape, and with only two hundred sick sailors to handle her, Commander Looff threw the remaining guns overboard and scuttled his ship.

We next passed Simaya Island, and finally arrived at lovely Songa Songa Island where a Canadian oil crew was said to be drilling for natural gas. After anchoring behind a white coral sand spit, we went ashore but were disappointed to find that the island was deserted. The weather deteriorated, and heavy squalls blew into the bay. In the morning we were visited by fishermen with whom we traded T shirts for fish, tangerines and shells.

We passed Kilwa which, in the twelfth century, was the wealthiest town in East Africa. It was the centre of commerce particularly for gold from Sofala, near Beira to the south of us in Mozambique. Here the Sultan ruled until invaded by the Portuguese in 1505. The ruins of this once prosperous city are the most spectacular and best preserved in all Tanzania.

As we were passing Mzungu Bay, Christine was reading in the cockpit. Suddenly she called "Isn't that a mast in the bay?" I couldn't see anything against the thick backdrop of trees and mangrove lining its shores. However, through binoculars, we confirmed the presence of a mast.

"It's strange," Christine said, "the mast is upright and totally still, yet there's breaking surf running on the beach. Could that be the French boat from Kilifi? Is it green hulled?"

We both looked hard but couldn't decide on the boat's colour.

"OK," I said, "we'll find a way in through the reef and get a closer look." Carefully approaching the surging white water crashing against the protecting reef, we followed it along until we came across a passage of deeper water. We pointed *Demelza* toward the shore and, surfing in with our hearts in our mouths, we hoped that the blue water would continue into the bay. It did. As we approached the boat we saw that it was green and that it was stationary because its keel was firmly planted in the sandy beach below a village. Dropping our anchor in calmer water, we noticed lots of activity ashore. A swarm of children were making for their canoes lined up on the beach. In no time at all they were paddling frantically towards us across the bay. The leaders came to a shuddering halt by running their canoes into *Demelza*'s side.

"Get those damned canoes off the boat!" I yelled as I danced about on deck to no avail. A further fusillade of hull impacts signaled the arrival of a dozen more canoes. None of the children spoke English. I waved my arms frantically in the air and assumed the stance of a policeman stopping traffic in downtown Vancouver.

The missing boat

All with no improvement except for a gale of appreciative laughter, and more resounding thumps as their outriggers hit our sides. Finally Christine, long used to my fruitless outbursts, calmly walked on deck, and using an admirable mixture of Swahili and calm gestures, located one small boat operator who understood enough to take off for shore to bring out somebody who could speak English. Furthermore she bribed the children to stop banging *Demelza*'s sides by giving one of the biggest boys a packet of cookies to share among the crowd, on condition that they stayed away from our boat. It worked like a charm. All unwanted attention was diverted to the little lad who had the hopeless task of sharing the cookies out fairly.

Anxiously watching the shore we were so relieved that, before the cookies were finished, a little canoe with a very large gentleman in the stern was being paddled towards us from the direction of the village. Christine was able to contact Tony in Kilifi on the radio, telling him the good news that we had located Roger's boat. The dinghy and our visitor, who was sitting up to his waist in sea water, drew alongside.

"My name is Shari Samuel," he said holding out his hand as he came aboard.

"We are so glad to see you," I said. "What is going on here?"

"The green boat went ashore three miles south of Ras Mwedi at Kisiwe Nongure," he replied. "That area claims many boats as it has a strong onshore current." We served him tea and shortbread biscuits in the cockpit, which impressed the lads circling *Demelza* in their canoes at a respectful distance. Shari explained that he was a visitor to the village himself and worked for FinAid building roads nearby.

"It is like this," he said. "This is a bad village, and you should get out of here as soon as you can. Roger and his wife abandoned their boat on the reef as he was badly hurt in the Zanzibar attack. Subsequently thirty men from Mzungu village worked for four days to get the boat off the reef, using empty oil drums as buoyancy. With the help of two dhows, and after taking off the keel, they managed to pull the boat into the bay. When they got her there, they stripped everything off her and sold all they could for very little money."

He further explained that *Mzungu* means white man in English, and that a stone located on a nearby point, marked the landing place of the Portuguese in the fifteenth century, and now marks the border between Tanzania and Mozambique. Shari described in detail what was left on the boat, and this information we were able to transmit over the radio to Tony in Kilifi.

"The villagers think you have come here now with money to reclaim the boat. They will be very disappointed. Whatever you do," he said as he left, "don't stay here after dark." This explained the excitement we had seen on the beach when we first arrived.

"I cannot thank you enough." I said as we waved him goodbye, escorted by a fleet of canoes.

The full moon was just rising above the trees and bathing the bay in an eerie light. Ashore, campfires were being lit to cook the evening meal and the sound of drums and dancing increased in volume as we looked on apprehensively.

"If we don't get out of here, we'll find ourselves in the pot for supper," I said as the drums beat ever louder.

Finally the moon was high enough for us to see reasonably well. We hauled up the anchor and headed out towards where we thought we had entered through the gap in the reef.

"I don't feel good about this," I said, "but staying here for the night is the worse option." We groped along the inside of the reef, trying to find the opening out to sea.

"If we get this wrong," I said "we're here for keeps."

Finally we found the gap. Thankful for the full moon shining a path for us, we made for the open sea. Ensuring we were at least four miles from shore before turning south we passed the spot where Roger's boat had gone ashore. We noticed the strong current that Shari had warned us about. A truly strange phenomenon as there was no obvious local land formation that could have accounted for it.

The Indian Ocean high pressure system was intensifying south of Madagascar, so we decided to push on before the trade winds intensified. At daybreak we found ourselves sailing into the long bay and river mouth on which the town of Lindi is situated. This is an old German colonial town in which the many period buildings have been kept in fairly good repair. Its main export is sisal. Entrance to the river mouth is over an extensive bar, which was rough in the prevailing fifteen to twenty knot southeast wind and ebbing tide. Carefully we motored upriver past a huge coral reef to starboard. We decided not to anchor off the town pier in case we ran into the same trouble Roger had had in Stone Town. Instead we motored on upriver for about two miles before dropping anchor in good holding mud. Not far away across the bay was a ferry dock, used to carry people across to town. In the morning we dinghied ashore and spoke to the ferry captain, who delegated a small boy to come across the river with us to introduce us to the Lindi Port Captain. Following introductions, the Port Captain assigned two English speaking boys to escort Christine to a produce stall and a local bakery in town. It seemed that the only items available that day were oranges and coconuts. On the radio, Tony had told us of the availability of Makondi carvings in Lindi, so we decided to try to locate the carvers.

The next day we took *Demelza* across to the town anchorage as we needed to get some diesel and water. After anchoring, we lowered the dinghy and put our diesel and water jugs on board. The town tap, to which we had been directed in the Port, was dry. Another boy, Masanje, who was waiting for us ashore, escorted us to the local gas station for fuel, and then to the town well for water.

The town well was some distance from the port, along high walled streets. Along these Masanje and I walked, while Christine kept an eye on the boat. Eventually Masanje darted through a gap in the high wall, and we found ourselves in a large enclosed courtyard. At the far end of this were terraces overlooking the well which had a concrete apron surrounding it. A crowd of local women were doing their laundry, lifting water up from the well in pitchers. Some of these they carried away on their heads. Both they and the crowd of children instantly stopped talking and laughing when they saw a white man carrying empty jerry jugs. Obviously this was neither the place nor a job for men folk. However, the throng of good natured children thought it very entertaining and tried to help. The women retreated as we approached the well, and would not entertain the idea of me waiting my turn. So I accepted the opportunity to get water. I lowered the bottom of an oil can that was being used to haul the water up from the well. Down and down it went for an eternity before a distant splash signaled success. Masanje cranked up the container, and I was relieved to see its contents were perfectly clear. One of the ladies, noticing my problem in transferring the water from the oilcan into our narrow necked jug, produced the top end of an old 7 Up bottle to use as a funnel. After many journeys down and up the well our jugs were full. I expressed my thanks to the crowd and beat a hasty retreat. The cacophony of noise resumed, as the ladies regrouped to discuss what had obviously been the event of the week.

Masanje helping with supplies

In the heat of the afternoon, Masanje asked if we would like to visit his home. So after putting *Demelza* and the dinghy in the care of the Port Captain, we set off on foot to his house. Here we met his brother Suku, the district engineer and his wife. Both spoke good English. We were served a delicious lunch of rice, roast meat and a salad of tomato, onion and spinach, followed by small sweet oranges. The house was spotlessly clean, and after lunch several more children appeared. Apparently they were not direct family members, but rather an extended family from all over the country. Suku explained that in Africa, if one family member is well off, it is their duty to look after any family member who asks for help. Later he drove us in his car to a park like area just out of town, in which there was a thatched shed where local wood carvers did their work. That day there was only one carver working. He explained that the others were in the bush collecting ebony. Most of their carvings were bought by a local monastery for shipping to Germany. After some persuasion by Suku, he produced a handsome two foot ebony carving of an Askari holding his shield and adorned with all sorts of attitude adjusting weapons.

Our lugubrious warrior

All this kindness we reciprocated the next day by inviting Suku and his family to visit us on *Demelza*. For this occasion we opened up a tin of fruit cake which Penny and Shaun had given us in Australia, and which we had saved for a special occasion. Washed down with paw paw juice, followed by pretzels, nuts and raisins, our visitors looked well satisfied. Just as our meal was over, a local fisherman brought his small boat alongside offering us a lobster.

Later as I replaced the engine's fuel filters, Christine treated the scratches on *Demelza*'s hull with Penetrol. We cleared customs and immigration, and waved farewell to Masanje, who had got up early to see us off at dawn on the ebb tide.

A thirty mile sail southwards brought us to Mikindani Bay, and a further five miles of motoring through its narrow entrance led us to the shelter of Mikindani Harbour. Several houses nestled among the baobab trees around the bay. In one of these, Livingstone was said to have lived for two years prior to leaving on his last expedition to Lake Tanganyika.

Farewell to Lindi

CHAPTER 18
Comoros Islands and Madagascar

COMOROS

Cruising on south, the *Razs* on the charts became *Cabos* denoting that we were now cruising around capes in Mozambique waters. Rounding Cabo Delgado was very rough in spite of it being the early morning when the wind was light. Huge clouds gave the shoreline a rather bleak look, and the sea had lost its appealing blue colour in heavy showers. The stretch of coast between Cabo Delgado and Cabo Diabo is made up of one hundred and twenty miles of unspoilt reef with plenty of sheltered anchorages and incomparable diving. The coast itself is low and uninteresting, but pristine coral islands are arranged like a necklace along its length.

It was at this point that the south going Mozambique Current joined the coast, its full strength being felt five to ten miles off the fringing reefs. Close to these the current was normally between two and three knots. Cabo Delgado had the first working lighthouse we had seen on this part of the coast.

The weather remained unsettled, with the wind blowing between twenty to twenty-five knots from the south. This made the anchorages a little uncomfortable. At one of them, on Vamizi Island, we touched a coral head lightly with our rudder on the incoming swell, and had to move to a clearer but less protected spot in forty feet of water.

When at last the weather did clear, we set out eastwards to cross over to Mayotte in the Comoros Island group. Our water-maker was working hard as we travelled. We had an excellent sail, and soon were able to pick out the volcano Mt Zamboro, on Grande Comoro Island about fifty miles in the distance. A beautiful tropic bird flew out to greet us as the sea became unsettled. This meant there were storms around somewhere. The boat pitched and rolled, which made all tasks difficult and frustrating, as we struggled against wind and current, only achieving between one to three knots over the ground. Off Grande Comore Island the current suddenly changed, and we found ourselves going in the right direction at twenty two knots over the ground! The clouds cleared and the seas settled. Past the islands of Mohere and Anjouan we sailed through flat water, getting into a bay on the north end of Mayotte Island at midnight, where we decided to anchor for the night.

In the morning I dived under the boat to inspect the rudder for any damage following our touching the coral head in Vamizi Island. All was well. So we motored to Pamanzi Islet and dropped anchor outside Dzoudzi harbour. In her best school French Christine called "Charlie Tango," the Port Captain, radio operator and local weather guru, to tell him of our arrival. That afternoon, a boat with Charlie Tango and three smartly dressed Comoran Douane, came alongside. Formalities over, we started the engine to relocate closer to shore in the harbour only to find that our cooling water pump wasn't working. As it was only a short distance to our new anchorage, we persevered. All the overheating alarms were sounding before we shut down the engine. Sure enough the fan belt to the water pump had broken. Replacing it with a spare involved the usual dismantling of half the boat to be able to get at the appropriate area. This was the first time since being in Dar harbour that we had seen other cruising boats.

Postcard of Dzaoudzi harbour

By now we had accumulated a fresh crop of maintenance jobs. A split hose, a leak under the galley sink, and a fuel leak at the top of the main diesel tank in the bilge all needed attention.

The Comoros Islands are volcanic, rising twelve hundred feet straight up from the seabed. Their name derives from the Arabic *Gamar* meaning moon, which shines with brilliant clarity out of clear night skies. A tropical storm was forming and moving down from 9S to 11S just to the east of our island. This gave us some concern, as we re-inflated our dinghy and went ashore to Pamandzi. At the boulangerie we bought baguettes, and at the Superette a bottle of Pastis, a favourite drink of Christine's. Being a French possession among an otherwise Arabic island group, Mayotte is well stocked. Restaurants serve excellent French cuisine, and boat parts were readily available. It was an oasis and such a pleasure after a long absence of these items.

One of our favourite pastimes here was to sit, relaxing on a restaurant's terrace above the ferry landing, watching the colourfully dressed Arab women moving about below. They carried everything from food to livestock on their heads. As well as their all encompassing dresses, many of the women wore sandalwood paint on their faces, which was considered a sign of beauty. They also wore copious amounts of golden jewellery.

Dzaoudzi ferry

On the radio we heard of a British boat lost off the South African coast. Regular calls were going out for *Transgression*, and the overseas service of the British Broadcasting Service was asking Penny to call home. Finally, an air search was mounted for the boat, but was called off after forty days had elapsed since she had been sighted.

When the Comoros Islands voted for independence from France, only Mayotte Island voted to stay a French prefecture. The entire colonial infrastructure had to be moved from Grande Comore to Mayotte, including the airport, travel agencies, and telecommunication centre. This put all but Mayotte into an economic nosedive. The banks were a short ferry ride from Pamandzi islet over to the main Island, where most of the retail and wholesale outlets were situated in the town of Mamoudzou. Getting our propane tanks filled proved quite a hassle. Firstly, the fittings for the gas bottles were not compatible and secondly, riding with gas bottles on the regular ferry was not allowed. Instead, we should have waited for the "dangerous goods" ferry which went over once a day. Needless to say most people carried their bottles concealed in backpacks on the regular ferries.

Word had gone out on the radio from us via Durban to Canada, telling our family that we had arrived safely in Mayotte. This was received with much relief by everybody at home as they had been hearing stories of the search going on for the British yacht.

Being in Mayotte provided us with an opportunity to visit the capital of Madagascar. We arranged to leave the boat for four days as reports were favourable about security in Dzoudzi. This was not a great surprise as there was a sizable naval base nearby. There were lots of healthy young French sailors running around in the shortest, tightest shorts that one could ever imagine. With friends keeping an eye on *Demelza* we booked tickets on an Air France flight to Antananarivo, and arranged to stay in the Hilton Hotel!

Madagascar

Suddenly we were flying over the sea, a flight which took seventy five minutes across the Mozambique Channel to Madagascar. As the large island came into view, we were amazed to see steep terraced mountains and paddy fields along the sides of its central plateau. We had one stop on the way to collect entry visas at Majunga. Antananarivo is located on the high plateau in the interior. Madagascar had its origins one hundred and fifty million years ago when it split off from the Gondwanaland super continent leaving a space between Somalia and South India before moving southwards. Early Malay and Polynesian settlers mixed with raiding Bantus and later, Arab traders who plied their wares and slaves throughout the area. Madagascar served as a base for pirates in the seventeenth century attacking European trading ships. A turbulent history followed involving French colonizers, warring tribes and British missionaries. The latter devised a written form of the Malagasy language. French money helped develop the island's infrastructure. In 1947 an abortive rebellion for independence was put down with great savagery by Senegalese mercenaries paid for by the French. In 1958 a referendum was passed making Madagascar an autonomous republic with full independence following in 1960. French influence was replaced by the USSR and China, which caused turmoil and hardship to the economy. With the fall of the USSR in 1989, a new approach was made for trade ties with South Africa which culminated in the beginnings of a new era of democratic rule in 1993.

Antananarivo

We were met at the airport, and whisked away to the Hilton by John, who spoke good English. In the twenty minute drive into town he persuaded us that he should be our guide while we were in Madagascar.

The double storied brick houses, with no chimney and smoke stained upper floor windows were a surprise to us. Every town and village had brickworks outside its boundaries. Along the way rice paddies were everywhere on the terraced hillsides, fed by very brown streams. Land erosion is a huge problem, as all the covering trees had been removed and the heavy rains were exacting a horrific toll on the quantity and quality of soil.

Brick houses

Down below our hotel's window, the flower market decorated the sidewalk surrounding Lake Anosy in the centre of the city. The cobbled streets wound up from the lake to the old President's Palace and the modern commercial area. The city is built on twelve hills, so the streets are steep. One hill dominates the rest with the burnt out Reva Palace ruins at its summit.

John's brother, also John, whom we called Jacques to avoid confusion, drove the car. With John as our guide we went to a village north of the city where the old royal Marina family's palace stood. The next day they took us on a walking tour of the Zoma market, and were most diligent in protecting us from its infamous pick pockets. The market was packed solid with people, and every time Christine agreed to pay for something, John would jump in and beat the price down in an embarrassingly long harangue in Malagasy. The following day we drove one hundred and ten miles south to the spa town of Antsirabe, with its wide boulevards and elegant spas. Rickshaws all vied with one another to carry anybody showing the slightest inclination of walking anywhere. Behind plain doors off the streets, men sat at tables, cutting and polishing semi precious stones dug out of the local mines. Exquisite jewellery was being made which sold for a very reasonable price.

Hurrying is not a concept in Malagasy life, and *'mora, mora'* (slowly, slowly) is the saying of the day. Social rules are strictly adhered to, especially the high respect in which elderly people are held. These rules or *'fady'* dictate all aspects of life. Taboos abound unexpectedly, some of which make sense and others do not. *Fady* varies from village to village and must be determined early in any visit.

Soon our trip was over, and we were walking the docks of Dzoudzi again finding our way back to *Demelza*, and being greeted by new and old friends. We felt totally at home again. Dzoudzi anchorage on Pamandzi Islet is quite a gathering place for yachts cruising the western part of the Indian Ocean, because of its security and its readily available facilities. Longtime cruisers Humphrey and Claire from Burnaby, near Vancouver, had just arrived from Richards Bay in South Africa. They were kind enough to share their knowledge of that area with us as that was where we planned to make landfall in Africa.

Becoming increasingly sensitive to the quickly changing weather patterns in that part of the Indian Ocean, we decided to pack our sick laptop and send it home to Canada for repair. This, along with all the many chores of repairing sails, varnishing, oil changes and filter changes kept us busy. We had the occasional break for sightseeing to Lac Dziani, the local volcanic crater, and the annual craft show in Mamoudzou. Many of the boats that had left turned back because of the frightful weather outside. We were also invited to the home of Philippe, the Port Captain of 'Charlie Tango' fame, his wife Sonya, and daughter Nicola who was going to Police College. Philippe was a mine of information on local weather, and between his broken English and our broken French, we learnt a lot.

Bruno, at the Information Centre, drove a Taxi Brousse. He agreed to take a group of cruisers on a day's safari to a village called Ngoudja at the south end of Mayotte Island. Eight of us packed ourselves into his vehicle before driving through the lush countryside. We stopped to look at *Bangas* (bachelor pads), where teenaged boys lived alone apart from their families, to prepare themselves for manhood. Swimming off the beautiful beach at Ngoudja, Christine spotted a huge turtle with two remora attached. Apart from the cost of a can of beer, $6 at the local resort, the place was a dream.

On returning to the boat, we called in at the Port Captain's office and sent a Fax home asking them to send any future correspondence to the Zululand Yacht Club in Richards Bay in South Africa. By this decision we made the necessary commitment to the next leg of our journey. We had to seriously prepare for the upcoming cruise to Madagascar and then on to Richards Bay. First a thorough check of the boat. Every inch was gone over and the discovered deficiencies remedied. Christine spent a lot of time using the hand cranked Singer sewing machine, mending the head of our jib which was in danger of coming off, and repairing several parting seams. It was a thrill to meet Delwyn McPhun on his girl friend Sylvia's boat *Gabian PV* which had dropped anchor in our bay. Delwyn, after three years cruising the East coast of Africa, has published his book *East African Pilot*, a beautiful testament to his perseverance. He was kind enough to sign our copy and Christine's photograph of him now graces its front page.

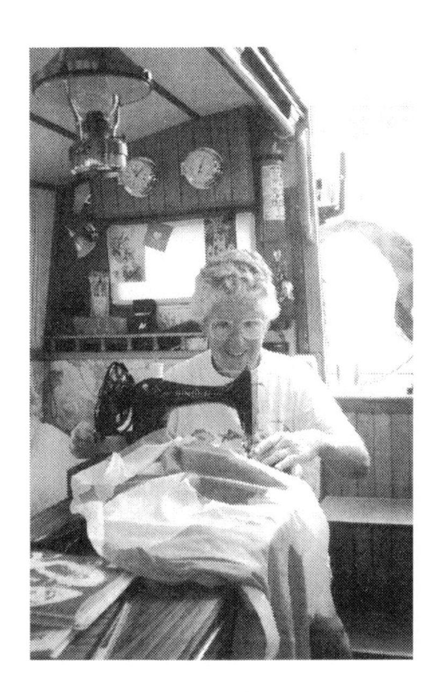

Christine and her trusty sewing machine

Having almost completely re-sewn our number two jib, the stitching of which had rotted in the tropical sun, Christine then started re-provisioning the boat, as basic supplies would not be available to us again until we arrived in Richards Bay. Being a great fan of Eric Hiscock's books, and in the present dodgy state of our refrigerator, Christine decided to salt lean beef and to bottle it in brine, as mentioned in Eric's books. We also tried drying meat in direct sunlight using aluminum reflectors for greater heat, but this was not so successful. Meanwhile I did the usual replenishing of fresh water, diesel oil, and propane from widely scattered and distant sources, using our folding German built trolley. This received a fresh coat of paint and a new wheel bushing in recognition of its invaluable service carrying heavy fuel, water jugs, and bags of groceries. Christine stitched a new Q flag, as the original had fallen apart having flogged itself to pieces. She also replaced worn out panels in the French courtesy flag that we had used in several countries on the way. We pored over the upcoming charts of Madagascar and of the coast of Mozambique and South Africa.

Nancy on *Tethys* kindly shared a series of daily local weather fax pictures with us so that we could get an idea of the best time to leave. Although some boats had left, I was not happy with the picture we had been getting. So we decided to wait a couple more days. I took a trip to the top of the mast and found that the lower forward shroud had sprung one of its wires. Peter, from *Shemali Blue* gave me a hand replacing it using Norseman fittings, which were new to me. Soon the job was done. Now we were ready to leave! That day we celebrated our wedding anniversary with a lunch at a local restaurant in the company of seven friends from three other boats, English, Swedish and Australian respectively.

After final farewells to "Charlie Tango" — *Demelza*, *Shemali Blue* and *Lutana II* pulled up their anchors and rendezvoused at Bandele Island at the entrance to South Pass. The wind was blowing strongly from the south west and it was a rolly anchorage. By the next morning however the wind had gone around and we were off on a great sail until two in the morning, when the wind died.

We motored under a quarter moon all the way to the beautiful island of Nosy Mitsio, off the Northwest coast of Madagascar, anchoring in forty feet in mud. Low rolling hills overlook the many beautiful pristine anchorages, and this anchorage was well protected from all but northerly winds. Most of the covering of trees had been cut down on the island, except for a small area at its south end. Mangoes and coconuts were delivered by outrigger canoes in the mornings. Along with three other boats from Britain in the bay we felt quite crowded after all our travels alone in Kenya and Tanzania. Three days here, swimming, eating lobster, walking and socializing, soon passed with only one hiccup. When reversing to set the anchor near one of the beaches further up the island that we had visited for a swim, I managed to wrap the dinghy's painter around the propeller. This necessitated jumping over the side of the boat with a sharp knife to physically remove the resulting solid knot, piece by piece. The other damage caused by this incident happened as the propeller tightened the line, which was unfortunately over the top of one of our stern lifelines. This increased tension had snapped the lifeline.

We sailed past four huge basalt rocks, the Four Brothers, which emerged from the depths as round naked rock. Rising vertically from a depth of one hundred feet, these were home to thousands of frigate birds and boobies.

After half a day's most pleasant sailing we arrived at the channel between little Nosy Sakatia and the larger Nose Be, a beautiful anchorage with excellent snorkeling off the boat. Both islands are carpeted in cane plantations and Ylang Ylang groves.

Sakatia anchorage

The latter's fruit is distilled for perfume, and the former for rum. Here, coffee, vanilla and spices grow in profusion. The main town is on Nosy Be and is called Hell-Ville. We paid a visit there by taxi from a beach close by. The town has a relaxed, meandering, colourful, faded kind of atmosphere, where people watching seemed the main preoccupation. The market was full of exotic fruits, and visiting tourists from many resorts on the island were well represented. Excellent restaurants were well patronized by us all. Here we purchased fuel vouchers to take to the bulk oil terminal in Crater Bay along the coast. As we had to buy a minimum two hundred gallons of fuel, *Demelza* joined four other boats in sharing that quantity.

Hell-Ville lace market

The next day we took all the boats around to Crater Bay and, while the first yacht tied up at the fuel dock, the rest idled around. After a few minutes there was a lot of shouting on the dock, with waving of arms, and rushing about. The fuel was stored in huge tanks at the top of a cliff, about two hundred yards away from the dock. It was transported to the dock through a four inch hose which had no nozzle on its end. The only control of oil flow was by a tap between the bottom of the tank and the beginning of the hose at the top of the hill. At an appropriate moment, the owner of the British catamaran who had gone first, shouted to the fellow up the cliff who controlled the tap. With an increasingly loud rumble, diesel fuel came in a torrent down the pipe and into the bilge tanks of the catamaran at far too great a pace for the tanks to take it in. By the time the shouting and dancing on the dock had registered with the man controlling the tap, the boat's bilges were half full of diesel fuel, and the skipper's mate a slithering smelly copy of her former self. The biggest problem of all was that, even when the tank man had turned off the tap, the huge hose still kept disgorging its contents over the hapless receiver at the bottom end. It was then I decided I wouldn't take *Demelza* anywhere near that apparatus, but instead filled four jerry cans, badly, from the hose, thoroughly coating my self, our dinghy and the dock in oil.

At various times during our stay, cruisers were suffering malaria-like attacks of intermittent fever, and dashing off to the local hospital for appropriate tests and treatment. Fortunately, with careful precautions, Christine and I were able to avoid all those problems.

Beach BBQs, snorkeling nearby reefs, collecting empty sea shells, swimming to keep cool, shopping and sightseeing kept us busy for the week before we left for the neighbouring island of Nosy Komba with its village, Ampangorina. The weather on this island was exceptionally good, and we landed at Rogers Beach, walking up through the trees to a delightful nearby waterfall. The village was quite small but busy and packed with black lemurs. We bought a carved mask of a lemur from one of the local craftsmen, made out of Paliscundia wood, and also a lovely wooden model of a dhow. A visit to Nosy Manoko at the south end of Apasindava Bay was exceptionally well sheltered, with not a hint of the roll that we had been experiencing in some of the other anchorages. The beaches were scattered with rosy-hued crystals from fallen cliff faces. Picturesquely set, with a back-drop of mountains and mangrove lined sandy beaches, it was a perfect isolated spot to spend a few days. We took the dinghy up a cut which wound its way through the shoreline mangroves for about three miles, going up it on the swirling flood tide. Madagascar Bee-eaters, fish eagles, black parrots and a curlew like bird flew ahead of us as we motored along the narrow waterway, which wound quietly onwards. Lemurs gazed and called at us from the tree canopy. This was truly a very special place.

Peter, Carda and Ellie Best

Abdullah, from the little village at the head of the inlet, brought crabs out to *Demelza* that morning and on another occasion, a carved wooden prawn for which he seemed pleased to accept T shirts, fishing line and lures. It was a very quiet and isolated community, and as we returned down the waterway, we spotted the occasional fishing outrigger canoe parked in the many little backwaters off the mainstream. Traveller palms grew everywhere, and seemed to be the particular favourite of the Bee-eaters that fluttered about in the sun with their beautiful iridescent olive plumage reflecting the light as they darted around us.

Nosy Tanikely is a particularly lovely little island, with quite exceptional diving reefs just off shore. Its marine life is incomparable. On the well treed island, flying foxes and exotic birds abound. Our anchor, set in sand in twenty feet, was clearly visible from onboard. It is a truly lovely place and one which we visited many times.

"Charlie Tango's" weather broadcasts still called for reinforced trades. So we hung about for another week. Those yachts that had left for Russian Bay, the jumping off spot for South Africa, encountered fifty knot winds and miserably rough seas with some boat damage reported. So we continued our blissful pottering around the little islands and beaches in glorious weather. A huge ray swam under our boat on one of our expeditions and then gave us a display of jumping out of the water before splashing its wings on the surface.

A forty five foot English catamaran joined us for a few days. She had a hired crew taking her to meet the owner in South Africa. They very kindly took us for a spin on the boat to show us how well she sailed. We were very impressed at her speed as she traveled in the strong winds across the smooth water between the islands.

Finally, after a total stay of four weeks in this idyllic cruising ground on the northwest coast of Madagascar, we tore ourselves away. We moved to Russian Bay readying ourselves for the Mozambique Channel. The winds continued to be heavy during the day but it was time to be moving on.

Russian Bay (known locally as Helondranon Ambavatoby) is a huge sheltered bay with a narrow neck between Point Antsiriaka and Point Makambi. This is a traditional hurricane hole. The surrounding forest had many lemurs, which called loudly at night, and plentiful birdlife inhabiting the tree lined shores.

Suddenly it was the end of September. Cruising boats from all over the Indian Ocean were moving south to avoid the Cyclone season which begins in October and most frequently occurs between January and May. We had spent many happy months cruising in this delightful area, and many of the boats that we had met along the way, with whom we had shared so many rich experiences, had already moved south. We had spent hours with them planning tactics for the crossing to South Africa. In the end, the decision as to the best day, hour, minute to leave was an individual one. Some had tired of waiting for a good forecast. Some didn't bother with weather forecasts at all. Some just dithered and waited for somebody else to take the plunge before following along. For our part, we did not leave until the weather charts looked favourable. *Shemali Blue* left Madagascar on 22nd September and *Magnum Bonum* on 23rd September. We left on the 29th September followed by *Wind Magic* and *Cynosure*, who left on October 3rd. In spite of all the planning, the boats followed different courses across the Mozambique Channel, hoping to find and use the south flowing Mozambique Current to best advantage, while getting across quickly enough to be able to find shelter on the mainland should it become necessary.

Dolphins leading the way

CHAPTER 19
Mozambique Channel

The Mozambique Channel, lying off the coast of East Africa between 12°S and 26°S, is two hundred and forty miles wide at its narrowest point at Cap St Andre on the west coast of Madagascar. Unlike the sheltered cruising grounds off the northwest coast that we had been exploring, the Mozambique Channel presented some unique conditions which had to be considered for a safe crossing. The cyclone season precluded crossing this channel for almost six months of each year, so we were comfortable, after spending most of September in Madagascar, to plan the channel crossing for October. We had to be prepared to do without the help of any functioning light stations to confirm our landfall on the African side, but hoped to be able to pick up salient land features as we approached. We would be traveling at the end of the South Monsoon, and could expect SSE winds of fifteen to twenty knots, which would make our southwesterly course a reasonable point of sail. Along the Madagascar coast we would be affected by land and sea breezes at different times of the day before getting into the southeast trades further out. Our decision was to sail down the coast to Cap St. Andre before heading out into the channel to catch the south flowing Mozambique current. Because of the constant threat of coastal low pressure systems and associated cold fronts from south of the Cape of Good Hope in South Africa, we had to watch the barometer closely to anticipate problems. These cold fronts brought a few hours of northerly wind, followed by strong south westerlies of gale force which reach as far north as Beira on the Mozambique coast at 20°S. To lessen our exposure, we thought that after passing Cap St. Andre, we would cross over quite quickly to take advantage of anchorages at one of the two available sheltered locations, one at Punta da Barra at 24°S, and the other at Cabo Inhaca at 26°S, both in Mozambique. While crossing, we wanted to make the greatest use of the Mozambique Current, flowing southward at four knots, until it passed the south end of Madagascar where it is joined by the South Equatorial current from the Indian Ocean to become the Aghullas Current. This would hurry us on to Cape Town at a later date. The Mozambique Current was about one hundred miles wide for most of our proposed route becoming stronger as we approached the African mainland.

On the morning of 29th September everything was ready. Our everyday cruising things were stowed away, all locker doors fastened, floorboards secured, and jack lines rigged along the deck to which we could clip our harnesses in rough weather. The dinghy was deflated and stowed down below. A beautiful dawn and gentle breeze saw us out of the excellent anchorage at 1000hrs. More long haul cruising boats had appeared overnight, and were getting some sleep before leaving for distant destinations, mostly in South Africa. The trip began with us motoring through still water in glorius weather. As we listened to the radio reports on weather and currents from yachts aheaed of us, they reported it was blowing thirty-five knots at the north end of Madagascar. We, a hundred miles to the south, had light north westerlies and a weak northerly current as predicted. By the light of the moon, Christine watched dolphins playing in the calm water ahead of us as *Demelza* steadily slipped south. Throughout that first night the wind continued to drop, so that at the start of my watch at 0100 hrs we stowed all sails, unhitched the tow generator, lifted up the wind vane steering blade, engaged the autopilot, and motored on into night.

By early morning the wind and sea had picked up from the south. Christine didn't get much rest as the waves were banging on the hull. So as not to disturb her further, I didn't put up the sails or reverse all the previous evening's work until she finally woke up and came on deck.

Just when we could have done with a weather fax picture, Pretoria didn't put one out on schedule. Apparently the transmitter towers had been hit by lightning during the night. Instead we relied on our ham radio contact with Tony, who was able to receive weather fax pictures from farther afield on his land based radio. We were able to pick up our friend "Charlie Tango" in Mayotte. His forecasts were always excellent, even if we lost something in the translation at times. We spent many hours translating the audiotapes that we always made of his broadcasts.

Gradually we lost the southeast wind which changed, over the next couple of days, to a favourable north westerly. We picked up a couple of Booby birds on our masthead one evening, and during the night one of them scared Christine half to death by landing next to her in the cockpit. They must have come out from the Island of Juan de Nova that we had passed during the night. In the darkness we could hear birds flying all around us, but couldn't see them. Their calls sounded almost human at times, maybe because we had been at sea too long. In another week we would reach Richards Bay in South Africa. Christine had daily radio schedules with several other boats, some of whom were ahead of us and beating into twenty knot winds with rain and lightning as they approached the mainland coast near Punta da Barra. We decided not to get too close to the African shore.

On the sixth day out we had seven hundred and forty one nautical miles to Richards Bay, and were in the main Mozambique current which was running at about three knots. By evening, our speed had picked up to six knots over the ground. Gradually the wind switched to the southeast and began to build. We took a reef in the mainsail at 0100 hrs at the start of my watch. As the night progressed, with twenty-five knots of wind, I had to take a few tucks in the furling jib in an attempt to calm the boat's motion so that Christine could get some sleep.

By 0900 hrs all was calm, leaving a residual nine foot swell and a restless sea. I always found these conditions disconcerting, waiting for something to happen. I was glad of the calm, yet frustrated that progress was not speedier. During our morning radio schedules we heard the other boats arriving in Richards Bay in thirty-five knots of wind from the northeast which, with the southerly current, had pushed them along at eleven knots over the ground!

Sure enough as the day gave way to evening, the soft clouds began to band across the sky. By 2300 hrs we had put away the genoa, and had locked its pole onto the mast. On the radio we heard of a low pressure system and associated front making its way up the coast toward us. We hoped that it would have tracked further north by the time we closed the mainland at Punta da Barra, which was now only one hundred and fifty six nautical miles ahead of us. Our search for weather forecasts was reaching fever pitch. Every few hours or so the weather rapidly changed. Durban Radio, "Charlie Tango" and amateur radio stations ashore, all helped to provide a picture which we recorded so that we could mull them over at leisure.

Ninety miles off Punta da Barra the wind deserted us. Heavy clouds glowered above. A sloppy sea threatened of winds to come and made the sails slat back and forth. "Bang, bang, slat, slat" and the odd crash from inside the cabin as something took off on a journey of its own. No matter how carefully we tried to secure everything to everything else, there was always an errant item. Progress slowed to about two knots. Surprisingly a dragon fly circled us as we watched from the cockpit. Chafe was a constant feature in these conditions, and it happened so quickly. I noticed that one of the jib sheets was beginning to chafe where it crossed the lifeline.

Sixty miles from land the wind picked up again. Out to sea a huge cruise ship idled by northwards about six miles away. It was the first ship we had seen for days. All around us a family of dolphins frolicked in the spray from *Demelza*'s bow. Alistair, in Durban told us that our cold front was leaving the area, and that we should have four days clear before the next one arrived. What a relief. Meanwhile, to the south of us, our cruising companions continued to arrive in Richards Bay in twenty-five knots of wind, and persistently recurring lightning storms. All we could think of was how lucky they were to have an uninterrupted night's sleep ahead of them in a quiet boat, firmly tied to land.

Punta da Barra looked like a long low sandy peninsula sticking out from land along the horizon on our starboard side. It was nice to see land again, but combers were visible crashing along its length. As I watched those crashing waves, they seemed to be getting closer. The wind was building. This was a lee shore, so we were galvanized into closing everything down. The bronze caps replaced the dorade vents, hatch covers were closed and drop boards put in place. We worked at all these jobs, securing everything down below. Daylight was fading and a mist developing around us. Checking instruments, I noticed that we were indeed closing the beach at a rapid rate, and that the wind was now blowing at thirty knots from the south. Hard on the wind, we sliced into the oncoming waves. Their noise increased with every minute that passed, and occasionally one caught us hard on the bow with a shuddering thud and flying spray as gallons of water raced down the deck. The sea was now white as we hunkered down in the cockpit to watch the maelstrom develop. All around us were crashing waves. The sail juddered as a new gust hit, and we heeled over before its strength. Our white wake coiled erratically behind us as the wind vane struggled to keep us on course. Out to sea we noticed whales surfacing, rising out of the tortured water to crash back again in an arc of foam, which was soon dispersed by the now screaming wind. One after another they rose, cavorting in what was to them a perfect environment for a bit of fun. One whale was slowly approaching us. Christine went below to radio our position and conditions to a contact ashore. Suddenly I looked up and there, twenty feet above us on a mountain of sea, was a sixty foot whale swimming alongside.

"Hold on" I yelled. "We've got a whale taking a great interest in us about twenty feet off our port side."

Just then the whale turned and passed across the bow of the boat. Frantically I disengaged the wind vane, turned on the engine, and swerved the boat sharply to port. The wind spilled out of the sails to an accompanying deafening roar. *Demelza* sat bolt upright without the pressure of wind on her sails, and the sea seemed determined to inundate us as we were broadside on. Meanwhile our visitor came to a stop abreast of Christine's window as she talked on the radio. The whale returned her startled gaze with a seemingly all knowing eye. Satisfied at last, it raised its enormous fluke, and sounded as I turned the boat back to a sailing course again.

"He's gone." I called into the cabin.

"Perhaps you should take in the tow generator's line," Christine suggested "the whale might think it is something to eat." We had heard of people losing trailed propellers, and I had already noticed tooth marks on ours. However it was such a hassle bringing it in for short periods of time, especially in rough weather, that I decided to let it be.

Sailing as close to the wind as possible we were still edging inshore because of the onshore current.

"I don't think we'll clear Punta da Barra light on the end of the spit. Or maybe we just might." I called. After two hours of shamelessly pinching the boat into the wind, we passed the point at a respectable distance, and continued on towards the Baia de Maputo.

Tony, on the radio in Kilifi far to our north, told us that the front, which was supposed to have passed us by, had stalled right on top of us. So we double reefed the main, and struggled on with a very small jib, heading as high into the wind as possible to avoid getting too far into the Baia de Maputo.

By now the waves were huge, roaring as they broke all around us. By day,

I felt it was possible to steer between such breakers (maybe wishful thinking), but at night that seemed a remote possibility. The noise was deafening as spume flew everywhere. How Christine produced meals in those conditions always amazed me. They were needed to keep up our strength and I always appreciated the effort that went into producing them.

By morning we were both feeling tired. The wind had dropped to twenty knots, the barometer was rising, and we were only two hundred and forty five nautical miles from our destination, Richards Bay. Having lost the helping current in the bay, we were only progressing at four knots over the ground. We had to get out into the current again as we needed all the speed we could muster to get into harbour before the next storm. As I pondered this latest conundrum, a Royal Albatross did a slow and watchful circle around the boat. How graceful this large bird was and how agile as it glided among the wave tops, disappearing and then appearing again unexpectedly at a distance. A variety of Petrels mimicked the Albatross' acrobatics but somehow, they could not emulate the breathless performance of the larger bird.

Restless morning after Punta da Barra

Our log showed that, on this passage, we had covered one thousand and forty five nautical miles at an average of one hundred and four nautical miles per day. Not breathtaking but OK. In the evening, we received a dreadful forecast from Alistair, along with an anxious query as to how long it would take us to get into Richards Bay?

"A coastal low is making its way up the East Coast of South Africa, and its rate of progress toward your area off Mozambique is unpredictable. Associated winds are blowing at thirty six to forty knots from the south at present, which will make the sea unbearable in the contrary current that you presently have." he said.

Our nearest bolt hole was behind Cabo Inhaca, east of Maputo (formerly Laurenco Marques) in Baia de Maputo. This was the one area of which we had no suitable scale chart. Christine, with uncanny foresight had, months before, traced another boat's chart using tracing paper. This had become our most important document. Cabo Inhaca is located on the north end of a small island about four nautical miles east of Maputo. Sandbars, which constantly change their position, are sprinkled all over the bay behind the low lying treed island which is deserted except for a lighthouse. A tide of about two knots flows over these bars. Although there was an anchorage well into the bay behind the island along a navigable channel, the advice we received was that it was not suitable for sheltering from a southwesterly *Buster.* Rather, we should stay off the northern tip of the island, anchoring on a leading line half a mile offshore in twenty three feet over sand. Deciding against this we turned on the engine and bent on all sail. This raised our speed to seven knots over the ground. Soon we had found the current again, and in twenty four hours covered one hundred and fifty five nautical miles. On the following morning's radio contact with cruising friends who were already safely in Richards Bay, they sounded so worried about our predicament that we almost dissolved into a jelly of anxiety ourselves.

Off Cabo Inhaca

The wind moved to the northeast at thirty knots as we passed Cabo Inhaca before pressing on in the helpful wind and current. The seas became confused and the ride became most uncomfortable. We were now only forty nautical miles away from our proposed landfall, and the boat was traveling in excess of her hull speed. The water swept past us almost up to the deck on either side as we careered along. Nevertheless I was pleased that the boat still felt steady and responsive to the helm. So we persevered rather than shortening sail for safer speeds. By early afternoon we had arrived outside the long stone breakwater which indicated the entrance to Richards Bay. The end of the breakwater was hardly discernable through the flying spray and mist. Christine went down into the cabin to check the GPS coordinates for the harbour entrance, and I disconnected the wind vane.

"That must be it," she shouted from the navigation station. Immediately I put the helm down and turned for shore, racing down the huge waves. By now the wind was blowing at forty knots out of the northeast. The huge seas were getting bigger by the minute as the water shallowed, and the noise was unnerving. Fortunately the sun was shining. Christine and I always felt less anxious in heavy seas during fine weather. Maybe it was because the air wasn't as heavy, or maybe that our general mood was more optimistic. Phalanxes of breaking waves stretched as far as the eye could see along the coastline. Looking forward was far less disconcerting than looking behind, where the waves seemed to build higher and higher. Towering above the stern of the boat, and still a few feet away, the tops curled and, with a hissing roar, disappeared under our transom. Spume flew all over us and the boat was enveloped in a tumult of white water. We surfed down these mountains of water until they passed under us at breakneck speed, leaving us behind to await the next onslaught from astern. By looking at these wave trains approaching us from behind, I thought I could pick out their patterns, frequency and position. This allowed me to steer the boat between the mountainous crests of water. Whether that was a fact or not, it was a comforting exercise to go though, as it make me feel I could do something useful.

Approach to Richards Bay — never has our jib been so tightly furled

The greatest concern at these high hull speeds was that a breaking wave from behind would broach the boat over to one side or the other, bringing her broadside on to the wind and waves with the resultant risk of a knockdown. The risk of damage to the boat would be high. As expected in these conditions, the rougher it got the more whales appeared all around, breeching and playing in the white capped water. Wandering albatross appeared from and disappeared within the maze of huge seas around us.

After asking for and receiving permission by radio to enter Richards Bay Harbour, we made straight for the waypoint of the harbour entrance, which had at last become clear to us. At 1600 hrs, after an eleven day passage from Russian Bay, twelve hundred and seventy five nautical miles away, we roared behind the breakwater at the entrance to the harbour. As we rounded the end of the wall the water flattened. The noise of the sea had gone, to be replaced by the slatting of our running rigging on the mast, and the clatter of our burgee and ensign in the whistling wind.

At the wharf an enthusiastic crowd of fellow cruisers was assembled to take our lines at the Tutsi Gazi Marina. A cold beer was pressed into my hand, and the smiling faces of welcome will remain with us as one of the special moments of our lives. Once secured and formally checked into South Africa, we all marched up to the local Portuguese restaurant ashore to celebrate our safe arrival as only the cruising family can. The hubbub of conversation, punctuated by intermittent gales of laughter, continued as experiences of the passages on different boats were exchanged. We felt fortunate to belong to this warm and caring fraternity of "yachties." Eventually Christine and I had to call it a day. We were worn out and needed a good night's sleep. So we said goodnight and walked back to *Demelza*, sitting quietly at her wharf, and tumbled into our bunks for a good twelve hours uninterrupted sleep in a perfectly still and silent boat. What a thrill it was for us to finally be in South Africa.

By morning the wind, which had continued to blow, had switched to the south as predicted. This resulted in dangerously huge seas in the Channel which are even a threat to large commercial ships. By radio, on schedule, we contacted all those people ashore who had been so concerned and helpful to us, to tell them that we had arrived safely before the *Buster*, and again to thank them for being there. Christine also called her brother, Nicky, in Cape Town to tell of our arrival.

An enthusiastic welcome to Richards Bay

We have arrived!

Demelza at Zululand Yacht Club

Myself, Josef, Linda and Herman

CHAPTER 20
South African Landfall

Gateway to South Africa for cruising yachts from the Indian Ocean, Richards Bay is located on the Tuzi Gazi coast just south of the border with Mozambique. It is a major coal port, situated across the bay from the small craft harbour. Around Pelican Island the Zululand Yacht Club shelters from southerly storms in its own little bay. It certainly was a luxury to walk on firm dry land again, and to have access to so many of the amenities we had not enjoyed for so long. The Portuguese restaurant in the small boat harbour was the mecca for the sailors in this area. Good food and congenial company were always available, and each visit provided a wonderful opportunity to meet local sailors who knew South African waters well. Meerensee, a town just a short cab ride away, was the main shopping centre and a little further on across the Parkway was the town of Richards Bay. This area, with its coastal sand dunes and huge estuary is a major stopover for migrating birds. Over two hundred and forty one species of birds can be seen in its Bird Sanctuary. This was to be our home for the next two months, as we did maintenance and repair work on the boat, as well as using it as a base from which to make safaris to the surrounding area.

Within twenty four hours of our arrival, Christine had befriended a very nice Afrikaner lady in the car park and her dog. Linda, Herman and later their son Josef, were to become great friends. They willingly helped us work on *Demelza*, extending to us the hospitality of their lovely home overlooking the bay. They ferried us about all over the area to show us the sights. Not only that, they introduced us to many interesting South African dishes.

Above us in the boatyard, Hornbills nested in the overhanging Casuarina trees. They make a frightful noise, and deposited large, black and white feathers all over our deck. Beside the usual cleaning and maintenance, we repaired our refrigerator, had the engine exhaust system replaced, and replaced the tri light navigation bulb at the top of the mast. All this to the accompaniment of a series of southwesterly gales that made living on the boat ashore almost as exciting as being at sea. The tow generator windings had to be replaced as sea water had got in through one of the seals. The Autohelm was repaired so that it would keep a steadier course. We also replaced the boat's audio system, as the old one had rusted out. We had a slight shock when we found galvanization in one of the bronze through hull fittings. If left to a point of failure this could lead to a serious hole in the bottom of the boat, with the resulting danger of foundering at sea. Although it had not progressed too far, it did show the importance of taking the boat out of the water regularly to check underneath. The cause turned out to be a break in the bonding wire connecting the through hull fitting to a zinc anode under the boat. On restoring the anchor chain after having had it re-galvanized, we found a ninety five percent break in the main electric cable servicing the anchor windlass at the point where it passed through the chain locker. It had been cut by the working chain. We had the pilot house cushions re upholstered, as the constant heavy wear and exposure to sea spray and wet clothing had taken its toll.

In tackling these jobs, Herman was so helpful and very skilled.

"Let's make a plan." was his usual response when we discovered yet another new challenge.

Herman's plan for windlass wiring

At the Zululand Yacht Club, which we were able to join as temporary members, we collected all our mail, faithfully sent out to us by our son Nick. We so enjoyed catching up with the news from home. The Club was an excellent venue from which to sell our used charts of the Indian Ocean and to supplement our stock of charts of the South African coast to help with the next leg of our journey.

One day, John's parents (we had met him in Dar es Salaam) arrived at the yacht club to invite us to their home in Eshowe ('the place of breezes'). That evening a storm hit the club in the middle of the night, tearing off the yacht club's outer dock and blowing it out into the bay with boats still attached.

Our visit to Eshowe was so interesting. The family was third generation sugar cane farmers, who also operated a creosoting business on their land. One of the sons had found the derelict equipment in the bush and had taken it home, reconditioned it, and then secured a government contract to creosote telephone poles. The government had recently announced that there would be a concerted effort to bring telephone services to thousands of homes throughout KwaZulu/ Natal. Although creosoted poles were thus readily available, providing the telephone service was still a problem. The local residents were removing the copper wiring at night faster than it could be put up in the day. From this they made bangles and necklaces which they sold for cash in the local market.

Eshowe was built on the site of the birthplace of the King of the Zulu nation during the Anglo/Zulu war of 1879. We enjoyed being driven through Zululand seeing the verdant hill country with Zulu kraals scattered over the hillsides. We stopped at a sugarcane mill, where we were shown around by a farmer who was a friend of the family, and were almost overcome by the overpowering smell of the sugarcane. Craft shops were everywhere selling finely woven Zulu baskets and personal adornments of all kinds, all of excellent quality. Next we called in at the historic Fort Nongqay, a reminder of the Zulu wars, and new home to the Zululand Historical Museum.

Back at the yacht club, we secured boat insurance for the South African coast. Our laptop computer arrived from Canada and we were both thunderstruck and disheartened to find it still didn't work.

"We just cannot get the weather pictures we need for this stretch of the journey." I moaned. Apparently it had worked well before it left home. All we could do now was to see if we could get it fixed on our arrival in Cape Town. Our confidence for the next part of our travels south was not helped by the recurring arrival of vicious southwesterly *Busters*, and I would lie in my bunk at night listening to the wind whistling in the rigging, and the halyards slapping the mast, thinking we'd be grounded for ever.

Alistair (ZS5GC) 'On Air'

We took a two day trip to Umzumbe to join Alistair and Davina, his wife, on their sugar cane farm outside Durban. We were invited to attend their annual sailor's party, and wished to thank him for being such a reliable source of weather and general information on our trip down the Mozambique Channel. We shared the hire of a car with Dietrich and Peta, whose catamaran was also moored in the yacht club. Alistair's party was for the local ham radio operators as well as visiting sailors, so Christine was in her element. There was a goodly gathering of offshore sailors present, some of whom told us of their experiences in the recent gales. In one of the barns near his house, Alistair had a most elegant brass and copper apparatus in which he made his favourite drink from cane sugar, called "Umzumbe Dew." It was delicious, and we were given a bottle, much to our delight.

The next morning we drove away after a sumptuous farm breakfast, heading for the Drakensberg Mountains. Jacaranda trees were in full violet bloom and set off well by hosts of flamboyant trees along the roads. We booked into a delightful thatched cottage at the Hlalanthe Resort which looked up the Tugela valley to the Amphitheatre in the Drakensbergs. We could see the flat top of the mountain range, a remnant of the old super continent of Gondwanaland. Christine linked up with Dietrich for a hike up to the Cascade Falls. They reported back in the evening that Protea was in bloom everywhere and they had heard the *piet ny vron* call of the red breasted cuckoo. The drive back to Richards Bay passed Spionkop, Blood River and many other historical reminders of the Boer War.

First view of the Drakensberg mountains and our cottage

On the 4th December the wind suddenly died. After saying farewell to our friends we left Richards Bay at 1615 hrs for the overnight run to Durban. All clearing out procedures had been completed. Water and fuel tanks were full. The weather chart at the yacht club showed nicely spaced isobars around a large undisturbed high pressure system, centered southeast of Cape Town, and gentle southeast breezes of five to ten knots. The barometer was rising. It was time to leave.

Dock lines were taken onboard as we left to face gentle, sunlit seas outside the harbour wall before turning south towards Durban. At midnight, under a full moon, the wind changed to the northeast. We put up all sail and poled out the genny. Dolphins leapt in our bow wave as we sped along. We traveled about three miles offshore, watching lights on the land as we passed by. The following morning we were approaching the city of Durban. There was a long stone wall breakwater that we had to locate at the harbour entrance. Durban is a big city with much commercial shipping. Our destination was located beyond all the big wharves, with their container ships, where much loading and unloading was going on as we passed. There are numerous sandbars in the harbour, so attention to the navigation markers is crucial. We tied up at the International Wharf with many other cruisers and local boats. The city lay just across the train tracks, enabling us to explore with ease. Next door was the Royal Natal Yacht Club with its exotic facilities and well tended lawns from which we watched spectacular sunsets. Durban is a bustling, dirty port city. Crossing the railway tracks is to be undertaken only in daylight, and only in company. The whole area had been taken over by street dwellers, whose numbers alone were daunting, and whose reputation was worse. Several good chandleries were nearby, and a great find was the Ocean Sailing Academy. On hearing that we were offshore cruisers they invited us to join the student's "weather" class each morning for an hour, to discuss the day's weather chart and forecast. This was invaluable, and gave us an opportunity to discuss items of mutual interest with the students.

Durban Harbour

Clearing in and out of Customs and the Harbour Master was confusing, as the offices were at different locations around the perimeter of this huge harbour complex. This necessitated cab rides to all locations, but avoided having to walk the streets of what was undoubtedly a rough neighbourhood.

On December 6th we heard from Alistair that there was a weather window approaching in two days time, for us to move south along the Transkei coast. The following day a front passed gently over us as we enjoyed a walk around town looking for charts, and an Internet café from which to send emails home. By the end of the second day, having previously seen no sign of officialdom to sign us in, a uniformed officer finally arrived, carrying a form for all thc new arrivals on the wharf.

Sure enough the weather window arrived, clear and calm, while Christine was readying the boat for sailing. I took all our boat papers by cab to start the round of clearing out for the next leg of our journey. First I went to the Ocean Terminal Building; then to Immigration three miles away at Home Affairs; then back to Customs in the Ocean Terminal Building with the completed form; then on to the Harbour Revenue Shop to pay harbour dues; back to the Port Office to file all the papers along with our sailing plan at the Harbour Signal Office. This completed we had to leave within thirty hours or start the process all over again.

The forecast was now not that certain, and the wind was from the southwest. We decided to wait another night before leaving at 1045 hrs the following morning in a gentle ten knot southeasterly breeze. This stayed with us and, aided by the Aghullas current, we maintained a speed of nine to ten knots along the Transkei Coast toward East London, which was two hundred and eighty nautical miles away. The barometer was steady, but we heard on the radio that the wind at the Cape of Good Hope, south of us, had changed to the southwest by our second afternoon out of Durban. As night set in the sea roughened up and our speed increased to over eleven knots. We stayed approximately ten miles offshore, close to the two hundred meter depth contour line. Threatening thunder clouds gathered as sheets of lightning began to streak across the sky with an accompanying drenching downpour. In spite of this the barometer was steady and, having heard reports of the problems some yachts had had finding mooring in East London and reports that the southwest *buster* down south was still two days away, we decided to keep going toward Port Elizabeth. That afternoon the seas calmed down, and our speed fell to between seven and eight knots as we lost the current.

At 0215 hrs the following morning, while Christine was asleep, I put on the engine as our speed was dropping in the lighter air. Suddenly I noticed smoke pouring out of the cabin. My heart pounding, I turned the engine off and almost vaulted over the drop boards into the cabin to rouse Christine. It always seemed to be 0200 hrs when I woke her up for some emergency or other. Understandably it is never very well received as she had usually only just got to sleep at the change of watch at 0100 hrs.

"Darling, wake up, I think we're on fire!"

As we both scrambled to the cockpit, smoke continued to billow out of sundry cracks and crevices around the engine compartment. While Christine steered the boat, I got a flashlight and tentatively opened up the engine room, brandishing a fire extinguisher and a fire blanket that were located nearby. I peered into the gloom.

"No flames visible down here," I choked. Gradually the smoke cleared.

"Would you believe it," I shouted up the cockpit "that brand new exhaust system we had put on in Richards Bay has fallen off!" Following an hour of playing with wire, lots of aluminum foil and hose clamps, I managed to suspend the length of exhaust pipe approximately where it was meant to be, before gluing it in place with special glue from our spares locker. Black greasy diesel exhaust was everywhere. I was covered in it and spread it around on everything I touched as I emerged

"Do get cleaned up before you get it on everything." Christine admonished. That done we started the engine again and, although considerably better than it had been, there was still a terrible smell of exhaust in the cabin. We kept it as well ventilated as we could, and stayed outside as much as possible making all speed to harbour before the next change in the weather. The wind had dropped considerably so we really needed to use the engine.

With the next *Buster* approaching, and having passed East London which was the last bolt hole before Port Elizabeth, we had no choice but to keep the engine going with all sails up. Clocking eleven plus knots over the ground in the current, we raced towards Port Elizabeth. Intense thunderstorms were all around us. Lightning made the large swells look quite scary. In the morning the wind settled, the sea calmed down, and the sun came out to cheer us on our way. We were delighted to recognize the small birds swimming around us as Jackass penguins. They darted and dived all around the boat, giving us a great welcome. A squadron of gannets from nearby Bird Island also came over to inspect us as we crossed the vast Algoa Bay toward our destination.

By the morning of the second day we were surfing in a strong easterly breeze towards the harbour entrance of Port Elizabeth. We could see the Yacht Club as we entered. Stowing all sails and putting out fenders, we thankfully handed our mooring lines to several men who appeared on the wharf to receive us. One of them happened to be a stainless steel machinist! He kindly offered to sort out our exhaust problem. After a trip like that there's nothing quite like a good hot shower, a glass of something to drink with the local yachties, a good meal and then finally bed.

Sure enough, within twelve hours of our arrival, the wind changed to the south and the sea got up, setting all the boats at the wharf bouncing in the surge. In the morning Christine managed to make an 0725 hrs radio rendezvous with

Tony, in far away Kilifi, to tell him we had arrived before the *Buster* and that all was well. We thanked him for taking our positions as we had moved along the coast.

Port Elizabeth, on the Baakens River, marks the approximate half-way point between Richards Bay and Cape Town. So far we had managed to keep out of trouble. But there were plenty of challenges ahead, and we had to press on if we were to get to Cape Town for Christmas where Nicky and Penny had kindly invited us to share their festivities. We had been so impressed by the Aghullas Current, flowing as it does about ten miles offshore like a huge river of water, taking us south at unheard of speeds over the ground. Otherwise we would never have been able to have reached sheltered water in the time to avoid the frequent southerly storms.

We caught a ride into town with club members Felix and Claudia. The town has a lovely older section built on a hill overlooking Algoa Bay where the Portuguese explorer Bartolomew Dias landed in 1498. An ancient cannon points its muzzle out to sea from the cliff tops; a reminder of this area's turbulent past. On our return to the boat, a series of people came to look at *Demelza*. Some were seasoned sailors, and some had never set foot on a boat before. We offered coffee in the morning and accepted an invitation to a BBQ lunch at the club. We served tea in the afternoon before sunset brought relief from all our visitors. Before supper we enjoyed a quiet glass of wine in the cockpit. Not much achieved but a lot of wonderful local friends made. At 0900 hrs the next morning we took a mountain of washing to the local Laundromat, followed by a picnic at Sardinia Beach, south of town, with some new friends. The next day our stainless steel man arrived, took out the exhaust pipe and went off with it to his workshop. Later in the afternoon he reappeared looking very pleased with himself, having fashioned a much more complicated looking join. With appropriate gaskets at each end, he was confident it would do the trick. Sure enough it all fitted together, and a cheer went up as we started the engine. Suspended upside down in our cockpit locker, with his feet sticking up in the air, he inspected his handiwork. Our faith in South African workmanship had been restored. After all that motoring, we needed diesel. A club member ran me up to town in his truck with our four empty jugs that we carried on deck. Meanwhile, Christine accepted a ride to a local shopping center to stock up on provisions, before getting a cab back to the club. She stored everything away in our inventoried lockers. The following day was maintenance day, spent changing engine oil, oil and air filters, and topping up the boat batteries with distilled water.

A huge low-pressure system had settled over us, covering the lower half of South Africa. We had some more time to look around. One of the club members took our laptop computer to his shop to see if he could persuade it to give us more reliable weather fax pictures. Meanwhile we had developed more problems with our exhaust system. Our stainless steel man went off to make a special tool with which we could tighten the bolts on the new prosthesis, as regular tools didn't fit. This done, the problem again seemed to be fixed. My confidence level in the whole assembly was not that great. In the evening we were taken out for supper to a very gracious home on the headland, in an area called Schooner. We were given three stones as a gift. One from Wales, which had been picked up on the beach below their house. It was thought have come from a shipwreck's ballast. The other two were lovely pieces of local quartz bearing rock from the headland nearby. This area was the site of the 1820 landing of British settlers.

A low pressure system speeding down the Transkei Coast had caused a tornado which destroyed a local hospital, killed sixteen and injured over a hundred people. As the system moved south towards us we began to experience heavy southwest winds and rain. What was most disconcerting was that none of this appeared on the previous day's weather forecast. This made us feel very uncertain about leaving on the following day as planned.

Our laptop was returned with an assessment that we had a problem with the weather fax modem itself. This could not be fixed. In the morning the winds were light and from the south, so it was becoming increasingly unlikely that we would be able to reach Cape Town by Christmas.

With one hundred and seventy four nautical miles to our next destination in Mossel Bay, the coastline took a sharp turn to the west along the southern end of the African continent. On this stretch we had two possible bolt holes, Knysna and Cape St. Francis. Timing entry into Knysna between the narrow Knysna heads was critical, as it was only possible to do so at slack tide. We left at noon, rounding the light on the end of the breakwater, and headed west along the long beachfront to Cape Recife. We kept well offshore, but within sight of all the holiday makers swimming in the calm waters near the land.

The weather chart at the clubhouse had shown widely spaced isobars around the low pressure system in the Indian Ocean to the East, and an approaching high pressure system coming in from the west. The only slight concern was a cold front, coming up from a low in the Southern Ocean. If we could keep up an average speed of six knots over the ground, we should be in Mossel Bay before it could cause us any trouble. With the engine on, and the sails up, we were making between six and eight knots in flat seas under clear skies. This continued throughout the night.

The next morning we were treated to a beautiful sunrise but the wind seemed to be settling from the southeast and rising as the barometer fell. The wind picked up to twenty-five knots by lunchtime and the seas were getting up. We were now moving along at eight knots over the ground, with a reefed main and small jib. We noticed two other sails visible a few miles behind us, also making for Mossel Bay.

Twenty seven hours after leaving Port Elizabeth we approached the entrance to Mossel Bay to the accompaniment of spray flying downwind in great clouds.

From the end of the wall, light coloured shallows showed underwater for some distance, which necessitated keeping clear of them before rounding the wall. To complete the rounding we had to make a ninety degree turn to port to get in behind it. This threatened to put us broadside to the huge incoming waves. We closed the boat up tight as we inched as close as we dared to the shallows, before turning sharply to port along the trough of the waves. A huge wave passed under us but a second one looked so threatening that we paid out sail and turned offwind allowing it to roll under us before turning for shelter again. The large ketch following us didn't quite get the timing right. As we looked over our shoulders we watched, horrified, as she was laid flat on her side while rounding up to pass behind the wall. We had radioed ahead of our arrival, so a worthy band of local sailors was able to guide us into a sheltered wharf. What a relief when all was secured. We dashed along the wharf to lend a hand receiving the following ketch with its rather shaken crew. This larger boat had difficulty maneuvering in the confined space available so that, on their second attempt, they raked a neighbouring yacht with their bowsprit, which resulted in a sickening twanging of shrouds and screech of metal on metal, as she scraped along the other hull. With a thudding impact she finally came to rest with her bowsprit intertwined with the neighbouring boat's running rigging. By now the long suffering crew was hysterical, and there was much sobbing and shouting as they attempted to untangle the mess and make their boat secure. The recipe for soothing all our frayed nerves was a hot shower, salt free clothes and a good meal of fish and chips in the welcoming clubhouse ashore.

The next morning brought sunshine and a lot of concern for the other yachts behind us who were still experiencing heavy winds and huge seas. We walked up to see the Post Office tree, an historical drop off point for the sailors' mail in the early days. The nearby maritime museum recounted the exploratory visits to this area by the Portuguese in 1488, as well as having a wonderful display of seashells from the Indian Ocean. The Portuguese explorer Bartolomew Dias will always be remembered as the man who paved the way for the eventual discovery of the sea route from Europe to India. He traveled from Portugal in a Caravel, the favoured vessel used by the Spanish and Portuguese for exploration as well as trade. Its later version, developed for ocean crossing, had three masts, with a square rig on the two forward ones and a lateen rigged mizzen sail aft. It carried a crew of thirty.

As we became used to the relaxed life ashore, the days to Christmas were creeping by. I was anxious about rounding the Cape of Storms in the uncertain weather so as to arrive in Cape Town on time. We anxiously watched the weather chart at the yacht club. On Sunday, 21st December, the wind died down so we planned to leave the next morning. But when we woke up the boat was tugging at her lines, and the rigging chattering in yet another gale. Our ham radio weather forecasters said there was no hope of a window to get us to Cape Town for

Christmas. Downcast after all the effort we had made to reach our goal, we knew the wise thing to do was to leave the boat in Mossel Bay, rent a car, and drive to Cape Town. Sure enough, the next morning the weather had deteriorated further, and we watched an intense low front pass overhead as we walked into town. Later, returning to the boat in the ensuing gale, I was concerned about the violent working on the mooring lines due to a significant surge in the harbour. We decided to stitch leather chafe pads around all contact points on the mooring lines. The weather fax showed a cold front right over us, and the barometer had dropped to 968 milibars, so we felt justified in our decision to leave *Demelza* here. Friends offered to keep an eye on her for us, especially her mooring lines, until we returned in a few days. Christine signed off from all her regular radio schedules explaining we'd be ashore until after the holidays.

Penny has her husband back

Nicky put to work

CHAPTER 21
Cape Town

Our bright red rental car was waiting for us, so we set off through rolling hills leading to the Langeberg Mountains. We stopped at Swellendam to see the museum of early Dutch settlers, and to have lunch in the warm sun on a riverside restaurant's patio. We had not felt such warmth for weeks.

The Sir Lowdy Pass had exciting vistas as we drove down into the community of Somerset West, before crossing the Cape Flats at the entry to Cape Town. Our family holiday with Nicky and Penny was idyllic. We especially remember our walk up the hillside to Silvermine through the Fynbos, with its colourful Watsonia in full bloom. All the colours of the rainbow covered the hills as we climbed, until finally reaching a ledge overlooking the sea, and down into the little port of Hout Bay. Chapman's Peak Drive wound its precarious way along the steep cliffs below us. It was here that Nicky decided there must be something to this ocean cruising for us to have devoted so much effort to it. He asked if he could accompany us from Mossel Bay to Simon's Town, just for the experience.

On our return to Mossel Bay after four happy days, we were horrified to find that *Demelza*'s mooring lines were almost threadbare, in spite of the leather chafe pads. Three of the lines were almost severed. Fortunately I had doubled up the lines to cover this unlikely event. We worked to bring *Demelza* back into cruising mode, refueling, replacing filters, and topping up the batteries with distilled water. Nicky was put to work on the innumerable jobs that always seem to accumulate on a boat when left on its own.

Next morning, the wind blew gently from the northwest. Weather charts looked passable, with two high pressure areas located one west and one east of the Cape, with wide isobars between. Even the meteorologist on Cape Town Radio sounded optimistic for the next few days. By the time we left harbour the wind was blowing briskly. We had been warned not to attempt rounding Cape Agulhas, the southernmost tip of South Africa, in unfavourable weather. The prevailing southeast wind was ideal.

On this coast there was an inflowing current at all the major capes, Infanta, Agulhas and Hangclip. Outside Mossel Bay, we began to lose the helpful effect of the Agulhas Current as it made its way out to sea to dissipate over the Agulhas Bank. We missed its helpful flow, and had to get used to slower speeds over the ground once more. By Struis Bay, the wind was up to thirty knots from the east. Nicky, unused to the boat's motion in the swell, was pitched across the cabin and was brought up sharply by a tooth grinding impact of his head on something solid. Looking shaken and seeing stars, he carefully explored the point of impact on his head, while I cast a surreptitious glance at the point of contact on the boat.

No permanent damage had been done to either.

The wind dropped, so we turned on the engine as night fell. We could see the Cape Agulhas light ahead, but it seemed to take forever to come abeam. The lighthouse was built in 1848, and Christine was thrilled, as we passed, to be able to raise a ham radio operator who lived just down the road from the light. He in turn was happy to have contact with a Canadian yacht passing his window.

The sea continued rippled as we motored along in the dark, keeping watch for coastal shipping and unlit buoys. As dawn broke, huge rafts of kelp appeared all around us, and seals lay on their backs with their flippers in the air acting as sails. The vivid blue of the Indian Ocean gave way to the dark grey of the Atlantic, and the water temperature quickly plunged from 80°F to 60°F. Whales appeared in the distance, and albatross glided from swell to swell around us. Occasionally the head of a penguin would pop up in alarm, before disappearing again on seeing us. Other than the lighthouse, Cape Agulhas was a disappointment. Low lying broken rocky shore, with flat grassland above on which sheep grazed, stretched on for miles. In horrific weather it would look quite different.

After passing Cape Handclip, with its steep cliff reaching for the sky, we entered False Bay which stretched ahead of us for thirty miles, and were met by a brisk head on breeze that slowed us down considerably. To the west of the bay the spectacular rocky cliffs of the Cape Peninsula appeared. To the east was a line of suburban beach resorts, with a magnificent backdrop of the Hottentot Holland Mountains. Ahead of us, in the distance, were sand dunes and the beaches of the Cape Flats townships, with the busy Cape Town airport behind. False Bay is renowned for its Great White Sharks, which feed on seals that abound on Seal Island. Continuing to motor into the strong headwind, we headed across the bay to Simon's Town. As the day passed, and evening began to fall, we watched as the confusion of the town's lights developed in the twilight. Pinpointing the harbour entrance was becoming more difficult and, by the time we had arrived, it was almost invisible. The light at the end of the breakwater was not working, so we approached very cautiously. Carefully rounding it, we almost ran into a floating black plastic boom snaking its way around the enclosed harbour.

"This approach in the dark is a bit unnerving." I observed aloud to myself as Christine and Nicky did stalwart work on the bow finding our way in.

"The lights of the town make it impossible to see." Christine called. Fortunately she had made radio contact with cruising friends who had arrived before us so that, on our approach, they came along to the end of the wharf with flashlights to indicate the way. At 2100 hrs we pulled into our slip, and willing hands caught *Demelza*'s mooring lines. Penny was on the dock to claim her slightly damaged husband, who had endured his first cruise with fortitude. He was the first to admit that he couldn't imagine what the longer passages must be like. Christine produced the bottle of champagne given to us by Herman and Linda in

Richards Bay for this very occasion, to celebrate our successful transit along the Wild Coast of South Africa.

Simon's Town, named after Simon van den Stehl, an early governor, has been a recognized anchorage since 1741. The British turned it into a naval base in 1814, and it is now the base for the South African Navy. In spite of the dockyards presence at one end of the town, it has a seaside resort atmosphere. Its main street runs alongside False Bay, and is connected by an electrified commuter train to Cape Town. Our first berth was exposed to winds whistling down from the hillside above us. This caused a lot of wave action against the side of the boat. So when we were offered the use of a club member's berth which had power and water, behind the black wave boom, we jumped at it. The False Bay Yacht Club extended us a temporary membership which allowed us to use all their facilities. It was a very welcoming, friendly place in which to base ourselves for the next two months. We celebrated the New Year as the Navy sounded all ships horns, firing parachute flares up into the night sky. Yacht Club members lit out of date flares on the Club's lawn, followed by a special *braai* (barbeque) to mark the occasion.

Enjoying a morning coffee in *Demelza*'s cockpit soon afterwards, we were startled by a nearby pistol shot. The club was hosting an International Dinghy Sailing Regatta in which there was a team from Canada. One of the sailors was a young lady from our yacht club at home. She was able to tell us news of our club. We shared some of our experiences and asked her to take messages home on her return.

Three days of strong southeasterly gales followed. These tested the wave barrier to its maximum. The water in the bay was smoking, and the dinghy sailors were having difficulty deciding whether and when to sail between the heavy squalls. Finally the weather settled, and we were able to cheer on the Canadian boats.

The town's streets wound their way up the hills behind. From these we had spectacular views as we worked on our aerobics following our confinement afloat. Above the town was the grave of a dog. A memorial stone put up by the Royal Navy during the Second World War, commemorated the life of a Great Dane called "Just Nuisance." He had been adopted by sailors entering the port during the War. His claim to fame was his habit of riding on the little train into Cape Town with the sailors on shore leave and, after a concentrated evening of pub crawls, escorting the stragglers back to their ships. Toward the end of his life he had been officially taken on the Naval Base's strength and awarded the rank of midshipman.

Just Nuisance

Nicky offered us the loan of his new car to explore the area north of Cape Town towards Namaqualand. This we accepted enthusiastically. As we drove north the heat became quite uncomfortable. By 1500 hrs, steam began to pour out from under the hood of the car as we climbed a very long hill north of Garies. Finally the engine stopped. Fortunately we had noticed a garage as we had passed by the tiny town. As I steered to turn us around, Christine pushed to point the car's nose downhill. I felt ashamed when a car, and then a truck, drew up to offer to help Christine and her seemingly handicapped husband. Finally, with the car pointing downhill, Christine quickly hopped back in and we glided down the ten mile hill, to draw up at the only garage in town.

Nicky's car was in bad trouble. I had to make the most uncomfortable telephone call of my life, to tell him that his three month old car's engine had blown up. As the local garage could do nothing for us, we arranged a free tow to the larger town of Springbok. Commiserating with one another in the nearby hotel, over dinner that night, we met a most delightful couple from Bloemfontein. They had just arrived for the husband to start work as manager of the local granite quarry. Next morning, after a ride with the tow truck to Springbok in forty degree heat, we were glad to learn that Nicky's car was under warranty. As some of the seals had failed, it qualified for a replacement engine.

In the Springbok hotel we met George Swanson, a mining prospector in that area for the past thirty years. He had a most wonderful collection of minerals at his home. His prize was a globe of Blue Lace Agate, which had been adopted as the symbol of World Ecology following the Apollo 17 astronauts' observations from space that: "If ever there was a fragile piece of blue in space, it's the earth right now."

Nicky's dead car

George Swanson holding Blue Lace Agate Globe

Our new friends from Bloemfontein had some free time. They drove us through the arid country around Springbok to visit the Geogap Nature Reserve where, in the right season and under the right conditions, the desert floor is covered with a colourful mass of flowers of over six hundred indigenous species. Here we saw gemsbok and springbok in their natural environment before driving on to Namabeep, where Cornishmen had played a large part mining copper. The old shaft, called the Glory Hole, had been sealed off. We were told that George Swanson's father had ordered two thousand men out of the mine twenty four hours before a total collapse of the shafts. At the Okiep mine, the 1882 Cornish Beam Pump house was still standing, and next to it the smokestack built by the Cape Copper Company in 1880. We went to the aptly named Cornish Pub for lunch.

Another memorable trip we made with Charmaine and Peter was a visit to Port Noloth. We drove through an arid and sparsely populated desert where white goats roamed at will. Eventually, on each side of the road, we could see mine workings where miners looked for diamonds. We arrived at Port Noloth, established as a small vessel harbour and railway junction in 1854. This shallow harbour is the centre for small scale diamond recovery from the seabed. Boats ply the shallows, on the decks of which are large pumps with suction hoses which pump tons of sand through filters to retrieve the diamonds that lie on the sea bed. Quartz veins were readily visible, running through the rocky outcrops on the beach. Since its inception, forty five million Rand had been paid to the contractors for diamonds recovered at Port Noloth. After days of waiting in Springbok for the replacement engine to arrive, Nicky became impatient and drove Penny's car from Cape Town to take us home.

Diamond dredging boats Port Noloth

While we were enjoying ourselves on land, a friend of Penny's was working on our laptop computer. He had some limited success in that we could use it for retrieving weather fax pictures only. Christine was disappointed that we could not hook up the email equipment that we had bought to establish easy contact with home. At least now we should have reliable weather pictures for our passage across the Atlantic.

Many of our cruising friends had joined us in the marina, having negotiated the continuing storms along the Wild Coast. We had a major overhaul of the boat's engine, which included tappet adjustment, compression tests, new belts for the alternator and the cooling system's raw water pump. We replaced two engine mounts that showed some signs of deterioration.

We visited the Royal Cape Town Yacht Club to spend time soaking up its history and hospitality. What magic that name conjured up. It had always been one of those places that had excited my imagination. It is a club rich in maritime history, being closely tied to the Dutch exploration and colonization of South Africa. It was here I was to learn of the derivation of the word "yacht." In 1660 the Dutch gave Charles II of England the jacht *Mary*. He enjoyed sailing her so much that he built a second jacht *Jamie* to the same design, racing her against his brother, the Duke of York, in the first recorded Jacht race for amateurs. In 1664, the Dutch East India Company had sixty jachts scattered throughout its trading posts in India, Ceylon, Batavia and Cape Town. They were used to carry messages, ebony from Mauritius, slaves from Madagascar, and ivory, gold and ambergris from South Africa.

The earliest recorded amateur racing in Table Bay was in 1850, with the first formal regatta in 1857. The first club was founded in 1861 by the Cape Town civil service. Many of these boats were involved in whaling, rescue and salvage work in the nearby dangerous roadstead. In 1882 a local enthusiast built the forty three foot copper sheathed *May* at his home. He took out a wall to enable him to load her onto a bullock wagon to take her to the launching site. She had beautiful mahogany paneling, with gleaming mirrors and a piano. She was cutter rigged, with a long boom and bowsprit, and was considered very fast.

The Southern Cross Yacht Club was founded in Table Bay in 1882. This sponsored a local regatta week, and in 1883 a Boating Association was formed to regulate regattas. The Southern Cross Club closed in 1888. In 1898, the visit of Captain Slocum to Cape Town primed public interest, and this was reinforced by the visit of Captain Voss in 1904. Cape yachtsmen were presented with an illustrated book of the Americas Cup in 1905, involving King Edward VII with *Britannia*, and the German Emperor with *Meteor*. Sir Thomas Lipton was also a great protagonist. As a result the commodore of the Table Bay Yacht Club, founded in 1905, defied all the dislocations resulting from the development of Cape Town Harbour, promoting the Royal cipher for the Club as the premier yachting organization in South Africa. Gradually the number of yachts increased through imports from England, Norway, America and Australia, as well as through locally built boats.

They bought a corrugated iron shed, home of the defunct Southern Cross

Yacht Club, as their new club house. It had originally been used as an army hut in the Boer War. They began organized racing events, and an Easter Cruise which continue to this day. The greatest threat to the Cape yachts was their exposed anchorage. After 1906 the club's fleet was required to pass a design inspection before admission. The first organized Ocean Race was from Cape Town to Simon's Town in 1911. In 1914, Table Bay Yacht Club became the Cape Yacht Club and later received its Royal Charter to become the present day Royal Cape Town Yacht Club. In 1908, Sir Thomas Lipton presented "The Lipton Cup" to the club, to encourage and develop yacht racing in South Africa, and the first race for this Cup was held in 1911. It was won by Durban Yacht Club. By 1929 new facilities were developed. After a gale in 1931 had blown the roof off the old Club house, the move was made to new quarters. The Royal Cape Town Yacht Club was officially credited with being the main source for recruiting wartime South African sailors as regulars and reserves, and one of their members is credited with sighting French Vichy warships off the Cape, which later led to their capture off Port Elizabeth.

On a visit to North Sails in Cape Town, we were lucky enough to pick up a brand new light air gennaker drifter, which had been made to order for another boat. It had been rejected because the colours chosen didn't match their boat. It didn't match *Demelza* either, but who was to worry at half price! This sail was to prove a godsend on our passage across the Atlantic.

Boats were beginning to set out to round the Cape of Storms and Cape of Good Hope. We picked up their radio messages, concerning the wind and sea conditions. Meanwhile Christine and I pulled up daily weather fax pictures. In between many interesting trips into Cape Town with Nicky and Penny, we continued to prepare ourselves for the long journey across the Atlantic. We planned to make the first port of call in Trinidad, before working our way up the Caribbean entering North America in Florida. After a great deal of discussion however, we changed our minds. Should our good fortune of the past six years hold up for one more year, we would have had enough excitement and it would be time to go home to our growing family of three grandchildren, whom we hardly knew. The new plan was to cross the Atlantic from Cape Town to Charleston, South Carolina. From there we would go up the Intracoastal Waterway on the East coast of North America. The following spring we would enter the Great Lakes before ending our sailing journey at the Lakehead, before trucking *Demelza* home.

Christine was persuaded by the Hout Bay Women's Agricultural Society to give a talk on our adventures. This proved to be a most entertaining and cheerful experience. We also appeared on a Cape Radio talk show for an hour. Originally scheduled for ten minutes we received so many calls from listeners that our host decided to extend our time for a further fifty minutes. He told us after the show that he was feeling a bit gun-shy when extending our invitation because the previous week he had invited a guest comedian for an hour's show which he thought would be hilarious. It soon transpired that the comedian hadn't an ounce of spontaneous humour in him, so after a ten minute excruciatingly dull interview, they had terminated the show.

One big disappointment was that our propane stove, which I had taken into town for repair, came back in a worse condition than when it left. Only the top two burners worked. We hadn't either the time or inclination to contemplate installing an expensive replacement.

The weather remained fine and windy. One night a seventy knot squall hit Cape Town harbour causing an oil rig, that was in for servicing, to break loose and be blown down onto four ships as it drifted across the harbour, causing a spill of eighteen tons of oil.

More gales continued to pass over us, lifting water off the surface of the sea just outside our marina, turning the bay misty white. With all this wind my confidence in rounding the Cape of Storms was ebbing and I felt as though we might be stuck for a long time.

We received an invitation to visit *Bright Waters*, a beautiful original family home standing on its own beach on the Cape Peninsula. It belonged to an early pioneering family. When the South African Government bought the private land from this family to establish the Cape Peninsula National Park they had agreed provided they could keep their home and thirty surrounding acres. Nicky was a friend of Dawn, the daughter of the family, whom we had met previously on a visit to the local workshop for the Handicapped where Nicky worked. After lunch we went for a walk on the beach to look for blue trade beads, which continue to be washed up on some of the nearby beaches after storms. They are much prized, as they were used as ballast in the holds of the returning sailing ships carrying silks and spices from India to Europe around the Cape of Good Hope and used as trading currency in those "far off" lands. We found a few bits and pieces of beads, but with characteristic generosity of the people that we had met all over the world, Dawn gave us two complete beads for luck.

Work continued intermittently on *Demelza*. I disassembled the wind vane, the delicate mechanism of which is constantly exposed to salt water during passages. After examining all its parts for wear and tear I cleaned and greased it lightly with special grease. The wind vane had proved its weight in gold, reliably steering the boat in all conditions better than any extra crew could have done.

Among the supplies we needed for our long Atlantic passage, was a good stock of wine. Where better than the vineyards of the Southern Cape? We drove with Egan and Sylvia, who had sailed to Cape Town in their Swedish boat *Magnum Bonum*, into the wine country. We spent a hilarious but fruitful day testing and buying bottles by the dozen. This episode had an unusual result for, after we had left South Africa, Nicky sent an email to our yacht club in Canada telling them we had just left, and suggesting if they should have any difficulty locating *Demelza* on the Atlantic crossing, they could follow the line of empty wine bottles bobbing in our wake, starting from Cape Town. Cheeky fellow!

One of our favourite places to relax between boat jobs was Bolders, not far from Simon's Town. Its two beaches are the most protected on the peninsula, which makes them attractive to people and penguins alike. Known as Jackass penguins because of their donkey like braying call, over two thousand of these appealing birds make their home in the sand under low lying bushes overlooking these beaches. The bushes shade the nesting birds and chicks in the summer's heat. Penguins are hard on the bushes they value so much, over fertilizing them, and trampling the young shoots underfoot. Bolders is the only one of twenty four known breeding colonies that has shown an increasing population. Globally, there has been a ninety percent reduction in their numbers, classifying them as an 'Endangered Species.' We spent many evenings sitting on the sand watching the birds return home after a day's foraging at sea. It was obvious they had a lot to talk about as they waddled up the beach making their way up to the bushes under which they roost in holes they have dug in the sand.

Jackass penguins in from the sea

Harry, whom we had met at the yacht club and who lived with his wife Margaret in a house on the hill behind the town, kindly took me in his car to Fish Hoek, to refill diesel jugs and propane tanks. Christine continued to re-victual the food lockers, mend sails, and make new country flags from blanks she had made to accommodate our revised cruising plan. Having done that, she cleaned the boat and etched the aluminum foot rail around the deck before painting it. She serviced the winches, and in fact turned her hand to any job that needed doing to prepare us for the passage. So what was I doing? Oh, there was plenty left over. Up the mast to replace the wind vane, thread through replacements for worn halyards, replace a worn shiv under the masthead cap, and check all the standing rigging. We cleaned under the boat and replaced the anodes. I greased all the bearings on the rudder, and tightened the stuffing box on the propeller shaft, replaced all filters on the fuel lines and engine and worst of all, crawled into the bilge to check the through hull bonding wires. Between us we felt we had, in the prevailing heat, done a creditable job of getting *Demelza* ready, and were confident that she was in fighting form to face whatever the Cape of Storms and the Atlantic would throw at us.

We took Harry and Margaret, who had never been on a small boat before, out into the bay for a sail. Coming home, and approaching the end of the breakwater into harbour we noticed a South African naval vessel coming out of Port.

"OK crew," I said, "let's see what that ship makes of us. Margaret and Harry stand to attention along the port deck facing the ship. Christine lower the Canadian ensign as we pass." Quickly the ship passed along the port side, and on seeing that we had dipped our Canadian flag, sent seamen scurrying aft to their ensign to reciprocate. The next day, through the yacht club, we received an invitation to visit the minesweeper *East London's* captain, Captain Andrew Blake, to have a conducted tour of their ship.

"We've never had anybody salute our ship before," he told us when we met him the next day. "It certainly woke us up."

Time was running out. We presented a letter to Customs and Immigration in Cape Town from the Yacht Club to say that we had paid all our bills, and they issued their Clearance to us to Charleston, South Carolina, which seemed a world away.

Cape of Storms

For the last time

CHAPTER 22
Crossing the Atlantic

On February 28th, we pointed *Demelza*'s bow out into False Bay turning toward the Cape of Storms. Nicky had come down to the wharf to cast us off from the shores of South Africa for the last time after an unforgettable, action-packed two months. It was so sad to say "Goodbye."

The wind at the outset was from the west, changing almost immediately to southeast, perfect conditions for crossing the Atlantic. As we sailed along the Peninsula's shore which had become so familiar to us during our stay, the sun shone warmly, and we were feeling very optimistic. We sailed past Bolders, home of our friendly penguins. They were totally absent, fishing out at sea. Following the cliffs, we sailed to Cape Point, which was sitting bathed in the morning's sunshine with its two lighthouses clearly visible. The older of the two, high up on the cliffs, had proven too unreliable in bad weather as it was often obscured by clouds. The newer one was almost on the beach. As we passed the Cape of Storms the air became noticeably cooler, and an ominous mist began to form around us, obscuring the sun. The wind changed again to the north northwest, and began to build in strength becoming so uncomfortable that, in spite of our good weather forecasts, I was fearful that a southwest *Buster* might follow.

By the time we had turned north, approaching the low lying Cape of Good Hope on the western shores of the Peninsula, the effects of the northward flowing Benguella current flowing up from Antarctica was noticeable by our increased speed over the ground. The wind continued to build, and a new weather forecast was issued for forty knots.

"There's no point staying out here to get beaten up," I said "Let's make for Hout Bay just ahead of us, to take shelter." It took us a while to motor deep into Chapman's Bay, at the end of which the fishing village of Hout Bay is located. In spite of the gathering gloom, we could not but be impressed by the precipices of Chapman's Peak lowering over us in the gathering storm clouds. We savored the last few miles of sheltered water before tying up at the marina in Hout Bay, to enjoy one of the best fish and chip meals we had ever had. Sure enough, within an hour of our arrival, the wind was howling around the little fishing port. Snoek and crayfish boats scuttled in for shelter. Torrential rain lashed the boat all night, and we were thankful to have made the right decision to wait for calmer weather.

In the morning we realized that there were quite a number of offshore cruising boats sheltering in the same marina. Some were to continue sailing up the west coast of South Africa before heading across to the island of St. Helena, Napoleon's prison island. Others were going to head more directly for St. Helena. For our part, we had decided to sail west of St. Helena and Ascension Island and head for the island of Fernando de Noronha off the north coast of Brazil. We had been advised not to arrive in the North Atlantic too early in the year. Thumbing through *Ocean Passages of the World*, our planning reference book, there was a two hundred mile long stretch of water along the equator off the coast of Brazil. This was supposed to be the shortest gateway through the Inter-tropical Convergence Zone which would move us from the southeast to the northeast trade winds. On hearing of our predicament, Nicky drove to Hout Bay to take us home for supper. He must have been wondering if he would ever see the last of us. After two days sheltering from the latest storm in Nicky and Penny's home, they accompanied us back to *Demelza* in Hout Bay to see us off yet again.

"Not being rude," said Nicky "but I hope this is for the last time." We all laughed and waved our goodbyes. They had been such wonderful hosts, and had done and shown us so much to make our stay in South Africa very memorable.

Turning north in light air and warm sunshine, we sailed along the coast past the seaside town of Llandudno, across Camps Bay and past Clifton to Ships Point. The sight of Cape Town with a backdrop of Table Mountain, its tablecloth of cloud streaming down its sides was an unforgettable sight as we made out across Table Bay into the Atlantic. The radio was alive with 88s, the sailor's radio jargon for 'best wishes for a good passage.' Christine re-established radio contact with all her friends ashore, including Tony in Kilifi who had asked her to talk to him every day during our Atlantic crossing to see how far out he could maintain contact. We had our usual disturbed first night at sea, getting little sleep because of the boat's motion, all the past excitement, and in anticipation of the voyage ahead.

The cruisers going up the west coast of Africa had run into bad weather, which we had been warned about. The others, going directly to St. Helena, seemed to be progressing well and we had daily contact with them. Our friends from Victoria, Coryn and Tony on *Taonui*, were twenty-five hundred nautical miles west of Cape Town on their way up from Antarctica. The last time we had seen them had been in French Polynesia.

Buoyed by the idea that this was to be our last major passage, Christine had posted a "gloat chart" on the wall of the pilot house on which she crossed off each day of our passage as she came on watch in the mornings. After two or three days, we had settled into our normal passage making routines, had regained our appetites, and were both feeling well and rested. Christine had managed to send a shortwave message to the family at home in Canada, that we were on our way, and should reach Charleston, South Carolina within the next two months.

The weather forecast was now calling for more wind. We were experiencing typical trade winds of fifteen to twenty knots from the southeast, and were making between one hundred and thirty and one hundred and fifty nautical miles each twenty four hours, under poled out genoa and main. The seas were quite big at times but, under the clear blue sky and fluffy white clouds, we were enjoying ourselves, reading books, enjoying regular meals, listening to taped music and in radio contact with many friends.

Whisker pole at work

One night we heard *Shemali Blue* had done an unexpected gybe, which put a serious tear in their mainsail. The boats leaving Cape Town behind us were experiencing thirty knots of wind and rough seas as a weather front passed over them. Further south, Coryn reported that they had a gale of sixty three knots, six meter swells, and snow. They were travelling much further south than us, catching the storms moving from west to east below Cape Town. One of the boats making for St. Helena reported that they had broken two Autohelms, and were having to steer by hand until they could get one of them fixed. For our part, we were trucking along nicely in the Trades. At night these would calm to between five and ten knots before rising again each morning as the sun rose over the horizon. At night, the boat's progress could be heard as a steady 'swish' through the water over the huge swells. Behind us the Southern Cross, which had been our nighttime companion for so long, was getting perceptibly lower in the sky as each day passed. Christine found that steering a steady course by night was most easily checked by eying a star behind the mast from a selected position in the cockpit. Her favourite star was a rather brown looking one just above the cross trees. Our friends on *Cynosure* continued to endure rough seas on their way to St. Helena. Christine heard them say to a neighbouring boat on the radio

"This milk run is turning into a milkshake!"

We crossed the Greenwich meridian, and changed the boat's clock to Greenwich Mean Time. This made our waking hours more compatible with sunrise and sunset. Christine was thrilled when the radio operator on Tristan da Cunha Island contacted her on the radio. She had several conversations with him about his daily life on a small, isolated island in the South Atlantic. Born on the island, he had gone to the UK for two and a half years training before returning home to his present job. In 1967 the island's population of three hundred had been evacuated because of its volcano's activity. Thankfully it returned to dormancy, and many residents had now returned to the island. Fresh streams of drinkable water gush out of the volcano. The island's economy depends on exporting crayfish to South Africa, raising sheep and cattle, and growing vegetables. This made islanders reasonably self sufficient. They used collie dogs to round up their sheep, and raised geese and ducks as an additional source of meat and eggs. He tried hard to persuade Christine to change our course to visit the island.

We passed three hundred nautical miles south of St. Helena. It was six days since we had had to touch the set of the sails. The water-maker was put on each day to fill our water bottles with drinking water for that day. In this way we were able to check our daily water intake as well as regulate the supplementary minerals that we were taking.

By the ninth day, in a lessening breeze, we were nineteen hundred and eight nautical miles from the Equator. We had seen no rain, although we noticed there were more clouds as each day passed. We ran the engine for an hour after ten days just to spread the engine oil around its insides. The tow generator was putting excellent charge into the batteries, keeping all our lights and instruments functioning. Reports were coming in of the arrival of our friends' yachts in St. Helena, and we enjoyed their stories of trying to get ashore from their dinghies and up the impossible seawall in the strong surf. We envied them the experience of visiting the island, but we had had enough of strange anchorages, and wanted to get on with our passage. Next morning a tropic bird circled overhead as Christine signed on with Trudy's short wave radio net from Barbados. The sea was calm and all was well. We were now fifteen hundred and seventy nautical miles to our waypoint off the coast of Brazil. Our GPS had a fit of reversing our heading, which was a little disconcerting, and I hoped that it did not herald our first failure of the trip. We had a spare should the worst happen. After a morning of playing with it and reprogramming all our waypoints, it recovered, much to our relief. Using radio nets in Barbados and Mississauga, we were able to send a message home to our family in Victoria to tell them where we were. Meanwhile Coryn and Tony were due in Gordon's Bay, in South Africa the following day.

Finally we took down our South African courtesy flag, our second one, as the first had been blown to pieces sailing down the Wild Coast. Within twenty four hours the barometer started to fall, the wind backed to the south and began to rise, and a mist was rising off the sea. We put a reef in the mainsail, and it wasn't long before we saw a series of rain clouds marching along the horizon. However, within a few hours, the barometer climbed again, the clouds disappeared, and we were back in the southeast trades doing one hundred and forty nautical miles a day. Two weeks out of Cape Town we encountered our first heavy squall. It just would be that we had chosen that very morning to fly our light air gennaker for the first time. This huge sail billowed above us in the light air, putting our speed up a couple of knots. Just as we were getting used to its power, the wind picked up, so we hastily took it down. Looking up from handling this mass of unruly material into its bag, I noticed a dark black cloud ahead of us, with a slant of grey water pouring down from its flat bottom into the sea. Gradually it came closer as Christine and I scuttled around the decks, shortening sail, closing all the ports and hatches, and checking all the tie downs of the spare fuel and water containers on the deck. Soon the sea on the horizon under the cloud had changed from black to white, enveloping us in an eerie light. The margin of this whiteness was reaching out towards us at an alarming rate. The trade wind dropped and the sea around us sank into a slate grey, restless swell. Suddenly, the squall slammed into us. Spume off the surface of the sea was flying in clouds all around. The boat heeled over as I reset the small jib to accommodate the new wind direction, and to stop its alarming flogging in the howling wind. Sheets of rain cascaded down the sails, and flattened the sea to a smooth swell coming at us from all directions. The wind could not decide which way to blow, confusing the poor windvane which I could imagine calling out

"Make up your mind can't you?"

The wind would seem to blow for a while from one direction, sending us across the ocean at breakneck speed. Then suddenly changed its mind, switching to another direction, so causing havoc to the sails and the course steered. This continued for about twenty minutes as we retreated to the shelter of the pilothouse to watch and hang on. Then, as quickly as it had appeared, it suddenly left us slopping about in an indecisive swell, until the gradual return of the trade winds. They sorted out the chaos and sent us on our way again as though nothing had happened.

In flat seas, the preparation of light meals was no great problem, nor was doing the necessary deck work. Each morning as Christine got breakfast, I would do a tour of inspection of the sails and rigging. This would be repeated in the last light of day. One night, three Lesser Noddies (Terns) spent the night on our aft rail, which was great company on night watch. Unfortunately, the exertion of waking up, facing a new day at sea, and taking off, precipitated an explosive discharge of what smelt like foetid fish glue all over the cockpit. This took some time to remove, returning the cockpit to a habitable condition. After one rambunctious night's sailing, when the trade winds had stayed with us, I found dozens of flying fish scattered, either moribund or dead, all over the decks. Even squid had found their way aboard, to hide themselves behind jugs or in obscure crevices, where they bled their blue staining ink all over our white gel coat.

Light air sail

By day, in the boisterous waves of the trades and under blue skies, we delighted in watching squadrons of flying fish propel themselves out of the leading side of the waves, before flying downwind in a silver cloud for fifty yards, to disappear back into the sea. We never got tired of watching this display. At night we heard birds, seemingly talking to each other as they flew around the boat in the stygian darkness of the night, or in the reflected light of the moon and stars above. It was so remarkable to watch the phases of the moon cycling nightly as we moved along our passage. The amount of moonlight made such a difference to night sailing.

The boats visiting St. Helena had enjoyed the experience, going on bus tours around the island, and meeting the islanders in the pub at night. Now they were leaving, most of them for Ascension Island.

A sudden squall snapped one of our jib sheets which had frayed where it passed over the life line, and which I had missed on my daily inspections. Resolving to be more careful on my tours, I replaced the jib sheet. Squalls were becoming more frequent as we progressed. At night their approach was heralded by a green echo on the radar screen which was quite distinctive from the echo of a solid ship. Most often squalls appeared spontaneously in groups of four or five on the screen. The targets on the radar popped up at random. They marched in procession ahead of us, inexorably making their way to the centre of the screen, which was *Demelza*'s position, no matter which way the boat was steered. While alone on night watch, I could become quite paranoid watching them approach. All the experts talk of making use of these occasions to chase the squalls so as to replenish the fresh water tanks and to have refreshing showers. However squalls have a nasty habit, having wetted down the naked body trying to maintain balance on the swinging deck, of shutting off the water just at the point where a healthy all encompassing lather has been achieved. The resultant bubbly expostulation from the victim above never failed to raise a howl of merriment from the crew below. As to filling the water tanks, I did not seem to possess the necessary skills to stop the blowing spray from contaminating the rain cascading down the sails. From here it was supposed to flow off the boom into either a bucket, or into a rather crafty funnel and hose contraption that I had devised for transferring the water into the fresh water tanks. Even if I did achieve this miracle, my success was usually totally negated by taking a wave onboard. This had no difficulty at all finding its way through the water tank openings on deck. Fortunately this was not so much a crisis as it seemed, as we only drank water made by the water-maker .

We now started plotting the daily position of the Intertropical Convergence Zone (ITCZ), given out over "Trudy's Net" from Barbados. Diligently I would copy all the details down on to a blank paper chart of the Atlantic including the location, positions and progress of all the weather systems that might affect us. One day the wind moved to the northeast so we took down the pole for the first time in sixteen days to proceed on a fast reach in confused seas. As soon as we had it down and stowed away on the mast, the wind switched back again so we had to redeploy the pole. By now we had seven hundred and thirty-five nautical miles to go to Fernando de Noronha which we would pass to the north. We had so many flying fish on the deck one morning that Christine, who hated the daily unintentional carnage, suggested she try frying some for breakfast. The general consensus was that they were quite delicious, a little like herring, but oh so many small bones.

The ITCZ was taking the shape of a wavy line above and below the equator. Our interest in this area was twofold. Firstly it is associated with unsettled weather and squalls, and secondly it moves about quite dramatically, oscillating north and south of the Equator. So once having crossed it, which we would have to do in crossing the Equator, there was no guarantee that we would not cross paths again any number of times.

One night, in the northeast part of the sky, we spotted the Plough, guidepost to the northern hemisphere. We could still see the Southern Cross to the south. This made us feel just a little bit nearer home, our emotions being honed by the expansiveness of the ocean.

"Look!" shouted Christine from the companionway the following morning, pointing behind the boat.

There, unmistakably following us was the fin of a large shark. It was either eyeing our generator propeller or looking for smaller fish that sheltered in the shade of our boat as we moved along in the hot sun.

"No swimming today." I said.

On Trudy's Net, we received news that our friends and neighbours from Victoria, Val and Peter, were arriving in Barbados for a two week holiday, beginning on the tenth of April. They were hoping that we could drop in for a visit. We were now at 5°S so a meeting was theoretically possible, depending upon how our journey progressed, and on the weather. We were now seven hundred and ninety seven nautical miles from our waypoint on the Equator, and had, for the first time, been able to hear the Mississauga Ham Radio Net and its excellent weather forecaster, Herb. We tried for a couple of days to make contact with him, but without success. There were dozens of boats, all wanting their individualized weather forecasts, crowding the airwaves. We reported our lack of success to Trudy.

"Try again tomorrow." she said, "In the meantime I'll email Herb to ask that he listens for you to pick up your signal."

Sure enough, the next evening on Christine's second call, Herb came back.

"I think I hear *Demelza* in the background. Are you there *Demelza*?" Our link was established, and we began to receive a most detailed and personalized weather forecast for our reported position each day. What a wonderful service. At the same time, contact with South Africa was becoming more problematical each day. We often had to use Tristan da Cunha as our relay station.

Small tuna fish were following us, darting past the boat and having a fine old time. We saw one jump out of the sea to catch an unsuspecting flying fish in midair. Noddies were making a habit of spending their nights on various parts of the boat and, in spite of our previous unfortunate experience with them, we hadn't the heart to deny them a resting perch. Sure enough, a cleanup was most often needed. Perfect downwind sailing continued, pushing us along at a steady six knots. Sometimes ocean currents would either help or hinder us as we closed the Brazilian coast. We were able to leave the gennaker up night and day in the settled weather, which helped our daily mileage.

"Look at the size of that ship." I gasped, as a huge tanker went gliding by at a distance of four miles. It was the first ship we had seen since leaving South Africa. Christine called it up on the radio and spoke to the radio officer.

"This is the *Jahr Viking*," he responded, "the largest oil tanker in the world. We are sailing to Cape Town from the Gulf of Mexico, then on to Durban and the Persian Gulf.

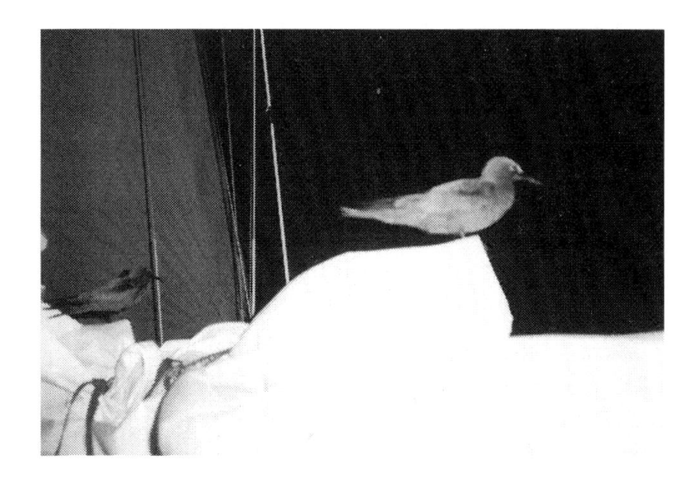

Noddy hitch hikers

We are five hundred meters long and are carrying five hundred and fifty four million gallons of oil. The ship is registered in Oslo, has fifty Filipino crew and Norwegian officers. Now I'll make you jealous, we have a gymnasium, swimming pool and TV lounge." It transpired that he, the radio officer, came from Bangalore in India.

The next evening we received the shocking news that Margaret, a neighbour of Tony's in Kilifi, who had befriended us and had been so very kind and helpful while we were staying in the lagoon, had suddenly died. We just couldn't believe it. She had always been so full of energy and wellbeing.

The compression post under *Demelza*'s mast developed a squeak with every movement of the boat. It was loudest next to the ear of the occupant of the passage making berth in the centre of the boat, but proved maddeningly difficult to locate. However, after a few nights of disturbed sleep and an increasingly grumpy crew, I was convinced that it had to be taken seriously. After lengthy periods on hands and knees in the rolling sea, I applied a shot of WD 40 down the whole length of the post on either side. Perfect peace was restored.

When we were one hundred and fifty nautical miles from Fernando da Noronha, squalls became the norm. Gannets put on awesome diving displays all around *Demelza.* Crafty Frigate birds would wait for them to rise out of the sea holding a tasty morsel in their beaks, before setting upon them in midair with aggressive aerobatics causing the prize fish to be released. The Frigate bird would then dive to snap it up before it hit the water. The rolling sea, and the consequent violent rolling of our boat, firmly wrapped the spare topping lift around the furler. I realized that unless it unwound itself without delay, it might present us with a problem in the event of a squall, as we would not be able to furl the big headsail. I untied the end of the topping lift on the boom and, with one hand holding on to the boat, and the other the end of the topping lift, I staggered along the deck, in a most ungainly fashion, to reach the drum of the furler on the foredeck. Then began a very wet and frustrating half hour trying to anticipate the roll of the boat to loosen the line's grip on the top of the furler. Eventually I was successful and it unraveled. It taught me a lesson never again to have loose halyards on the boat at sea.

The next excitement was Christine's observation one morning.

"Hugh, there's the most awful smell in the boat." Thinking bad thoughts, I again sank on my hands and knees on the cabin sole, inhaling sharply as I progressed unsteadily around the boat. Ultimately, I ended up at one of the lockers. In it Christine had stored the pork and beef in brine. Unfortunately the pork had absorbed more brine than usual, which had resulted in the meat being exposed to the air in one of the bottles. Putrefaction ensued producing the smell. No harm had been done, and the fish loved it I'm sure.

Next, just before one of Christine's radio schedules was due, the radio went completely dead. Now that was a real problem. Being without a radio would be a major loss. I spent varying lengths of time peering at, and poking at the connections before finding that a contact between the radio and the backstay aerial had corroded. A good clean and greasing fired up the radio again.

Our twenty four hour watches continued to be shared. I slept between 1900 hrs and 0100 hrs, and Christine between 0100 hrs and 0700 hrs. This didn't always work out, as the onset of squalls or rough weather often seemed to occur at 0130 hrs, which did nothing to improve intercrew relationships. When the weather was calm, I would catch another rest later in the morning, and Christine would disappear for a break in the afternoon. This system worked well. Through trial and error we had found that, using my natural predilection for a snooze after supper, and Christine's preference to stay up until all hours of the night, we were able to utilize both traits to our mutual advantage. On watch we would read or listen to the radio in the pilothouse, check our course, keep an eye on the radar which was on "watch," and go up on deck for a 360 degree scan of the horizon every ten to fifteen minutes.

Chafe was beginning to show itself as enemy number one. Even the slightest contact of the sail or running rigging with something else on the boat would cause chafe in no time at all due to the constant swaying and movement.

We had loaded up with fifty books for this trip, and with the pleasant sailing we were experiencing Christine, always an avid reader, was making great inroads into the pile.

After one session on the radio Christine said "I cannot figure it out. There's something falling into my hair whenever I use the radio." The radio station was situated directly under one of the dorade vents, which when I took it to pieces, revealed dried red earth. It was probably the remains of a mud wasp's nest from Africa. Bits of this had shaken out with the boat's motion.

The wind continued to die, one of the worst conditions at sea. The rolling of the boat in the cross swell shook the wind out of the light air sail, which magnified the boat's movement. This made working in the hot galley a most uncomfortable exercise, as the utensils had a nasty habit of sashaying across the counter tops. Christine always kept her cool and, when she occasionally came up for air looking a pale shade of green, she managed to recover after a few minutes above deck to produce delicious meals. We arrived at the ITCZ after nothing but days of 82 F., calm blue seas, and clear skies with fluffy clouds. We had enjoyed the experience so much, and were now about to pay for it. A large low pressure system was located over the Brazilian coast, and its effect was reaching out into the Atlantic. We had not yet reached the point where we thought the narrowest north south distance across the doldrums was located, so we turned west toward the Brazilian coast, parallel to the equator. As if the deteriorating weather were an ill omen, we heard on the radio that our beautiful German shepherd Tessa, whom we had left at home with a great friend, had died. It was hard to throw off our mood of depression.

Huge dark convection clouds began to develop all around us, which made for dazzlingly beautiful sunsets. These moist towers were lit up by the changing colours of the sun. As we moved parallel to and south of the equator at a distance of one hundred and sixty nautical miles, the nights provided us with a distant display of fierce electrical storms along our starboard side. We motored westward toward the coast of Brazil. Suddenly the electrical storms stopped, and the skies north of us cleared. We put the helm hard over at midnight and motored slowly northward with storm clouds once again on both sides of us, but clear skies overhead. There was not a breath of wind, and by 0800 hrs the next morning we felt the first breath of the northeast trades. We crossed the equator at noon, on April 1st.

After unfurling the jib in ten knots of wind from the northeast we continued northward to reach 2°N before turning northwest. By doing this we hoped to get out of the clutches of the ever unpredictable north south movement of the ITCZ, with its attendant hard work.

All around us at night, the sky over the horizon was lit by fish boats. We hoped that we could find our way safely through their nets. Christine continued to talk to Tony, who gave us news of Margaret's funeral, and told us that they had passed on our condolences to the family. We were now two thousand seven hundred and sixty three nautical miles from Charleston, South Carolina and had traveled four thousand and forty two nautical miles from Cape Town. The seas began to build again, and Christine began to feel a bit battered and bruised in the rough seas. Even running our radio wasn't that much fun in this weather. Often, after a prolonged conversation, she would appear, dragging herself over the companionway's lower drop board, looking a bit sick.

More oil tankers were passing about two miles on either side of us. At night, if the radar images suggested that these behemoths were too close, I would turn away for safety. But they had a nasty knack of turning towards us to find out what was giving them a radar blip. This could be disconcerting as they were so huge, and moved along at such speed. We had been at sea for five weeks and Christine's gloat chart was definitely filling up as we continued sailing parallel to the north coast of Brazil. The tuna fish swimming below us created flares of phosphorescence in the dark water at night. They easily kept up with us, and indeed it often looked as though they were waiting for us to catch them up. Gannets were all around as we roared along in the northeast trades.

Christine's gloat chart

We sailed past Forteleza, covering one hundred nautical miles in a day. We still had two thousand seven hundred and sixty three nautical miles to get to Charleston, which seemed forbidding at the time, but reinforced the idea that we should do it in one shot rather than spend another season in the Caribbean. With the trades consistently blowing at night, the sea was uncomfortably lumpy. Christine had sore arms from hanging on to the hand rails while working around the cabin. Occasionally we would reduce the size of the jib just to make our progress more comfortable in these boisterous conditions. Gradually we began to shake off the squalls that had dogged us intermittently since the equator. We had time to reflect on the old trade sailing routes between Cape Town and North America, which we read all about in *Ocean Passages of the World.* Faithfully following it had served us well getting us through the ITCZ. In lighter air and the large cross swell, the rolling of the boat became fierce in the absence of the stabilizing wind in the sails. Putting up the gennaker was an option, but I was afraid that, with all this motion, it would chafe to pieces. As soon as the cross swells diminished in the light air, we did put it up again, alert to the possibility of an errant squall pouncing on us. We had been playing intermittently with a counter current for a couple of days, which had reduced our progress. I did wonder whether or not we had entered the Equatorial Counter Current which runs between one and two knots at this location.

One day we launched an empty wine bottle with a note in it, sending greetings to an unknown beachcomber somewhere in the world, giving our names, the name of our boat, homeport and the date. Weather reports from the Caribbean were not good. They were experiencing a lot of electrical storms as we continued to make about one hundred and thirty nautical miles a day on smoother seas.

Message sent

Charleston was now two thousand and two hundred nautical miles ahead of us at the end of our 41st day at sea. Drawing abreast of Tobago, the Caribbean Radio Net became available, with George the regular weather man. In calm periods, as we bowled along, we solved anagrams over the air with other yachts, and distinguished ourselves on one occasion by being the day's winners. This made a pleasurable break from reading books on our long passage.

By now we were beginning to make contact again with boats that we had met in the Pacific who were cruising the Caribbean. Jack and Sandy on *Utopia* were in the Bahamas at Green Turtle Cay. We had last seen them in Puerto Vallarta in March 1994. Gradually the wind backed to the north, making us take down the genoa's pole to study the weather fax pictures coming out of Boston. There seemed to be a change on the way, but it was unclear what it was. Changeable weather conditions kept us busy adjusting sails until the trade winds returned on our 42nd day at sea.

The Southern Cross was now only just visible above the horizon at night. With all the gear hanging on the stern rail, the weather vane was having a problem picking up enough wind to make it work effectively in the heavy swell. The nights were moonless and, in the steady but light wind, we continued doggedly northward over a flat sea. At 17N we made direct contact for the first time with our own home radio net, the DDD net. Christine, after being roused from her bed in the middle of the night, was able to talk to Peter Thomas, finding it difficult to get back to sleep afterwards. To add to our excitement Val and Peter had been invited to Trudy's radio shack in Barbados so that we could talk on her radio. Not quite as good as a visit, but close.

Abreast of Antigua, the squalls returned. With thirteen hundred nautical miles to Charleston, the wind vane kept rounding up the boat in the heavier gusts. I spent a lot of time readjusting it and the sails to achieve a better balance. Our radio contact with Kilifi failed for the first time, mainly because of interference from a lot of radio traffic. Herb, on his weather net, wanted us to close in to the Caribbean islands as he thought we were in danger of losing the northeast trades. Veering off to the west from our straight course for Charleston really rankled. I split the difference. We turned half-way toward meeting his advice, hoping he wouldn't notice.

"I see you are keeping out from the islands," was his opening remark on contact the next day. "Don't do it or you'll lose the wind." Crestfallen, and feeling very ungrateful not to have taken his advice, we steered towards his suggested waypoint.

Christine had been able to talk on the radio by telephone patch to our friends Harold and Virginia in California. She had told them that we should arrive in Charleston within nine or ten days. Still the gennaker flew, drawing us ahead in the light breeze. Really feeling bold, we now left this huge sail up night and day as the likelihood of squalls seemed slight. Herb's weather forecasts remained good. With eight hundred and sixty nautical miles to go to Charleston the next hurdle would be crossing the Gulf Stream. The day was remarkable for seeing vapour trails from two high flying aircraft for the first time since leaving South Africa. The wind was now so light that our gennaker was sashaying about in the cross swell as there wasn't enough wind to support it. On bringing it down, it wrapped itself around the forward navigation light, which was fixed to the pulpit, and snapped it off into the sea.

Herb was not sounding so confident the next morning.

"You'd better hedge your bets," he said "and get closer in to the Bahamas. I'm not at all sure about Charleston over the next week." We entered a new waypoint into our GPS off Nassau. What rotten luck after all that way with only six hundred and ninety nautical miles left. It was then we received news from *Shemali Blue* that our friends on *Magnum Bonum*, off the coast of Brazil, had not been heard for a few days. They had been making for Rio de Janeiro.

On Herb's next contact, he sounded cautious.

"An intense low pressure system has formed over the Gulf of Mexico, and a gale warning has been issued for 32°N. This system will move eastwards towards Florida, and may cross your intended track on the way to Charleston at 33°N. You would not want to meet it in the Gulf Stream."

Proceeding along the east coast of the Bahamas, we were only doing three knots, and still hoped the weather would hold. We had no good charts for the Bahamas, our best only showing deep water into Nassau.

"If cruise ships can get in there, I'm sure we can." was Christine's unfailing logic in the face of my growing pessimism.

"Hang on," said a voice from the islands, as we chatted to Trudy about our dilemma. "I think I've got a proper scaled chart in my attic. Can you hold?" While he went scurrying off to his attic, Jack on *Utopia*, who had been listening to our conversation, popped into the airwaves.

"We're sitting in Marsh Harbour in the Abacos," he said. "Give me a waypoint outside the reef and a time of arrival, and we'll be out there in *Utopia* to meet you, to guide you in." What an offer. All our worries dissolved as we made for our rendezvous with *Utopia*. The sea was now flat calm, so I took advantage of the moment to transfer diesel from the jugs on deck to the main fuel tanks. Then we continued to motor in the eerie stillness of the day. To the north of us that night we could see intense lightning lighting up the sky ahead. Thanks to Herb's advice to slow down, the storm had passed north of us.

The fifty seventh day of our passage dawned. Land came into view and, with nineteen nautical miles to go, we spotted *Utopia* waiting for us on the horizon near Loggerheads just north of Marsh Harbour. We talked to them on VHF radio. What a thrill.

With many thanks to all the people who had helped us on the radio, especially Trudy in Barbados and Herb in Mississauga, Christine signed off.

We followed *Utopia* closely in seven feet of water over the reef. This was a shock to the system after the more familiar ocean depths.

"I'm not sure I like traveling at six knots in seven feet of water." I fussed.

Suddenly we were back. Boats were everywhere, sailing those placid, sheltered waters. Helping hands took our lines and secured us to the dock at the Triple J Marina. After eight weeks at sea we had arrived.

Utopia waiting for us off Marsh Harbour

Demelza dwarfed by her neighbours

CHAPTER 23
The Bahamas

After we had reported into the Customs and Immigration, and had taken a most welcome shower, we shared a meal with Jack and Sandy, catching up on the past five years cruising. This was followed by a twelve hour sleep in *Demelza* that was quiet for the first time in eight weeks.

We cleaned and tidied up before going into town to replenish our supply of fresh food. In the marina, we were surrounded by huge sport fishing and power cruising boats. They towered over a *Demelza* who looked well worn after fifty six days at sea. News of our journey had spread around the harbour so that we were stopped frequently for a chat.

Sandy and Jack

"How much fuel did you burn on the trip?" the owner of one behemoth asked one morning.

"Twelve gallons." I replied.

"Geeze," he groaned, "I use that getting out of this harbour."

Gilbert

We were adopted by Cliff and Bezy on the sailboat *Ceilidh*, who shepherded us around the town and local eateries. The weather was fine but the forecast was for forty knots of wind. One morning we had the greatest surprise when tuning in to the regular morning chat net on the VHF radio, to hear Keith and Helen, whom we had last met in Opua, New Zealand calling us.

"Is that the *Demelza* we met in New Zealand?" they asked.

"Yes, it is." we replied. In a trice they were down at the boat with big hugs all around.

Up the road from the marina was the local watering hole, the Jibset. Here, while enjoying supper one evening, we were thrilled to meet two Canadians, Eileen Quinn and her husband David. She writes and sings sailing ballads for a living, and entertained us all during our evening meal. She is so talented, and her songs capture the very essence of cruising life.

Hearing that we planned to go up the Intracoastal Waterway, on the East Coast of the States, one of our neighbours generously gave us a set of Chart Kits of the area. Over supper at the Tiki Hut, a dramatic thunderstorm rattled the windows adding atmosphere to the occasion. This was the big storm that we had avoided by coming in for shelter. It caused a lot of damage to the island, and created waves which completely swamped the restaurant where we had had our supper. It would not have been a pleasant experience being caught in the Gulf Stream in those conditions. Fierce storms had lashed the Southern States, with tornadoes causing many deaths before spinning across to Florida and out over the Gulf Stream, right across the path we would have taken

Because of the stir that *Demelza*'s arrival had caused in the harbour, we agreed to do a question and answer session at the Jib Set Club House. Cliff introduced us to forty people on the appointed morning. We talked of our adventures, followed by answering a lot of questions from the audience. Afterwards, people from all over town arrived at our dock wanting to look at the little boat that had just sailed in from South Africa.

Following the meeting a man approached Christine.

"Would you consider coming on my radio talk show on Radio Abaco?" he asked "Certainly, she said. "When?"

"Tomorrow afternoon. See you there."

The following morning we went swimming at a local beach to cool off before the talk show in the afternoon. Gilbert, the interviewer, met us at the door of the radio shack on the hill overlooking the town. We spent a happy hour with him and his listeners talking about the thing we loved most – cruising.

We tried to clean off the encrusted salt on *Demelza*. Christine worked on the wind vane while one of our neighbours went over charts of the Intracoastal Waterway with me. He knew it well, pointing out some of the anchorages he had enjoyed over many years.

With Jack and Sandy we visited the quaint Hope Town Harbour Lighthouse with its gorgeous view of the island. Attractive cottages painted in soft pastel colours, with contrasting trim, lined the streets. On our return down the wharf, we saw a streak of light in the sky which we later found out had been the launch of an Atlas rocket from Cape Canaveral.

After ten days reacclimatizing to life ashore, and getting used to the overwhelming generosity of our American neighbours in their grand boats, we tore ourselves away to relocate *Demelza* in Green Turtle Cay, New Plymouth. History tells us this was the site of Loyalist landings. We enjoyed the simple pleasure of looking around shops again, and Christine emerged from one with a very sporty sun hat, complete with a broad Bahamas ribbon, to keep off the hot sun. Our plan was to stop off at Great Sale Cay for the night, before an early start across the Gulf Stream to Florida. Most of the boats we had spoken to during our stay in the Bahamas had regaled us with horrific tales of their many crossings over this stretch of water.

A day of sailing in eight feet of water across the Bahama Bank to Sale Cay, during which every detail of the ocean's floor was clearly visible through the crystal clear water, was totally unnerving. How thankful we were, yet again, for *Demelza*'s four and a half foot draft. In the clear water of our new anchorage, I jumped over the side to clean the bottom of the boat as a prelude to crossing over to Florida. Severe thunderstorms were still plaguing central Florida, with wind damage being reported from many locations. Twenty four boats were gathered in our anchorage waiting to dash across the Gulf Stream at the appropriate time. We had watched many of these huge vessels making for our anchorage earlier in the day. Every one of them appeared to be on automatic pilot, following exactly the same course on their chart plotters. Often we saw nobody on the bridges as they steamed along at breakneck speed. The same was true of boats on a reciprocal course for the islands. How they never met head on we could never make out. We had taken *Demelza* two miles to one side of this stream of traffic to be sure that we were not accidentally hit by one of them.

We left Great Sale Cay at first light and, as there was no wind, motored to the north end of the Little Bahama Bank, a distance of sixty nautical miles. We arrived at 1530hrs, and found ourselves off the Bank and in deep blue water where I felt much more relaxed. As the afternoon wore on, lightning began to flicker among the dark clouds forming ahead of us. Squalls began to affect us, and the sea became uncomfortable lumpy, throwing spray about. This was quickly swept away by the northwesterly wind. By 0130 hrs the next morning we were forty seven nautical miles from Cape Canaveral. The sky had cleared, revealing brilliant stars above, and the street lights of Florida lit up the sky to the west. As light dawned at 0630 hrs, we could see the buildings of the Cape Canaveral launch site ahead as we entered the Canaveral Barge Canal. Here we encountered our first opening bridge before passing huge Casino Cruise ships tied up alongside the canal. Below us we saw our first manatee swimming slowly about in the murky green water.

CHAPTER 24
The Intracoastal Waterway

We were on our way to Titusville Marina in Florida, which had been recommended to us by friends in the Bahamas, before we realized that it was not a Port of Entry into the States for clearing Customs. On calling the Coast Guard on our radio to tell them of our dilemma, they told us to continue on to the Marina where we would be checked in. What excellent service.

A short cab ride into Titusville the following day allowed us to replace some of our travel worn clothing, which compared poorly with that of the local population. Advice on traveling the Intracoastal Waterway was readily available from neighbouring boats moored in the marina, as most of them had done the trip up and down the coast many times. We made notes on the information they gave us as we pondered the charts together. Preferred anchorages, access to shops of various sorts along the way, fuel stations, points of interest, difficult areas to transit, and places to avoid were all included.

By email, we received the sad news of Virginia's illness from Harold in California. Life was going on outside our little world on the boat, and it was sad to hear such bad news. Why did these things always happen to the nicest and kindest people? Harold's request for us to break our journey, to visit her, put us in a bit of a quandary. Because of the upcoming hurricane season, we were advised to get *Demelza* north of Florida by half-way through June. It was now the middle of May, so we needed to press on before leaving the boat to fly to Fullerton.

Our first experience with the severe thunderstorms that affect the east coast of the United States occurred the day before we visited the Kennedy Space Centre on Cape Canaveral. It was a warning of things to come.

News arrived that our Swedish friends on *Magnum Bonum*, last heard from en route to Rio de Janeiro, had suffered several severe knockdowns. Their heavy forty eight foot ketch had lost its main mast and radio aerials. They had been found and towed into harbour, where the boat was currently under repair. Both of them were tired but unharmed.

After five days in Titusville, where we had cleaned everything on the boat and ourselves, we motored out of the marina and turned north along the waterway.

At Daytona Beach, we caught up with Sandy and Jack who had arrived from Marsh Harbour. We anchored next to them for the night. Being a prudent skipper, Jack had let out a 10:1 scope for the night, so he was soon swinging down on top of us in the fickle evening breeze. We moved, in the twilight, to the other end of the anchorage to keep out of his way. Next day we motored fifty four miles north to St. Augustine, passing lovely homes along the waterway. Roscatc Spoonbills watched from the trees as we motored by. At the current rate of progress we calculated that we had enough time to leave the boat in Charleston, South Carolina before flying to California in June.

We enjoyed travelling with Jack and Sandy. They showed us around the delightful town of St. Augustine, where Jack and I were happy to support the local Irish Pub, while Sandy and Christine toured the shops. Much can be written on the history of this pretty place. Suffice it to say that we would like to return one day to spend more time exploring. When the bridge opened on the morning of our departure, we set out across the St. John's River and entered the St George River. That evening we found a recommended anchorage in ten feet of water. An Island Packet sailboat, the only other boat in the anchorage, went aground in the night as the tide fell. However they only had an hour heeled over before the tide turned and they were floated off again. What I found amazing was that, being a regular on the waterway, going aground was of no concern to them. To me, it would have been the end of the world. Another lesson learnt on the Intracoastal Waterway.

As we motored on, we passed huge storks' nests in the marshes. On past Fernandina on the Florida/Georgia border, crowded with shrimp boats, to the Breckhill River anchorage. With the engine turned off, we were serenaded by birdsong in the evening light, and sheltered from the north wind by tall trees along the shore. Wild horses grazed in a nearby pasture, and raccoons rummaged along the shoreline for their supper. Three dolphins glided past in the riffled water. The wind dropped, and a glorious sunset preceded a quiet twilight in which we heard the curlews calling.

Passing Terapin Point on the north end of Cumberland Island, we wended our way south of Buttermilk Sound. Here we spied a six foot alligator lying on the surface of the water, watching us as we slid by. After a further forty eight nautical miles of motoring, we anchored in New Teakettle Creek. Our friends on *Utopia* were twenty miles behind us, nursing an overheating engine. Pelicans were gliding over the wide bay looking for tasty morsels in the water below. Suddenly they would dive, surfacing with their catch in their large bills. A big French boat preceded us as we reentered the waterway in the morning, heading into Sapeto Sound. The wind had switched to the southwest, and the prevailing currents seemed to be helping us along. By mid afternoon we had reached the attractive suburbs of Savannah, Georgia. We passed the exit of the Moon River, made famous by the song of the same name, sung by Andy Williams. We slipped past the elegant Savannah Yacht Club to arrive at the Herb River anchorage located in swampy grassland beside the wide waterways.

The next morning we moved a short distance to the Palmer Johnson Marina, which was crammed with magnificent yachts, owned by a most welcoming group of people. At our first meeting, one offered to lend us his car to go shopping. How could we not enjoy being guests here? It was their custom to put a daily newspaper and six delicious donuts into our cockpit every morning before we awoke. People's generosity was sparked by stories of our cruise, as many had the ambition to do something similar themselves one day.

Utopia's engine had finally given up on the outskirts of Savannah. Jack had to tie their inflatable dinghy firmly alongside the boat, which helped them reach the nearest marina for repairs.

Savannah was a most fascinating place to visit. The main post office was built of Georgian marble. It was both huge and ornamental. Jack and Sandy joined us as we caught a red trolley bus into town, where we learnt some of its history. The architecture varied from 1700s to the present day, giving a most attractive overall effect to the city's appearance. The old Cotton Exchange, with its cobbled streets, graced the waterfront. We found a large book shop, where they served excellent coffee as we browsed happily among their well stocked shelves. Reluctantly we had to leave Savannah, vowing to return one day. We said farewell to Jack and Sandy who would be travelling more slowly than us. We would meet up again in Charleston after our visit to California.

The waterway was totally clear of other boats as we made our way first to Beaufort, in South Carolina before continuing on to Charleston, our originally planned landfall from South Africa.

The temperature was in the mid 80s°F as we called ahead on the radio to book into Charleston's City Marina. Passing one of the navigation markers at low tide, we nudged bottom in a very narrow stretch of the waterway. The sailboat following us went hard aground, and immediately asked two following boats to 'wave him off.' This procedure entailed asking a power boat if they would kindly speed past the grounded vessel at many knots and, in so doing create sufficient wash to float the grounded boat off the obstruction. In this case it was a shallow sand bar at a curve in the waterway.

By now we were used to making radio requests to the various bascule and swing bridges along the waterway, asking them to open to let us through. The John Limehouse Swing Bridge, south of Charleston, stayed open for an extra eleven minutes to let us pass. I think they had seen us going flat out as we approached the open bridge, and they didn't have the heart to shut it before we arrived.

We entered the approaches to Charleston pier to the sound of the Russian National Anthem and cheering crowds. Thinking it a bit odd that they bothered to make such a fuss of our arrival, we looked to starboard and saw a weatherbeaten sailboat, flying the Russian ensign, being towed in. The boat was the last of several competitors in the "Round Alone" race that had recently arrived at the Charleston finish.

Bridges opened for our passage

The waterfront was gaily decked out in colourful balloons, bunting and banners. The band was playing enthusiastic music, and we were soon caught up in the crowd inspecting the racing yachts and munching ice cream on the harbour wall. Nearby a local advertisement exclaimed "Charleston is where the Ashley and Cooper Rivers meet to form the Atlantic Ocean."

Charlestonians are immensely proud of their heritage, and "Hey y'all" echoes in the streets all day. We found the people we met extremely friendly and happy to make us feel at home in their town. It is loaded with history of the founding years of the United States.

With such crowds and ongoing hubbub in the marina we decided to relocate to the Maritime Centre. From there the walk into town would be much shorter. On our arrival, we met an artist setting up a show of his work in its opulent facilities. He took us in his car to visit the Carolina Yacht Club, which turned out to be more of a social club for wealthy power boat owners.

In the evenings, we sat on the Maritime Center's lawn to get out of the ninety degree heat in *Demelza*'s cabin. We envied the luxury of the local boats which had air conditioning units keeping them cool in the heat of the day. Here we met Connie and Jim walking their two small dogs, Samson and Delilah. With them, we watched the firework display the city had put on for the ocean racing celebrations going on downtown.

Mary, our crew on the first leg of our adventure, drove down from Washington DC where she was visiting her daughter, to stay for a couple of days. She was able to meet the curator of the Natural History Museum who was a friend of a friend. We took in an art show before we all had a superb supper at 'Blossoms' in the evening.

I took our small two horse power outboard for servicing before joining the girls to see Julia Roberts and Hugh Grant in the movie Notting Hill. Later the Maritime Centre hosted a reception for those yachts staying in its basin.

We were invited to Connie and Jim's apartment overlooking the Marine Centre. It was two floors of sheer luxury which we really appreciated after living on *Demelza* for six years. Following drinks, they whisked us away in their nice little Mercedes to the Charleston Country Club, which was very exclusive and for which we had to put on the best clothes we possessed.

Back to more mundane things on the boat. Engine maintenance in 90°F made working conditions in the 'hellhole' even more demanding. After cleaning it up, oiling the moving parts, checking and greasing the bonding wires and cable steering mechanism, I felt comfortable asking the local Yanmar mechanic to come to check the engine.

Connie picked us up one morning, and drove us to Drayton Hall, a lovely freestanding Palladian house built in 1733. Its huge plantation had been worked by slave labor, growing rice and indigo, and was the only surviving completely restored mansion of its type in the whole area. During the civil war, the owner had told the Union troops, as they arrived, that the house was being used as a smallpox hospital. Whereupon they left it well alone. Earthquakes and hurricanes had taken their toll of the outbuildings over subsequent years. Tall trees now obscured the once magnificent views from the mansion's windows. The grounds were redolent with flowering Magnolia trees and handsome old live oaks covered in Spanish moss. Back at the marina, Jim showed us over his beautiful forty two foot tuna fishing boat, before taking us for supper in their lovely home.

That evening a tropical depression had developed over Bermuda. Everybody started to worry. The Maritime Centre gave us a pictorial sheet of all the river and swamp sanctuaries in the area, to one of which *Demelza* had been assigned in the event of a hurricane threatening Charleston. Over the next twenty four hours tropical storm Arlene developed, which seemed to be heading northwest rather than southwest towards us.

We serviced the winches and the anchor windlass before being invited out to dinner by a retired couple who had sailed out of Scotland for Morocco in their younger days. They had cruised in their boat for ten years in the Mediterranean before moving to the States.

I replaced the bow navigation lights that had been ripped away by the gennaker off the Bahamas, and the replacement parts for the gas stove's oven were installed. Thunderstorms and heavy rain signaled a change in the weather, as we struggled in the humidity and heat preparing to lock up the boat for our flight to California.

Following a sad ten day visit to see Virginia, who did her very best to make us welcome in spite of being so ill, we bade her and Harold a fond farewell. It was the last time we were to see her, as she died a week later. We felt so fortunate to have been able to say goodbye to such a sweet and loving soul.

On our return to Charleston, *Demelza* looked fine in spite of all my worrying. No storm had hit in our absence. Jim, with the Maritime Center's help, had looked after her well. We sent a diver down to clean under the boat and to replace the anodes. He reported all was well down there.

"Be sure to come up to meet us in Maine," were Jim's final words as together we pored over charts of the east coast. "It's fabulous sailing up there, and totally beautiful."

Demelza had been in Charleston for a month, and it had been a wonderful place to stay. The Ben Sawyer Bridge opened early to let us through, and we motored all day to anchor in the South Santee River under overcast skies. We had passed a huge Corps of Engineers barge during the afternoon, which was busily dredging the waterway in an attempt to create a minimum depth of six feet at the centre of the waterway.

The wind developed into a full blown gale by the next morning and, as we moved out of the anchorage, threatening black clouds were marching across the surrounding land. Turtles sat on exposed rocks in the Wacamow River, and ospreys watched from the surrounding tree canopy. After fuelling at the Wana Wachee Marina we continued north, the tide helping us along, until we drew alongside Barefoot Landing, where we stayed for a couple of days.

Waterway mooring

Motoring along the waterway is not the relaxing preoccupation we had anticipated. Breakfast; up anchor, motoring all day lining up the day beacons, keeping out of other boats way in the narrow channels, especially the wide commercial barges being pushed along at great speed by large tugs; staying off the shallow banks; making best use of the currents; finding a suitable anchorage; anchoring; and maybe an anchor watch at night during the squalls that accompanied the fierce thunderstorms. It was all quite exhausting.

We went past the notorious "Rockpile," a particularly shallow stretch of the waterway, then carefully navigating past Little River on the North Carolina border where fish boats were roaring out to sea. We passed Southport along the Cape Fear River, anchoring in Shaw's Cut in front of a new waterfront condo development. We rested for an extra day there to explore the area. The local pastime of the residents was to honk a Freon horn at the many speedster boaters spinning past their development, leaving a huge wake which damaged the Cut's banks.

The bridge was open at 0800 hrs as we motored through on the incoming tide. The day was hot as we thundered on for the next fifty miles, before finding a pool off the waterway, dredged out by the Corps of Engineers for one of their service Centers. The heat and humidity was ferocious in the absence of any breeze.

Through the Onslow Swing Bridge we went at 0645 hrs. They opened it especially for us. We were overtaken by a severe thunderstorm with hail, which caused property damage in Wilmington, about a hundred miles north of us. As we entered Bogue Sound, the wind was blowing at twenty-five knots from the southwest. The chart showed very shallow water. Our course was indicated by a series of widely spaced numbered markers across the Sound. Straying slightly from this marked channel would inevitably lead to grounding. Some of the markers were so far apart that at times, it was hard to see the next one ahead in the driving hail.

By evening we had arrived at Beaufort Town Dock, North Carolina, where we stopped for a day to restock the boat, and to allow another gale to blow itself out. We took the opportunity to visit Moorehead City to find an internet café from which to catch up with news from home.

Through the next bridge we motored on the next day in hot and muggy conditions. We crossed Pamlico Sound and the Neuse River, with its fascinating city of Oriental. We had been advised to visit here, but felt inclined to keep moving while the conditions were favorable. Again the Sound was shallow and the markers far apart. Biting flies were everywhere, and thunder threatened in the distance. We anchored in six feet of water in Eastham Creek. Lightning closed in all around us, and heavy raindrops bounced off the water in the accompanying downpour. The anchorage was somewhat exposed, with flat reed covered land surrounding us, and our mast was the only feature sticking up into the lightning fractured sky.

"I don't think I like it here," I said to Christine "Let's move to a less exposed spot." Eventually we arrived at the River Forest Manor's marina in Bellhaven and enjoyed a delicious supper in their delightful old Southern style mansion. To visit town, the Manor provided electrically driven golf carts for their guests. This we had to try. The remains of July 4th decorations still adorned the tree lined streets of this charming little town. The cool of the air-conditioned Helmsman coffee shop was just the place to enjoy lunch as a strong hot wind persisted all day.

River Forest Manor, Bellhaven

By noon the next day we were roaring north along the Alligator River using our small jib, praying that the central swing section of the next bridge would be open on our arrival. It was, and after passing through it, we turned into the Alligator Marina. Next day a cold front arrived in the early hours of the morning with a lot of associated northerly wind and thunderstorms. The air immediately cooled off, which was such a relief after weeks of oppressive humidity and heat. The next challenge was crossing the vast Albemarle Sound. We waited for the weather to settle. Some boats arrived later in the day telling us of their tempestuous crossings in the shallow turbulent water.

For two days it rained and blew, with the crests of the waves in Albemarle Sound blowing away downwind, creating a haze in the air. As the wind had settled by the following morning, we left the Alligator River Marina at first light to cross the Sound, along with a flotilla of other boats. But after an hour of bucking into a rising northeasterly gale which had suddenly sprung up from nowhere, we turned into the Little Alligator River to shelter. By 1230 hrs the wind had left as quickly as it had arrived. We raised the anchor and set off again using our jib, to arrive at

Elizabeth City's town wharf in the centre of town. After a quiet night at the dock, we awoke to another grey, rainy day.

Two gentlemen appeared riding on a golf cart. They knocked on the boat introducing themselves as the "Rose Buddies." They asked if we would mind having our photographs taken with them in the rose garden, with the Elizabeth City sign as a backdrop. We readily agreed and accepted their welcome gift of a long stemmed red rose. In a nearby pub, I found ale with the quaint name of "Weeping Radish" The town had some pretty streets, and several gardens were adorned with pink, white or red Crepe Myrtle bushes.

The Rose Buddies reappeared the next morning. They tried to persuade us to extend our stay, but at 1100 hrs, feeling the need to move as the bridge opened, we motored on up the Pasquotank River. Tall trees towered over us on both sides as we carved our way through the glassy water.

Arriving at South Mills Lock just as it opened at 1500 hrs, we entered The Dismal Swamp. We motored five miles to the Visitors Centre wharf. Here we met a couple from Durban, South Africa, who had left that country six years earlier in their boat *Bijou*. They were returning to their boat in Florida after a holiday in their campervan up north. They knew Tony in Kilifi and several other people we had met in East Africa. What a small world.

Motoring the Dismal Swamp

On we went through the "Dismal Swamp," a long, straight, still, tree lined route of dark water that had been carved out to form a canal on the orders of George Washington. It would save smaller boats from having to go out into the ocean around Cape Fear, which had a reputation for being very inhospitable in bad weather. We reached Deep Creek lock, and had to wait an hour for it to open. Once through, we motored to a marina in Norfolk, Virginia for a noisy night. We met a couple in a neighbouring boat who kindly invited us to join them at their much quieter Yacht Club on the north shore of Hampton Roads. On the way to the club, we passed dozens of naval vessels at the wharves along the seaway. We crossed the wide Hampton Roads, where the two ironclads *Merriman* and *Monitor*, had fought their sea battle in 1862. On we went into the Hampton River, passing the University of Hampton, which was the first university opened for black students after the abolition of slavery. We tied up at the Hampton Yacht Club. Here we were met enthusiastically by our new friends and other club members, who all wanted to hear of our adventures.

Most of the boats at the club were sailing vessels. We were soon given the name of an excellent boat canvas firm nearby which could design and make a new bimini for *Demelza*. Our old cockpit cover was exhausted. At night the temperature in the cabin again rose to 90°F, sleep came fitfully at best. The gardens of the well appointed homes nearby were full of flowers. We were thrilled with the new bimini design. It had three sections, joined by heavy plastic zips and Velcro. This would provide a permanent cover forward over the entrance to the pilot house, a shade from the sun in the aft steering position, and a removable middle section for use in heavy rain.

Two days later we were lent a car by Darienne to visit Yorktown, site of the British landings in 1781 and led by Cornwallis. The resultant rout of the British led to his surrendering to the Americans, and the United States gained its independence soon after. The battlefield where the army of George Washington prevailed is now a grassy open field where small deer graze. From there we visited Williamsburg, site of early colonist settlement, before driving the picturesque Colonial Parkway leading to the island on which Jamestown is located. Here the first settlers landed from three small ships, the fifty foot *Godspeed* with fifty two people, thirty nine foot *Discovery* with twenty one people and the eighty foot *Susan Constant* with seventy people aboard. It was nothing but a struggle for them to get established. Fires gutted their new homes but eventually, with reinforcements and help from Pocahontas, daughter of the local indigenous chief, they succeeded.

We paid a visit to the exemplary Mariner's Museum in Newport News before joining club members Rene and Dick to look over their lovely home and gardens. Jo, another friend from the club, drove us all over the area where she had lived since being a young girl. She showed us her family home which was then being repaired after being damaged by a tornado. Jo drove us around the town looking for a VW Campervan which we planned to use after hauling *Demelza* out of the water in the Chesapeake. On advice we had chosen Deltaville on Chesapeake Bay as our final destination for the year.

Following our busy and enjoyable eight day stay at the Hampton Yacht Club, we said our goodbyes before entering the East River and Mobjack Bay where we tied up for the night. Because of thunderstorms, we stayed for two days before sailing along the Chesapeake Bay to Fishing Bay Marina, and the end of our almost seven year odyssey afloat.

At Deltaville we spent some time exploring the village on borrowed bicycles in the ninety five degree heat. We looked at all the local marinas, all of which were located miles from town. It was our intention to leave *Demelza* on land for the hurricane season and winter, while we returned home in time for the arrival of our newest grandchild. Our plan was to resume our cruise in the spring, heading north up the Chesapeake, making our way into the Hudson River, the Trent Eerie Canal and the Great Lakes, before sailing as far west as Thunder Bay in Ontario.

The unforeseen problem with this plan was that the winter weather would not allow us to enter the Trent Eerie Canal, due to ice, until May. Our one year's cruising permit expired in April. I applied for an extension, which was refused by the American authorities. They told us that our only option was to take *Demelza* out of United States waters for twelve days, before reapplying for a new permit. Because of this, we decided to truck the boat home to the west coast the following spring. Instead we would enjoy the journey home in a campervan.

Scanning the newspaper advertisement in Richmond, Virginia, we saw a VW campervan for private sale. We rented a car, and drove to Richmond to look at it. The van was definitely old and dirty. It had rust both underneath and in the exhaust system and on one panel of the body. The vendor was a nice young man, who allowed us to have the van vetted by his garage. It passed as sound and it was ours! The insurance company was very helpful and gave us a form to take to the State Motor Vehicle branch to apply for registration.

"Sorry," said the nice lady behind the glass panel "you cannot be issued with a vehicle registration as you are not residents of Virginia."

"But, I've bought the vehicle," I protested. "Its insured and I want to drive it out of Virginia as soon as possible."

"Sorry." she said.

"I'd like to speak to your supervisor please," I said, trying to be on my best behavior. Along came an even nicer lady. The situation was explained to her as I looked on.

"No problem, Sir," she smiled. "We'll issue you with a T number."

"Great." I said. She typed in all our details, checked our driver's licenses and attempted to enter our postal code on the computer to complete the deal. It was rejected as it only had six digits instead of the American seven.

"Oh no," I said "now what do we do?"

"No problem, Sir." she said, adding a digit. The machine was satisfied.

On driving the van back to the marina we cleaned it, and replaced critical rusted parts. As luck would have it, the boatyard manager at the marina was a VW enthusiast, having had one himself for many years. He was able to provide all sorts of helpful advice about each problem as it appeared, and a few problems that did not. One of the most significant was that in the 90°F heat of the day, it was not possible to turn off the interior heater. Another was it was that it was only possible to lock and unlock the van using the driver's door. This entailed some gymnastics when we wanted to get in and out.

We moved *Demelza* across the bay to Fishing Bay Marina, which we thought was more sheltered even though the dry storage area was only twelve feet above datum tides. This could be a problem in any surge accompanying a severe hurricane. We had a complete marine survey done on the boat before moving her to the dry storage area. *Demelza* came through with flying colours after her long and arduous journey. Once settled, we divided the days between packing the boat for the winter and cleaning up and servicing the van before starting out on our cross country land cruise.

On one of our numerous trips into town, the starter motor wouldn't work.

"Maybe we've bought a lemon after all," I moaned, "He seemed such a nice young man." At the time, I was parked at a gas station having just filled the tank. I was mortified to find myself pushing our new prize possession to one side contemplating our next move. The boat yard manager, Charlie, sped to our assistance, after I had phoned him to explain our plight. There followed a quick lesson on how to hot wire a car, a new skill for me, which resulted in a gratifying roar, or the VW equivalent of such. We were in business again. Having bare wires dangling around my knees was not something I needed all the way across North America, so we put "tidy up wires" on our "must do" list before we left.

By now *Demelza*'s cabin was so full of equipment and gear for storage that we had to transfer ourselves to the van. We rigged suitable close fitting mosquito nets to keep the varmints at bay. These let in a cool breeze at night.

It was time to leave. We gave *Demelza* a farewell pat and started on our long trip back to British Columbia.

CHAPTER 25
Homeward Bound

Dry Storage at Fishing Bay Marina

As we drove through Richmond the van's speedometer and odometer ceased to function. Without delay, we called in at the "The Bughaus" in Richmond, the previous owner's garage. They were able to fix both these problems while we waited. We found a pleasant trailer park to spend the night after a sweltering day of a hundred degrees. Leaving on the following morning, we stopped in Cumberland for gas. You've guessed it. The starter wouldn't work. I phoned AAA, who sent a very large flat bed truck to take us back the hundred miles to Richmond, as there was no mechanic any closer. Then I phoned Bobby at the 'Bughaus' to say we were on our way.

So there we were, on our second day out, atop a flat bed truck, sitting in its cab with all our possessions behind us, making it speedily back to "Go."

On our arrival four men in overalls greeted us at the door and, after half an hour of "work," Bobby appeared and seemed satisfied. "That should do it," he said "If you have any further problems, squirt a bit of this Quick Start into the carburetor. There's no charge, but I don't want to see you again. Knowing what you have achieved on your boat, if anyone can get this van across North America it's you guys." With that, we set off for Cumberland once again.

Needless to say, we didn't stop there a second time. In fact we didn't stop until the gas tank was gasping for fuel. Sure enough, following a drink at the Amherst McDonalds to counteract the effect of the heating system, the van wouldn't start. "Right," I said, stomping off into the distance. I came back, brandishing a can of Quick Start which I squirted in the appointed hole after having removed all our belongings in the back of the van to get at the engine. Immediately she roared into life. I re-stowed our belongings, and leapt aboard before she had time to stop again.

"This is going to be one of those trips I can tell." I groaned.

On into the Blue Ridge Mountains we rode, finding that the heavily loaded van was pulling better up the hills with the encouragement of Premium fuel. At Waynesboro, we were able to stop and start spontaneously without making an exhibition of ourselves in the local gas station. However on descending the hill out of town, a fearful noise developed in one of the front brakes. "That's all we need," I said. "First we couldn't start, and now we won't be able to stop." Our enthusiasm for driving the sixty miles of the lovely Blue Ridge Parkway, was somewhat tempered by intermittent screeching of brakes at every turn in the road.

Tropical Storm Brett, out in the Atlantic, was causing a stir on the east coast of the States, and our thoughts flew back to our lovely *Demelza* sitting all on her own in the boatyard in Virginia.

Into a garage we drove for the fourth time in a week. On baring the inner workings of the front wheels, we could readily see that there was practically nothing left of the brake pads in either front wheel, and the bearings needed replacing.

"If we go on at this rate," I said, "we'll have replaced the whole van by the time we get home." For good measure, we picked up a set of new windshield wiper blades, improving our visibility as the others were worn out especially the one on the passenger's side! As Christine was the only one aboard who had the faintest sense of direction, it was imperative she could see out of the window.

By email, we received an invitation from Jim and Connie from Charleston, to visit them in Portland, Maine on specific dates. It would all depend on how many garages we would have to visit en route. We heard on the radio that Tropical Storm Brett had now developed into a hurricane, and was heading straight for *Demelza* (or so it seemed to me).

Finally, considerably lighter in pocket, we got away from Waynesboro to arrive at Harrisonburg where "Pep Boys" had a fantastic sale on tires. We just couldn't resist as, of course, ours were rather threadbare. The van looked almost new with its four new tires.

With new confidence, we motored to Gettysburg. The information on the history of this famous place was beautifully presented. We looked at the electrical display of the battle between Robert E Lee and the Union Forces. We walked the battlefields and the Peach Orchard. We saw the Round Top, Seminary Ridge and

Memorial Stones, before visiting the Eisenhower home, which was close by, and the bridge where Lincoln made his Gettysburg address in the cemetery four months after the battle.

On then into New York State, crossing the Hudson River on which we had hoped to cruise, to Vermont. We camped at an exceptionally lovely place in Bennington, in a grassy meadow which sloped down to a pond below, surrounded by trees on the rolling hills. The nights were getting cooler. We could hardly believe it was the end of August. We visited the Norman Rockwell Gallery in Sandgate, crossing a classic red painted covered bridge over the shallow Batterskill River. Here we met a gorgeous black lady who, as a girl, had been a model for some of Rockwell's paintings, as had many of the local residents at that time.

Through the hills of Vermont and into Maine, where we met up with Jim and Connie in their gorgeous apartment at the end of Chandlers Wharf in Portland. This development overlooked the active harbour. We spent three happy days with them sightseeing and enjoying lobster feasts. With Jim's professional eye, he painted a new VW emblem to fill the hole in the front grill of the van. The original one had been stolen before we bought her. After a visit to the maritime museum together, we returned to Jim's car to find he had a flat tire. Try as we may, we could not remove one of the lug nuts on the wheel. Christine and Connie went off to buy a can of tire inflator, which worked beautifully. So I decided there and then to buy two cans, for any future emergencies in our van. Our final breakfast with our kind hosts was spent watching lobster boats coming and going, offloading their catches at the wharves below. Goodbyes were as hard as ever. We fired up the VW and reached Booth Bay by evening. After a night's rest, we visited the charming seaside town of Camden with its Marine State Park.

Meanwhile, Hurricane Dennis, which had been looking very threatening, was now downgraded to a tropical storm and located at Cape Hatteras.

At Bucksport, we camped on the shores of a lovely lake. Fall colours were just starting to appear. Loons called to their young in the cool evening air. Life was bliss, until we spotted a leak of antifreeze appearing from under the van. One of the hoses had perished. Naturally, it was located in the most inconvenient place. However, after much struggling, I was able to splice the two rotten ends together sufficiently well to stop the leak.

It was now the beginning of September. Littleford Beaches were packed with tourists, so we were lucky to find a vacant place to camp. I phoned ahead to our next destination at Onion River to make sure they kept a space for us for the following night.

The other call I made was to Peter, the editor of the Vancouver 32 Newsletter, whom we had known by mail ever since acquiring *Demelza*. His home overlooked Lake Champlain and he was glad at the prospect of a visit from us. On waking the following morning, we discovered we had a flat tire and one of the lug nuts would not come off!

"Out with one of your trusty spray bottles please." I called to Christine. It worked like a charm until we arrived at a garage in Bethel.

"How many garages is that so far?" I asked.

"Seven," Christine replied.

"Not bad in a month."

Peter and Diane's house, on the outskirts of Charlotte, looked west over Lake Champlain. A backdrop of the Adirondacks, in New York State, was reflected in the lake's calm water. Peter was working as a volunteer at the Maritime Museum helping restore the old paddle steamer, the *Ticonderoga.* She had plied the waters of the lake, carrying people and cargo long before the present roads had been built. The small communities around the lake had depended upon her for supplies.

They took us for a sail on the lake in their Vancouver 32 *Wind Rose.* The feel of the light, un-laden boat sailing through fresh water, came as a surprise. At the museum we watched a film of Benedict Arnold's gun ships being surveyed on the lake's bottom. Our hosts, on our way home, kindly offered us the use of their ski cabin at Waterbury, in the Green Mountains, for a few days.

Sailing on Lake Champlain

Waterbury looked a picture as we approached, with the lovely church spire pushing up among the trees with their Fall colours. Water tumbled over a weir at the centre of the college town as we passed on our way to Rochester. Talcum powder and marble were quarried here in the past, but now it is a ski destination. The cabin was situated in a quiet wooded spot, and was ideal for resting after our hectic travel schedule. On one of our walks through the meadows we found twelve graves dating back to the Revolutionary wars.

Nearby Woodstock, with its covered bridge and art galleries, and a tour of the Quechie Glass and pottery factory, provided us with all the entertainment we could take in a day. The following day we visited the Rutland Marble works, which used Vermont marble to fashion the most beautiful art work in both green and pure white.

After returning to Charlotte to thank Peter, we made the half hour crossing by ferry to Essex in New York State. At Wilmington, near the White Face Mountain, which was the 1982 Winter Olympics venue, we visited Lake Placid to see all the facilities, including the skating rink where Sonja Henie had skated in 1932

We entered Canada across the St. Lawrence River at Cornwall, Ontario, as Hurricane Floyd was picking up strength in the Bahamas, and yet again we worried about *Demelza.* The casual way in which people living on the east coast treated hurricanes continued to surprise us. Having heard of two hurricanes and two tropical storms threatening the East Coast during the short time we had been travelling by road, it was apparent that it was just a part of life in that corner of the world.

Crossing the St Lawrence, back in Canada

Crossing the border had been easy. But because the VW had been built in Germany, we had to pay import duty. However, as it was over fifteen years old, we didn't have to have it inspected. I was so relieved not to have to unload everything.

We went to Ottawa for a few days and included a visit to see the Group of Seven paintings which Christine, as an artist, found truly magnificent. Saturated with culture, we moved on to Bancroft, south of Algonquin Park, mineral centre of Ontario. As the chips in our van's windshield were being fixed, we visited the Chamber of Commerce's mineral collection before driving to the Princess Sodalite mine. Lovely pieces of Labradorite from Madagascar, local Rose Quartz and Amazonite from Quebec, Calcite with Apatite, which was a pink and green crystal, and local Dropsite, as well as many other minerals, fascinated us. In 1901 Queen

Mary, on a visit to Canada, was presented with a piece of Sodalite. She so admired its rich blue colour, that one hundred and thirty tons were shipped to her in England in 1906. This event had resulted in the mine's name.

Our journey continued to the Big Chute on the Trent Severn waterway. This bodily lifts transiting boats over a huge rocky outcrop and the road below. As a boat was making this transit, I hitched a ride on it to enjoy the experience. Following a stay at Sudbury, we drove on to Sault St. Marie through brightly coloured woodlands, and soon afterwards experienced morning frosts for the first time. We continued on to Wawa beside Lake Superior. The lakeside was a tapestry of Fall colours, and the lakeshore made up of tall inhospitable cliffs, interspersed with attractive coves.

We had camped next to a newer VW campervan in Wawa, and met up with them again in Thunder Bay. Joy and Bob, experienced VW campers from Prince George, British Columbia, were returning home from a summer in Labrador. We spent many cheerful evenings camping with them along our way. In the evenings we would watch great V formations of Canada geese noisily making their way south. Winter could not be far behind.

In Winnipeg, it was blowing hard and cold at Portage and Maine, living up to its reputation as one of the coldest spots in Canada. Our friend Jan, whom we had met in New Zealand, showed us all around. Housing seemed reasonably priced, but their taxes were exorbitant. One of the highlights was a visit to the Leo Mol Art Gallery and Gardens. These were adorned with his bronze statues. An excellent artist in many media, he came to Canada from the Ukraine sixty years ago and had just celebrated his eighty fourth birthday.

We continued across the prairies through Brandon to Regina. Here the mornings were crisp, with a carpet of frost on the ground. In bright sunshine and clear cold days under the huge blue dome of the prairie sky, we continued past countless grain elevators and across the border into Alberta, stopping at Medicine Hat for the night.

Two days later we continued on to Calgary, calling in at the prairie town of Brooks. In Calgary we stayed with Christine's younger brother Martin, his wife Claire and their two boys George and Scott. We heard of the ninety car pile up on the Deerfoot Trail in snow and ice, and I wondered how our van would make out crossing the Rocky Mountain passes. On 1st October, snow continued to fall, so we decided to stay for a couple more days to let the weather settle down. We busied ourselves around Calgary visiting other friends.

After another parting, we motored through Calgary's urban sprawl over clear roads up into the dramatic Rocky Mountains to Lake Louise, over the Rogers Pass and down into Revelstoke for an overnight stop.

On the way to Enderby we stopped at Craigallachie, site of driving the last railway spike connecting the rails from the east to the west coast of Canada. Ray and Margaret gave us a warm welcome and two good nights sleep before we continued on to visit other friends Janet and Ian in Naramata. Suddenly we were heading home to Victoria where we had been invited to stay, until our home was available, with Mary and Bob, the indomitable crew on the first leg of our voyage.

What a welcome we received from family and friends, and what celebrations. We were home again after six and a half years.

ON REFLECTION

An unforgettable six and a half years seemed to have passed in a flash, and in that time I had realized my childhood dream. The company and help of the only person that could have made it a reality, Christine, had been the deciding factor.

We had discovered for ourselves many lands and places of which we had only read or heard.

We had discovered that the peoples of those lands who, no matter what their circumstances, had been unfailingly welcoming and generous spirited.

We had discovered the majesty and power of the vast oceans of our world.

We had discovered the unique support and friendship among our fellow cruisers, a homogenous group from very different backgrounds. They had varied aspirations for, and expectations of, the cruising life. All had a common goal – a successful cruise. Many of these newly acquired friendships last to this day, and through visits and the magic of electronic communication, we never tire of their continuing exploits either on land or on the sea.

We had rediscovered the magical value of family and friends ashore.

Above all, we have discovered more about ourselves, our strengths and weaknesses, and have learned to harness them to enhance our love and support of one another.

POSTSCRIPT

In the spring of 2000, I flew back to Deltaville, removed the mast and all its attachments, and loaded the boat onto an Associated Boat Transport flatbed truck. Not only did the driver and his rig arrive a day earlier than booked but, rather than sitting around doing nothing, he helped me considerably in getting *Demelza* prepared for the journey. When all was secure, he drove his huge red vehicle out of the marina's tricky driveway, to disappear from sight with a throaty roar.

Four days later *Demelza* was back in the Pacific Northwest, having seen us safely through our amazing adventure.

If you have felt the salt spray,
Flung to the face by a whistling wind,
From a wild green sea in the waning day,
With a trailing white churned wake astern,
If you have heard the sea birds cry,
In swirling swarms on a hazy shore,
Then you have life – yet life holds more.

Author unknown

Demelza continues sailing the oceans of the world with her new owners David and Elizabeth. May she continue to inspire happiness and good fellowship wherever she goes.

GLOSSARY

of nautical terms used in this book

Aft	Towards the stern
Anchor rode	Anchor line, rope or chain connecting anchor to vessel
Antisyphon valve	Device that prevents liquid from returning to the line from which it came
Autohelm	Electrical steering device
Backstay	Long line or cable reaching from stern of vessel to masthead
Bar	Large mass of sand or earth formed by surge of the sea.
Beacon	Lit or unlit aid to navigation.
Beam	Width of vessel at widest point
Bearing	Horizontal direction of a line sighted between two objects on the surface of the earth
Beat (to beat)	To sail upwind using a series of alternate tacks across the wind
Bilge	Bottom-most compartment of hull
Binnacle	A stand on which the ship's compass is mounted.
Bitter end	Last part of a rope or chain. When anchor rode is fully paid out the bitter end is reached.
Bollard	A land based post to which mooring lines are attached
Bommies	Australian term for coral heads
Bosun's Chair	A chair device to haul someone up the mast using halyards
Bow	The front (sharp) end of a boat
Bowline	A type of knot
Broach	A sharp uncontrolled turn made by a vessel under sail, which often leads to a knockdown
Buoy	Floating anchored object of defined shape and colour, at a given position, serves as an aid to navigation
Cabin sole	Cabin floor
Cleat	Stationary device used to secure rope aboard a vessel.
Close hauled	Sailing close to the wind
Combers	Large ocean waves approaching land
Cross trees	Cross beam athwart the mast to spread the shrouds leading to the mast from below
Cutlass Bearing	A bearing on the driveshaft of a vessel, lubricated by water as it rotates

Dodger	Cover for cockpit
Doldrums	Also called Equatorial calms, sometimes with light variable winds
Dorade vents	Ventilation fittings on deck
Drop Boards	Boards sized to slip into hatchway leading into cabin of vessel
Ebb tide	Falling tide
Fathom	A unit of length equal to six feet (1.8m) used to measure depth
Fender	An air or foam filled bumper used to keep boats from banging into docks or each other.
Fetch	A distance of water which allows waves to build up
Flood tide	Rising tide
Flopper stopper	Device to reduce boat's sway caused by waves
Following sea	Wave or tidal movement going in same direction as ship
Forestay	Long line or cable reaching from bow of vessel to masthead used to support mast. Standing rigging connecting bow to masthead
Galley	Kitchen of vessel
Gennaker	Light air foresail
Genoa (jenny)	Large sail attached to forestay
Gooseneck	Fitting joining mainsail boom to mast
GPS	Global Positioning System. Satellite based radio navigation system giving continuous worldwide coverage provides navigation position and timing
Gybe	To change from one tack to another away from the wind, stern of vessel turning through the wind
Halyard	A line used to raise the head of any sail
Hanks	Fittings for attaching foresail to forestay
Hatch	Entrance to vessel
Hawsepipe	Pipe for passage of anchor chain within vessel
Head	A marine toilet
Headsail	Any sail flown in front of the mast
Heaving (hove) to	Stopping a vessel by lashing helm in opposition to the sails, vessel will gradually drift downwind
Hull speed	Maximum efficient speed of a displacement hulled vessel
Hull	Shell and framework of body of a ship.
ITCZ	Intertropical Convergence zone
Jib	Triangular sail attached to forestay
Jury rigging	The act of rigging a temporary mast and sails
Keel	Central structural basis of hull

Knockdown	Condition of a sailboat being pushed abruptly to horizontal with mast parallel to water surface
Knot	A unit of speed. One nautical mile (1.8520 km, 1.1508 m) per hour.
Lazarette	A small stowage locker at the aft end of vessel
Lee cloths	Support on side of berth for use in rough seas
Lee shore	Downwind shore
Leeway	The amount the vessel is blown to sideways downwind
Life raft	Raft used in event of vessel being abandoned
Line	Nautical term for majority of "ropes" being used on a vessel
List	Leaning the boat to one side
LOA	Length over all, length of vessel
Luff up	To steer a vessel towards the direction of wind to reduce pressure of wind on the sail
Lying ahull	Vessel allowed to ride unaided on water's surface
Magnetic bearing	Absolute bearing using magnetic north
Mainsheet	Line controlling the main sail
Making way	When vessel is moving under its own power
Med moor	Anchored from the bow, tied to land by the stern
Nautical mile	1.1 statute mile. Approx the distance of one minute of Arc of Latitude on the earth's surface
Oilskins, oilies	Foul weather gear worn by sailors
Outboard motor	Motor mounted externally on transom of small boats
Pinching	Going too close to the wind
Pooped	Swamped by a high or following sea
Port Tack	When sailing with wind coming from port side of boat. Must give way to boat on starboard tack
Port	Left hand side of boat, denoted by red light at night
Portholes	Windows of vessel
Preventer	A device to prevent accidental gybe
Radar reflector	A device to reflect radar waves to sender
Range lights	Land based lights, when aligned, show path to follow
Reach	Sail position with the wind aft of the boat's beam
Reefing	Reducing sail area.
Rigging	*Standing* – Shrouds and stays. *Running* – lines controlling the sails' positions
Rode	The line/chain attached to the anchor of a small boat
Rudder post	Connects the wheel to the rudder
Running	Sail position with the wind following the boat
Scanner	Revolving radar antenna

Sextant	A device for navigation using stars or midday horizon
Shivs	Fittings to guide over masthead pulleys (blocks)
Shrouds	Wire mast supports from the side of the boat
Sou'wester	A wind from the Southwest
Sounding	Measuring the depth of water
Southern Cross	Constellation of stars in the Southern hemisphere
Spinnaker pole	A spar used to help control spinnaker or other headsail
Stanchion	Vertical post near deck's edge that supports life lines
Starboard	Towards right hand side of vessel facing forward, denoted by green light at night. Vessel on starboard tack has right of way over vessel on port tack
Staysail	A sail whose luff is attached to the forestay
Stern	The rear of the vessel
Stuffing box	A seal between the propeller shaft and hull
Swage	Pressure fitting attaching standing rigging to boat
Tacking	Sailing upwind by zig zagging course
Through Hull	A valve in the hull of the boat
Toe rail	Rail around the edge of the deck of a vessel
Toggle	Swivel fitting at the end of standing rigging
Topping lift	Line holding up the aft end of the boom
Track	Slotted guide holding leading edge of the mainsail
Transom	Flat after end of vessel
Traveller	Small fitting that slides on a rod or line. Most common use is for inboard end of the mainsheet
Tri sail	Small mast mounted storm sail
Trim	Fore and aft relationship of a ship's hull to waterline
Vang	A device holding the boom level
Wake	Turbulence behind a moving vessel
Wash	Waves created by a moving vessel
Wearing	Tacking the boat with the wind from behind
Weigh anchor	Heaving up the anchor, preparing to sail
Whisker pole	A pole to clip onto the clew of the foresail to hold it out from the boat allowing it to catch more wind
Wing on wing	Foresail and mainsail on opposite sides of the boat going downwind

ACKNOWLEDGEMENTS

To all friends and family that made this adventure possible, and saw it to a successful conclusion. A special tribute and thanks to my wife, **Christine**, with whose help, support, companionship and encouragement this dream came true.

Most especially I should like to recognize the contribution of:

Robert Harris – for designing such a seaworthy and seakindly boat.
Peter Thomas – Controller of DDD Amateur Radio Net, and all those other amateur ham radio operators who helped us on our way.
Peter Coombs – who was my long distance cruising mentor.
Maurice Chazzottes – for his literary encouragement putting this book to paper.
Peter Kellond – for his help in assembling and organizing this book into digital and publishing form.
David Dunnet — for kindly agreeing to proof read the book for us.
My son Nicholas – for handling mail and dealing with all financial matters while we were away.
My son Chris – for all his help and encouragement with the computer.

Cover Photograph — Baie de Gadji, Isle of Pines, New Caledonia

Photography credits — Thanks to Christine Richards, Ann Ferriera, Paula and Vigo Anderson

PRINTED IN THE USA BY:
CREATESPACE
CREATESPACE.COM
INFO@CREATESPACE.COM

Made in the USA
Charleston, SC
22 March 2011